Screening
the
Sexes

Screening the Sexes

HOMOSEXUALITY IN THE MOVIES

Parker Tyler

HOLT, RINEHART AND WINSTON

NEW YORK   CHICAGO   SAN FRANCISCO

Published simultaneously in Canada by Holt, Rinehart
and Winston of Canada, Limited.

ISBN: 0–03–086583–2

Library of Congress Catalog Card Number: 71–155504

First Edition

Designer: Victoria Dudley
Printed in the United States of America

*Besides the Film Department of the Museum of Modern Art, Anthology
Film Archives and the Andy Warhol Studio, the following individuals
are owed my gratitude for help in collecting the stills used to illustrate
this book: Mr. Gene Andrewski, Mr. Bill Kenly and Mr. Jarry Lang. I
heartily thank them all and the three gentlemen, as well, for advice.*

CONTENTS

v

INTRODUCTION:

TAKING ON THE SEXES

This book is about an idea of sexuality; an idea of sexuality as mirrored in wide variety in given specimens of a certain medium. My belief is that an idea, any *idea*, is altogether a moral thing—it is an "image" with a positive, self-interested and self-indicating shape. Summarily, it is morality in its objective and literal nakedness. This metaphor is a happy one because my subject very much pertains to human nakedness, to the body itself, as a necessary and natural ingredient. Never, in the following pages, do I lose an implicit orientation to bed behavior between the sexes. The body and particularly the sexual organs are at once the earth and the earth's playground of my idea. I have wanted to free the sexual body and all its behavior traits from the straitjacket of conventional ideas that limit them for serious contemplation and cripple them on the open ground of the imagination.

It would be foolish to assume that the various moral and intellectual taboos illustrated by the movies, as a historical phenomenon, do not exist circa 1971. True, these taboos nowadays are being so rapidly relaxed and lifted that it is hard for print to keep up with what we call tolerance and liberality. Hence, one of the functions I necessarily undertake here is to make note of the progress of moral liberality as reflected by the movies. The emergence of sexual freedom in the medium of the movies seems to me tremendously important. If the mere "facts of life" were ever enough, mankind would always have been wisely tolerant and liberal! But the facts of life have always been moralized, penalized, arbitrarily damned and exalted, and in general hemmed in, distorted, and regimented by public institutions and official codes. In a way, indeed the most *important* way, the arts form a history of this same process: this evolution of mores from the primitive tribes to modern global civilization. This is why I seize upon instances in all kinds of movies that consciously or unconsciously revert to pagan attitudes toward sex, civilized attitudes (such as the one in *Fellini Satyricon*) that deal with sex as a thing naturally, perennially taking offbeat forms—truly *free* forms.

The basis for free moral forms—forms with essential balance, I mean, not forms merely oblique, wild, and uncontrolled—is instinctual behavior. What has happened during the civilized eras, those termed historic as contrasted to prehistoric, is that mankind in terms of behavior has perfected the faculty of molding sex into an infinite variety of tensions, shapes, characters, and styles. This true *erotic liberalism* renders absurd the sexual categories as determined statutorily by the organic male and female. As I say in subsequent pages, the sex organs themselves, as exclusive natural categories, pertain *only* to the fact of reproduction. As reproductive organs, they exist apart from erotic pleasure and its multiple variety of means. All rules of normalcy, obeying the rationale of reproduction by conjugation, are thus strictly limited and represent a limited idea of sex. I wish to *unlimit* this idea.

Thus the chief purpose of this book is to expand that limited idea (the pleasure of making and rearing children) with an idea of sexual behavior that achieves magnitude through variety of form, hence variety of sensation and emotion. To accomplish this, I have logically assumed that the basic genders are irrelevant. Per se, "male" and "female" are biological patterns, simple reproductive organs. These rudimentary patterns, these organs, are mere statistics telling us the minimum, not the maximum, about the sex of an individual. The strange irony is that the sexual organs themselves are exactly like musical instruments, things "manufactured" by nature, whose true value lies (aside from any status as decorative objects) altogether in *how* they are played and *what* they play. Sex depends, thus, on the sexual musician and the sexual music he plays.

To view the matter seriously and comprehensively, this qualification applies also to the sex organs as reproductive instruments. Children themselves can be valued as works of musical art that must pass through vicissitudes of growth decided by congenital nature, the forces of environment and the influences of changing experience. The whole body, not just the sex organ, is an individual's erotic instrument. The sum total of this human function is to be called *the sexual personality*. It is the style of this personality, not the incidental sex organ, that determines "gender." Film is so ideal a medium for expressing this truth because it offers us the human being's visible presence from head to toe, it brings us technically close to him and does so with increasing thoroughness owing to the medium's new body-candor: more and more nudity. As of this moment, this exploration has just begun.

Another fortunate factor here is that the film, being so recent an art form, had to educate itself and its public anew into the behavior patterns of sex. The movies had to fight over again the old civilized fight of élite intelligence against official taboo—the taboo of the bourgeois establishment with its hypocritical moral codes. Official, formal censorship of the movies has been simply the cover for unofficial, informal censorship: the instrument of society's paranoid fear of the true nature of the libido, whose genders are so variable.

This book's all-inclusiveness made it logical that heterosexuality, too, should be represented by its genders. While my deliberate focus is on the homosexes, it often happens that the heterosexes come naturally and relevantly into focus. In fact, in the chapter on transvestites, the standard heterosexual act of coitus is depicted as a paradoxical form of transvestism. The film version of *The Dybbuk* is cited to illustrate what I mean. Transvestism inheres in the fundamental act of the penis's penetration of the vagina, which becomes something "worn" by the penis, a temporary dress. The classic myth of Hermaphroditus is thus an image neither homosexual nor heterosexual, but *transsexual*, in the very sense that modern surgery changes organic gender. Heterosexual transvestism of the sexual act is passing, yes, not permanent; it is, as it were, a creative act capable of repetition and as such is an intense and sublime moment long celebrated in poetry and romance. It is precisely a great climax in which the sexes are fused to the point of losing their sense of identity and separateness; this is an element of the legendary love-deaths.

The higher erotics, the full tables of eroticism, inevitably point to a homogenizing of the sexes denoted by the contemporary term "unisex." Today unisex is the sexual parallel of racial integration. The modern love-ins, for instance, are unisexual; no gender distinctions are present except mechanical ones; there are no regulations regarding correspondence: every sex fits any other sex. We should note that racial integration has two aspects: one purely social, the other biological; the latter means literal assimilation. Political ideas like black power and black independence militate against biological assimilation and even social assimilation, sometimes even implying black apartheid. These extremist ideas are as puritanical in their way as the rigid norm of heterosexuality, which condemns offbeat sexuality as perverse, renegade, and sick. Black power may function as a political weapon, well or ill as the case may be. It may even function in the illiberal sense that heterosexual power has functioned under modern dictatorships, as a power artificially, arbitrarily imposing on society the delimiting heterosexual norm.

In Visconti's film *The Damned*, we can see how Nazism signally failed to impose such a norm and instead arrived at a deep-going cult of perversion and inversion. This means that anything basically natural, when frustrated, will resort to extreme strategies to maintain itself and will retaliate with means as authoritarian and special as the means used by the dictatorship seeking to suppress it. Today's outcrop of minority elements, such as blacks and homosexuals, belies the technical label of minority. Only in the most elementary, actually insignificant sense are blacks and homosexuals "minority groups." In a political climate which, for all its ambiguous wars, is democratically live-and-let-live, homosexuals, long viewed as a minority, are in fact letting the world know what a major human capacity they have always represented. Homosexuals tend to represent the free libido. And the free libido—make no mistake—is a human majority, not a human minority!

That the homosexes, and all offbeat sexes, represent sex as fully as do the heterosexes is what I particularly argue and seek to demonstrate in this book. If the movies, being the most rudimentarily, imperfectly developed of our art forms, can avail a host of evidence for the undiscriminatory power of the libido (and I think the movies do avail this), then we have at hand a gallery of live, very diverse illustrations of my sexual thesis, my *idea*, quite unencumbered by applied aesthetic criticism. The very force that made the movies a species of major entertainment, a vulgar orgy of the emotions, has compelled whatever was subtle and offbeat, strange and secret, to resort to the most devious strategies to preserve and, at last, openly express itself. In this respect, what today we rather facilely call the Sexual Revolution can be located centrally *in the movies*.

I must insist on one point: I have not chosen to associate homosexuality so closely with heterosexuality (which may be a disguise of homosexuality) in order to make the one as "respectable" as the other. I violently repudiate what is commonly known as respectability, which itself is an antiquated strategy of the dishonest bourgeois establishment. Realistically, sexual respectability resides in sexual virtue, and sexual virtue may reside in any sex, no matter which. Virtue itself, all varieties of it, is a most difficult human achievement. It is never given— it must be *won*. Virtue may be known under the generic label of decency. But decency, as used in daily language, may be only a mechanical gambit, a more or less trivial hoax without real substance. If, and only if, connected with true virtue can the word "decency" mean anything vitally real.

One of the great virtues is sexual integrity. In the widest and the strictest sense, sexual integrity is omnisexed. It is sexual without the least discrimination among the sexes. Only from this viewpoint do I consider homosexuality and heterosexuality worthy of each other: *when each in its own right represents sexual integrity*. And yet life is as full of playful disguises, tricks, and charades as are the movies. Films simply provide a very present, very available, very intimate index to the truths thus transparently disguised. However legitimate as an art, the movies too have the divine freedom of invention— and by his inventions shall man be known! One of his inventions, a very great one, is sexual style.

If we read aright the signs of sexual style in the movies —read them with intelligence and an open, enlightened spirit —we can descry the true, the actual, the varied features of the whole repertory of human sexuality. I have not meant to present this repertory here in any solemn academic way, a way lacking humor. If I introduce conceits, if I go for fun and strategies and innuendo, it is because that is what sex does, in life as in the movies. To honor the seriousness of my idea, however, I have thought it best to invent a god of homosexuality, Homeros, and him I treat with the awed respect appropriate to sacred rites. I confess Homeros is a pagan god; in fact, I think he has always belonged to the ancient Greek pantheon, and thus I have not invented, but discovered, him. Like Proteus, he is chameleon and therefore can take female as well as male form. Like most gods of his ilk, he can be as ridiculous as he is sublime. As for mischief, he is capable of more of it, as we shall see, than his natural brother, Eros. Yes: much more of it! In the realm of mischievous fun and grim mischief, the movies are never off the mark. All this makes for a poetry of sexual wit. In sexual matters, more than other matters, the movies become profound.

GLOSSARY

These lists, divided according to the organic sexes, are composed of scientific, religious, literary, colloquial, and slang terms for homosexuals, given in alphabetical order. In a few cases the slang has fallen into disuse. Speaking generally, specific usages depend on age or, especially in the male list, style or type of personality. Mood, of course, is also determinative; the slang terms may be downright contemptuous, simply familiar, or possibly (particularly nowadays) neutral. Most terms are international among the English-speaking.

MALE
athenian (*modern élite*)
auntie (*middle-aged or over*)
belle
"Bessie" (*personal familiar*)
"Beulah" (*personal familiar*)
bitch
bugger
butch number (*masculine type*)
catamite
closet queen (*double-lifer*)
cocksucker
daisy
faggot (fag)
fairy
floss
fruit
groovy guy (*1970*)
"Gussie" (*personal familiar*)
"Mary" (*personal familiar*)
nance (nancy)
nellie

pansy
pederast
poof (*English slang*)
queen
queer
sissy
sister boy
sodomite (sod, *England*)
swish
tante (*French*)
violet (*American Civil War*)
wolf (*active partner only*)

FEMALE
bull dyke (*aggressive type*)
butch
diesel dyke (*masculine partner*)
dyke
femme (*feminine partner*)
lesbian (les)
tomboy

MALE OR FEMALE
deviate
gay (people)
invert

"one of those"
pervert
"that way"

NOTE. In the following text, the author has licensed himself to embellish the above lists with certain terms of his own: sappho (as alternative to lesbian) and Homeros (Greek = Homo + Eros), a name for the homosexual deity, male or female.

1. MOTHER SUPERIOR OF THE FAGGOTS AND SOME RIVAL QUEENS

Almost everything, at last, has been or is about to be done about Mae West. Yet it was not till *Myra Breckinridge* that the pre occupations peculiar to a certain style of homosexual became literally a part of Mae's acting routine, which was always suggestive and always (she could hardly deny it) based on an obsession with sex—the male sex. I shan't repeat gossip, underground or over, to articulate the case of Miss West. The subject is already historical. It is enough for me to review and explicate the surface facts. Miss West's reaction to comments that connected her with female impersonators (apparently she wished long ago to present herself in a play called *The Drag*) was reported as the boast that, of course, she "knew that female impersonators imitated her." It is often hard, as everyone knows, to establish primacy of claims to originality, whether actually asserted or only indicated statistically. Perhaps one ought simply to say that Miss West's style as a woman fully qualifies her—as it always did—to be a Mother Superior of the Faggots.

This title is no facile invention of hip journalism, mine or another's, but an analogy based on historical truth. Once I spent several years among the fairies; e.g., those homosexuals

1

unafraid to advertise themselves socially though they seldom
went in drag except at drag balls. A running joke of theirs that
has its empiric reality was that an older queen would act as
oracle, authority, and admonisher to a group of younger, less
experienced members of the clan; in short, would boss them
around. "Queen," I may interpolate, was the quality term at
that period and "faggot" a more or less in-group contempt term,
like a black calling his kind "nigger." Yet the epithet "faggot,"
at times, was as much a sign of guild solidarity as something at
which to take offense.

Likewise, in camp homosexual circles, the feminine
pronoun was commonly tolerated and protested against only as
camp gesture on top of camp gesture. To this day, when even
serious and socially respected homosexuals get together informally, it isn't abnormal for the gayer temperaments to call
both heterosexual and homosexual males casually by the feminine pronoun: "She this—she that . . ." No serious disrespect, as
a rule, is intended; rather, it's a mannerism for putting the supposed "superior sex" (the heterosexual male) in its place, a kind
of fem-lib response among homosexuals indifferent to maintaining at any cost (as some still do) the unrelieved straight or
"butch" style. One might add that the generic term for an
ostensible "straight" who is really gay is "closet queen." According to the book, a great deal of at-home privacy is needed
to persuade a closet queen to let down his hair outside the closet.

It is too bad that the movies have reflected so little of
the true homo social resonance, the actual mores of homosexuals,
where camping can approach the literary level and the joyous
wit of a Wilde play. Mart Crowley took a big step toward re-
flecting camp nuances in *The Boys in the Band*, except that his
play's calculated tenor, for the purposes of drama, put the open
style of social camp in the attitude of having to defend itself
against "good manners," bourgeois heterosexual "decency" and
all that somber stuff.

What homo society in comic art would seem to need is
the perfect assurance of Mae West, its Mother Superior, whose
suavity is that of a candid diplomat and whose tacit authority
is that of the Commander in Chief of the Armed Forces. One

has to admit this is a very difficult assignment, requiring a subtle and powerful grasp of life style. The ease and authority of Miss West as a homosexual camp symbol speaks aloud of her unique privilege: she is, after all, a woman. In many respects she behaves like a homo with a lifelong dedication to putting on the ritz, while undeniably being a good fellow through it all. If anyone still active in the theater arts justifies bringing that ancient piece of slang—putting on the ritz—up to date, it's unquestionably Miss West.

In her films, she invariably shows the affability of a touring queen; this in fact was, and is, the supreme aspect of her public character. When she delivered quips like "Goodness had nothing to do with it" or "Between two evils, I always pick the one I never tried before," everyone (down to the twelve-year-olds) knew exactly what she meant. Today even the eight- and nine-year-olds may have an inkling of what she meant. Mae was "bad" only because she made herself out to be sexually available through natural inclination, which a huge ratio of the earth's population spontaneously believes, and perhaps rightly, is "good." Mae herself once confessed her goodness in a forgotten newspaper interview. But that offstage gesture was as superfluous as her newest publicity, which states that she is deeply religious and humbly turns to God for guidance.*

Obviously she was kind to everyone, good-natured toward all but the "villain," and even when tartly responding to some crude slur, she adopted the tone of royal rebuke that both closed the matter and made the quarrel into a violation of protocol. In *My Little Chickadee*, she and W. C. Fields were teamed as parlor antagonists to amuse their combined horde of fans. In a verbal exchange, ending the picture with a fillip, they adopted one of each other's standard gag lines as a sign of the beautiful underlying social truce. He asked her to "come up and see him some time" and she finished it off with, "my little chickadee!" Never before in her films had Miss West allowed a man to abuse her without awful punishment. Fields necessarily had to do his malice act, and without getting blasted out of the film, but this

* *Modern Screen,* October 1970.

was only because, being a clown, he was a rejected lover of Mae herself: to let him rant on was a veritable act of revenge.

Fields, of course, had become celebrated for being unkind to both women and children. There may have been a filmic instance of Miss West displaying kindness toward a child, but I don't recall any. Maybe this notable gap in her repertory of goodness was due to a postural handicap: she couldn't always bend over at the waist. Her perpetual upright slouch (that moved along to an insinuating jiggle) was her very own unique creation. Calisthenically, the most she could do was voluptuously to recline; this she did invariably, ritually, with regal composure and a touch of witty condescension, which time and custom have done a little—but only a little—to modify.

Why beat about the West? She always had the style of a good-natured, expensive, successful courtesan born out of her time. In the nineteenth century, her accent, vocabulary, and swagger, equivalently gauged, would have been, however gay or amusing, vulgar, and her whole manner socially impossible because ludicrous. Only a tolerant and decadent democracy, "progressing" into the twentieth century, could have taken her up as a social fetish, even at a distance. Up to the present, celebrity-collecting is *de rigueur* among the high sophisticates of cultural society and probably, despite *Myra Breckinridge*, Mae is still a catch among the ultras. If she isn't, it's only because she won't be, or because, like time itself, she isn't growing any younger; she is not even, except through artifice, youngish.

Mae's personal publicity as a Hollywood star was never standard. She was never married (to anyone's knowledge) except in the neanderthal haze before her rise began. She was never reported as seen regularly in night spots accompanied by the same man. Mostly she frequented nightclubs as an "act"—she toured extensively after retiring from stardom in the films— and her escort then was a tailing bevy of prize-winning muscle men, whose public contact with her was confined to presenting their muscles for her to feel. I doubt that Miss West was ever connected in the papers with a single known personality of her same professional rank.

Some years ago, an official of New York's Museum of

Modern Art told me of meeting her, however, in a nightclub, where she proceeded to explain to him (tacitly in the hearing of her escort, who may well have been her agent) how she directed her sex appeal toward the male in terms of the contrasting magnetic fields situated in her right and left breasts. The gentleman was amused—and also rather awed. Who wouldn't have been? *There* lay the secret of Miss West's absolutely unique charm: she projected a purely academic, even learnèd, sexuality as if she were nonchalantly tossing a nipple at you—which, literally, of course, she never did; that immodesty wasn't necessary. Everyone could see the size and shape of her maternal breasts, and that the pelvic region, however much unused for making babies, housed a seemingly ideal womb while it sported hips of the sort once termed well-cushioned. Besides, the counterpoint of swing and sway in those hips happens to be a musical achievement.

Unfortunately, despite the artfulness of camera and make-up, time looks out of Mae's face, circa 1971, a bit ghoulishly. One has the impression of features that have attained a miraculous restoration after disaster, as if she had been snatched from the clutches of a tribe of headshrinkers who have decided to begin their gruesome work before decapitation. If the Mae West myth, face and all, has been altered, it is because she returned to the screen in *Myra Breckinridge*. Some concentration is due on the physical mechanism animating this movie's odd erotic plot. For it involves a kind of "improved" female impersonation that is ethically opposed to Gore Vidal's devastatingly flip satire. *Myra Breckinridge* is satire superfreaked-up largely owing to the mechanism of the transsexual operation as something correcting, supposedly, an original error of nature.

But transsexualism to one side, if the female impersonator has one serious moral function, it is to inform the world that sex is a sense of style, a predilection of the mind and senses, and is not answerable to nature's dually blunt decision about gender. For this reason the case of Christine (né George) Jorgensen, as both film and life story, seems to make a moral/aesthetic correction of sensibility to be addressed directly to Myra and her original creator, Vidal. The female impersonator, surgically converting an aborted "he" into a legitimized "she," is theoretically purged of freakishness—insofar, that is, as a transformation of the sexual organ can achieve the trick. Here a minus sign dominates the surgical science of making a male into a female. This is why the style of *The Christine Jorgensen Story* (as a film) has the atmosphere of an operating room, a funeral parlor, and a society debut all in one: the butterfly solemnly unfolds her drying wings in a postanesthetic, chemically purified air.

We find, then, that the operation-room cutting which morally begins a Myra morally ends, that is "perfects," a Christine. Society's moral structure, obeying the natural gender decisions, must regard female impersonation as a vagary or depravity: a freakishness tolerable only because of that democratic tenet of individualism that guarantees the freedoms of choice and privacy. When Jackie Curtis, a female impersonator both in and out of his profession of acting, uses the ladies' room, it is a simple test of the workability of the concept of individual privacy and freedom; so long as, in general, Jackie behaves like a lady, he can get by almost anywhere. Police action about female impersonation, of course, varies from hour to hour, place to place, country to country. Usually, when they like, authorities can seize on disorderly conduct as a technicality warranting arrest of any male caught in the act of publicly wearing women's clothes.

The female impersonator's routine, before the beaver films made it into a home-movie charade, found its way into the movies in curious, sometimes oblique ways. *La Dolce Vita* (in its last episode) is one of the few films to have made it look like a commonplace feature of mixed-sex parties. On the other hand, think of Anthony Perkins either in the movie *The Matchmaker* or as the psychopath in the Hitchcock melodrama *Psycho*, addicted to dressing up as his dead mother and forthwith murdering young females. A harsh lesson: a little boy's jolly old pastime of raiding the attic trunk should come to this! *Psycho* is a deliberately far-out case, but its commentary on the ancient custom of female impersonation—should one care to take it seriously—might be construed as injuring the public image of impersonator-homosexuals. Quite of an opposite kind, the old-fashioned collegiate musical show, in which even athletic stars get into drag and cavort, has been nominally only a harmless romp: an indirect way of demonstrating just how far gone the boys are on girls. The sexual enlightenment, inexorable as time, has gradually punctured the innocent aura of college-boy theatrical drag and shown the Wolf beneath the Ziegfeld Girl. Even Little Red Riding Hood can get into pants and a butch manner—and sometimes, we find, the little tomboy means it. The reader will be apprised of examples as we go along.

The real-life legend of a Christine has a variegated background, both mythical and realistic, that touches—perhaps a little too closely for comfort—on the mad fictional legend of a Myra. Mythologically, fringe activity has somehow preserved the sheer fun-image of the male's addiction to imitating the manners and outward appearance of the female. The Charley's Aunt legend is a classic nerve center of both the innocence and the theatrical propriety of female impersonation. Probably we ought not to forget that once the young Prince of Wales, later the contemporary Duke of Windsor, got into drag on a British battleship and was photographed for the newspapers. That was grand-manner English camp. However, the modern era, with its new ultrapermissiveness toward the exhibition of all sexes and all sex acts, has compromised the traditional dignity of the theatrical drag act. Drag balls, for example, once served to bolster homosexuality as a sort of public charade reserved to a small minority of social ineligibles, as if the balls were the annual affairs given for themselves by élite domestics. Not that the social élite itself did not visit drag balls: I recall seeing Clifton Webb, resplendent in white tie and tails, at one of them. It was not expected, of course, that drag balls would in every respect live up to polite standards of behavior. They tended—if only because of their link with the gangster world—to get a bit rowdy; inevitably, their tone was a cutely disrespectful parody of high social style.

The female impersonator as a *rowdy* is an enigmatic image with many tentacles of interest. Myra herself seems to illustrate the transsexual operation as an act of female-impersonator violence. After all, she becomes a con woman with pretty rough methods. There was a noted female impersonator of the late twenties whose punch could be as fearsome as his apparition at drag balls, where he looked like a football player who had turned Follies girl, ospreys, shoulders, spangles and at least six feet. Soon he was a nightclub performer and ended up in Hollywood, where he was drowned when a car he was riding in catapulted off a pier. Ugly rumors accompanied the report of the supposed accident.

The world of crime inevitably has a masquerade element, therefore why not *transvestism*? The device of criminals to dress up as women to elude the police, in fact, is a classic stint for the bad guy hero in detective melodramas—in life as in the movies. It duly appeared in the transposition of "Dutch" Schultz's crime career to the screen. Humphrey Bogart's role as a detective hero in *The Big Sleep* neatly revealed how the plain homosexual, sans female dress, can be a masquerade. Not many years ago, incidentally, there were news stories, furnished with titillating photos, about policemen getting into full drag so as to trap mashers at their vicious work and nab a few purse-snatchers too. The point of the "masquerade" in Bogart's role was that nobody would expect a palpable pansy, however quiet-mannered, to be a detective on the prowl. To impersonate a homosexual, Bogart turned up his hat brim in front, wore glasses, spoke with a lisp to the clerk of the bookshop he entered, and sidled about nellishly.

More properly, perhaps, this phase of the discussion might appear in the following chapter devoted to the chameleonism peculiar to homosexuality. Yet these casual transvestments are somehow linked imaginatively to the violent, enigmatic motives of Myra's complex challenge to the homosexual as transvestite and transsexual. One recalls the way Frank Sinatra's role in *The Detective* (more of which later) becomes involved with a homosexual crime to the point of Sinatra's playing "homosexual" in the line of duty. Corollary to *The Detective*, a vintage French film had Jean Gabin in a role anticipating Sinatra's. Pursuing his clues, Gabin's detective flirts with two gay boys, a "pair," so as to split them up and gain evidence of their suspected complicity in the crime he has to solve. The feint succeeds: Gabin pairs off with one of them, and the other, out of jealous pique, promptly betrays his comrade.

Suppose we switch to the female as a corresponding fortuitous drag number. A favorite device of old-time, pretalkie Hollywood was to disguise a young woman's vulnerability to public insult and assault, whether or not in a man's company, by dressing her as a boy, usually a poor boy. A standard item of her drag was a large cap under which she tucked her telltale, adorable curls. The fact that nobody in the world, taking a good look, could be deceived by her disguise was only a regulation part of Hollywood camp, mechanically derived from a theater convention that, in the western hemisphere, dates back to pagan and Elizabethan times. Some of the fun was to see the charade boy "act tough" so as to get by. Similarly, the rowdy female impersonator is actually based on ancient clown routine; his face and above all his exposed musculature shriek out the failed impersonation: the bigger the biceps, the more surefire the shrieks. Historically, it is a matter of carnival hilarity as well as a theatrical institution. Men in drag are perennial figures at carnivals over the world and appeared at the antique saturnalias, where their absence would have been noticed.

On the side of male impersonation, the old naïve Hollywood convention I mentioned above was deliberately parodied, in terms of sophisticated comedy, by François Truffaut in *Jules and Jim*. There no less a leading lady than magnetic Jeanne Moreau got herself up like Edna Purviance doing a drag act in some early Chaplin film or Pearl White in one of her *Perils of Pauline* disguises. Like other elements revived and revised from old movies by the Nouvelle Vague, the Moreau bit of sex impersonation was aimed at piercing the spectator with nostalgia while providing him with an amusing updated satire on erotic foibles. Deception in the literal sense was no factor in Miss Moreau's charade, which was simply another item of camp symbolism to be "read" by savoring sophisticates of all sex persuasions.

The artificial routine no more indicated lesbianism than did those of Gabin and Sinatra, just mentioned, indicate male homosexuality. Drag, male or female, is a way of communicating as well as concealing something. There are few cases, in or outside literature, where it is meant as a permanent, impenetrable disguise. Among male homosexuals, the masculine dress of everyday is an automatic and unavoidable "disguise." Not till very recently has it become the thing to declare oneself homosexual, either as a matter of course or of public principle. Allen Ginsberg's example was probably influential, not long ago, in inducing a group of homosexuals, three males and three females, to come into the open and discuss their problems on a television panel.* The Myras and the Christines, then, whether or not they be "ladies," can be argued as incarnate strategies whose purpose is to avoid the prospect of declaring oneself a sex formally contrary to one's given gender.

Be that as it may, deception is not essential to male or female impersonation, inevitably related though it be to what must be called homosexual delusion of grandeur. This delusion may or may not lead to a surgical operation to convert the male (transsexually, not cosmetically) into a female. Here we should not pass over the existence of ladylike heterosexual males who have a yen to dress like the women they sleep with and sometimes marry. Doubtless this is the sort of compliment to women that fem-lib exponents find abhorrent. Note that it is not a Don Juanish device, whose only avowed object is to enable a man to get into a woman's bedroom; we shall duly come to examples of this. No, here the sexual disguise is ritual, ornamental, purely cosmetic, and *inner* in a sense which carnival disguise is not. Need we emphasize that heterosexual female impersonation is a recorded phenomenon and neither pure legend nor literary symbolism?

The vital point is that, as a habit, it does not conceal male *homo*sexuality but male *hetero*sexuality. Rare as part of the personal constitution, it is rarely reflected in art. As a legend it takes the form of some parent's decision to dress a girl like a boy because a male, not a female, child was desired. Played by Greta Garbo in the movies, Queen Christina of Sweden had this legendary cause for dressing as a man; as monarch, she had to

* National Educational Television, 1970.

shoulder a "man's" responsibilities. Encouraged by the manly charm of John Gilbert, there was no question but that Garbo, as Christina, should turn out a true woman. Film archives are loaded with transformations of this sort, and attention will be given this phase in the chapter devoted to all kinds of transvestites in the movies. Sometimes film actresses have taken it into their heads to invert the Elizabethan convention and play a straight male role. Leading example: Mary Pickford as Little Lord Fauntleroy.

Not infrequently, the impulse in heterosexual males to dress like women is translated, as it were, into a profession such as dressmaking or hairdressing. Legends of interior decorators and dress designers as "homosexuals" are common bywords; at times, the reading is correct, yet not always. Even in the homosexual calendar, these individuals may not be drag types at all. Homosexuality, in claiming them by virtue of their surface mannerisms, the general style they maintain, may be jumping to conclusions too hastily. However, homosexuals *can* be identified by such signs. It takes an experienced eye to be certain on first sight.

The physical type, with more or less burlesque manners, has been seen as minor characters in many films: the parody itself is "taken from life," and a face-value reading of it is automatic: "Here's a homosexual!" One such appeared as a stage director in *The Producers,* a movie farce about theater life. Behaving as if only shrieky homosexual conventions ruled society, he caricatures, in poker-face, mannerisms such as Harold's in *The Boys in the Band.* In the last-named film, realism has been the object, whereas in the usual campy gay taken straight from life, it is the quasi-professional clown who appears: the one whose social function is exclusively to entertain. The more polite his camping, the more socially eligible he is. In actual society he appears in less crude forms, where the female parody may even be an intact male elegance, a part of the personal style, like dandyish clothes. Gradually the type is being absorbed everywhere into society's normal texture.

In two French films, *La Poupée* and *Sweet and Sour,* the basic homosexual is seen in quite disjunct charades. The former, a heavy-fantasy farce, had a well-known female impersonator, Sonne Teal, playing a professional who doubles as a theatrical producer's wife. Here was someone with a high degree of impersonator talent who yet left his male identity tangibly visible. It seems as if the plot's inner dimension (the impersonation of a real female by a professional impersonator bent on deception) meant to ratify by oblique tour de force the overt tour de force of the nightclub act. Mr. Teal had enough sheer acting talent to make his complicated film stint amusing. Bear in mind that there is no serious effort in such cases to make the sex impersonation more than a meaningful, though perhaps ambiguous, illusion. One element of the convention—especially when seen in theater or movie house—is that the impersonator may be, but is not necessarily, homosexual. It is obvious to remark: "Well, nobody is fooled," and almost equally obvious to add, "and nobody is meant to be fooled." Yet life has the habit of really fooling people exactly when it only seems to pretend to be fooling them. In this light, the serious aspect of *Myra Breckinridge* would be its criticism of the transsexual operation as doomed because it is an aesthetic error. The error would be the unsuccessful effort to convert what essentially is a *playful form* (female impersonation) into a *serious substance* (being a female). In a moment more, we shall consider just what happens to Myra, Mae, and their friends.

As for *Sweet and Sour,* an offbeat independent film, it is actually a parody of cinéma vérité with psychiatric overtones. The plot involves a sort of fairy godmother, a "wardrobe mistress," of psychic transvestism; this male person, never in drag, discreetly yet naturally camps through both life and his job. As seen here, the type is not attractive; in fact, he is rather homely. But his features are of the "amusing" sympathetic sort. Nobody in the film calls him a queer or the equivalent, nor is he explicitly made out as gay, because the clear assumption is that he is a normal, accepted, even prestigious member of his professional community: he is a dancer and physical trainer. Is he supposed to be homosexual? The answer is implicit, that is, left to the audience. Humorous in personal key, a "performer" and good fellow, tacitly indispensable, the character is a lot like an actual off-off-Broadway director, John Vaccaro, as if nature had created a social archetype with given physiognomic traits. Mr. Vaccaro, who acts too, sometimes plays in drag, sometimes out of it; anyway, his total life role includes that of fairy god-mother (or godfather, if he prefers) and spiritual guide to the transvestites and others of his troupe. In homosexual mores, he stands as the male counterpart of Mae West's Mother Superior.

As either novel or film, and regardless of how evaluated, *Myra Breckinridge* is a vehicle of the great new permissiveness, in the media, about things sexual. Mae West was always avant-garde in this respect. She consistently wished to put sex to the front from all angles (even backviews) while legal constraints had consistently been foiling her. Part of her legend is that she actually spent a few days in jail for having put on a stoppable Broadway show, a "drama" called *Sex*, in the year 1926. Not even Miss West can be permitted, at this point, to beat about the public bush. Whether the gag line that is a dirty joke in *Myra Breckinridge* was written by her or not (one might assume it was, from advance publicity on the film), beyond doubt she delivered it in person in her usual nasally insinuating, blackout manner. She plays the book's role of the Hollywood agent, Letitia Van Allen, who finds a line of ambitious young studs waiting every day to be interviewed in her office; it is an open fact that jobs are procurable through the bedroom back of the office. One of the studs, ostensibly a Western number, informs her without ado in a fake rawhide accent, "I'm six feet, seven inches, tall."

My wording of the quotation may be slightly inaccurate, but the numerical quantities are exact. And Mae replies, in split-second reflex, "We'll forget about the six feet and concen-trate on the seven inches." Again I plead innocence of steno-graphic accuracy, but the sense of Letitia's line (the opposite of innocent) is colossally, crushingly present. I doubt if—in the confines of New York City anyway—there's a single adult soul (and that includes precocious children) who hasn't at least heard of that epoch-making wisecrack, while fifty percent of the children who heard it have made it a point to be wised up on it. Just think: it's on the lips of an actress who, on screen and off, has sternly emphasized that inside and out she was a lady—

and if not a "lady," you cad, then something better than a "lady"! To be sure, the wisecrack itself is securely a part of the dirty-joke repertory belonging to everyone. To speak in filmic parlance, it is verbal superbeaver and has the equivalence of stag-film status.

However, *Myra Breckinridge* is far from being a mere stag film, which in its pure form is a thing without dialogue. The movie is an elaborate satire on sexuality with the outrageousness in the homo key; nobody on the set could possibly have been unaware of this central fact. Myron, the protagonist, is seen becoming a transsexual, Myra, who eventually, inspired to sadism, sodomizes a heterosexual male, thus laying the groundwork for the young man's finally becoming (to quote the book) "a complete homosexual." As for heterosexuality, it ends up with Myra reformed back into a reactionary Myron, having good intentions and a rather unbelievably good penis: he marries Rusty's old sweetheart. So it appears that part of Vidal's myth is an even greater surgical feat: that of reconstitution of a transsexualized male by transplantation of a new male organ. Could it be that Mr. Vidal is mocking the legitimacy of many a contented heterosexual male who, now married, is convinced he has overcome his homosexual phase?

Another ambiguity—this one very visible in the movie— is that Myra's victim, Rusty (incarnated by beguiling Roger Herren) is chastened, tearfully submissive, and relieved after the anal rape, not outraged and physically sickened. A really revolted hetero male (in life or art) would have liked to turn on Myra, when released from his bonds, and beaten the silicone out of her. Technically, Rusty can't do this because he is on probation for having committed a minor crime, and Myra, who knows this, has the power to blackmail him. Yet I fancy Mr. Vidal is being awfully cute again. The rape incident is intended to be a revelation of sex disguised as a degradation of sex. Else why should he let Myra's scheme triumph by having Rusty, as duly reported by Myra to her journal, become "a complete homosexual"?—that is, become one of Hollywood's undercover homosexuals playing a cowboy star?

Myra Breckinridge, while a calculatingly outrageous fantasy, sustains a naturalism as built-in as Mae's own hidden but generous anatomy. It is *she* who supplies all the socially veracious notes—including the aforeside wisecrack—added by the movie. The movie does not brand Rusty as a homosexual convert. No, indeed! Still, in both film and novel, Rusty starts climbing the ladder of fame by putting his best foot forward in Letitia Van Allen's bedroom (the standard hustler motif). In the novel, he tries to take out on Miss Van Allen his technical grudge against the rapist, Myra, by brutalizing Letitia in bed and climactically (her orgasm is timed with it) throwing her downstairs; the result being that Letitia joins Myra in the hospital, where the latter is recovering after being run down by a car.

The novel's Letitia, though not the movie's, is a confirmed masochist who rhapsodizes to Myra that she has achieved her most supreme moment of sex . . . nothing, but nothing, can ever top what Rusty has done to her. All this is proper to Vidal's epic joke; for whatever else his book is, it is consciously an epic joke. Rusty's sadism was precluded from the film by Miss West's selection, or rather election-by-acclamation, to play Letitia. I imagine the lady would sooner die than even seem to suffer such a brute indignity as Rusty visits on Letitia. She has her own, Mae West way of seeming to handle the delectable Rustys of the world and, as we find, was not averse to indicating this way by lucid enough sight and sound.

In the film, we take farewell of Rusty and Letitia during what, in some *other* film, would be delicious rut of the now-approved, showily evident order. One wonders if Miss West realizes—though how can she not realize—the full license she has now granted her screen personality. We camera in on her session with Rusty when it has been interrupted by a telephone ring. Miss West is neither nude nor seminude; I doubt she has ever appeared in anything less than a filmy negligée or chemise and petticoat. Now, answering the phone, she wears a formal boudoir gown that seems fresh from the box it was bought in. Rusty, however, is visible lying supine on a huge bed, splayed out, as if exhausted, mute, naked except for a towel across his middle. We now learn just how academically inflected Miss West's sexual conduct can be.

Rusty may be only relaxing; he may even be "waiting."

But that would be unkinky logic, and nothing in *Myra Breck-inridge* is without kinks. His attitude may imply, rather, that he has been acting, or will act, the purely passive role in bed. His position is typically that of the heterosexual male ("trade" is the good old vulgar name for it) who graciously allows homosexuals to perform on him certain morally submissive but physically quite energetic acts. Now for the scene's payoff: as clear in verbal meaning as an efficient soundtrack can make it. After putting down the receiver—Is this the lace-curtain line, old-timers!—Mae turns to Rusty and says, "How about another trip around the world?"

There may exist local, specialized, arbitrary realizations of what is meant by this symbolic expression. But the intrinsic joke is that it does *not* mean anything to do with traveling in the broad geographic sense. There may be, too, some benighted innocents of all age classes who have not yet learned the import of this bit of the sexual vernacular—*but they will, Gore, they will!* Heterosexuals also do it, of course, but it has earned its superstar status, probably, from fervently articulate homosexuals. The point is that in the film's context, it makes out Miss West—and to me this is all to the good—a fairy godmother of fairy godmothers. There was never one to equal her and I am convinced there never will be. She is the White Goddess in metaphysically transsexual drag.

Myra, kindly step down . . . after, that is, you've finished the Ginger Rogers/Fred Astaire dance routine the film has wished on you and Myron.

Mae, kindly step up. *You* are the Queen.

2. HOMEROS

AS CHAMELEON

In the eyes of the public (I do not say its mind, as people seldom use their minds in matters of custom), being homosexual in our age, till recently, was anything from a moral calamity to a serious social embarrassment. Such conditions were due to what is still termed by some an aberration of nature, which frequently existed in the observer as well as the observed. Today, things are more sane and relaxed, to the point where it is possible to state, without provoking contempt, disbelief, or laughter, that being homosexual may have quite as much going for it as being heterosexual. This means, among other things, that it is always facile to judge any subject merely by its official atmosphere: said atmosphere is too likely to rest on legal statutes that both nature and society, in reality, freely ignore. Truly realistic observers have concluded that a discernibly sharp division exists between the floating public myth that is a "moral atmosphere" and the actual private conduct that is at the heart of the floating public myth. Less than a century after Oscar Wilde's trial, enlightened modern politics is trying to correct the inequity between myth and reality by passing statutes legalizing mutually consenting adult homosexuality. In brief, the joys of being homosexual are coalescing with its "rights."

Not that problems, by and large, do not still plague humanity: I know the world we are living in. Yet often social and

17

political conflicts involve matters not strictly relevant to *specific* conflicts. The point I am making is that human conduct in general calls into question practically everything that science and religious thought are used to postulating as "natural." I would dare say that we live, right now, in an age of imperative exceptions. I am aware that the naturalness of homosexuality (whatever its granted "pleasures") is still a scientific issue. In effect, the forces upholding public ethics have been compelled to retreat before increasingly publicized behavioral data extending from the realm of biology to the realm of ancient religion.

Psychiatry as a technical antidote to homosexuality is simply that arm of correctional public morality which has been established in order to combat the principal psychic evils resulting from all sexual problems, homosexuality being only one problem. It is no secret, nevertheless, that some practicing homosexuals go regularly to analysts as a smoke screen to assist them should they be caught someday in a legal trap, or else (as is supposed) in order to assuage an unhappiness which perhaps really is a specifically individual, not a specifically sexual, problem. One of the most exculpative of public situations for practicing homosexuals, in fact, is for them to be psychiatrists themselves; many homosexuals, of course, belong to that tribe of nominal good samaritans.

Meanwhile a louder and louder rumor exists that the breakdown of the world capitalistic structure—or at any rate the acuteness of its current peril—is only consistent with the threatened collapse of all ethical structures. Instant legal permissiveness toward old-statute crimes is conceivably only a symptom of an endangered political system attempting to prevent its dissolution all along the line. Tolerance of both sexual deviation and sexual promiscuity can be seen in the light of sheer political strategy. After all, that the Greek god Zeus had his Ganymede, or boy concubine, and that this reflected the widespread practice of homosexuality among the social élite of pagan and prepagan civilizations, is bound to suggest to an intelligent mind that there is nothing basically unnatural about homosexuality.

Furthermore, investigators of this subject, without a thought of political strategy, must defer to sexual phenomena

in the animal world, where homosexuality seems an act as instinctive, if not so typical, as heterosexuality. Something odd,
of course, inheres in such an entente between human sexual
practice and the sexual practice of animals. Granting that religion itself is an invention of social élites, it can still be argued
that the whole point about the historic emergence of man as a
"super animal" is that he is an improvement on the lower
orders of animal. And yet, to assume just this, we have to reason
that man sets himself up, historically, as a corrector of nature
and thus that he is *above* nature. Whatever man decides, then,
about sexual matters, "natural" or "unnatural" as relatively they
may be classed, has to be right. Another problem lies here, and
not a mere semantic one. Despite all the democratic progress in
the world, serious group prejudices exist, and one such is directed against sexual deviation.

The status of postpagan religions as a formula of improvement of and superiority over nature is to be credited
mostly, in the West, to the dominance of Judeo-Christian religion since the death of Jesus. If we scrutinize sexual phenomena
in the ancient Greek and Roman civilizations, either at their
strongest or weakest, we find, however, that homosexuality as
such was simply an easy and obvious scapegoat in scoring the
moral abuses of tyrants. This is easy to verify by the lives of the
Roman emperors, where homosexuality as a serious vice cropped
up only when the emperor was unpopular or political rivals
conspired against him. When an emperor was popular, and a
well-balanced individual such as Hadrian, he could not only
sleep with a man but also, in the case of his favorite, Antinoüs,
have temples built to him as a god. At certain historic periods,
power, prestige, and popularity decided everything. Today,
when everything is on the global plane, popular cults and many
other sorts of "interest" tend to crowd each other out and come
into confused collision.

Turning to Greece in the Golden Age, we see that heterosexual incest was a greater crime (as in Sophocles' Oedipus
trilogy) than any form of homosexuality. In the lost first play
of the Sophocles trilogy, Oedipus' father, Laius, is supposed to
have initiated the chain of family woes by abducting and raping

a young boy. Inevitably, we think of the deistic pattern that stood above the lives of kings and that, as I just mentioned, Zeus committed the same "offenses" as did the family of Laius: homosexuality, patricide, and heterosexual incest. So it is clear that, in considering homosexuality as a human problem arising from moral irregularity, we have to determine whether it is really contranaturam, as official religion has argued, or whether it is a simple abuse; that is, a vicious, evil, or contrary aspect of something which in itself is natural and therefore permissible. If we study the matter, it becomes compromisingly clear that man puts himself beyond nature, and stands as its improver and corrector, *only when it suits his incidental purposes to do so*. But what is the modern testimony against homosexuality? Let us momentarily consider this issue.

Respecting homosexuality as contranaturam, the chief argument propounded by the school of psychiatry is the biological view that it arbitrarily interferes with the structure of nature as would any other diversion or "abuse" in the true natural order. Logically, too, this school of thought would concentrate on the mind as the seat of the disorder: e.g., an act of the mind that obstructs and perverts the given heterosexual structure of mankind. When one realizes that this argument, so simple at first glance, is actually restricted *entirely* to the primary function of the sexual organs as such, and that—since mouth and anus are functional mechanisms alignable with penis and vagina—this "primary function" is *not* an exclusive organic convenience, then one sees that the contranaturam grounds must be remapped. Remapped, that is, as applying particularly to homosexuality, since the mouth and anus as instruments of sexual satisfaction are as much a potential of heterosexuality as of homosexuality. The contranaturam argument is thus left on very narrow ground, and that ground is unstable. In the human subject as the object of clinical attentions, there is only one factor to justify the aggressive antihomosexualism of psychiatry. This is the self-professed unhappiness of the sexual invert and his spontaneous desire to be treated for its supposed cause. The truth is that millions of practicing homosexuals, male and female, never have the impulse to seek the help of psychiatry and the reasons may well be that they do not consider themselves unhappy or that they locate the cause of unhappiness elsewhere.

There is another fact to influence thinkers on this subject. Homosexuality in the modern world has lately taken to crusading for itself as explicitly a natural and reasonable state of satisfaction, with normal possibilities of happiness. Of course there is a ludicrous aspect to moral crusades as to all moral obsessions instrumentalized by either group or individual. Whatever the degree of a mass expression, the obsessive psychology of its crusade is self-enclosed, its culture limited to propaganda for a "cult." The really odd, rather humorous truth of current homosexual affairs is that, while homosexuality duly inherits its puritanic social critics and its dogged medical opponents (who deem it a curable disease of heterosexuality), it also has its pop, quasi-political cults as evidenced in the gay-power newspapers (most as pornographically vulgar as they dare to be) and even by street demonstrations. For years, moreover, homosexuals in the United States have had an established organization, quite serious in temper, working for legal reform and social tolerance: the Mattachine Society. We need not specifically criticize the creed and the rhetoric of this society. The point is that nowadays it is reinforced morally by several new organizations and various sorts of public lobbying.

Our era is not cloudy in one respect. This is a day of democratically inflected let-live for minorities, all of which have reached the conclusion—with disconcerting simultaneity—that a show of aggression will make the point for them and perhaps win the day. Duly, male and female homosexuals have taken the hint and grabbed the gambit by "organizing." The obvious advantages of "victory" for homosexuals is freedom from legal prosecution, common social humiliation, and job discrimination. Clearly, then, as a common cause, homosexuality automatically joins hands with all other group disadvantages, whether race, class, or sex define the "disadvantage." This fact of our total society makes the recent concept of Gay Power more than an indulgence in pornography, self-advertising, and group hysteria. Not that large numbers of homosexuals are wholly exempt from those particular charges (the personals in the ad sections of the gay papers are proof of their complicity), but then so are large numbers of blacks open to charges of self-seeking and the modern obsession (still underestimated) for basking at whatever price in publicity's many spotlights.

Since "glamour" has become such a charged-up social value, with publicity its most potent agent, it seems a bit absurd to discuss homosexuality in terms of serious medical (and otherwise moral) prejudice against it. Yet exactly such prejudice remains a strong political factor. Else where would be the propriety of a thing such as homosexual propaganda, why the need in behalf of homosexuals for organized protest and lobbying for legal reform? We have to examine antihomosexualism in its own avowed terms and criticize it as objectively, as roundly, as possible. I wish this book of homosexual manifestations in the movies to be free of those mental reservations which may linger in a reader and spoil his receptivity.

To take up the matter of physical hygiene, while medically this may have progressed through the centuries, it has had to separate itself from various traditions of religious superstition. Some so-called hygienes plainly have originated in totemic mysteries. Obviously the sexual organs are involved with more taboos than simple "dirtiness" implies. Moreover, what we call cleanliness is a sort of puritanic supersitition. When I hear the word "dirty," meaning neglect of body cleanliness, I am apt to think of D. H. Lawrence's opinion, which I once ironically cited in an exchange with Marianne Moore. "Don't wash too often," Lawrence said, "it impoverishes the blood." Literally true or not, the opinion is a criticism of fetishistic cleanliness.

Aside from rudimentary physical hygiene, applying equally to homosexuals and heterosexuals, the antihomosexual case rests on a concept of natural sexuality designed to regularize and maintain the higher (that is, more complex) concept of the family. According to the social philosophy of the ancient Greeks (decisive in Western culture), homosexuality was socially tolerated precisely because it could coexist with the family and was a sort of safety valve for it, insofar as it represented merely a sexual displacement in the long-honored system of wife-and-mistress. In the Orient, of course, the harem system established a different pattern of home life.

The prime duties of a Greek or Roman citizen were to father a family and fight for his country in war; if he performed these duties he was free to seek what bedmates he chose from either sex. That, in the West, during medieval times, it was considered a superior individual's right to enjoy himself with either sex at will, is evidenced by a letter of advice (happily preserved for posterity) from a father to his son. When homosexuality was ridiculed or condemned in the ancient world of the West, that was because (as I implied above) it was a sensual abuse, like eating or drinking too much and making an unseemly public spectacle. The scene in *Fellini Satyricon* about the licentious old actor who buys Giton establishes the issue very clearly. When Roman emperors had luxurious vices, erotic excess could easily be one of them; whether the excess was homosexual or heterosexual in character hardly mattered to the offended and the envious.

What any society basing itself on the unit of the family has always had to fear is the breaking up of this unit through sexual infidelity (including, inevitably, incest). But historians and sociologists have had the opportunity to remark that wives may take a husband's infidelity with a man as less of a threat to domestic unity than his infidelity with a woman—and for an obvious reason: a husband, especially where legal divorce is possible, may sever himself from his wife, marry his mistress, and father children on *her*. He could not do the same with a man unless in some symbolically unreal sense. Only a very limited number of homosexual couples wish to emulate, through adoption, the pattern of a home with children. While some women may regard it a peculiar humiliation to have a man win the place of lover to one's husband, it is only good sense to realize that "another woman" poses a much greater threat of rift or demolition to the family fabric.

The tenor of current times prompts one to note how outdated such perfectly traditional reasoning sounds. Granted: it is somewhat simplistic. But this effect is partly due to the historic perspective in which I have put these matters by way of defining the ethical tradition they involve. Facilely one thinks, nowadays, of how endangered is the social institution of the family. This dire image (owed to much besides homosexuality) never departs from the subconscious of dogmatic antihomosexualists. Yet who are the *most* dogmatic antihomosexualists here and now? Surely not the politicians of democracies and republics! And if homosexuals are persecuted under dictatorships (although Hitler's world possessed a stark paradox in this respect), it is always because of the obsession of dictators to make their states ultra-cohesive by eliminating as many internal flaws and insecurities as possible. They sustain a psychology of permanent crisis. Hence, even in the American democracy, homosexuality used to be a publicized issue only during the crisis of war, when the Army turned down draftees for that reason, but more significantly, when it was assumed that foreign agents can suborn individuals in government posts through their "vulnerability" as homosexuals.

Since the state is but the superstructure of the family, times of crisis emphasize this structural link and elevate the idea of restrengthening the state (and thus the family) through purification and special ratification. This was the case with Hitler's Germany when the Jews became "alien" to the twin-family ideal of race and government. Cruelty, moral and otherwise, seems to mark all dictatorships, classic and modern, as a function of human sadism; the same sadism was in the medieval Inquisition and the American Puritans' burning of witches as in Hitler's persecution of the Jews and anything he considered "un-German" in nationally ratified Germans themselves. Sexual persecution logically becomes one instrument of sadistic dictatorships. This was precisely the empiric nature of Hitler's anti-homosexualism. That some loyal officer close to him, some talented exponent of Wagner's music, might be homosexual, were surely matters to which he was personally indifferent, whatever his public attitude. That Hitler was himself a repressed homosexual is a highly special argument and could probably never be satisfactorily proved. His obsession with absolute power is to be explained technically by virtually any internal aberration, one that might be homosexual or heterosexual.

The ambiguity of Hitler's case is keenly projected in shadow form by that imaginative if somewhat fallible film artist Luchino Visconti, in his movie *The Damned* (1970). It does not deal with Hitler in person; rather, it deals with persons somewhat more typical of sexual sadism, and pivots, politically, on the liquidation of the SA militarists by the SS militarists. History analysts have determined that this drastic action within the realm of German militarism was occasioned by crude power rivalry and the atmosphere of paranoia that reigned in German political psychology before and during World War II. Like all diffused and tolerable "vices," homosexuality became attackable here as one (if not the only) opportune pretext in the contest for power. Elimination of one's enemies (despite the longevity of Jesus' revolutionary doctrine) is still the basic principle of political success. It does not matter if the elimination is blind, caused by trumped-up scandal or technical error; it must be elimination, and preferably mortal. So, in *The Damned* (originally titled *Götterdammerung*), we find the politically lethal sexual personality an individual symbol of discrete and secret vices, one of which (the heterosexual group) triumphs over the other (the homosexual group). Yet neither history nor Visconti's film furnishes us with the clear political function of the sexual vices involved.

This ambiguity— brilliantly reflected by Visconti's film —is very fascinating but also rather personal, a way of juggling (like Fellini, while less overtly) with his own sexual hang-ups. I suspect three leading Italian directors—Fellini, Visconti, and Pasolini—of at least fantasy-homosexuality, even if it be no more than an obsession with transvestism, which may have a sort of ambisexual character. In dealing with the arts, some think it unseemly and indiscreet to attribute precise sexuality to a creative artist. Yet why should the biographic aspect of an art (especially one where the auteur film director is the subject) be eliminated from critical inquiry? It is one of the responsibilities in an age where candor as such is rated as a value.

One recalls the impressive transvestite incident in Fellini's *I Vitelloni* (1953) and that the theme there was young male fellowship and was supposedly autobiographical. Against his desire, Fellini had to submit to the cutting of a scene which indicated that one of the young comrades was really homosexual. Of course, with *Fellini Satyricon* one comes to explicit homosexuality in the two principals and notices that the beauty of the boy Giton, over whom the two quarrel, is very epicene. Visconti uses transvestism as a pathological symptom in *The Damned,* and in Martin von Essenbeck (Helmut Berger), its leading character, situates it as the other side of sadistic power obsession.

Young Martin's family is analogous to the Krupp family of worldwide fame. While Martin is deep in nourishing his pet vice, his mother's lover, Bruckmann (Dirk Bogarde), murders his grandfather and precipitates the coup which historically was the destruction of Roehm, the Nazi homosexual who headed the SA corps. Bruckmann then marries the Baroness herself (Ingrid Thulin), Martin's mother, and becomes head of the family and boss of the steel works. Yet Martin's blood rebels at this man's upstart villainy, and he successfully ruins both Bruckmann and his mother in a horrendous series of maneuvers in which he rapes his mother, gets personal control of the steel works, and reduces both his mother and Bruckmann to the state of helpless puppets, making the Baroness a sleepwalking drug addict into the bargain.

At first Martin is introduced to us in full drag as he imitates Marlene Dietrich, doing a song in *The Blue Angel,* for a stately family gathering. Later we find him an effeminate dandy, in love with a whore but also fond of seducing very small girls, with a tragic result exactly like that in Dostoyevsky's *The Possessed.* This stark portrait of an offbeat sexual personality is insinuated as part of the structure of German political frenzy at this period. Reliable history, however, does not verify the bastions of Visconti's artistic fantasy here. While mortal and merciless, the liquidation of the SA by the SS seems not to have been so sensational as Visconti makes it, if only because the holiday amusements of the SA men seem actually not to have been the veritable Roman orgy of transvestites that is set up here to paint the occasion with color and pathos.

If the SA had actually been so devoted to extreme homosexual pleasures (there's a male couple in every room of the inn, and more outside), they could hardly have been so potent and enviable a military/political organ. Be that as it may, Visconti provides the orgy as mainspring of the moral basis for the lethal political liquidation that sneaks up like a thunderclap. The film gives the impression that nobody was spared—films are so like that!—while actually, though some were executed on the spot, a few were only arrested and permanently or temporarily spared. The historic evidence seems to say that the SA corps was not simply a homosexual club in military uniforms.

In effect, the SA homosexual orgy functions as background for young Martin's private sexual obsessions and thus is a scapegoat for this antihero's repressed moral guilt. But, rather inevitably, dramatic action is the point of *The Damned,* not moral criticism or historical accuracy. Visconti has concocted a moralistic Grand Guignol. Ostensibly his logic seems to have been that the fierce activism of the Nazi leaders was a ploy to stave off a threatening outburst of moral guilt, and that this ploy was consistent with the "triumph" of a sadism like Martin's, displaced from sex to politics and back again. I think Visconti's emotional sensibility has led him to artistic license in making his orgy, first, simply gay and overtly heterosexual, then overtly homosexual and bloody. Realism of method, anyway, is foreign to this auteur director's baroque temper as an artist.

The strapping, good-looking, rank-and-file transvestites of the SA are remarkably male in personality, as becomes more evident when their female trappings are partly shed and one sees more of their athletic physiques. In a muscular manner, they are highly eligible for homo admiration. As a cast, they seem hand-picked rather than, like an army, a recruited set of good, stout, devoted fellows. Of course, the intimation may be that the homosexual leaders *have* more or less hand-picked those under their command. And yet, assuming the film has *any* realistic credibility, one pauses to wonder under what hypnosis such brawny healthy young German males could actually have lent themselves to the purported prostitution of the SA. One shivers to think that it might have been under their own compulsion! I mean: one shivers for heterosexuality.

Altogether the burden in the movie is made to seem light on those magnificent shoulders and chests, on those boyishly beautiful brows. The insistence of Visconti's artistic license (he photographs them as if they were by Michelangelo) makes one turn to the internal dimension of the acting profession as a "circumstantial" form of prostitution. Was this cast of males in drag privately motivated to be thus displayed on the screen? Or were they, perhaps, just (to make a figure of speech) hustling parts in big movies? Was it all a knowing continental camp, the sexuality a formal put-on? During the lethargy of the orgy's aftermath, when some of the poor pretty things seem genuinely tired out, thoroughly surfeited, as it were, Visconti has somehow persuaded a number of them to look like honest hustlers of homosexuals, really "gotten down" by the fate they have chosen, yet despairing of any other possibility. If one could take them instantaneously out of context, regarding them as single-frame pictures, one would register not "drag act," but "football locker room," and then ask, "What kind of a party could *that* be?"

It is just this male type, one observes, that becomes so professionally conditioned, because so successful, that he ceases altogether to think of ever sleeping with a woman and becomes the paid, even passive, homosexualized male so well known to our swinging, well-informed society. Stagger-staged homosexualization is *one* way for instinctive homosexuals, embarrassed by their outward masculinity, to be initiated into their real selves. As the reader knows that the present observer considers the movies as more than entertainment, the preceding passage must not be mistaken for a mere digression; rather, it is important evidence in the nature of a moral charade unveiled. The movie myth is designed to betray quite as much as it portrays. The same is true of life as it is lived rather than life as it be "analyzed" or "psyched."

I mention psychiatry again because it is precisely those simplistic thinkers, the arrogant clinicians, who like to imagine that they have the answers to all charades involving homosexuality. I doubt that they do have the answers, at least the precise ones. Therefore the point I wish to make now is that something very rudimentary is held in common by modern dictatorships and modern antihomosexual psychiatrists. This something issues, via Judeo-Christian sources, in ultrapuritanical, pseudo-hygienic ways of conceiving sexual customs. As I hinted above, the "crime" of sodomy is particularly a Judeo-Christian idea, converting male homosexuality from a tolerable vice, more or less reprehensible, into an unpardonable offense against God and the state. Incidentally, the professional hustler of homosexuals may be said to represent a social vice, but he has not the problem of a "homosexual patient," and it is a stupid affectation to suppose he has. He participates in homosexual practices, but with an economic, not an erotic, substructure; the erotic may eventually filter into his emotions, or it may be kept out.

We know that in Europe the Napoleonic Code started the reformation of the taboo on homosexuality, even within the statute books. It is a little amazing to reflect that once, in England too, homosexuality was punishable by death, and a little amusing to reflect that the application of this penalty made no discernible dent in the prospering of homosexual orgies and even "clubs." Both commoner and noble, however, did die for this "crime." Aside from social tolerance outside the law, and before the Napoleonic Code in nearly all European countries, we know of the brand-new law in England as well as the current agitation in the United States to provide a similar law regarding adult consent. All the more remarkable, then, the stubborn creed of the school of psychiatry that declares homosexuality contranaturam.

Once and for all, in view of the above considerations, what facts could the contranaturam judgment be based upon? It would seem, following the patriarchic theory of human custom, to derive historically from the rigor of phallic worship: the penis as supreme in nature and lord *of the vagina only*. But the pagan, non-Judaic aspect of phallic worship offered a patent danger, which was a simple one. In the worship of the phallus, males could make ritual community with females; as conversely, viewing the matter matriarchally, females could make community with males in worshiping the mother goddess, Cybele, or some cult surrogate. The existence of a hugely built Mother Goddess as object of mystic worship by both homosexual and heterosexual males is impressively, poetically illustrated in *Fellini*

Satyricon when Encolpius' impotence can be cured only by union with the incarnation of the female principle: a monumental black woman like a prehistoric Venus.

Historical logic in these affairs is much more mixed and ambiguous than the puritans of both modern psychology and the Christian tradition would have us believe. True, things such as Robert Graves describes in his reconstruction of the archetypal ritual of the White Goddess—a troupe of transvestite males dedicated to the goddess and presumably "sexless"—can be ascribed to timeless religious fanaticism. Males, in fact, dedicated themselves to Cybele by going into a riotous ecstasy and cutting off their genitals as sacrifices to her. Is Myra/Myron Breckinridge a sort of avatar of this type of fanaticism? Young Von Essenbeck, as seen in *The Damned*, may be regarded as a historically displaced, pathologically perverted devotee of Cybele; he does not part with his genitals, but, as if in contempt, uses them as quasi-destructive weapons.

A traditional semblance of credibility is lent both the male cult of Cybele and Graves's historic fantasy (he dubs his male troupe the Handmaids of Mari) by the monkish institution of castrati as church singers (naturally this spread into the profane theater) and even by the oriental institution of the eunuch as official protector and head-servant of the harem. Of course the eunuchs were not transvestites, and indeed are said to have retained, in some cases, the desire to love and marry women. Yet this very divagation of the psychic transsexual pattern serves to disprove the contention of puritan psychiatrists and orthodox religionists that the healthy and normal male sexual organ is really conclusive in pointing to heterosexuality as the supreme, the only, natural condition of man.

It is time to answer the question, not what does determine the "natural" condition of heterosexuality, but what does not—and what does not is exactly what the antihomosexual school of thought presupposes as the groundwork of its contranaturam criticism of homosexuality. What could this be? It's fantastically simple. It's the function of the penis and the vagina as *reproduction* organs rather than *pleasure* organs. The very nature of the proposition, as viewed empirically (that is, how it works), compels such reasoning to discount the pleasurable in favor of the reproductive. Psychologically, ideologically, ethically, it is plausible to maintain that the sexual organs in their reproductive capacity should be supreme icons if, *and only if,* the exclusive heterosexual will of nature is to be granted in advance. Yet we know very well that heterosexuality is socially established as a "supreme" will only through a statistical majority of opinion and not through any "natural law" residing in the male and female organs. It is the strategy of proheterosexual psychiatry to shift the focus of homosexuality, therefore, onto mental sickness and even "uncleanliness."

The propaganda for this position has been considerably, if mechanically, helped along by the common supposition of Freudian and other clinics that many cases of sexual neurosis are due to the suppressed guilt of having "sick" homosexual impulses, resisted and brought to a virtual impasse. Of course, these neurotic way stations are part of standard male and female homosexual experience; often the way stations are survived and the survivor turns out homosexual. As for homosexual "mental sickness" per se, it would seem primarily the result of a social difficulty, not the cause of a sexual difficulty. The shame of a child having homosexual impulses (they can begin very early, earlier than most imagine) is due to his fear of straying from the family pattern surrounding him, a pattern which at first he imagines determines all the world's reality. Then, usually, his neurosis (if he develops one) is due to his fear of that stigma, and perhaps the ridicule which, he can observe, is meted out to "sissies." I suppose that the stigma on sissies will never quite vanish so long as the heterosexual establishment endures. Yet, with the formidable rise in contemporary respect for all minorities, the stigma on "sissies" has less and less prestige; besides, few homosexuals grow up as sissies or, on the female side, as really "butch" tomboys. In any case, there is bound to be a fusion, a leveling out, of dissident traits in human types whenever tolerance and intercommunication gain sizable ground as social tendencies.

Common, or garden-variety, sexual neurosis is often involved with impulses toward mother or father; hence the homosexual child is in a confused state of fearful ambisexuality. A great deal of the way his sexuality evolves may depend on the character and behavior of his parents, both toward him and toward each other. Individual sensitivity and intelligence, moreover, have much to do with the style as well as the longevity and fate of the adult outcome of a neurosis. Sternness, aggressiveness, and dignity of character by no means always have the outward "masculine" trademark supposed by naïve idealists, innocents, and interested medical thinkers. Besides, many a victim of homosexual "mental sickness" survives to be a strong, successful, respected member of society; many a victim of heterosexual "mental sickness" is nonentitized to a pathetically low level or turns homicide/rapist. I think we are justified in giving the anti-homosexual team of psychiatrists a scoreless inning on mentally sick homosexuals who, hypothetically cured, would be restored to the total condition of moral and physical health known hopefully as heterosexuality.

Here another urgent piece of evidence from the movies is called for. It leads directly into an important phase of my thesis: the sexual joke. Varieties of this joke are basically what makes homosexuality in the movies morally ever more palatable and thus more aesthetic, even on its low levels. I have in mind the new gray, or theatrically de-Beckettized, comedies whose fun is much too orgiastic to be just plain, depressing black. My exhibit is not less a smash of a comedy than *M*A*S*H*. Sadly for the puritan psychiatrists, homosexuality appears starkly here as a sort of burlesque joke (like so much in the movies, it once *was* a burlesque joke) and is proffered to the audience as a naked nifty from the archives of jokes extracted from weird sexual ignorance. In our day of ultra-pop vogues, this particular joke is designed to register as the craziest, cutest of sophistications. The symptomatic ignorance behind it is at times so spontaneous that we dare not consider it a peasant's compulsive form of clowning.

Its initiation in *M*A*S*H* is priapic in the easy-going pornographic mode—something in which the reproductive-organ school of sexual thinking should take valid, if naughty, pleasure. The rather burly, normally masculine, but innocent

duffer of a dentist in an American Army jungle camp, in the late
Korean War, has the enviable reputation of being sexually the
best-equipped male of the whole lot. How so? Quite simple.
There is a typical dirt-colored tent in which, by turns, the males
and females of the Mobile Army Surgical Hospital, solo or in
groups, seek the brightest personal cleanliness to be had under
the primitive conditions. As we know to our surfeit, war is a
grim business, and since the days of archaic film, Hollywood particularly has sought to redeem that bitter fact with reels and
reels of comic relief, which as the "doughboy" rumpus could take
up whole films. It is a filmically accredited as well as common
prank that here soldiers should make a hole at one side of the
bathing tent and eavesdrop on the spectacle of the dentist's tremendous organ (he takes care, it seems, to shield it from the
vulgar gaze). As pure spectacle, of course, the male organ is
still hot news in Hollywood.

   "Tremendous" I say advisedly. One of the soldiers im-
patiently awaiting his turn at the peephole measures it along his
arm with the traditional symbolic folk gesture. The jammed line
of waiting soldiers ("all male" as they say of the beaver movies)
is so avid of the coming view that one might think they formed
a breadline in a country suffering from famine. This much of a
folksy-folksy sex joke *could be* only an incident. But it has a
development. And the development, with odd-mod stylishness,
draws directly on the crudest male-noodle sort of innocence
about homosexuality. It seems that the said dentist, while so incredibly well equipped, has failed, in his latest encounter with
the opposite sex, to produce an erection. He then confesses this
calamity to the resident pastor, and the pastor, while respecting
the secrecy of the confessional, applies for help in the victim's
behalf to one of the film's leads, a groovy intellectual-type surgeon (Donald Sutherland), telling him only that the dentist has
a "problem." The surgeon, you see, is a medical man, and thus
by training (according to the bias of another crude folk myth)
a sex-organ specialist.

   The dentist, when the surgeon arrives at his tent, is
prostrated with shame and grief. Now for the meat of the joke:
his confession, promptly wheedled from him by the surgeon,

is simply, "I'm a fairy!" If you are clever, reader, you'll laugh at that from more than flustered shock, because you'll have guessed that the sole evidence for this fatal self-indictment is the failure of his erection a night or two before. This is homosexual folk-lore at the nadir of heterosexual goofery. Like all such extremist symptoms, its sex is under suspicion. But let that pass. The larger wonder is that anything so antediluvian should be flaunted in a mod comedy. But, you see, that's why—"that's why" being the profoundly cryptic and efficient answer to all questions of "why" addressed to mod, really mod, sophisticates. Yet the makers of the film, plausibly, saw reason not to let it go at just *that* "why."

The dentist (here the comic style is rather like that in Ben Jonson's *Volpone*) tragically announces his decision to commit suicide; not, you see, because he has become impotent, but because he thinks that impotence is proof-simple of homosexuality. He says he can't bear telling the truth to three ladies back home in America, to whom he refers as his "wives" and whose photographs he shows the possum-playing surgeon. The latter immediately reports the affair to his cronies but adds that he "knows" the dentist won't commit suicide. But the dentist, with help, tries to do so. And it is a fake suicide only because the black pill he is given by the surgeon is not the poison it is alleged to be, but probably, as implicit, an aphrodisiac—at least, one supposes that the Korean War forces were supplied with a specific for an emergency of that sort.

Meanwhile—yeah, this *is* crazy!—a veritable Last Supper is composed before the pill-taking, with an open coffin waiting in front of the board, where bread is broken and (even as in *Viridiana*) the participants take the postures of Leonardo's masterpiece. With the pill downed, and the inert "suicide" wafted from his coffin to his bed, the joke needs only a happy denouement to be a triumphant sexisode rather than a mournful sexicide. It is achieved by sending a charitably minded nurse under the winding sheet to prove the effect of the aphrodisiac, which is duly confirmed in the next scene, when the dentist reappears on his feet, hale and hearty, as sublimely ignorant a male reproductive organ as you could imagine in the form of a person. I had to laugh at the peephole bit, and I grinned sardonically at the rest. After all, since many sex jokes have (like this one) long beards, they weren't born yesterday. But neither was I. I am reminded of this fact rather specifically because a mock funeral for dead virility is held elaborately as a banquet in J. K. Huysmans' highly respected fin-de-siècle avant-garde novel *Against the Grain,* but there the comedy is high and esoteric, not (as in *M*A*S*H*) low and out of *Joe Miller Revised.*

For low homosexual comedy, one at least ought to go to homosexuals, who have a lot of it stashed away, or else to cannily informed heterosexuals with more taste than the *M*A*S*H* makers have. The seemingly earnest suicide is really the silly-silly part of the movie, because even if some grown goof believes himself a fairy because of one failure in bed, there are only two at all plausible possibilities for his pursuant behavior: he will realize rather quickly that it is a sign of his true impulse toward men, and gradually succumb, or he'll fly to a doctor, and perhaps a psychiatrist, till he works himself back into his previous virility; or, less plausibly, he'll be content to hide the shame of his impotence behind a false social assurance and just wait.

The suicide is a farce joke typical, in the theater, of comical peasants only. The funeral for dead virility, as presented by Huysmans' hero, Des Esseintes, is an elegant social charade, an excuse for another excess of the aesthetic sensibility, which at the end of the book is renounced by the highly moral hero. Incidentally, homosexuality appears in that novel entirely as an aesthetic experiment, and finally is rejected by Des Esseintes along with all sexual and other carnal indulgences. Now, you may ask why, in an American film comedy of 1970, a contemporary American dentist should not fulfill the theatrical tradition of being a peasant clown. There again you have that self-answering service: "Why?" It's the same in either positive or negative form: Why not? That's WHY! Well, that's why homosexuality, too.

But all joking to one side, there are much better low sexual jokes around (in the movies too) than in *M*A*S*H.* In fact, on a close look, all the outrageous, or rhetorically obscene, jokes in *M*A*S*H* are dispiritingly square. Genuine homosexuality never gets a look-in, while the fairy joke itself derives from that classic view (held by a certain nether stratum of world population) which posits that homosexuality is no more real or natural or viable than the fairies in *A Midsummer Night's Dream*. Who'd ever want anything like that in one's own family?—or one's own army camp? Hence, in *M*A*S*H*, it is only a preposterous delusion, based on an error in medical logic by a touchingly innocent layman, and elaborated as a joke because it's so absurdly implausible; of course, the well-informed gang in the film knows better, but *how much better* remains a mystery to the audience.

Just here one may note something very curious about this movie and its viewpoint toward reality. The horrors of the bloody and perhaps mortal mutilations of war, swiftly dealt with in the makeshift operating room (another tent), are taken in as good-humored a stride as is the psychological trauma of the dentist. An awful mess is created, with lots of "realistic" red liquid and close-ups of wounds, embedded surgical instruments, and a general air of chaos and mute hysteria. One could even say there is a *M*A*S*H* syndrome: a use of low-grade aesthetics that is the film's highest moral achievement. Everything difficult, dreary, dying, and snafu in the milieu of war is tossed into one bag and shaken up for laughs. Eroticism (all the nurses, even the snootiest, seem to be, or end up, as orgasm valves) never leaves the realm of lusty burlesque fun. The precise syndrome? Well, the criminal absurdity of war, via the ideology of radical pacifism, induces grown men to resort to the strategy of the most primitive comic reflexes to maintain their human equilibrium. Actually, the *M*A*S*H* syndrome is hardly as serious as this pure rationalization sounds. The picture's last episode is the classic football-farce roughhouse so dear to old-fashioned movie fans. I'm afraid *M*A*S*H* is just a mod, and duly mashed, revision of the standard doughboy comedy. Laugh, man, laugh! If you can still laugh. And, of course, you *can!*

As for high sexual joking, one need only cite as superlative and typical, and cannily homosexual, Wilde's *The Importance of Being Earnest*. That work, duly transferred to the movies, is high stuff even in the new psychedelic sense; in it, the cucumber, though surgically dismembered for sandwiches before gestation, assumes rank with the banana, which took its classic place as a phallic symbol and psychedelic tool in Andy Warhol's *Harlot. The Importance,* of course, is the superstarred charade of all modern homosexual works in any medium, gauging the modern era as from the nineties to the present. Wilde's superbly styled comedy is really a precursor of the recent Hollywood charade (transparent bluff that it is) titled *Bob and Carol and Ted and Alice,* where the action is climaxed in bed rather than in the parlor. Again, in the new American work, a film that pretends to be mod and offbeat turns out to be dreadfully square. It's a light, sentimental propaganda piece for the sanctity of "couples," legally wedded of course.

One notes, with a single tear in the eye, that the little symbolic promenade of couples outside the hotel, joined by Bob and Carol and Ted and Alice after they've failed in the game of wife-swapping, contains two obviously linked men, one of whom looks like a slightly inflated Burl Ives, and both (not surprisingly) a bit hippie. One imagines a point in thus trademarking homosexuality as having a gently grotesque dimension. "Yes," the film says (catch-in-the throat), "even *those,* too!" Those too, that is, *if* they are as faithful to each other as are Bob and Carol and Ted and Alice. Ostensibly, one is not to speculate that swapping wives for this foursome just might have something to do with swapping sexes all around. For one thing, the switch is to be fought out in bed, where all four of them get together in their night clothes, only to have the two virilities realize, soon after hostilities have begun, that each is the victim of a technical knockout before a blow has been struck. To put it plainly: the right swap (one notes a certain ambiguity of sex in one man and one woman) might have been man-to-man and woman-to-woman. But, as usual, the possibility of subconscious motivation is not recognized unless the plot has an explicit use for it.

The homosexual reading of Wilde's great comedy (though perfectly good without such a reading) is surely no extravagant matter inasmuch as the work itself, the most sophisticated sex farce in the world, is heterosexually extravagant anyway. Its ambiguity is not inertly unsuggestive but actively insinuating. First, hoaxing is the very mechanism of the plot, and the great social hoax of Wilde's period (as his own trial on homosexual charges sadly illustrated) was dandyish womanizing as a cover-up for homosexual tastes. But Wilde's supremely egotistic temperament made him "pose," personally, not as a sodomite indeed (that was Queensberry's vulgar and malicious guess) but as a poetic connoisseur of males: one mask in Wilde's "truth of masks." The whole truth was more carnal. Yet Wilde's farce comedy, *The Importance,* was designed for the theater, and as a film produced in 1953, in England, it was champagnish enough.

I have also seen it done twice on the stage and conclude that it is virtually style-proof. The hoaxes of the plot involve entirely mythical males (might one say "fairies"?) to whom the two society suitors are regularly drawn and with whom they dwell in statutory secrecy. It is notable that what they *really* do in their absences from visible society is never once mentioned; it is only assumed tacitly. The beautiful and witty heterosexual silliness, if one shifts the focus ever so slightly to the left, makes (at least it did in Edwardian England) beautiful and witty homosexual sense. Moreover, that's just the way contemporary, or tacitly 1971, husbands behave on both sides of the Atlantic if they wish to marry, have children, and maintain a home as well as, in some cozy garçonnière, a homo: they invent mythical duties elsewhere and transiently disappear from the social surface.

As a game it is both heterosexually and homosexually hoary. In Hollywood and New York, it's much easier than it was in Wilde's London. All that such modern husbands have to do is to make harmless dates with "other women" and let them ritually be publicized, as they surely will be. That heterosexual scandals in Hollywood are not only normal but *de rigueur* is demonstrated by the existence of a periodical named *Modern Screen,* once an orthodox "fan mag" but now an important gossip-column arm of hot publicity. It is devoted exclusively to exposing (supposedly) the private lives of film celebrities: affairs, marriages, family crises, infidelity, divorce, death, and disease;

in other words, it is one long repetitive charade of celebrity-society at home to those who know nothing about the homes of celebrity-society. It meshes film celebrities with all celebrities (especially if it happens to be Jackie). One of its chief functions is to keep the heterosexual fires burning in the homes of the numberless audience of glamour-watchers and star-gazers. In this respect, *Modern Screen* is not only a scream, it's screamingly square—and quite straightfaced about its supremely unrelieved silliness.

I shall probably be pointing again and again at Mart Crowley's *The Boys in the Band,* which is a bible of homosexual manners. One thing it possesses is an earnest-Ernest, a pipe-smoking former athlete who is currently father of an intact family (you see, "I love my wife"). As he freely confesses, he has had an after-marriage conversion to homosexuality and at the moment is obsessed, as he likewise admits, with staying married to his frequently unfaithful boyfriend. This character, Hank, played by Lawrence Luckinbill, is probably the most altogether "serious" member of Crowley's band. We might add, in passing, that his particular homosexual formula, while rather tormented, seems the most practically successful of them all. For the moment, a complete discussion of Crowley's socially valuable work must be postponed. The wait won't be long.

Men and men, in *The Boys in the Band,* are respectively courters and courted, while men and women, in *The Importance of Being Earnest,* are respectively courters and courted. My point is that Algernon and Ernest (or Jack) in the latter work are courting, not only women for strictly social purposes, but also (unmentioned and unmentionable) men for strictly sexual purposes; furthermore, Jack has decided to initiate Algernon into the game: perhaps they'll make a team. I can't think of anything more *homelike* in the really worldly sense. And neither, I imagine, could Wilde or Mart Crowley. In Wilde's case, the fake logic is uppermost, and there is even voluptuous fun for the two males—with corresponding maneuvers from the two females—to carry on the sanctified War Between the Men and the Women.

Now, I don't imply that ambisexed homosexuals never

"like" their female wives, who may well satisfy a real emotional no less than social need. I would be the last to deny that enduring sentimental attachments may result from the heterosexual end of the homosexual's double marriage. In this, and in the relative security of the heterosexual relation, the doubly married homosexual is just like the doubly married heterosexual with his wife-and-permanent-mistress syndrome. Whose life, for example, is a more dazzling demonstration of this than Wilde's? He never wished to leave Constance Wilde, and in a way he seems really to have liked her; certainly he respected her and he wished her only good. It was she, following the scandal, who renounced him.

Offered quite without frivolity, the previous passages are my case for the symbolism of Jack's and Algernon's comic gourmandise in eating all those cucumber sandwiches, *supplied,* you will remember, by Algernon, but *consumed* mostly by Jack. The animal gusto of this scene (a perfect icon of repressed homosexual hysteria) does not come through so well in the British film; it was positively juicy as acted by Sir John Gielgud and a colleague in a British stage production I saw in New York. What best brings out the sex-charade quality in the movie, where Michael Redgrave is only a so-so Ernest/Jack, is Joan Greenwood's mincing doll-like artificiality as Gwendolyn. I didn't like her gimmick quality *as art* because somehow everything ought to seem preposterously straight in this work. Yet, as I say, the thing is style-proof, either homosexually or comically speaking. All it needs on which to base all imaginable innuendos is the grand, absurdly witty cohesion of the lines and situations. Wilde's unique gift of puckish playfulness has never been equaled in the comic theater.

Well before the nineties, especially in England, there were many homosexual scandals, but few overtly homosexual *works,* unless they were underground products; i.e., pornographic. Wilde himself is suspected of having inspired, perhaps laid the groundwork for, or actually written such a work: *Teleny.* A most fascinatingly ambisexual if also elegant product of this type was *Under the Hill,* a novella by Wilde's contemporary Aubrey Beardsley. But Beardsley, within the province of his elevated style, is much more explicit in the erotic mode than Wilde presumed to be in *The Importance*. Beardsley freely, exquisitely dabbled in obscene details and found the organic difference between the sexes a pleasant accident, an ambisexual convenience. The term "ambisexual" is liberal in the most useful sense because it frees one from the necessity of defining (that is, limiting) a person's sex, and so leaves room for tangible homosexuality. Verily, *Under the Hill* is ambisexually comprehensive and unquestionably is a serious work. Somebody ought to make a movie of it!

The phenomenon of the Marquis de Sade, who left a considerable literary legacy, is rather disarming, and disconcerts any history of homosexual art works that pretends to be suitably chronological. For Sade (1740–1814) was belligerently ambisexual, carrying into sex a cosmic promiscuity that disregarded, in total commitment, all sexual distinctions and had no slightest relation to the eminence of penis and vagina as reproductive organs. This is not stated as news but as pertinent documentation. Sade was a fanatic aesthete of antimoral (or if you wish, amoral) sexuality: perhaps the unique anarchist of sex. His version of crime was simply a ritually inflected ambisexuality that his villainous system, regardless of considerations such as life and medical health, raised toward omnisexuality—a concept of which the reader will hear more.

Sade's tradition, of course, is no mere aesthetic archaism. People with much less character and intellectual faculty than Sade seem to have inherited from the race's past excesses a truly mad orgiastic drive, inducing them to aspire, in ways futile but sincere, toward omnisexuality as a practicable idea. Should anyone claim that exactly these persons are the lamentable, hopeless perverts, I would reply that I privately know at least one who has ended up a zealous though cuckolded husband, and the earnest if frustrated father of a family. Yet a line, inevitably, is to be drawn between life style and art style in the assessment of an individual's sexual nature. In the train of thorough homosexual identification in the movies, there are a number of paradoxical facts to be threshed out.

For instance, to return to the *Satyricon,* this most pro-

foundly homosexual movie in all history was made by a heterosexual, Fellini. The work's free-form fantasy is very personal and
yet calculatingly liberal, not unconnected in this respect with
Petronius' own spirit. Conventional criticism calls the prose
work, obeying the overtness of its title, a satire. A satire, very
properly, it is—on manners, however, not matters. Like the
antique saturnalias, the original work is a celebration of sexual
drives, their orgiastic and eccentric license. Fellini has not departed from the "line" of Petronius except by personalizing the
material, making it (in the way more current now than ever) a
specialized charade rather than the objective satire it technically
was.

There is, as we shall continue to be reminded, both late
and latent homosexuality—something I doubt that Fellini would
reject explicitly and outright as one motive for his *Satyricon*.
He himself is responsible for the legend that he is fascinated by
the freaky applicants, male and female, which his routine casting
calls and fame as a big-time director always draw to his office.
He has told that he personally interviews as many applicants
as possible; indeed, that his interest in them is not necessarily
practical, that he delights in them for their own sake; that, as it
were, he "collects" them and that they form a suite of souvenirs,
both mental and as documents, for he has filmed and photographed applicants whom he has never used in a film. Surely,
his own *8½* (1962) well documents this feature of his temperament in its last, unaffectedly sentimental scene, when all the
characters appear (led by some musical clowns) as creatures of
his fancy.

In the *Satyricon,* besides creating a lush movie spectacle
of much charm and ingenuity, Fellini provides a lengthy choreography of homosexually inclined, young, admirable male physiques and physiognomies, interrupted by heterosexual erotics
only for an interlude. My impression is that he has not neglected
to insert at least one quasi-sexual surrogate for himself. This is
no other than the heroic, archetypally masculine figure of the
Minotaur, who is a handsome, towering Roman gladiator in a
bull headdress. The headdress is good-naturedly removed when
the Minotaur spares the life of Encolpius, who has been forced

to enter his labyrinth as a stunt of the circus entertainment, with court and rabble in on the climax and declaiming their feelings in salvos of sound. Encolpius' good looks, his gameness when the Minotaur finally has him at his mercy, and especially his desperate protest that he is a "poet" and a "student," induces his conqueror to hesitate, remove his mask, and embrace the astonished young man with clear enough innuendo. This is, the Minotaur says for the benefit of all, the beginning of a "friendship."

I can imagine the Minotaur as surrogate for the powerful Fellini himself, sitting Jovelike in his office, receiving all the eager, flashy, amiable young men who desire to be in his films. Fellini's fantasizing atmosphere in this movie might lead one further. Maybe he has projected an even more radical surrogate —purely fictional flesh perhaps—in the profligate, Lichas, admirably cast, acted, and made up in the person of Alain Cuny. This man, appearing in drag, converts his patent masculinity into the demure personality of a bride in order to be formally married to Encolpius, who, as a slave, is under his power. The rite is carried out in solemn ceremony on the deck of the ship which Lichas himself commands, with the ladies of his retinue attending. In the light of the later Minotaur episode, it is significant that before he finds Encolpius so bewitching, Lichas has established his male superiority by worsting him in a wrestling match that starts by looking lethal.

When I first drafted this passage, I had not yet seen an article in *Cinema* (No. 2, Fall 1970) by a close observer of Fellini's work, and his personal acquaintance. Called "Fellini's Continuing Autobiography," it quotes Fellini as having stated publicly, "My *Satyricon* is even more autobiographical than my *8½*." Encolpius, claims the author of the article, represents Fellini himself—a very beautiful "Fellini" indeed. Here I feel obliged to note something long known to the world and to Hollywood: the physical beauty of the enactors of "irregularities" of all sorts, from homosexual acts to murder, put a quite different complexion on the matter than would be there if the enactor were ugly. To be sure, Fellini did not *have* to choose exquisite types for his two homosexual heroes; supposedly they are bisexual, yet their heterosexuality is professional in drive, not emotional. Without ambiguity, the young men selected—Martin Potter as Encolpius, Hiram Keller as Ascyltos—are convincingly in character as well as handsome. In Petronius' novel, the beauties of Encolpius and Ascyltos must be imagined by the reader. In the film, they are constantly before us as literal imagery.

One might think that such ritual aesthetic conversion of those who commit conventionally sordid and wrong actions—something so typical of the movies!—might have received the earnest attention of film critics. Not so. Research into critical records reveals that what is a sort of chicanery, openly and habitually practiced by the film art, has seldom been taken into account. A case from life, involving a homosexuality that the film made from it ignored, appeared in *Bonnie and Clyde*. The legendary criminal hero is played by handsome, muscular Warren Beatty. Actually a homely specimen, the original Clyde, along with his Bonnie, once picked up a gas-station attendant, who became chief male assistant in his holdups. He made the third member, apparently, of a bedtime threesome. In the movie, all this was expurgated. The pickup and loyal henchman proves so homely that it would have been very implausible, anyway, for the beautiful Clyde to have had a crush on him. Besides, the movie Clyde is made to have an impotence problem . . . *Sic(k) veritas fugit.*

A grave defect of movies in general is the dishonesty with which they handle all physical beauty in relation to its actual roles. Doubtless, in the *Satyricon*, Fellini exaggerated what was monstrous and bizarre, as well as what was beautiful, in Petronius' Rome. Whatever the stringency of the original satire, however, Petronius created a lifelike balance among its elements. This quality, essential to conviction, is just what popular movies in all genres are cavalier about. The sordidness of Petronius' version of life was gamier, less picturesque, than Fellini portrays it, yet Fellini understood its playfulness and its permissiveness. The way in which the interests of morality and aesthetics are opposed is seldom really understood in artistic quarters. Instinctively, the entertainment industries seek to exploit public ignorance in this respect.

The function of the joke (sexual or not) is habitually distorted when its status is satirical. A preposterous mistake (coolly made and coolly received—I mean "cool" in the mod sense) took place when the English came out with *Oh, What a Lovely War!,* an extravaganza prodigiously parodying the manners and mortalities of international military campaigns. Of course, that movie had cute points: jokes annihilating the pomps of military decorum. Yet our age of sentimental radicals, canonically opposed to war, thought that, because it had those points, it was utterly devastating propaganda for peace. Public psychology about war is in as much a state of semi-idiocy as public psychology is apt to be, even now, about homosexuality. Probably the general public will be more swiftly enlightened about the latter than about the former. Wars will end when mass murder becomes abhorrent to the race, not before. Till then, national interests and their supposed economic functions will determine war-making. The principal grounds for opposing the war in Vietnam are not simple abhorrence for deliberate killing of human by human; it is, rather, that Vietnam is none of our business and that the billions spent on fighting in behalf of South Vietnam had better be used toward solving American problems at home. Surely, these positions are eminently arguable. But they have nothing whatever to do with the musical-comedy style with which war has been satirized in *Oh, What a Lovely War!,* which is an extremely silly and unimportant picture regardless of the skills expended on it.

To say that this film is propaganda against war is exactly the same as saying that the satiric fun provided by playing on the mystic art of picking winners in horseraces, the subject of the pop film farce *Three Men on a Horse,* is propaganda against betting; or that the ludicrous agonies of the Marx Brothers—when as theatrical producers in a run of bad luck they cannot pay their hotel bills and resort to fantastic tricks to get credit—are propaganda against producing plays or being deadbeats. My moral point about *M*A*S*H* is not that the joke about homosexuality is a "joke" but a corny and naïvely mythological joke imagined on a scale that would honor the Ringling Brothers. It is a feeble and an antique joke and dishonestly used in a comedy styled pretentiously in basic black and rudimentary red. But, then, sentimental radicals will put up with any degree of pretension or ineptitude so long as they believe the Establishment is being "annihilated." They don't know that the credit of the Establishment is being lost daily through events, but *not* through events that paint the Establishment as joyously, riotously absurd. All this makes the Establishment seem the more "human," the more "inevitable."

Aesthetically, a joke is a joke, but permanent and changing customs affect the on-the-spot laughter. As for destructive satire, homosexuality can no longer be ridiculed as alien to nature and simply contemptible. It took large-scale mortal persecution of the Jews to make Jewish jokes seem "anti-Semitic" to a certain segment of the public. By and large, the sexual joke tends to be propaganda *for* whatever "vice" or idiosyncrasy it may utilize, barring none. Making a formal joke of homosexuality is what unites even heterosexuals with homosexuals. Ten or twenty years ago, I daresay some damaging ridicule was attached to the vulgar "fairy joke," depending on the company to which it was told. Can the same be said today? Has not homosexuality become today, at worst, another all-too-human foible? Certainly, in the ranks of the cultivated and liberal-minded of this time, no longer is the social equation between heterosexual and homosexual a sort of public confrontation; rather, it is only another privileged get-together to honor the verities and the amiabilities. "Status," the great equalizer, is no longer even needed.

As, so far, the most outspoken of overt homosexual comedies, *The Boys in the Band* is a clear-cut case by which to confirm the above observations. And it is not at all the crude propaganda of poker-faced pornography. What is subtle about it in today's theater (fortunately, unlike *Myra Breckinridge*, it became a movie outside Hollywood's factory system) is that it welds together homosexual ranks and heterosexual ranks by emphasizing decency rather than indecency about its homosexuals, by joking pitilessly about them and their amours, and by sounding, on the serious side, the note of existential unhappiness which the more serious theatergoer has learned to recognize and tolerate because so obviously it has a catholic moral hygiene to it. It humiliates pride (and prejudice too) and restores a certain rational balance to the existence of all madcap excesses, regardless of sexual classification. For centuries, heterosexual infidelity, heterosexual "wickedness" in erotic and other fields, have taken it on the chin from comic satirists, so why shouldn't the sister vices in the consortium of homosexuals take it on the chin, and nobly?

There is a dimension in which, despite its high degree of specialization, *The Boys in the Band* joins the realm of the enduring Human Comedy. And it is the rare virtue of Crowley's work that it situates itself so solidly and sanely, if a wee bit sentimentally, in this wider dimension. The film version both loses and gains in the transfer to another medium. On the stage (where Robert Moore directed it) there was a special dramatic focus in the ensemble acting that is lost amid the close-ups and attention to detail in the movie, which has all the actors of the stage production, so that there is no lack of mellowness in William Friedkin's filmic handling, which is also nicely gracile. Perhaps what the play did not have, the clutter of the flossy little terrace and the storm intervening and messing it up, properly emphasizes the haphazard, confused frailty of some of the homosexual relations shown. Yet such environmental realism, when not carefully montaged (as it is not here), damages the dramatic element in the old, fallacious documentary way. The stage production's outlines are cleaner, more unified, and thus more satisfying. Insidiously, film technique has reduced the effectiveness of Leonard Frey's superb enactment of the big camp role of Harold, the haughty homo for whom the party is given. To some extent this is due to the altered timing of Harold's lines, whose continuity is broken up by the montage of camera angles. His grotesque yet understandable personality dominated the stage whenever the action put him uppermost, while in the film his funny style looks less naturally kinky and idiosyncratic, more like calculated acting craft.

Perhaps Mr. Frey, acting in his first film, could not adapt to the movie technique so well as did other members of the play's cast. A notable gain is the sympathy engendered by the role of the outsider in the band, the "straight guy" who has been homosexually tempted but stands firm, especially firm when he gets a load of what really goes on in gay life. On the stage the actor, Peter White as Alan, came through a bit thin and priggish, his choked-up declaration of fidelity to his wife over the phone (during the telephone game) looking rather stagy. In the film, owing to the opportunity of Mr. White to convey his dilemma in close-ups and special timings, I believed rather than disbelieved in his character as really heterosexual. Of course, this ambiguity brings up an inevitable metadimension in theater, especially homosexual theater.

Is an actor doing a gay part really homosexual?—and conversely, is an actor doing a straight part perhaps relying on his craft to let him get away with what technically is a sexual put-on? Surely it is a fascinating problem for the buffs of gay life, and just as interesting as the psychodrama motif that has made modern theater a crucible for testing an actor's personality and character in private life. For example, is Lawrence Luckin-bill—enacting the double-life father-of-a-family in town doing his gay bit—privately heterosexual and only doing here a professional job? The point is that any heterosexual actor who does sustain homo tendencies will find acting a homosexual an inner moral test no less than an outer moral test, the latter being that of doing a good acting job. So, unless we the audience wish to play possum, the aesthetic/moral dimension of *The Boys in the Band* has several layers intercutting each other as quite real factors; for instance, a homosexual actor—*is* there one in *The Boys in the Band?*—has to decide, backstage, whether he is going to pose as a heterosexual engaged for a homosexual role, or somehow or other will let his fellow actors in on his true sex. I trust it is superfluous to add that I am totally unacquainted with the members of this cast or any hearsay about them aside from what I read in the papers.

Still another public dimension of homosexual meta-theater is the matter of desirable publicity for actors perhaps compromised by acting a fag role *so* brilliantly that the audience is supposed to conclude: "Well, that's the real thing: no doubt of it!" Hence the actor playing the flaming faggot or plain campy part of Emory, Cliff Gorman, enjoyed publicity stories in which he was quoted as indicating his private heterosexuality by stating that he was married, etc. No matter what angle one takes on homosexual theater, the distance between the professionally gay and the privately gay must be somewhat clouded by inherent paradoxes.

Public policy by actors and their agents is apt to forget, in such cases as *The Boys in the Band*, that heterosexual marriage is well known as a routine masquerade (again consult *The Importance of Being Earnest*) for homosexual actors whose careers supposedly depend on their seeming straights. When playing ordinary juvenile leads or starring parts, they usually have to be passionately in love with a woman, and the women of their audience, it is logically reasoned, have to believe in the heterosexual so as to believe in the actor. In *The Deer Park*, Norman Mailer's novel about Hollywood, we can see what a hullabaloo may be raised about the problem of a popular homosexual actor who balks at seeming heterosexual off the screen as well as on; usually, the Hollywood powers that be insist that there must be an official off-the-screen guarantee that a popular male actor *is* privately what he *pretends to be* publicly. The existence of *Modern Screen* (see above) sufficiently attests to this ordained public policy in the sphere of professional let's-pretend.

Going into the complexities of artistic make-believe, one risks losing sight of the substance of the ideas in homosexual theater per se. Mr. Crowley's idea in *The Boys in the Band* is important because of its social veraciousness, in that he has shown modern homosexual society as a unit of complexly interacting factors. He has tried to cross-section his homosexual society at the point where more or less outrageous homo types touch and mingle with acceptable ones; those, I mean, who have sustained enough natural masculinity and personal dignity to pass, if required to, in heterosexual society. Such homosexuals, of course, are, contrary to rumor, in the social majority. The two overt fag roles in Crowley's play represent the kink in homosexual compulsiveness to recklessly advertise its nature. In this sense, personal aggressiveness inevitably takes the social form of grotesquerie, discursively mannered (as we see in the two instances here) according to temperament, but still flamingly homosexual.

The more masculine and conventional homosexuals— even those who keep their camp moods and mannerisms on private tap—may scorn or deplore the flaming types while frankly being fond of their wit and personal ingratiation. One must realize how clever, in fusing themselves with the social and business worlds, homosexuals are in adapting an innate effeminacy, seeking outlet in innuendo and mannerism, to regular polite standards of behavior. As such moderated "clowns," they are welcomed because they relieve tensions, supply diversions, in the way jesters once did for kings and queens who had matters of state as well as sex on their minds. This social vein is brought out in Mr. Crowley's play quite well and with deft lightness. What is rather statically heavy and narrow in his play emerges as the more serious, agonic side of homosexual comedy-drama. One easily detects here that homosexual camping (which, by the way, need have no topical reference to sex) is a little theater in the midst of life; as such it is enjoyed, and a bit patronized, by the more masculine and dignified members of this boyish band. But the willing homosexual audience of life's camp theater, we learn, has its own differing problems; some such problems, as the play validly tells us, are settled summarily (even as in heterosexual relations) in bed. Others must overflow into tomorrow's loneliness, lovelessness, and bad conscience. The play, and the film made from it, tell us that, too.

Unfortunately, a weak spot in *The Boys in the Band* is the central role, Michael, the plot's motivator. It is he who gives the party, and getting uncustomarily drunk and overexcited, invents a telephone game which unsparingly puts everyone on the rack—with the sole exception of the Midnight Cowboy, the male whore who has sold his services to be Harold's birthday present; this hustler motif is not peculiar, of course, to Crowley's play. Michael, it finally appears, is a lapsing Catholic and as typical a fugitive from a psychiatrist's office as from the premises of God. As a scion of homosexual culture, he is palpably a chic failure, and presumably this failure is to move the audience on the side of pathos. It moves one not so much, I think, as the author intended, because the stakes themselves are not high enough: they're simply "chic." Finally *The Boys in the Band* must be rated an unusually entertaining and truthful social observation—impressive and yet faulty as a pathos comedy. Still, on the whole, the brilliance of its dialogue and its character-drawing survives. Crowley can supply laugh neatly on top of laugh in a way to recall Wilde's consummate gaiety. It is an artist's virtue and has nothing to do with social levels or genders.

At the end, after a fit of hysteria, the much chastened Michael tells his friend, a former lover, that to cap the all-too-eventful evening he's going out to catch midnight mass. Now the planned audience response is to weep for, or with, this morally naked homosexual, desperate in just the way that millions of heterosexuals with parallel problems are. Just so have homosexuals and heterosexuals in the audience been expected at least to laugh at, if not with, the preceding display of homo high jinks, which have been so many sex jokes given an extra lift, a superior tilt, by the lifeblood of drama. This is why, when the final note sounded by the author is overdeliberately sad, film and stage audiences would come out smiling and murmuring, "Brilliant, brilliant . . ." Throughout modern homosexual literature, one finds these elements and their contradictoriness displayed much less cannily than here.

Still, a vice lurks at the heart of the work: the overall air of pleading for homosexual tolerance by showing the promiscuously human, diffuse side of homosexuality. "Look!" the characters seem to say, "we're just like you, really; our problems are honest and we suffer for our moral flabbiness as for our sins." Gauged by more recent developments, that is a bit timid. Despite the rigor of his observation, Crowley cannot suppress a bias that today (more than yesterday) takes on the look of political coating, of propaganda. One thinks of the gay-power movement and its organizations: the elder Mattachine Society, the Gay Activists' Alliance, the Gay Liberation Front. It is not that this moral extension of the play's theme is "bad." But if it had been more intact and decisive as drama, it would not situate itself ambiguously in the social context, one would not think of it as special pleading. Doing so seems only natural; for example, wouldn't the slogan that appeared on a homosexual picket sign do for a joke in *The Boys in the Band*: "Have you tried one?" Current propaganda, in fact, has converted, updated Mr. Crowley's emotional bias. It has become the opposite of homosexual political strategy to seem a "sinner" or even "unhappy." By and large, as another slogan uncompromisingly says, "Gay is good." Anyone disagreeing with that is in for a fight. Events have indicated as much. Five homosexuals, dubbed "the Rockefeller Five," sat-in at Republican state headquarters in New York City and were arrested, as they expected to be. During a big rally staged for them, one shouted out: "Gay is not only good, gay is angry!"*

Mr. Crowley cannot help it. Homosexuality as a sex joke, a realm of happy porno violence, is firmly related nowadays to the new homosexual militance aligning itself with black militance and student militance as symptoms of our time's revolutionary temper. However impurely, *The Boys in the Band* links the outright joke with a dual moral: homosexual humanism and homosexual belligerence. Glance at the proliferating sex mags, gay, nongay, and split, that fly the flag of pornography as a thing washed clean of both sin and legal offense. These have formed, as of 1971, a propaganda front with conscious political platforms advocating untrammeled sexual empression.

Every sexual organism (and this is a charged pun) is a two-way mechanism. So is history, which, like the vibration of time, flows backward and forward at once. We do well not to risk overlooking the continuity of historic context when discussing seriously anything at all. The nonhomosexual homosexual joke sequence in *M*A*S*H* is part of its stark violence, a facet of its sophisticated-leer burlesque. Let us not ignore this historical vibration. A given social truth (e.g., homosexuals *do* exist) is turned into a brainless folk myth by the impotent dentist's absurd logic: "Since I'm impotent, I must be a fairy!" The stunt would technically resist depth analysis (is the dentist really homosexual?) because it fits so well the high-low farce style of

* Quoted by *The Village Voice*, August 13, 1970.

the film. Morally, *M*A*S*H* is a pure cock-and-cunt tract, sex being shown everywhere in Americanized Korea on the stale, horny-porny doughboy level. And yet this same level, freshened with the new permissiveness and appareled in new dress styles, is now all the rage. Is sex in *M*A*S*H* funny? One could scream with *Screw*. Is it also, in sober sense, highly moral balling? Glance aside at the official morale of the Gay Liberation Front. *M*A*S*H* reminds us, no kidding, just how old-fashioned in all ways that Korean War was. Today, from Vietnam, we hear of marijuana and harder drug habits among soldiers, indiscriminate sex orgies, and reports of mortal sadism with material consequences. As for cutting sex capers, those surgical jokers in *M*A*S*H* are somewhat closer to Dr. Kildare and company than to Now's high or low sex fashions. Anyway, how high (in more than one sense) all low fashions have become! Consider hallucinogenic sex, paraphernalia wear for males and females, highbrow rock, high-low bohemia as unisex life style, and so on.

As must be evident by now, my own prejudices are aesthetic and historical. Homosexuality, like a virus or a chemical poison, is often a technically qualified "disease" just where, it is hoped and presumed, heterosexual health technically reigns. Unhappily there persists an ecological mental prejudice against homosexuality like a cloud on the social horizon. One of the most irritatingly brassy and self-righteously sentimental of mod films about the sex scene was the successful *Midnight Cowboy*. Whether being funny or sad, it is as artful a piece of claptrap as ever came from honest craftsmen bent on making a fast buck. I willingly concede that Jon Voight and Dustin Hoffman gave excellent performances in view of the requirements imposed on them; in fact, Hoffman made such a wily portrait of a mentally and physically sick Broadway rat that I would have indulged myself by admiring it had it not been for the high-suds moral detergent used to finish up the action.

Jon Voight's role—a Texas big boy who falls for the idea of hustling in fabulous New York and buys one of its mod uniforms, a cowboy's outfit—might be thought a version of the traditional Fool of Fortune who wins out through innocence combined with virtue. But even great fools of nature as far up as the nineteenth century (take Prince Myshkin or even Lucien de Rubempré), while they may be heroic, are portrayed as pathological and end tragically without winning fairy-tale triumphs unless anticlimactically. In this century, existentialist fiction remolded such heroes into dreary suicide-suckers. Not so Voight's cowboy, who wins a fairy-tale triumph of sorts; that is, he's cured of the hustler hallucination and returns to decent society (believe it or not) after being initiated by the equally pathetic but magically virtuous hallucination of his found friend, Ratso, who believes that Florida is the earthly paradise the travel folders say it is. *Everybody* had to see that to believe it. In a day when all decent ignorant male critters like the Voight Cowboy are fashionably considered cannon fodder and the voluntary or involuntary victims of President Nixon, this particular victim is presented as a humane hero beautifully, cleanly redeemed from the filthy fleshpots of New York. "Wow!" as that cigarette commercial says.

"Filthy fleshpots"? Don't take that too seriously, although it's consistent with the film's corny logic. A point passed over with ingratiating ambiguity, but essential to the plot, is that finally the Cowboy, to aid Ratso in his Florida project, willfully and brutally victimizes an elderly homosexual and utters profanities in so doing that would have caused the president of the Mattachine Society, had he taken them seriously, to go through the roof. Of course, by the aesthetics of popular entertainment, nothing can be more easily laid aside, on instant notice, than one's morals. But why should this be so very easy a trick in our day of militant minorities, always getting bigger and impregnated with, among other things, the rights of sex—all kinds? What, in brief, is virtuous or decent or pardonable in killing, or almost killing, a homosexual patron who (in *Midnight Cowboy*) not only begs for mercy but rapidly offers you the contents of his bulging wallet without having received any favors? A parallel exists between the dreadful-duffer psychology of the dentist in *M*A*S*H* and the Midnight Cowboy's bray of outraged masculine virtue in the very midst of his bloody act. Let's not underrate the entertaining intrusion of blood in both movies.

Frankly, all entertainment values to one side, we'd have to apply to a mythical Office of Sadism Unlimited for a license to defend our Midnight Cowboy's morality. Anyhow, his film definitively washes him clean: deodorant-clean, because the perspiration of guilt is visibly absent on him.

Notice that one doesn't have to take a "gay-activist" attitude to condemn the vulgarity and moral abracadabra of *Midnight Cowboy*. One has only to reaffirm perfectly clear and traditional cultural and moral sanities. The film is as trivial and mixed up in all historical dimensions as it is irrational and immoral if strictly criticized by the principles of existing homosexual organizations, politically oriented or not. Notice this too: a depth reading of the Cowboy's emotional friendship for Ratso (doted upon by sentimental film reviewers) could aptly postulate that this friendship is subconsciously homosexual—the more aptly so because the Cowboy takes the trouble, again and again, to deny the rather too close implication. Sophisticated citizens: look about you. The evidence is in many recent novels and probably will be caught on even more screens before this book gets into print. The trade of hustling women (the Cowboy's original great ambition) sometimes evolves into hustling homosexuals—after all, it's easier— and this, in a good proportion of instances, eventually creates a homosexual in the hustler. There's nothing esoteric or forced about this logic; on the contrary, it can be justified by careful observation or checking.

Support for it has appeared on three Underground screens, these understandably being more genuinely confiding than commercial screens. However, commercial films are quick to sniff a trend, especially if a ready-made play is at hand. In *The Caretaker*, an interesting film with an attractive, obviously sinister Leather Boy (Alan Bates) going about his appointed business, the homosexual hustler lurks not altogether mutely just under the surface. The homosexual terms of the plot are decidedly and deliberately offbeat, so that, as homosexual life style, the doings in this movie assume the homosexual charade form of a guessing game for in-group spectators, homosexual and heterosexual. To grasp the full message of such a work, in other words, one must be a sexually well-informed observer as well as an astute reader of plots. Pinter's art style, of course, shares in the moral apocrypha invented by the existentialists.

As over and over we may notice in films, this homosexuality in code (because partly under wraps) is but another facet of life itself. We discern more clearly how it works by grace of a candidly devised film also from England, *The Leather Boys,* touching more honestly and clannishly than does *The Caretaker* on the Leather Boy as a masculine homosexual cult, masked, but putting forth the buddy-buddy stuff as unabashed bait. This is the ploy we see being used in the final sequence of *The Leather Boys.* It fails. The prospective convert, stubbornly heterosexual, is quietly shocked when the words and mannerisms at a Leather Boy bar give away his ardent chum's true purpose and personality. It is all unsensationally accomplished and even has the fadeout of the stock frustrated-romance film of the heterosexual world.

Revelation in art uses such a code at convenience, typically for creating an atmosphere of mystery or, perhaps more frequently, as a facile comic touch. The repertory of male nellies used as a titillating adjunct to farce has expanded with time in the film medium. I have already mentioned one such, cut from the male manikin pattern, in that wild, self-consciously kook film, *The Producers,* whose chief kook is Zero Mostel. The nelly-clown type, regardless of occupation, has a classic illustration in American films: the late, well-remembered Franklin Pangborn. Toward Pangborn's usually minor but unmistakable impersonations, the average spectator had the tolerant but touch-me-not attitude of certain adults whom I recall from my childhood. The permissive-minded witness, in life or in art, would laugh at such impersonations without drawing judgment to his side. In those days, this was possible because homosexuality in the media was still decorously hush-hush, still, even at its most daring, a politely obscene joke. In the seventies, one can look back on the way homosexuality has progressed in the movies from casual joke to something judged, moralized, and "treated," and now to an explicit aesthetic quantity, welcome or abhorred.

Homosexual code films have become mass distributed and may break out in wanton or coy clarification. Three films which I presently have in mind are of the Andy Warhol school of social realism: one part camp (for far-far cult laughs), one part literalist, one part old-fashioned tell-a-story film-making. This is the current, aesthetically primitive stage of the Warhol "school," of which the maker of *Flesh* and *Trash*, Paul Morrissey, is a postgraduate. It is not so much that these works are coded as that their protagonist, an attractive young male hustler given to states of homosexual mimesis, evolves a sexually fluid, indecisive libido. Warhol's *My Hustler* preceded Morrissey's films, and was, I believe, the first Warhol-trademarked movie to offer something like standard plot as an ingredient of his formula. Like everything about the Warhol factory, of course, *My Hustler* is insidiously, obsessively homemade, but here with an ingenuity related to life style in action rather than kept, like the Campbell's soup cans (so dear to the Beautiful People), in perpetual deep-freeze.

According to his odyssey in *Flesh* and *Trash* (where he is played by one performer, Joe Dallesandro), the Warhol hustler is a Midnight Cowboy sucked in and down to what traditionally passes for a low vice: indiscriminate male whoredom. But the Warhol-factory milieu is not a place where moral judgments are made or even remotely recognized; it is a place where questionable city morals assume an Arcadian innocence, even preciousness, not to say also some presumptuousness. Both Morrissey and Warhol like to think they are concerned with the facts—facts which already have been found bona-fide, and of course mesmerizing. In the Warhol prototype of such film odysseys, *My Hustler*, the protagonist, Paul America, is a pure male-physique type, tall, platinum blond, and as sweet, languid, and easygoing a number as a homosexual client might hope to dial. He *is* phoned up in the movie because he has joined a business called Dial-a-Hustler.

The communication media have grown sublimely pop. Nowadays you can order either a lay or a poem, as well as a steak, by phone. I'm not sure of the actual existence of this sort of call-boy house, but that want-ad sex has surfaced is a presumed fact now, for many months, according to columns in the porno sex mags. It is likewise a regular part, more or less tacit, of the much advertised dating services. Naturally the term "Dial-a-Hustler" is a fag gag; still it fits Warhol's film like a very tight T-shirt. Mr. America's longish euphonious muscles are not rhetorical like those of more gymnastic specimens, but the sight of his nakedness in swimtrunks (and less) instantly wins friends and influences people on both sides of the screen. I should say that, for an amateur actor, Mr. America is a most acceptable professional; in fact, casting so natural and modest a good-looker was a stroke of directorial genius, if nothing more. I can't imagine anyone who'd find him at all offensive, while many (as the plot implies) find him absolutely seductive, though all he does is stretch out and wait.

Lying on the beach in front of his client's Fire Island cottage, the youth is cruised by a female bather while his anxious host, who keeps a zoomy eye on him from the porch, discusses the situation with a friend who himself happens to be an old-pro hustler. The object of everyone's interest, the long lush blond, is quite new at the game. Will he be really "professional"? His suspicious client fears urgent propositions from other directions, and soon others materialize in a scene of hi-fi vérité in the cottage's snug little bathroom. Here novice and old-pro chum up for a shower and a shave, and for once Warhol's prolonged mini-action style pays a dividend in coin other than dullness. Mostly by ear alone (Warhol has a most economical way with technique) we witness golden propositions from two women and the frantic host himself. What none of the three incursive suitors knows is that during the previous part of the scene (the showering and shaving) the old pro has quietly made his own golden proposition, which includes, as counterpart of his offer to initiate the other into the high finance of hustling, a nominal fee for the initiator. What is the fee? Nothing, as we've learned from the delightfully discreet dialogue, but a "cut" in the form of the novice's body, available and free (at least once) to the old pro himself . . . not a bad looker in his own right. *My Hustler* could have been called *The Hustler Hustled*.

The cuteness of the idea, put across with dry camp irony, is that "my hustler" is everybody's property in the abstract, since after all he's a professional, but he retains, in concrete fact, the chancy independence of his own sexual preference, undeveloped though it still seems to be. What the prospective clients least expect, however, is that the proposition likeliest to succeed should come from *another* hustler. But it does. And, cutely, the mum reaction of the shower-fresh novice to the regular propositions made him indicates, at the deliberately cliff-hung fadeout, that he'll accept the veiled, though not *too* veiled, proposition of his new-found buddy. Decidedly: a different version of buddy-dom from that exploited in *Midnight Cowboy*! It is one altogether much more plausible—certainly as seen from the standpoint of the hustler's typical experience; it's also, I think, decidedly more palatable. Which, for the spectator, should make a tangible difference to the aesthetics of the matter.

A sort of specter spreads its Hollywoodian wings over the activities of the hustler, especially as he represents an all-male cult, and this specter (with a bow to Freud) is impotence; psychic impotence, traditionally, but nowadays, as we find from *Trash*, an impotence technically precipitated by drug addiction, and thus fuzzily psycho-physical. This is the sexual focus of Joe Dallesandro's hustler as he is made to evolve from *Flesh* to *Trash*. In respect for corollary evidence and the rights of beyond-camera truth, one must add that situations such as Dallesandro's in *Trash*, a development of the professional-sex logic of *Flesh* and *My Hustler*, are not founded on mirage but assumed to exist in the real world surrounding Warhol's studio.

While *Trash* was in the making, a well-known transvestite, Jackie Curtis (who makes a brief appearance in *Flesh*), was supposed actually to be married to a youth-type similar to Dallesandro, except that the expected groom did not turn up for the ceremony; therefore another young man stood in for the lugubriously gay occasion as it was reported in *The Village Voice*. Mr. Curtis is also an author of produced plays, incidentally, and thus in every way legitimate as an entertainer. The whole marriage idea might have been a simple publicity stunt. However, the situation in *Trash* has another transvestite, Holly Woodlawn by name, shacked up with Dallesandro. He is still a free-lance hustler, but now, in the main, is the service end of a shabby arrangement with his transvestite sweetheart, who for the camera plays "straight woman." The arrangement is shabby if only because of the accented factor of bohemian poverty— "trash," you understand. But trash, like gay, is "good," and sometimes even "angry." You should see Miss Woodlawn in her gay-activist (Women's Lib to you) moods. She's a veritable Vesuvia.

In *Flesh,* Dallesandro's relations with males are literally illustrated but they are almost pedantically professional. In physical stature he is rather petite but very well made: a slightly undersized Adonis. Once he merely strips to be aesthetically ogled, and chastely lectured, by a senior male artist, who seems to want only to sketch him. Since in this instance Dallesandro has been picked up on nearby Union Square, the artist's validity is presumably beyond dispute. In the later film, the same young hustler, whose hair has grown three or four inches— and hangs straight down like an Indian brave's—has become a junkie so that he can't always get it up for bed action, at least not for his inamorata, who supports him. Gone are those halcyon days of *Flesh,* when he could flirt with adjacent transvestites while being sucked off by a female whore. Debonairly free-lancing and laying females en passant, but out of commission one night because of drugs, Dallesandro is tossed out of bed to sleep on the floor; whereupon the lady (Miss Woodlawn) proceeds, in one of the most voluptuously tacky scenes in all film, to masturbate (anally, if she's to be taken as a transvestite) with a soft-drink bottle, an empty one. Meanwhile, Dallesandro desperately tries to sleep in his exile on the floor. The spectator may be moved to sympathize with both mistress and man. I didn't, if only because I was shocked that nobody in the film seemed to have considered what may happen to helpless soft-drink bottles when thus abused: by breaking or creating a vacuum, they cause accidents in their abusers, ranging from minor to major. But stop! I'm forgetting that such considerations certainly are part of the intentional fun. There comes to mind, unbidden, some paragraphs from an antique issue of *Time,* which boldly (for then) reported just such accidents. Yet the victims, I recall, were not transvestites or fragile fags, but rugged sailors, tragically if momentarily isolated in anal deprivation.

The course of true hustling, one might say, never drinks smooth.

In the continuity of real life, Paul America, actor, can contemplate the fate of Joe Dallesandro, actor, with the aid of a torch the size of the Statue of Liberty's. And if Jon Voight's Cowboy hadn't made his escape to Florida, and thence (plausibly) to Vietnam, a look-in on *Trash* might provide him too with the moral lesson smashed home by that film: sexual deracination by drugs doesn't combine with good hustling (unless, of course, Warhol presents the film). The prostitute's fortunes, like the true lover's, must depend in no small degree on virility. Virility's sudden or gradual loss may signal the operation, not of a knife, but of fate. Its role in homosexual experience, seen via the movies, is not to be overlooked.

In *Fellini Satyricon*, the loss befalls Encolpius as a tragicomedy of enigmatic origin requiring the approved offices of contemporary magic. One device is whipping—that is, rhythmic switching—another, sorcery. After being fortified with an aphrodisiac, if slambang confrontation with a passive female's open legs didn't bring you up, only black magic would. In such cases, from that century to this, aphrodisiacs have not only the odor of medical sanctity but the odor of tacit homosexuality. In Encolpius' case, the fun—once more—lies largely in his given status as a homosexual.

The most reliable, heterosexually oriented remedies might well be expected to fall short of effectiveness with homosexuals. Through the above-mentioned office of the Earth Mother in Fellini's film, we see that the computer of heterosexual tradition could mysteriously work even with a man who, when the show is down, elects to be homosexual. We see this happen when, after the sport with the charming Negro woman they find in the abandoned villa, Encolpius and Ascyltos turn to each other when it's bedtime. That black Prehistoric Venus is a wonderful image of a sexual computer. Yet we know that this same computer, as a heterosexual divinity, continually and utterly breaks down, never to be repaired. The old muse of Aphrodisia would rightly be shocked to learn that certain males, programmed homosexually, won't react to her herbs—or herself. The incident in Fellini's film may be construed as a fantasy projection of incest as integral with the homosexual drive but ultimately dispensable. Impotence is not necessarily a hetero- sexual disease. It may be a sign (army dentists, take note) that the star of homosexual health is rising to its apogee.

The facile ambisexual habits of pagan times are beauti- fully incarnated by Encolpius and Ascyltos. Yet these habits sustained their own mental fallacies, based on an old phallic worship whose origin, of course, had been heterosexual. In the *Satyricon*, Petronius felt free to play on this "phallacious" ambiguity and Fellini proved that he is not one to lag in such matters. The truly extraordinary plastic beauty with which he imagines the adventures of his homosexual couple may dazzle us so much that the astute moral essay he has written on sex (including a sacred and a profane fable about heterosexual love) tends to dissolve in the beguiling optical flow. Fellini has opened up homosexuality on the ambisexually poetic level without neuterizing it (we shall be discussing this development) or strait- jacketing it with morbid repressions, such as guilt complexes, or giving it, as does *The Boys in the Band*, a contemporary moral nudity. In Crowley's play, there is no basic sexual freedom; everything is straitjacketed into the struggle with invading con- ventions, as if today's homosexuals were pressured to duplicate the wife-and-mistress institution with a change in sex.

The so-called Roman decadence of the *Satyricon* was the ideal milieu for Fellini's purpose since it was a time and place when sensual license, being the order of the day, could indulge the entire repertory of sexuality from obscenity to sublimity, from the lyricism of low comedy to the dithyrambs of high tragedy; homosexuality, in this repertory, was simply one ingredient. The banal word "lusty" renders poor service to Fellini's achievement in homosexual aesthetics. "Virtuoso viril- ity" may sound too literary to describe it properly. All the same, virtuoso virility is the exact charge with which he has endowed his debonair, altogether charming pair of gifted love-makers. They are more romantic, less "satirically" sordid, than Petronius' originals: more flesh transmogrified to fantasy. Once, they have to be paid to lay the nymphomaniac wife of a despairing hus- band. Even so, they are the hustlers of timeless fable rather than the hustlers of current fact.

Lest we forget (for it may be an "accident" not so funny as it is deeply relevant), Voight's Midnight Cowboy is embarrassed in mid-bed by the same humiliating failure as overtakes Encolpius when, spared by the Minotaur, his "prize" is laying "Ariadne." The Cowboy has been picked up by a good-looking slumming female sophisticate in a Village rock palace and duly taken home with her. The movie has already set up for us the hippie works with some fast and furious psychedelic photography (even Viva and her halo of hair was enlisted), so that the intake of pot plus liquor just *may* account for the Cowboy's totally unexpected sex failure. Who knows? Surely not the blushing Cowboy himself. In any case, the disappointed lady turns out to be a right guy because she forks up the fee which the pretty Cowboy's patent willingness has earned. A meaningful point, it seems to me, is that the Cowboy has no drive toward a specific sex object. Encolpius has. It is the girlish youth Giton (like a Cupid from one of Caravaggio's paintings) over whom he has seriously quarreled with Ascyltos. Impotence may be due to the sudden realization that the *wrong* sex object is in bed.

No longer are commercial films reluctant to portray the moral and psychological difficulties of the hustler, whether his clients be male or female. In a Hollywood film, *Advise and Consent*, and a more pioneering film from England, *Victim*, there are credibly candid accounts of married men who have had, or are tempted into, secret homosexual lives—one (in *Advise and Consent*) was an episode while afield in the Army, and the subject had since reformed and been married; the other (in *Victim*) is set to live the double erotic life so well briefed for us by Hank in *The Boys in the Band*. The two present films show homosexuality as a socially stamped vice receiving its indelible character from the statute books, with the result that it is a ready-made incentive for blackmail. Both the films concentrate on mores and the law. Both are discreetly reactionary by settling on homosexual love its old moral onus and exploiting the sensationalism of its exposure.

I say "discreetly reactionary" because no longer do modern cultures take the outright (once *de rigueur*) viewpoint of outrage toward the private and public misfortunes incurrable by practicing homosexuals. Films have taken over the easy, empiric morality of journalism, where the homosexual victim, like other victims, is not so much a social or contranaturam "criminal" as a loser in that game somehow played by all private individuals with the Law. Political liberalism, in fact, opens the way toward total moral liberalism through the basic democratic theory that the private individual should be the ultimate arbiter of his conduct; hence what are called "obligations to the state" tend in our time to be more and more debatable.

What is the widest meaning of the recent emergence of so many militant minorities supposedly representing solid group interests? Technically they do represent group interests, but only as group interests seem to favor the maximum freedom of the individual to assert not merely his right to make his own moral decisions (within sane and reasonable limits) but moreover his right to reasonable privacy in his pursuit of total integrity. During the last few decades in the United States, the emphasis placed on the legal issue of "invasion of privacy" is but one sign of the principle of moral license that especially benefits homosexuals at a moment when public opinion leans so much weight on all aspects of individual freedom.

For example, to extend the range beyond sexual behavior, income-tax manipulation to reduce one's tax liability carries no really criminal stigma unless it takes the form of large-scale cheating. Even then, the "victim" is heard protesting his innocence as if he had only been apprehended committing an "indecent act" in a Turkish bath. Income-tax evasion, in the public consciousness, has become (like homosexuality itself) an excusable vice or at worst a venal crime; at the same time, we see people (perhaps at the celebrity level) openly refusing to pay an acknowledged portion of their taxes as a protest against the annual sums being spent on the American war in Vietnam.

Very palpably, as of 1971, we live in an ever-growing climate of moral exoneration that includes "Christian forgiveness" as a very minor tenet of its expanding rationale. Preponderantly, it is political and social. On the social side, homosexuality is now one of its intense focuses. In *Victim,* a parting scene between the obviously bisexed, possibly really homosexual, husband and his homosexual lover is exactly like counterpart partings in movies about romantic (heterosexual) love: it is sentimental, solemn, "empathetic." One motive of the film is to presènt the homosexual "side of the argument" as morally, legally compromised, sometimes tragically so, and yet exonerated by nature. As put by one character in the movie, a poised and forensic homosexual actor, homosexuality is "a part of nature."

Oh, yes, this is parti-pris, very much and very intentionally so! It is the underlying dominant tone of *Victim*. Two British producers, Michael Relph and Basil Dearden, expressly decided to make a film protesting the English law by which homosexuality was a criminal act. A way to dramatize such a protest, they logically reasoned, was to package it into an adventure romance. The right theme was pressingly ready to hand: simply the statistics that ninety percent of all blackmail cases in the English courts were homosexual in origin. And a formula was equally obliging: a brilliant lawyer, happily married to a devoted woman, but having secret homosexual tendencies, is (along with his known homosexual partner) threatened by a blackmail gang. Who but the tried and true actor, handsome and just manly enough Dirk Bogarde, should be the protagonist?

The movie's desire was to put homosexuality in its most respectable light, morally and humanly, while revealing it as typically victimized by criminals. This was done thoroughly and with indisputable sincerity. However, no production strategy in filming such a subject could avoid the trap of conscientious reviewers thinking of themselves as publicly appointed guardians of family morality. In 1962, when the film was released in the United States, the moral rating system of films which we have today had not yet been invented. In any case, critics on the American papers had to feel as much ostensible concern for middle-class adult sensibilities as for minors in the audience. The New York film reviewers were painfully liberal about *Victim*. Bosley Crowther was so indiscreet as to burst out with a defense of homosexuality unintended by the film itself; e.g., that a homosexual is one "afflicted with a condition beyond his will and control." Even outside the limits of this movie, that opinion is a subjective interpretation on the lips of condescending liberal ethics; conservative heterosexuality, tacitly, is "speaking out."

Granted that, after all, *Victim* is a commercial package, it makes its objective point with considerable ingenuity. Who could fail to sympathize with an actor as personable as Dirk Bogarde, dedicated in this role, where he is so humanly "vulnerable," to being a man of honor in every respect? The story's great honesty is to be praised because the compromising photo taken of the lawyer Melville Farr (Bogarde) with a known homosexual, young Jack Barrett, when they are tête-à-tête in a parked car, might have been argued a misleading appearance; and consequently, Farr's determination to protect his companion and hunt down the blackmailers, interpreted as a publicly inspired gesture of indignant morality. On the contrary, Farr, as the action has shown from the start, is emotionally if not physically involved, and later he confesses this fact to his nobly understanding wife. What matters is that he proceeds to defy the blackmail gang and risk his career and reputation by cooperating with the police so as to run down and convict the criminals.

That the gang itself is sexually compromised is conveyed by camera inquiry into the lives of its various members. The blackmail collector is a full-suited, motorcycle-equipped Leather Boy who keeps a statue of a Greek god in his room. The blind spy who collects information to entrap homosexuals is a seasoned habitué of gay bars. Thus the "villains" are made portentously sordid and suspect symbols of perversity. Young Barrett, the victim, has fallen deeply in love with Farr, and wants him, above all, to save himself; when Farr declines, Barrett grows frantic and steals in order to pay the extortioners; finally arrested and jailed, the youth hangs himself, from despair, thinking he and the man he loves are ruined.

In the light of the latest information about homosexuality, it is grotesque to go back and read the strange words uttered by Paul Beckley, late critic of the late New York *Herald Tribune,* about this film. "The dramatic drawback to its basic theme, homosexualism," he wrote, "is the difficulty of audience

identification with any of its principals." Oh, dear! *Any . . . ?*
What about that extremely well-behaved wife who is told by
her husband that he has been morally unfaithful with a man?
Suppose she were *your* wife! Newspaper reviewers have seemed
to live in a wide, wide world of their own, which only recently
identifies itself, to a noticeable degree, with the cruelly close
real world, and all its aggressive homosexuals.

Advise and Consent presents a different but related case
of homosexuality in a compromised heterosexual who is conventionally married. The homosexual affair of the reformed,
now married, male is treated as a peccadillo of the sort apt to be
pointed up by the moral statisticians who believe the vice of
homosexuality a mere hangover from youthful indulgence, or
else mechanically contingent, as when the subject (or should I
say "the victim"?) is isolated from women in prison or during
military service. We need not criticize these statistics as such;
they are valid only as applied to a slight minority of the millions
who practice homosexual acts. We know that what (as in the
hustler's case) begins as a circumstantial or professional temptation, yielded to more or less involuntarily, may turn into a
reflex-habit, then into a way of life, and often, even in the bisexual dimension, into the chief thing desired and consummated
with "adult consent." Referring this aspect to life, there is much
evidence for the homosexualized hustler's life style—cold-
hearted, perhaps sadistic, even criminal, but no less a life style,
and at times warm enough. In *The Boys in the Band,* we have
the benignly innocent version of the hustler, content with his
trade and a veritable big-baby who, when asked by his faggot
client if he is "good in bed," artlessly replies, "Well, I try to
show some affection." For some inscrutable reason, this mild,
true-to-life question and answer was omitted from the film version.

Another relevant fact of life to notice is that when the
homosexual seducer turns to blackmail, he may do so out of
frustration, as a sort of revenge at being a discarded lover, or
just as an extension of that amateur practice of hustling that
heterosexual and homosexual may engage in. Regardless of
precise sex, the gigolo traditionally has equal status with the

courtesan. So let us avoid any trap of naïveté about human sexual morals. Within moral relations, especially those at home between the sexes (any sexes), there are abundant opportunities for tactical blackmail of the subtle as well as crude kind; some are morally innocent insofar as these sorts of blackmail are often a mere strategy to hold a mate who wishes (maybe subconsciously or tentatively) to sever the relationship. For instance, what is known as psychological cruelty, a frequent charge in divorce action, may be the product of a one-sided match where the "cruel" partner has found a modus vivendi for forcing the issue; then the "victimized" partner, to save self-respect and perhaps pride in the bedroom, at last sues for divorce or just says pathetically, "Go, leave me! I know you want to. I can't stand your cruelty any longer!"

Aside from the hustler's theme, we may note of explicit homosexual films that they tend to put a brave, self-vindicating front on the homosexual, whatever his social or cultural status and whatever his story's dramatic issue; if frustrated or arrested, he may try to destroy himself. If we liked, we might trace the fortunes of the suicide-syndrome among homosexuals. Doubtless the movies have overdramatized this. But Tennessee Williams has been particularly fond of it to dramatize (or would it be "moralize"?) the "mad" extravagance of being a homosexual in the heterosexual establishment. Note that I do not say "in the heterosexual world." It is strictly establishment atmosphere that has made Mr. Williams introduce "tragic" homosexual episodes into his works by remote control. There are Blanche Dubois' former fiancé in *A Streetcar Named Desire* and the college roommate who has ended it all after the marriage of his lover to a woman in *Cat on a Hot Tin Roof*. Then too, there is the remarkably tasteless climax to *Suddenly, Last Summer,* where Elizabeth Taylor was persuaded to compromise her public image by appearing as a bait to lure boys to the side of her homosexual cousin. I suppose the motivation was so fuzzy, anyway, that the point was only that Miss Taylor should play a sex bait. I shall take up this particular matter when I talk about the fatal kinks of homosexuals.

It is not a kink, not emotional shock or guilty conscience,

that causes the "homosexual victim" in *Advise and Consent* to end his life; it is only because his homosexual past, technically buried, is being used by political enemies to blackmail him into disqualifying himself as the appointee for Secretary of State. Though this frustrated politician (played by Don Murray) is but one victim in the film's great mesh of political intrigue, his former homosexual partner should not escape our interest here. He is a very attractive physical specimen, handsome of face, manly of muscles. In fact he is the underground "orthodox homosexual" whose existence, quite plentiful, heterosexual psychology invents so many excuses to deny. Precisely because he is unequivocally masculine, not even oblique effeminacies or camp mannerisms adequately define his sex, since those things are characteristic of certain heterosexual varieties. Naturally, the shrewd observer can always "read" the small, small give-aways, but that often comes about through the special context in which they appear; for example, if the subject in question is flirting with *you*.

Cultivated, men-loving women and bisexually vulnerable heterosexual men, I suppose, account for most of the established moral hypocrisy about the stark realities of homosexual behavior in the male. Be that as it may, frivolity, the sin of a constitutional weakness, emerges as the most serious vice that can be imputed to the troublemaking homosexual in *Advise and Consent*. Those "indecent acts" are pushed into a dark corner and the young man himself becomes the cat's paw of his quondam lover's political enemies. It is the would-be Secretary of State, the sexually reformed ex-soldier, who is so unfortunate as to be put on the griddle for those distant "indecencies." Nor, in fact, is *Advise and Consent* the only recent film to make a politician's homosexual past the basis for his political rivals to cancel him out.

The same situation (here, too, the shady romance was an episode while in the Army) is featured in the film adaptation of Gore Vidal's play *The Best Man,* where Cliff Robertson, playing a presidential candidate with intermale dalliance in his past, has the veil torn from his hidden Achilles heel by Henry Fonda as a rival candidate. There is the usual machinery of buying the

incriminating evidence and threatening to spring the scandal—
a blot on the political escutcheon in which, as a satirist without
compunction, Vidal obviously delighted, and which the film
portrays, but which New York newspaper reviewers almost
unanimously found unnewsworthy. Even to this day, certain
reviewers are cued to adjust their optical transformers when
reporting screen visibilities embarrassing to those in high places.

The film version of *Advise and Consent* made a picturesque contribution to the grantedly grim occasion. Here the
homosexual first appears in his mythical habitat, the gay
bar, this one being glamorously misty with shadows and romantic with background music. On confrontation with the
accusing politician, who seeks him out, he breaks down with
emotion and rushes after his "victim" to explain and beg forgiveness; he really always loved him, it seems, and is as much
a victim as the anguished politician, now revolted by the sight
of his past. The gay bar is supposedly a gaudy symbol of Sodom:
the home of vicious lust. Disengaging the homosexual from this
symbol, we are forced to gaze on the Homosexual as His Own
Victim. Sexually he is a sort of disadvantaged adult, a handicapped child-man, safely in a spot where one can feel superior
to him, fluff him off as one of the déclassés, the "unfortunates"
of social prejudice who still manage a brave, gay front. After
all, he is not only handsome but also healthy, as if he exercised
every day. As for being "wicked," well, he obviously isn't. I
doubt if even God could make him out wicked when Hollywood
hasn't.

The old saw that a homosexual is simply one variety of
sick person, like a pathological murderer, only commensurately
less punishable, is slowly dying a natural death, I believe, despite
its being a reflex habit of plots bent on apologizing for their
own sensationalism. Another film, *The Detective,* a hard-hitting
murder melodrama, seems both to hasten the demise of "the
homosexual as sick person" and to give him reason to survive.
Here homosexuality is cross-sectioned as (1) a not unexpected
luxury vice of a rich man's son, who (2) is murdered by a pathologically trapped married man resisting his own homosexual
urge, while the search of the police to track down the criminal

(he has mutilated his victim) automatically involves and incidentally "incriminates" (3) the rank-and-file young faggots who nightly, on deserted streets, hold their orgies in parked trucks. The last is a familiar urban custom, utilized here as part of the routine police hunt but also serving for the observation that homosexuals, while bearing the group stigma of social inferiority (condescension again), haven't really committed any crimes worse than disgustingly unnatural acts, a description which, as we well know, is itself in dispute now and widely condemned as a legal fiction and a puritan prejudice.

I doubt there could be a more naturally ennobled acting personality to represent the viewpoint of liberalism than the man who plays "the detective" of the film: Frank Sinatra. Like the famous Sam Spade (Humphrey Bogart) of *The Maltese Falcon,* the Sinatra character is most knowledgeable and sophisticated about human weakness and its many vagaries; in fact, like Spade, he seems a good-hearted cynic about all vices. There used to be an underworld term, "gunsel," for a big gangster's personal bodyguard, attached to his master like a dog and, in some cases, sexually subservient, too; at least, the emotion guaranteeing the gunsel's perfect loyalty was tacitly either his or his lord's homosexuality, or both. I recall how amusingly and swiftly, in *The Maltese Falcon,* Bogart as Spade cased the master crook's gunsel. What made it the funnier was the gunsel's juvenile solemnity and his getting an instant, terrified whiff of the fact that Bogart's way of putting him down showed that he had guessed his identity to its depths. On top of that, the master crook was played by the incredibly majestic Sidney Greenstreet, of the enormous girth and insinuatingly fastidious style.

The exemption of Sinatra's detective from prejudice is technical as well as moral (which makes him doubly free to "condescend"), but in this case, where he has the chance to display lenience to "poor harmless faggots," he assumes an especially heroic humanity. One of the men under his orders unnecessarily roughs up (sign of low heterosexual bias) one of the young orgiasts dragged from the trucks being searched. Sinatra witnesses the cruel incident. Then he enacts one of those priceless scenes sacred to the Christian tolerance so deeply, anonymously embedded in popular sentiment and classic, of course, in the movies. Silently beckoning the brute, Sinatra takes him behind a car as if for a private word, and after a curt, pointed reproof, lays him out with a punch to the jaw. Perfect mark for Sinatra from the Gay Liberation Front! Need one be told that Sinatra gets his man, the pathological murderer? He does, but not without sexily insinuating make-believe along the way.

In *The Detective*, homosexuality serves much the same purpose in crime movies as do drugs and prostitution, those other "bad habits" of humanity: it supplies the provender, the atmosphere, and the motivation of a tough melodramatic plot. As I have said, this attitude is basically journalistic. These days newspapers, even conservative ones, have few scruples in reporting the most horrendous crimes. The moral rationale is that a crime induced by drug addiction or homosexuality—crudely aligned with each other as dangerous sicknesses—are curable; hence crimes committed in their name, as it were, are pathologically excusable and avert the death sentence from the criminal. This is why—and it is the rationale of *The Detective*— providing the most pornographic details of a murder is justified by the tacit function of portraying social evils so as to help prevent and cure them; for it is also tacit that society is permanently organized—nominally, of course, it *is*—to cleanse the public body of the special taints leading to crimes.

Overt homosexuality is thus neatly absorbed into the journalistic pattern echoed by the movie showpiece. An especially flavorsome charade is performed by Sinatra in *The Detective* after one crime suspect is run down, taken to police headquarters, and subjected to grilling. By all implications nominally homosexual, he is butch enough in looks while his "weakness of the flesh" is portrayed by signs of craven hysteria on being discovered and captured. After futile grilling in which he denies any connection with the crime, Sinatra walks in, clears the room, and stages a flirtation with him, very insinuating, and employing caresses, so that the suspect, duly vanquished at the prospect of a new conquest, breaks down and obliges: he has been the victim's boyfriend, having parted from him just before the crime, though he is not the murderer. The scene is acted convincingly by Sinatra and his colleague, who portrays a simpleminded butch homosexual out to hustle sleepable partners who pay well. In the sight of this kind of fiction, the homosexual is easily joined to the tribe of love-crazies, those who are professionals (and possibly criminals) because sex has driven them a bit off their rockers. Just so, not every drug addict commits a crime, not every pimp is engaged in a crime racket, yet their occupations *potentialize* crimes.

The large-mindedness of *The Detective* is notable. We are allowed to visit a homosexual hangout, where the fairies (none of them flaming) are going about their business with casual poise and discretion; that is, they are bar-cruising. *Their* only crime would seem to be accountability to the law punishing acts of sexual indecency. As for that, what fictional mode—from *Oedipus Rex* to the works of Spade and Sinatra—ever recognized the law as a deterrent from a passion strong enough to defy it? After all, the chief traditional image of the Law is that of avenger, not deterrent. The important thing is that the popular crime story is perfectly willing to be fair, even generous to the homosexual, if only because most detective heroes have to demonstrate their great humanity so as to compensate for their unpleasant profession.

Still, in naming homosexuality as another brand of pathology through passion, the world of films joins it firmly to the list of psycho-physical diseases. An after thought, a minor motif, appears in some cases as it appears in *The Detective:* the disease *may be* harmless even while, technically, it is on the records as a perpetual threat. This is why, after all, one must call *The Detective,* sex-wise, a curiously ambivalent crime flick. It might seem that the repressed homosexual—the "heterosexual" married man who has murdered the homosexual, and sexually mutilated his corpse—illustrates the *greater* evil of frustrating one's true sexual impulse. In line with Sinclair Lewis' evangelist, Elmer Gantry, the culprit here denounces flagrant signs of the very "vice" of which he eventually becomes guilty. Obviously, he has submitted himself sexually to the pickup before, in a fit of revulsion, he bludgeons him to death. On the benign side, prose fiction entertainment has given us a cheerfully homosexual *and black* detective,* but so far he has not been debuted on the screen. To put him there might offend the Black Panthers and the Young Lords, not to mention the NAACP.

Of late years, more films than one can count on the fingers of a dozen hands have given homosexuality a look-in as a sort of sophisticated bow to life as it is lived, rather than life as discreet arbiters of our morality would have it seem. Yet sometimes homosexual phenomena are tolerated in the movies the way society itself tolerates such things. It's just there. *Let it be.* A beautiful mod sentiment: exquisitely "today" in feeling! Technically, homosexuality benefits from it. One needn't count the female-impersonator bits, used in the movies as condiments or gags, but there should be mentioned a whole, soberly conceived documentary film, *The Queen,* devoted to what really went on behind and in front of the scenes when a contest for a transvestite Miss All-America was held, a few years ago, in a New York theater. The film looks very authentic, with only the most modest programming for the camera, while incidental business with the transvestites, informally seen off stage, seems just as convincing.

On the side diametrically opposite the transvestite kick, the David-and-Jonathan story has been held up (and duly treated when the movies came: there was a *Damon and Pythias* in 1915) as the traditional ideal of male friendship. Basically the legend was always homosexual in spirit, historically deriving its platonic status from the well-known Athenian custom. With the usual innocent and sentimental inflection, it has shown up in countless Westerns. An especially dramatic one, in which rivalry over a woman figures and "hate" disguises "love," appeared in the old Howard Hughes film *The Outlaw* (1947).† There, as sometimes still happens in these affairs, the film-makers betrayed that they were quite aware of the homosexual implications and carefully

* Pharaoh Love by name. He appears in a series of novels by George Baxt, the first being *A Queer Sort of Death*. Another homosexual detective, this time white, appears in a superior murder mystery called *Fadeout*, by Joseph Hansen. It seems to me the latter would make a most interesting movie—but perhaps the time is still not ripe.

† See *Sex, Psyche, Etcetera in the Film* (Tyler) pp. 32–36.

manipulated them. I would be the last to claim that such homeroic fictions may not be as innocent in life as they are in the
movies. But innocence is notoriously a fragile thing; a thing living, as it were, on borrowed time. Thus, while filmdom must
have its sentimental charades, must constantly assert its all-too-
public discretion, the innocence of really chummy, enduring,
and drama-fraught relations between men has to register as a
speculative factor, always subject to development and outcome
(not always visible to the naked eye), and above all, to analysis
that gets under the skin of mere appearances.

Who could believe of those staunch hetero personalities
John Wayne and Robert Mitchum that one day they'd find
themselves together in a movie that implied an ambiguous if
also hardy affection for each other? But they did. Concerning
such movies, if it doesn't occur to one of the pair of semiattached
heterosexuals on the screen, it will to someone in the audience
—and who is to say that certain acknowledged public suscepti-
bilities are not being deliberately sexploited by possum-playing
movie makers? A man to whom I was introduced while writing
these pages, on being informed of the subject that preoccupied
me, spontaneously burst out: "Oh! Well, you *do* remember that
Spencer Tracy was in love with Clark Gable in *Test Pilot?*" I
confess that my mouth dropped open a bit as I shook my head in
the negative. I had forgotten *that* one.

Suppose, reader, it's all a charade—this cowboy and
soldierboy business of being buddy-buddy, with conscious insinuation by the film fiction always a speculative matter. Still,
some cowboy charade is technically qualified to reflect a similar
charade among cowboys in real life, at least in the Old West as it
comes down to us. This point, again, has nothing necessarily to
do with the private lives of the actors, playing such parts only
because they are being paid to do so. The issue is: If we don't
recognize the existence of the real-life charades, we must take
the fictional phenomena, only implying their *possibility*, as
vacant romantic myths, a difficult, elusive reality abstracted
into inferior, simple-minded stereotypes. Consider: man-likes-
man, great-chums, hate-because-of-rivalry, narcissistic-jealousy,
and so on and so on. Meaning? Chop-chop. Guys-love-same-girl.

And so on. Add to vague and not so vague emotional involvements between males: *Hatari, Red River, The Big Sky, The Sleeping Car Murders, Z,* and . . . You finish naming them. If you don't, your friends will. Especially because, as in *Wild Rovers,* they're getting more and more overt.

Even in commerical American movies, the poignancy of platonic male friendship, ambiguously homosexual, is no very recent phenomenon. We might take a bee-line to some Museum of Modern Art revival of Garbo's films and witness it in one of that star's earlier triumphs, *Flesh and the Devil,* between two men who were great buddies before Felicitas von Kletzingk (Garbo) came along. Married to Ulrich von Kletzingk (Lars Hanson) she splits him apart from Leo von Sellinthin (John Gilbert) like a knife. This is done neatly by sleeping outside with Leo—and liking it, in a style rather new to the American screen, tremendously. Finally, when Ulrich surprises the adulterers in the act, it is *de rigueur* for him to challenge darling Leo to a duel. Both romantic fellows become grim about this in the larger romantic style; also, infinitely morose. Since Felicitas cannot bear the thought of her lover killing her husband, and/or vice versa, she rushes out desperately into the snowbound landscape to prevent it: she, after all, is *to blame.* As she crosses, on foot, a frozen lake to reach the island where the duel is to take place, the surface of ice (as surfaces of ice are known to do in the movies) gives way, and Felicitas, with startling but decisive suddenness, drowns. When the would-be duelists are stopped in time, they don't just solemnly shake hands and go their separate ways in mourning. They seem to think their lady's death a blessed deliverance and gratefully fall into each other's arms. Charles Hoffman, the pianist who accompanied these revivals at the Museum with ingeniously apt music, underlined the sad beauty of that embrace by playing a pathetically joyous tune that more normally might have accompanied a reconciliation between Garbo and her leading man.

Only sublime innocence could be expected of Hollywood when, in 1927, two leading men (rather than Garbo and a leading man) were found in what justly used to be called the final clinch. I hope, incidentally, that such satirical language, deriving from the technical idioms associated with commercial films, doesn't drop me into a pocket with the reader, who may think this camping too homosexual or just too campy. I remind my reader what my inquiry here is, what its focus, and that camping is part of the critical game I play with certain films which, deliberately or undeliberately, themselves go in for camping. My longtime position on Hollywood art has been that serious movies may be unwittingly, though not always unrewardingly, pretentious. Their unsophisticated pretensions tell us something, and the game is to guess just what it is.

To show that script writers are not consciously foreign to the situation in *Flesh and the Devil* as a plausible occasion for offbeat emotional relations between men, I shall cite later a film where the quarrel over a woman, literally and explicitly, is the upshot of a homosexual's intrigue to keep the love of an ambisexed male inclined to renounce their onetime relationship, though not for the reason that the latter is now in love with a woman. The woman who intrudes on the situation becomes a pawn in the curious struggle staged by the two men. This instance provides, along with the broad insinuations of another film, *The Outlaw*, a serviceable index to a persuasive substructure for certain feuds between apparently heterosexual males.

Of course, when a critic is convinced of such a thing by evidence in an art medium, he should first have been convinced thoroughly by evidence of it in life. In this respect, life is, and must be, a criticism of art. I emphasize this, in bringing this anticipatory chapter to a close, only because I believe there is a subtle heterosexual will to think categorically of homosexuality as a myth invented by the perverse minds of frustrated, tangled individuals: the sort of person who just doesn't know his sexual way around a bed. There surely ought to be an antidote for this heterosexual distortion of the facts. Obviously, the antidote would be the equally subtle *homosexual* will to debunk that deplorable hetero antimyth. I suggest that the reader look up his current neighborhood movie listings. The antimyth is probably being debunked somewhere nearby at this very instant.

I find my conscience speaking for the skeptical reader himself. I verbalize his objections something like this: "Good

God, man, do you mean that in all the movies that have been made since the dawn of the so-called homosexual enlightenment, not one of them has had just a plain, unkinky, naturally committed homosexual who goes, romantically or unromantically, *but as the hero,* about the simple business of making another guy? That would help your case a lot." Someone (I take up the reader's viewpoint) who isn't a flaming faggot, or an object lesson, or crucified for his sins, or desperately flirts with temptation, or brutally hustles, or has to play the villain of the piece? And who didn't live in the Roman decadence? Someone who's just in it for the regular thrills sought by anyone who's on the make? A homosexual, in short, who is a "chameleon" out of normal modesty, normal discretion, one who is *not* a closet queen. . . .

I could not sympathize more with such a desire for reasonable enlightenment, and I am very happy that I can oblige. It may be that the hypothetic reader missed a foreign film of Italo-French collaboration called *High Infidelity.* It is composed of short pieces by different directors on the same theme. The episode I shall relate, "The Scandal," is charmingly if a bit self-consciously *insouciant,* though that last expression belies the fact that an Italian made it: Franco Rossi. Nothing could be more ordinary than the basic situation. An attractive young heterosexual couple, married and spending a holiday at a rustic pension, meet a young man, another guest, who by all the signs starts to flirt with the wife of the pair. Played by John Philip Law (who was Private Swanson in *The Sergeant),* he is tall, blond, slender, handsome. He is merely like thousands of male homosexuals who could safely and stylishly model men's clothes and stir the innocent blind emotions of some orthodox female, like the attractive wife of this very movie. But, as you have guessed by now, he is really after the husband, and somehow is trapped by conventional manners (not to mention guile) into seeming to be, in restrained gentlemanly fashion, after the wife.

It is all accomplished on the right, light level of mild boulevard comedy, nothing broad or sensational, no nude scenes, no outbursts or hints of violence. The couple are a little intrigued by the assumed "pursuit" of their fellow guest. The only violence turns out to be psychological: when, at a party where the homosexual dances with the wife, then has a drink at the bar with the husband and is compelled by desire (though with well-bred compunction) to make his move by an unmistakable pressure of the man's hand, and presto! the husband gets the point. He is properly *bouche-bée* as he gives the young man an emphatic, if polite, brush-off and rejoins his wife, who is unaware of the furtive little scene, since she has been dancing with another. The young man has actually sent her roses: she thinks he is still flirting! While now the husband feels obliged to trump up a reason for cutting short their vacation, he elects to leave her with her romantic illusion. The pair drive off with the idea in the air that he is wafting *her* away from temptation. . . . It is really very cute, very bland. But who wants to be *bland* nowadays? It isn't box-office.

On the female side, something not so bland, but oh! so Continentally incontinent, is the routine seduction that opens *Les Biches*. A cool sophisticated number (no diesel dyke but a suave sappho) picks up a naïve sidewalk artist doing her stuff on a bridge over the Seine: faint irreverence of gay Parisian dalliance toward the "artist's" tradition. At home, the seducer proceeds to unzipper the passive girl's Levis, and the rest is understood if undisclosed. Male gallantry, as in other French films, stages its determined interference, bringing complications bitter, morbidly erotic, labored, and vague. Yet so far as the girls went, it began with straightforward cruising and a simple bedroom motive. Here was honest enough reporting—but spoiled by mysteriously emergent needles and not at all sure of its pins. If only plots were to be made and undressed, rather than dressed and made up!

3. FOUR HOMOSEXUAL MYSTERY STORIES AND A VERY QUEER NON-MYSTERY STORY

CONSCIOUS?

When I say that *The Great Escape* is a homosexual mystery story, I am prepared to hear the worst charges against me that could possibly assault a critic's integrity. People may go so far as to say that I'm not only homosexual myself, but a systematic fantasizer determined to use the movies as propaganda to slander normal sex and completely innocent motives. I shall be brave. I shall present my case and let the individual reader decide whether a tacit assumption of normalcy of sex and innocence of motive is justified by this movie's curiously focused version of military and human phenomena. *The Great Escape* is about a concerted and fabulously systematic attempt of prisoners of the Allied forces during World War II to make a massive escape from one isolated German prison camp. In a foreword printed on the film, its producers assert that, aside from certain compressions of time and place, every detail of the great escape we are going to see is a matter of record. Seemingly, nobody realized

80

how much leeway is given the invention of details when script writers go about "compressing" time and place.

But that difficulty to one side, it may be said by my critics that everything I shall point out below is really "coincidence" and can be accounted for without ascribing any role to homosexuality in the story's action. My answer to that is that nothing in art should be so *insistently* coincidental as the action here would have to be if it is viewed without sexual motivation. Sexual motivation, even minor sexual motivation, is formally absent. As for what is plausible or implausible in the action— well, that *is* something else. Let's allow the facts as much throughway as possible, left-handed though they be as art.

People are fond of saying that nothing, at times, is so implausible as the facts of a bizarre yet accredited truth; moreover, that, however documentary a screen fiction may pretend to be, it is the business of the entertainment industry to be as entertaining as possible without violating anyone's sense of fact. Well, a curious thing intrudes itself here. There is one thing *The Great Escape* proves aside from its theoretic fidelity to the records it claims to be based upon. I'll express the point this way: I would willingly stake my life that said records could be reconstructed otherwise than they have been in this film *without violating the letter of the existing statistics.* I'll go even further. I'll say that they could have been reconstructed *as I shall imagine them* with equally little violation of those statistics, and besides, by means of a plausible and reasonable version of life, whereas the version of life we are shown here is implausible and unreasonable.

The first thing to state is that the movie's entire action has nothing in it except scenes devoted to showing how the highly organized escape conspiracy took shape, proceeded, and at last manages to effect the immediate freedom of exactly seventy-six men, some dressed in complete civilian outfits and all fully equipped with forged identification papers and enough knowledge of the German language (and training in the German accent?) to get by as Germans. This group of facts alone strains credibility. Bizarre, if true. Naturally we aren't given evidence that every man is an expert in the German tongue.

Some may have had to get by without that, and so on. Suppose we could believe, however, that this particular prison camp was really manned with stupid and lazy supervisors and guards: officers and men perhaps blinded by the German superiority complex. The unlikely fact remains that never, save in curiously accidental ways, does anyone detect that a complete tailor shop is daily converting all kinds of materials into business suits and laborers' outfits; that the most complicated means are being employed by dozens and dozens of prisoners to create, not one, but three, tunnels of escape, and that incredibly the most acceptable materials are being found to forge identification papers for, not 25, but *250*, men; this implies not only paper but a duplication of some kind.

One point about this that speaks very badly for German efficiency is that it seems not to have occurred to the commanding officers, or anyone else, to plant a spy or spies among the Allied prisoners. Several good spies would have made the Great Escape impossible. Of course, we are asked to believe something that is supposed *morally* to account for the success of the fabulous project, of which British officers are almost wholly in charge; only one American has a prominent part in the action. This moral factor is—as the highest-ranking prisoner sternly informs the camp commander—that the sworn duty of British soldiers is to make every possible effort to escape. This determination supposedly accounts for the escape's miraculous success. Yes, it is foiled in process by discovery, but (as I said) seventy-six men do break free, while only a very small minority, as we learn in much detail, manages to get safely out of Germany. Fifty are captured and summarily shot in a group by the Gestapo; about twenty are returned to the prison camp, leaving roughly six who make good their escape. These statistics, despite their prominence, do not matter. What does seem to me to matter is the following:

From the outset, we are shown men who are certainly human and likeable enough, perfectly good fellows with all the traits one might expect from movie heroes as well as courageous soldiers; the actors are competent, the separate characterizations credible enough. Yet one anomaly peeps out like an unofficial, unlisted member of the cast. This anomaly is that these men, while so obviously human, and in different ways attractively human, seem programmed, like computers, to be only Soldiers Dedicated to Making Their Escape. Their *humanity* is what seems really coincidental! Why should this be? Exactly because, it seems, they have forgotten all about the human relations which they once had when they were free men; that is, before they were put in soldier uniforms and fought a war.

Surely we have seen enough of soldiers writing home and getting letters from home; nostalgic, embittered soldiers; rebellious soldiers; soldiers who manage affairs with women no matter what the circumstances; soldiers who miss wives, sweethearts, parents, and friends and talk about them. . . . Yet the soldiers who are concentrated on here are characterized by not a single one of those objectively displaced moral and emotional concerns. In brief, these soldiers are programmed to have no sex lives, no nostalgic memories, no yearnings. It is striking that only one of the protagonists, a very homely Scotchman, even mentions "women"; the mention is singular and fleeting, and perhaps it is significant that he is the *one* prisoner who "falls apart" and makes that insane dash for the fence in broad daylight, to be duly gunned down. But he is inferior stuff and sadly is characterized as such: a mere good-natured simpleton. The rest are altogether—with one neurotic exception—entirely Spartan, entirely sexless. Ostensibly. Only one ordinary object of impassioned concern is indicated throughout the entire film, which lasts two hours and forty-five minutes. This object is a cup of coffee or tea. Coffee or tea seems to satisfy all fleshly cravings of the daily sort among these wonderfully dedicated soldiers.

Here is a vivid illustration. One prisoner (acted by Donald Pleasence) is growing progressively myopic, and by the time the escape plan is ready, he can see nothing clearly if it is not two inches away from his eyes. This man happens to share a two-bunk room with a prisoner enacted by James Garner. When the escape leader—a British officer whose great reputation as an escapist entitles him to his post—informs Pleasence that he must stay behind because of his blindness, there is a pathetic scene which abruptly ends with Garner taking the noble stand that he will be entirely responsible for his roommate and provide eyes for them both. The buddy-buddy sentiment is surely a tried (and trite) one, but theoretically sound. When the leader, showing a nice understanding, reluctantly consents to the arrangement and leaves the room, the choked-up Garner suggests to his roommate the daily object of passion tacitly shared by both: "How about a cup of tea?"

Which brings me to the ineluctable point. Eight of the protagonists (the most conspicuous) have fallen into looking like "couples." It is the buddy-buddy thing that seems to have slipped unobtrusively but surely into this much-programmed "great escape" as if it were an automatic part of it. Yet going in pairs is not mentioned as a feature of the strategy; in fact, most escapers are solo. Precisely in the case I have just mentioned, the pairing off becomes highly inconvenient, and therefore one of the two must insist that their status as a couple be maintained. . . . All right! Some emotional drama is always in order in the movies. Yet why this oddly specialized drama? For it's not in the strict programming. The fact is that Garner is quite a desirable masculine type: tall, dark, handsome, well built. There is no particular sign that he is not heterosexual. Very good. But *if* he's really heterosexual, doesn't be logically have, and bear in mind, a wife or mistress (not to mention a family) who would dearly miss him if he never came home?—some persons or person whose existence might induce him to forgo helping his roommate escape, considering that his blindness will make him an albatross about his buddy's neck? But no. There's no apparent conflict of this sort. The only problem seems to be getting the leader's okay to let the seeing-eye buddy take along the blind one. We are obliged to conclude that Garner has not been programmed for sexual attachments or any moral commitments outside the prison camp; he has been programmed only for his part in the escape, and, coincidentally enough, for his exemplary devotion to his roommate—who, while a very pleasant fellow, is bald, rather homely, and older than he is.

Here it might be mentioned that *The Great Escape* reveals a military aspect of World War II which we must take on faith as shown. British war prisoners apparently became career men of escapism. They were rated by their prominence as escape-heroes, more particularly by the number of times they had effected escape; the number applying to the protagonists here ranges from ten to as much as twenty. I concede there was something logical about the script conceiving the principals as Career Escapists. But, just as logically, there is something rather inhuman about that. Another big black mark against the Army as a dehumanizing machine?—a hero-manufacturing machine? So what! But previously, American movies about Army life have limited the mass ethics of robotism *to the enemy*. The logic must be that robotism on *our* side ceases to be robotism: it becomes heroism.

One might ask if the case of buddy devotion I have just mentioned is perhaps alone in this movie, a unique exception. No, it is not! There is another couple, one of whom shows a most dramatic attachment to the other. Both are very masculine types; one (Charles Bronson) is quite muscular and agreeably, primitively "butch" in temperament. Yet he has an Achilles heel. When he was a boy, he was trapped somewhere, and therefore has latent claustrophobia, which so far in the war (since he is a great tunnel digger) he has overcome. But one day a load of earth falls on him as he digs; a sort of fright seizes on him and lingers. He can hardly be induced to start digging again. His crisis comes one night when his chum discovers him outside the cabins, all set to make a personal break through the fence. Because he seems out of his mind, his chum struggles with him, they slug each other, and almost get caught. Every few seconds, searchlights are being passed over the encampment, so that the two men, while struggling, are risking their lives, and at least one of them well knows it: the one who is so fiercely devoted to the other. He induces his friend to go back, and at the appointed time they make the escape as a couple, although that is only after another seizure of fright, overcome only by the grim devotion of the protective chum.

Is that all? That is *not* all. There is a third case of buddy-buddy, although this is nipped in the bud before the escape: the little Scotchman has acquired a chum in the American (Steve

McQueen) through repeatedly being confined with him in the "cooler," where they can talk to each other from cell to cell. When (as already mentioned) the Scotchman makes his hysterical break for the fence, McQueen irrationally tries to prevent what he rationally knows to be a virtual certainty: the man, already climbing the fence, will be gunned down. Yet he delivers some karate footwork to the guard who first takes aim; fortunately, he is only kicked in the groin for this futile piece of daring.

I imagine that by now some must really think I have a distorted, evil mind. Yet in the interests of truth and humanity, I refuse to give up my position. Why are these personal attachments—thus abstracted, isolated, and framed as they are—the *only* emotions which these prisoners are allowed to display for the duration of many months? Otherwise they show only the most routine of comradely feelings. I am far from imputing to the film-makers here a homosexual conspiracy. On the contrary, I am specifically imputing to them a definite type of innocence the sort that has combined formulas of commercial film-making with the robotism of making out war prisoners as career escapists. It is the hypnotically acting facts themselves, not any conscious creative motives, that betray the inhuman anomaly prevailing among these prisoners of war. It is not a whole human picture that we get in *The Great Escape,* but only an elaborately executed trick plot. Yet, given the *complete form* of this plot, the only logical thing to infer, humanly, is that beneath the visible surface, hiding as it were in the unphotographed interstices, is buddy-buddy homosexuality. No one need bother to pretend that such a thing doesn't exist in armies: it is more than amply documented.

My point is that precisely this factor fills in for the motivation lacking to the behavior of certain prisoners, who are made the principals. Humanly, sexually, emotionally, such deep personal attachments are not to be accounted for by the dedication of war prisoners to escape; as we saw in one case, the attachment is an *impediment* to escaping. One can offer the obvious excuse: the human factors of sexuality and related emotions have simply been eliminated here. But why should they have been? Why should artistic representation *ever* eliminate those factors?

Since when does a melodramatic plot have to be so skeletonized as to be asexual? Would it be "homosexual" to assert that at least *one* man should have mentioned how much he loved and missed his wife; or *one* man have complained bitterly of sexual starvation; or *one* man have hinted that he had something so normal as an Oedipus complex; or *one* man have allowed himself a bit of mock sex-play? Even if a man had said to his roommate, "Gosh, I wish you had a pair of tits!", that would have sounded corny, yet, in the context, reassuringly heterosexual. But no! *Absolutely not!* These men are phenomenally satisfied with each other, exactly as they are, through months of nominal sex privation.

I must add one thing because of its waywardness as the sole show of homosexual insinuation. There is one really implausible detail to it which stamps the whole incident as most suspicious. An important item of escape equipment is lacking: a complete set of identification papers. How to get hold of one so that it can be photographed to enable the forger on the escape team to provide the needed 250 documents? This is how the identification document as well as the camera to photograph it are obtained: The prisoner acted by James Garner (the prettiest of the lot) strikes up a sly buddy-buddydom with one of the German guards, a patently neurotic, rather mind-loose fellow. Garner gets very cute, boldly pals him around, and offers him chocolate from a cache of illicit foods. According to the way Garner does it, it shouldn't fool a child. But technically it is "courtship" in the palsy-walsy hetero manner, and, seemingly, stops there. However, the guard is so taken in by it that he has to summon all his lurking paranoia to refuse the bribe of chocolate and other foods (as yet, he can't guess what Garner is up to) and hurriedly scuttle out. Now, what is supposed to have *also* happened while he was in the room with Garner?

Physical contact between the men has looked very casual. All the same, Garner is supposed to have lifted the other's identification papers, his most precious personal possession, whose loss, if discovered, would have grave consequences. The papers, naturally, are carried in a buttoned-up jacket probably in the form of a wallet; or at least, in a back trouser pocket covered by the jacket. How could Garner—even as "the scrounger" he is nicknamed—have lifted the wallet in such circumstances? Only the two of them are in the room, and the German, however much fascinated, would naturally be wary (indeed he *is* wary) of a prisoner who is transparently making up to him. Somebody, and not in the movie, seems to have slipped.

Later, on discovering that his papers are missing, the guard returns to Garner's room when again he is alone, and agitatedly reports the loss, begging the prisoner to look everywhere in the room for the "lost" article. The guard seems not only distraught, but silly and sheepish. Is it mere silliness that prevents his reporting the loss that occurred, presumably, when he was in Garner's room? He should have enough sense to know that he will only receive a mild penalty for having chummed with the prisoner as compared to the penalty he will earn if the loss of his papers be discovered without his having reported it. Moreover, only an idiot could not know that Garner was up to something, and that reporting him might well be instrumental in uncovering an escape plot.

Incidentally, the whole function of this particular prison camp, we are told, is to herd together notorious escape careerists so they can be watched in one bunch. Why does the guard's panic and sense of guilt not only prevent his reporting Garner (which he could do on the basis of the food cache alone) but actually induce him later to steal a camera and present it to Garner? There is one simple hypothesis to explain all these things. At least, it would lend some plausibility to what otherwise is a fantastic degree of sheer idiocy in the German guard. Maybe the script writers didn't slip at all, maybe they just sleepwalked through. It is merely that (it could have happened in life, if not in *The Great Escape*), the prisoner played by Garner actually got the guard to go to bed with him, or at least remove his jacket for some hanky-panky. That would make fairly credible Garner's capture of the identification papers as well as the guard's guilt and conceivably his sentimental reasons for gratifying Garner with the camera he asks for. Did I say *The Great Escape* is a homosexual mystery story? Well, I did not also say that the mystery could not be solved by an alert critic who is entirely impartial and objective about sex.

I hope I have solved the mystery to the reader's satisfaction. But where my own satisfaction is involved—and I trust the reader will continue to bear with me—there is another dimension in which to consider the commercial charade that is *The Great Escape:* the purely aesthetic one. In film fiction to be rated as "G" (for the whole family), this dimension is very apt to be situated in or near the unconscious. Yet one must never assume it is *absent.* Nature is thoughtful where man is careless or indifferent; nature does not neglect the aesthetic but seems the more vigilant about it where man, egotistic "script writer" that he may be, is apt to lag. Unless this movie's makers were very devious, indeed, it was nature's "plot" which supplied all the aesthetic underpinnings of this melodrama.

One thing that struck me about the consistent pairing off of the principals of the film—all male, since women do not appear except fleetingly as mere background figures—is that the prisoner played by slim, platinum-blond David McCallum never gets hitched up with anybody; that's odd, for surely he's a nice-looking fellow. Yet a startling act of heroism does characterize him. Among those who escape (including the escape leader and his traveling companion), McCallum and a few others board the same train. Being well behind the escape leader and his friend when they all get off, McCallum sees that, ahead of them, Gestapo men are stopping all passengers to look at their identification papers. Does he have a secret yen for the leader? Anyway, at this point, McCallum creates a sudden diversion by assaulting a German agent standing isolated by the train and manages to shoot him with his own revolver. Within seconds, the men who have been scrutinizing the passengers' identifications have gunned down the fleeing McCallum. His act has been one of self-sacrifice and technically in the line of a good soldier's duty: in the confusion, as doubtless anticipated, his superior officer and friend have seized the chance to escape. No special challenge to this pattern. Its notation seems enough.

However, we follow the fortunes of the other escapers, see them caught or not caught. The American escaper has an exciting experience that symbolically is very suggestive. As I said, he was deprived of his chum by the latter's open dash for the fence. So now McQueen has the status of a "loner." Through some curious design of fate, he manages to acquire that symbol of Leather Boy sexuality, a motorcycle, on which he whizzes along over hill and dale as if he were a cowboy on a horse. One might think, according to a familiar romantic pattern, that he'd meet a woman who would hide him or even ride with him. Not this time: something in nature and the script combined to decide otherwise. He is detected by frontier guards, and the Gestapo as well, so that we witness a merry chase through open country with half a dozen vehicles zooming in pursuit of him. It's calisthenically exciting, and it occurred to me that this deprived chum was in a bitterly ironic fix, being chased by so many men who were out to do nothing more sportive or sexy than bag him. The sequence is well photographed and ends when McQueen approaches, I should guess, the Swiss frontier, which is provided with a double, very formidable set of barbed-wire barriers that his motorcycle can't crash through. Yet finally cornered, like someone in a game, he does dive the motorcycle under the barrier, and while uninjured, tangles himself dexterously in a lot of barbed wire; threatened at once by leveled weapons, he has to give up, and smiling a little, extracts himself gingerly from the barbed wire—but not before he has given the (doubtless still warm) seat of the stolen motorcycle an affectionate caress that's like a "Thank you, old fellow, we almost made it!"

It was this, I think, that caused suddenly to dawn on me that the whole escape maneuver had been anally oriented rather than vaginally or womb oriented. I mean, of course, the existence of the subterranean passages of the three tunnels dug by the prisoners. They are not nicknamed Sal, Mary, and Ann, or anything of that sort, but Tom, Dick, and Harry. Thus the film script, not I, designated them as masculine. One might, heterosexually, think of the tunnels as symbolizing a return to the womb (Mother Earth), and the emergence of the escapers through the man-sized hole, near the woods outside the fence, as a token of rebirth. Freedom = rebirth as free men, as soldiers. There's nothing wrong with this pattern except that any structure of the unconscious or subconscious ought to take its cue from the structure of the conscious *with which it is technically connected*. For some reason, women are entirely excluded from any significant role in this movie's conscious structure; as I say, memories of women apparently have nothing to do with the principals' emotional life.

Hence it seems more apt to consider the tunnels as excretory passages and the escape itself as an anal climax. A prisoner of war is a wasted, frustrated soldier. Through the benign function of this artificial colon and rectum, however, he is freed to function again, normally and properly, as an active, free-moving soldier. The sexual analogy of homosexual relations (which are "underground," according to the pattern supplied by the film and analyzed above) would fit exactly the term of anal intercourse between males. The Bronson character's claustrophobic problem means, in this light, the bowel stoppage that sometimes results in homosexuals from guilt feelings, or indeed, from fright feelings (like: "I will be caught" or "I will get a disease" and so on). It can also mean the anal retention that causes constipation when the passive sodomist resists, for whatever reason, the idea of intercourse. Aesthetically, in terms of the movie's action, all the business of getting the men through this laboriously achieved tunnel by having them, one by one, lie prone on a little sled moving on small wheels and having it pulled by someone at the other end, all the shocks of stoppages, accidents, and the anxiety of the whole experience, can be aligned equally well with bowel movement or anal intercourse.

Fright is curiously, but very relevantly, associated with a soldier's total experience, whether or not his experience has a specific sexual (here homosexual) extension. Familiar to soldiers is the experience, on the field, of sudden or creeping fear which, in so many, must be overcome so that he can conduct himself properly in battle. There are no bones about the colloquial expression used to describe his sensations at such times: he feels, to employ the classic expression, like shitting in his pants. Reliable statistics tell us that not only does he "feel like it," occasionally he does. We must be careful to be grave about these matters. No doubt a certain Hollywood contingent will take my apt and logical speculations either as a set of dirty jokes or an evil, scandalously impudent critical attack. I am not evil, I think, because I believe so much *good* of the movies. As for being thought scandalous or impudent, I don't mind that at all. To the "critical atack," I plead guilty, because always I speak for the truest aesthetic values I know. But by all means, and in any event, the matter here is *no joke*. It is humanly fine and has a considerable majesty of its own, this symbolic substratum of *The Great Escape*.

A rather elegant piece of symbolism has been provided by the movie's overt action. One important technical problem of the tunnel diggers is the disposal of the earth dug up to create the passageway. Eventually its accumulation makes impossible any practicable form of the camouflage hitherto employed. Everybody is really stumped till one day McCallum walks into the thinking room with a perfect solution. It is greeted with delight. Suspended on cords inside a prisoner's trousers, one in each leg, will be two long thin bags like unfilled sausage skins; when these are filled with the earth to be disposed of, a cord manipulated by the wearer will be pulled, a mouth opened at the lower end of each bag, and the dirt spill out. Of course, this operation has to take place outside the cabins. But the pounded empty ground of the encampment is too flat and of a different color. Patches of fresh dark earth on it would easily be noticed. Now, what solution? It soon comes. Start a series of garden plots to grow flowers, so that while the compound's dirt is busily being dug up, men can casually pass over the plots, stop for a moment, and relieve themselves of their load.

No anal problems here.

It works. In fact, it's beautiful. So to speak.

UNCONSCIOUS?

Homosexuality is insidious. It's there, seemingly uninvited, in *The Great Escape*, or technically built in, in an Italian film, *Investigation of a Citizen Above Suspicion*, as one variety of human pathology. Rather too eagerly, at times too snugly, it takes its appointed place in crime melodramas. Yet I shall not be moralistic and claim that decent homosexuals, not suffering from dangerous complexes, have been slandered by the alert, ambitious auteur director of the present film, Elio Petri. To do so would be aggressively partisan. Petri's film seems meant as a serious indictment of the concept of police bureaucracy—and, by one remove, the police state—as the existential symbol of human corruption in the name of authority. In a way, by introducing its particular homosexual, *Investigation* portrays deviate sexuality as just another form of human frailty that is victimized by the dominant form of the unnaturally constituted and impelled police machine. No alternative to this all-powerful machine, which governs the lives of heterosexual and homosexual citizens, is suggested by the film explicitly. It appears as the most malign form of human fate at this stage of our civilization, with the only elements actively to oppose it seen as the revolutionary youth who throw bombs, shout songs, and write slogans on the walls of public buildings.

Many plot ideas could be written from this general angle and these biased, rather simplistic assumptions. Petri has devised a plot (in collaboration with Ugo Pirro) as consciously peculiar in the role it assigns homosexuality as *The Great Escape* was peculiarly unconscious in the shadowy role it assigned homosexuality; that is, the latter compromised all sexuality by automatically involving homosexual premises that were in no way openly acknowledged. Petri's film quite deliberately acknowledges homosexuality, so timed and treated, however, as to make it integral with the enigma of its central character. This Police Inspector (as the credits term him) is chief of the homicide squad in Rome. In the opening scene, he celebrates his promotion to Chief of Political Intelligence by murdering his mistress and adding a case for the new homicide chief to solve. The character of the Police Inspector is very special and very devious; the more so because his stock characterization as a Machiavellian little Napoleon—hard, tense, overbearing, outwardly cynical and jocular by turns, a very machine of authoritarianism treated by his aides with servile awe—is first seen as an invulnerable surface concealing a profound guilt-neurosis, with "sexual inadequacy" at its root.

The film's realization of this is not altogether happy or

convincing, but it is much in earnest. As we learn by a series of flashbacks showing his relations with the young woman he has murdered, sexual inadequacy has been the specific charge of his mistress when once, in a fit of temper, she turned on him and beat him till he cried like a punished child. The affair began because, a total stranger to him, she made a series of telephone calls urging him to come to her home and "interrogate" her just for "thrills." Their sex has become a game in which he plays master, and she, slave, so that when she turns on him and beats him up, the pattern is suddenly broken. A particular feature of their game was for her to impersonate the victim in some current or typical murder, when he, "playing" Inspector, takes police photographs of her "corpse." In at last making a real corpse of her, he grants his sexual inadequacy and the crime assumes the quality of a mechanism by which he takes her place as an aggressive masochist, whose ultimate motive is to provoke harassment, be arrested and "grilled," confess and suffer punishment. In short, he is a persecutor who, through some vague but persistent compulsion, wishes to take the place of the persecuted, his own victims. To this end, he immediately arranges glaring clues to his identity as the murderer. The gimmick by which Petri justifies this pattern of guilt-neurosis is the criticism of supreme authority, especially punitive authority, as not being "above suspicion" except on its own terms as a subjective irrational myth.

What seems naïve about this is that Petri has apparently misunderstood the fatalistic irony of Kafka's statement that formally closes the film, to the effect that the symbols of human authority "elude judgment." That was a paradox Kafka himself never pretended to solve because his conception of the law was divine, not human. For Judeo-Christian thinkers, God is as enigmatic and absolute as any supreme dictator who formulates the laws. Nevertheless the deity's power flows from some timeless, unearthly source, something transcending even "God." Thus the law is incomprehensible through inherent mystery. To the pagan, however, the law was not thus transcendent: its authority derived from arbitrary humanoid will. The Greek gods did not obtain their authority from a stainless virtue or from being identical with a supreme, primordial mystery; they obtained it as "original ancestors" from whom mankind "inherited" it as the sons of kings used to inherit kingship.

So if, in his film, Petri is saying that the tragedians were right in their criticism of the vainglorious pose of human infallibility (this is the theme of *Oedipus Rex* and *The Bacchae*), it is only what political militants chant every day in the streets of modern cities. In fact, Petri brings these same militants into the action when a bombing takes place outside police headquarters and as a consequence droves of suspects are arrested and jailed. Yet the supposition that all civilized authority is well within suspicion (as tacitly capable or guilty of wrongdoing) does not account for the specific form Petri had given his protagonist's story. This form lies in its motivation and style, the human significance of the exact illustrations it affords. After all, the Police Inspector is known to us as guilty *from the start*.

As it happens, the new Intelligence chief has to try hard to induce the police to overcome the very myth of authority which he incarnates. It is long before they consent even to suspect him and follow up the clues which he has stray impulses to complicate so as to make them look baffling. Finally he has to openly mock and bait the police chief and his aides, then freely confess before they can grasp the idea of his guilt. If all this were undertaken as an intellectual experiment, an existentialist game, it might have a genuine Kafka look, though not the true Kafka philosophy. But Petri has deliberately loaded the intellectual experiment with sex motivation and strongly implicated unconscious homosexuality as part of that motivation. Is this a criticism of Kafka or a criticism of society with "improved" Kafka methods? That hardly matters, because Petri has cornered his protagonist in a web of explicit sexual motivation. Just what, then, is so far off-color as to make the Inspector a very curious protagonist indeed?

I am duty-bound to say that the evidence points to suppressed homosexuality; a masochistic drive so deranged, that is to say, that submitting himself sexually to a man seems the only possible climax to a paranoia of guilt that craves supreme and utter degradation. The film ends with a climax and anticlimax that make it look as if the reigning police system of our time will refuse to admit the guilt of one of its own agents of authority. Such seems to be the guilty protagonist's own *more secret* wish: that his guilt will ultimately be denied or ignored. This could be a form of the delusion of grandeur which has always been opposed to his guilty desire for humiliation and punishment. The issue remains: By just what factors of motivation have his concrete actions been achieved? Petri plainly says these actions are *sexually rooted*. What are the sexual roots?

Well, from the account I have given, it is heterosexual inadequacy, a pathetic infantilism tempted to assume temporarily the master role in pseudo-sadistic sex, a role fated to collapse. Surely this is glaringly present unless we are to take the numerous flashbacks showing it as actually wishful thinking, only a fantasy. But the murder itself, which cannot be fantasy or wishful thinking, ratifies the recollections as perfectly credible. One might well think that this completes the pattern of sexual motivation. But it does not. For some reason, Petri has complicated the situation by having his Inspector's mistress married to a homosexual from whom she has been estranged, and who is duly arrested as a suspect in the crime. The Inspector does not know him, has never met him, but when he appears, the Inspector identifies with him and denies the man's guilt, as for the time being he tentatively, formally denies his own guilt. Like all victims of severe psychosis, he is prepared equally to exonerate and incriminate himself. Why is the homosexual husband, however, necessary or appropriate to the plot pattern? Technically, as the movie stands, he could be dropped from it without disturbing its pattern, without damaging the completeness of its statement.

All the same, his presence fits conspicuously into a telling bit of action which Petri has provided as part of the Inspector's motivation in deciding to kill his mistress (who, by the way, is most satisfyingly attractive). This is simple jealousy of another man, a good-looking revolutionary youth who has encountered the Inspector exactly when he left the apartment building after the murder, because the youth himself happens to live in the building. The previous connection the two men have is that once—though the youth does not know it—the Inspector glimpsed him in the showerbath of a cabana making love to his mistress. Because the youth has seen the Inspector on the scene of the crime, he might be expected to come forward with this information. He doesn't, presumably, because he shares the revolutionary creed that the power bureaucracy will never dare incriminate one of its high members who are "above suspicion." But when the bomb explosion takes place and many young radicals are arrested, this youth is among them; and when the Inspector has him brought in alone for what we expect will be a display of sadistic revenge, it is the youth who denounces the Inspector, the youth who explicitly and violently indicts his "persecutor." What happens is that, isolated with his "victim" and accused by him, the Inspector abruptly turns into the masochistic child-adult he was when his infuriated mistress had belabored him and flung at him the charge of "sexual inadequacy."

Once more, the bugaboo of *impotence!* Again a desexualizing that suggests reversal of the sex roles if not of the sexual identities. Yet why is a reversal of sexual identity *also* indicated? Precisely because the homosexual has been dragged into the situation. If he is not extraneous to it, then he represents the suppressed homosexuality that is the true, the deepest, source of the murderer's motivation. As it is, the Inspector's jealousy of his mistress can be interpreted according to an accredited pattern: a heterosexual married man, repressing homosexual impulses, sometimes becomes reasonably or unreasonably jealous of his wife because he really wants to sleep with the man with whom he accuses her of sleeping. It is one of Freud's formulations, and case histories of the sort have richly confirmed it. Everything fits here: the Inspector's sudden conversion into the cringing, whining attitude of someone who imagines himself trapped, repeats what we have already witnessed: the homosexual's whimpering behavior when he has been grilled; to be sure, he is protesting his innocence (which we know for a fact) and claiming an alibi. But so does the Inspector, at times, pretend he too is guiltless, has no complicity. Plainly the Inspector has a schizoid personality. Not only is he a strutting bully, ready to crush his subordinates like worms, he also suddenly begins being jovial and habitually makes a point of affectionately pinching the cheeks of his aides and associates. When, during the questioning, the police are trying to pin down the murdered woman's husband as homosexual it is the Inspector who, with a traditional camp gesture of homosexuals (parody of the way a woman primps her hair), delivers the positive verdict on the man's sexuality. . . . A time-honored term in crime mysteries—now uncommon because we take it so much for granted—is "Cherchez la femme!" (Find the woman—and you'll solve the mystery!) I suggest a new version that is not—at least, not quite yet —a cliché: "Cherchez le pédéraste!"

SUBCONSCIOUS?

Perhaps the question mark is superfluous. Even the word may be wrong. It's the involvement that decides. . . . We see the profile of a middle-aged, ambiguously middle-class blond woman with some of the picturesque quality of a Roman coin. It looks brooding. That is instantly communicated. One is involved. A cheap, showy woman sits on some shabby steps near a landing. There's a door back of her. It opens and a hand tosses out some paper money . . . more money . . . and then a crucifix on a necklace. She sniffs, glowers, picks up her heavy form, and leaves the house. On the street, she passes some nuns and their little charges, singing and turning in a circle, with joined hands. The woman is grim, weary. She pawns the crucifix. . . . She climbs the steps of her home . . . and her first speech is *récitatif*. She is Madame Flora, the heroine of Gian-Carlo Menotti's opera *The Medium*, in its filmic version (1951). Marie Powers is her real name. Powers of Mary, truly enough!

But Mary come on hard times; Mary: a fat medium, a charlatan. The White Goddess, to be sure; the same one who, in *Satyricon*, Fellini made black and pagan. Menotti's Christian goddess, basically pagan, has no visible past. She needs none. She is the Timeless Woman, dense in her natural atoms, broad and authentic of bosom. Marie Powers is void of the vanity of great actresses, but she is a great actress because she found this part. The singing voices which, in others of the cast, are so shocking—especially during the close-ups that are foreign to stage vision—seem incidental when set beside Miss Powers' authoritative, overwhelming instrument. It is a voice that dominates what is sung. Menotti's music is very canny in this respect; the libretto is also his, so everything is planned. Unfortunately for film, it remains a stage-built, if wonderful, contrivance. The Christianized goddess is the spirit and substance of a dateless matriarchy, slightly (as if for fun) also dated.

Age, clothes, the supernatural myth integrate this effect. Madame Flora has a daughter but she has long ceased to be a mother in the ordinary sense. When her life is first revealed, she is already a complete symbol. It is too bad, in a way, that she must be the central energy in a work in which one medium of artistic expression, the opera, struggles throughout with another, the motion picture. But this lack of formal cohesion reveals all the better a myth (still contemporary) of which Marie Powers came along as the foremost agency.

It is a myth of homosexual guilt in which a serious and realistic "Mae West" plays the very opposite of a nightclub personality: a betrayed Female Principle incarnate. Mae West is the image of the "good mother" which the homosexual's instinctive imagination makes into a "whore"—first because of Oedipal jealousy; then, because he desires the man with whom he imagines her flirting and bargaining. An artist may not realize he is doing this sort of thing; nevertheless he *is* doing it. Madame Flora is the same image as that, made into the sinner which the mother's personality may become, may represent, in this particular myth of a young male's imagination. The "Mary" of Madame Flora has the powers both of the Madonna and the Magdalen. She is the vociferous Magdalen to whom, in her state of agonized conscience, the Madonna comes paradoxically as a demon and a blessing. The myth becomes true *in* Madame Flora.

Alike, the dramatic line and the musical line of *The Medium* are too strong to be destroyed by the self-conscious filmic form. This must be said even though the camera vision (by Alexander Hammid) is fine and tactful, sometimes brilliant.

Menotti's opera is like a dream in that it is compact of elided, irrational, significant images. A perfectly apt inspiration made the operatic convention of loud music and bizarre melodrama into the "medium" of a quasi-dream. The special artifice is justified not by art, but by symbolic psychology. The film has made the original stage conception the less artistic because the more realistic. At the same time, the very realism of the film brings the dream symbols into the sharp, immitigable focus of the close-up. The foster son of Madame Flora (played by Leo Coleman) is first seen in grotesque female costume at play with her daughter, and the foster mother's first words here are reproaches for being in "woman's clothes."

Toby, the foster son, is, significantly and precisely, dumb. He is a sort of cosmic outcast, the more emphatically so because, while supposedly a "gypsy" picked up by Madame Flora "on the streets of Budapest," his native blood (to judge by his physiognomy) is African, assuredly in part. Like other, more important heroes of ambiguous personality, he is also a sort of idiot, and even as Prince Myshkin, notably infantile. The style in which Coleman acts the part plays up a calculating theatrical motive: he choreographs, in outline, every movement and unmistakably shows a dancer's training. There are times when he seems a cross between a Katherine Dunham dancer and the Favorite Slave in *Schéhérazade*. Yet no one else in the cast practices an equivalent style. Is it chance which found this way of making Toby more strange as an outcast, more a symbol of homosexual guilt than otherwise he might have been? But chance is one way of nature, homosexual or heterosexual.

Toby is as he is not just because he is physically handicapped but also because he is hypersensitive. If he idolizes Monica, his foster sister, who innocently provokes his love, it is out of completely uncrystallized if sincere sexuality. The scene before the mirror in which Monica, to help him express his love, takes first his part and then her own, denotes the fluid nature of the boy's gender. As an image and an idea, Toby has that sensitivity which justly or unjustly is commonly characterized as feminine, and his character, however deliberately, has been accented toward this aspect. Notice, on the other hand, that

Madame Flora is curiously masculine, if only because she is the absolute authority in her house, a sort of tyrant; she is much more powerful than the mild male who, with his mousy wife, listens during the séance to the "transcendental" laughter of their little dead son. Indeed, Madame Flora has no difficulty in creating an atmosphere of cosmic domination, subject only to her own fear of the supernatural—of whose supposedly real forces she becomes suddenly aware after a career of pure fakery.

The film has been able to show one important point which the opera omitted: Toby's psychic agency in terms of the "hand" felt by Madame Flora at her throat during the crucial séance. In his hidden compartment, where he takes part in the hocus-pocus of the séance, Toby actually, we observe, makes the gesture of choking someone. It is an oblique but plain enough hint of voudoun (the popularly known voodoo) magic. Madame Flora has enslaved both daughter and foster son as adjuncts of her profession, yet she is not especially unkind, apparently, till after the incident of the ghostly choking, of which she persistently suspects Toby. The point is that the content of her crisis is psychic, or more realistically speaking, spiritual and psycholog ical. It is the nemesis of her own guilt feelings that attacks and haunts her. The further point, clearly, is that this guilt centers upon her foster son. Why is this?

Imaginable are equally eloquent alternatives which the dream structure of Menotti's opera seems to make rather indistinguishable while utterly vivid. Madame Flora's anxiety is the projection of Toby's guilt feelings as symbol of the homosexual son and/or the suffering of a mother who hallucinates her son's betrayal of his sex and thus of *her* sex as his mother. As a foster son Toby represents the fostering of guilt. That Flora's experience should be thought simply a resurgence of Christian conscience would make the work as it stands into a pretentious, external, arty melodrama. No: I think this opera much more than theologically inspired. The clammy hand pressing her throat at the séance, thinks Madame Flora, is the hand of her foster son. This is hardly a theological suspicion. What should be a warm caress, in any case, is applied as if in cold aggression, "evilly." This is how a son might betray his normal relation to a loving and loved mother: by turning technical caress into actual assault.

Consciously, Madame Flora expects no aggression from Toby, and Toby himself may not be precisely aware of his own magic "projection." Evidently, something unconscious or super-conscious is speaking in the relation between foster mother and foster son. The quality of the incident is enhanced by the super-stitious awe associated with the weak-minded. Toby as a helpless victim may be the very crux of Madame Flora's psychic anxiety and the sudden shock of its climax. Maternal authority may be deposed by paternal authority in more than one way. The matri-archy may suffer defeat by the mere sexual default of a son. Doom can be in this arbitrary motion of the malé psyche. It cannot be wholly nonhuman, or supernatural; the human is too securely present for that. To begin with, the ghostly, inimical touch at the séance logically corresponds to an *incestuous* son's caress, which in the abstract or moral sense, even if tender, would be aggressive, and to the devout, particularly, an over-whelming sin. Magic and morality are the same: the caress is an *attack*. Here a special and decisive ambiguity rests in the fact that Toby is an irresponsible epicene in Flora's eyes, and thus outside consideration for the sin of incest or pseudo-incest. Hence the "ghostliness" of his touch would signify sin or mis-demeanor by *omission* rather than *commission*. This ineligibility for sin assumes a corresponding ineligibility for virtue. So Toby becomes a symbol of sin by simple default of virtue.

Madame Flora's religious conscience, the "manifest con-tent" of the opera's dream art, is likewise not the result of posi-tive sin, but of the sheer default of faith. This default has led her to her professional mockery of the supernatural. So might the default of sexual validity lead Toby, or anyone else, to homo-sexuality through the consistent mockery of heterosexuality. Manifest homosexuality can be interpreted socially as a "positive aggression" against sexual normalcy, just as atheism or agnosti-cism can be interpreted religiously as a positive aggression against God. In the present case, the specific aggression would be against Mary, the Mother of God.

Surely, Menotti must have felt, perhaps meant, the laughter of the little dead boy at the séance as analogous with the divine exuberance of the Christ Child. Madame Flora, whether or not she ever had a real son, and whether or not he was homosexual, has never taken motherhood seriously. Thus she feels guilt not only toward her living daughter (in contrast with the parental love felt by her clients) but also guilt toward the hypothetic son symbolized by Toby. An access of guilt feeling, coming at a period of physiological crisis for all females, is all that could naturally account for Madame Flora's terrible spiritual ordeal with which the opera ends.

In terms of psychoanalysis, Menotti has supplied a mythic-religious superego structure for his work, one bearing relation not only to Freud's system but also to Jung's. Besides the Divine Child and the Divine Fool, Toby the foster son is the Divine Foundling, who in the opera's first scene wears a jeweled crown. We know in what respects the myth of Jesus' birth corresponds to the legend of the royal or divine foundling. At the same time, as an actual person, Toby is disqualified by his peculiar defects. Madame Flora's spasmodic tenderness for him signifies the symbolic or supernatural phase of her own personality as it likewise does of his. In the condensation of the dream technique, she systematically confuses, too, her own defects with his. Her defects, moreover, have a perfectly sensible human aspect: maternal guilt may base itself on the simple premise of having neglected one's offspring. The imaginative organism of the film, allowing one kind of abnormalcy to translate itself easily into another, only repeats the workings of standard human psychology. The intimation of Toby's homosexuality (or just the technical incest suggested by his feelings for his foster sister) might well have been interpreted by the superstitious Madame Flora as the retribution for her own latently present sins.

Nor does this basic aspect change when we shift to Toby's viewpoint and observe Madame Flora's agony rather as the hallucination of a guilty homosexual son who has visited pain on his mother through his sexual apostasy. Madame Flora is one facet of the work's complex dream art; Toby, another. On the high symbolic level, a conscious idea of drama has been used subconsciously to express a moral myth. The component parts of the opera-film show this particular myth transparently, beneath the varied surface, as the true psychic mechanism animating it. Menotti's impulse toward the legendary field of psychic phenomena was in no sense approximate or incidental, but on the contrary inseparable from the symbolic message he sought to formulate. The structure of psychic phenomena as practiced by mediums aesthetically corresponds to the oblique and often ambiguous structure of abnormal (that is, offbeat) sexuality. Persons may behave, as well as think, like dreams without knowing or caring if they do so. Madame Flora, surely, is an Earth Mother. Her very name suggests the fertility image of the Demeter myth, whose human implications are those of parental responsibility and anxiety.

This woman, indeed, is a commodious symbol. As Madame Flora, the Earth Mother has become afflicted with a barrenness which allies moral failure of the self with moral failure of one's sex, as witnessed here by defective male progeny: Toby the mute, the childish, the unmanly. As the eternal foundling, Toby is an equally large symbol, susceptible to the homosexual fantasy of symbolic release and apotheosis through a supernatural idea; exactly so does he represent the mundane ecstasy of the male child who raids his mother's closet and parades before the mirror in her clothes. All this constitutes a powerful tribute to the female principle as well as a point of immense crisis in the life of a developing male: something to be seriously considered, I think, whenever a female impersonator presents himself on the screen.

It is foolish to believe that the mythic forms cannot be "modern"; automatically, they modernize themselves by offering the varied evidence of fresh growths, showing, as in double exposure, form within form. Here the human crisis predicates moral failure, certainly a dilemma, both tormented and tragic. Sex, through such a masquerade, is both subjective and objective. As we shall see, later on, the male-transvestite form carries an impressive *parody of* the female, an impressive *compliment to* her. Fixated on Toby as the very image of her own mystery, Madame Flora sets forth this elusive ambiguity in her final madness.

The woman with Demeter's face of melted wax and the fat of the ages has lost all normal bearings. . . . She flees in her drink-sodden mind from a lethal ghost. She sings, magnificently, her despair, bringing up from a fabulous bosom the triumph of Marie Powers' voice. Yet Madame Flora is defeated. She is the foil of a spook that incarnates the conscience of the world itself: the world of woman with its insidious maternal guilt. This world moves around Flora and brings its awful exile into the house in the material shape of Toby. Now he is driven away, so fearful is she, but he lurks about in the rain and finally sneaks back, dodging behind his habitual curtain as Madame Flora rushes into the room too late to see him. But she sees the curtain tremble, and wildly she accuses the ghost while the unseen Toby cowers hysterically.

Flora opens a drawer and grasps a revolver. Toby dare not emerge. She shoots repeatedly at the shaking curtain. Senseless and bleeding, Toby pitches forward, dragging the curtain down with him. Automatically, in the fall, he half-wraps himself in it as if it were a dress. . . . This is no mere detail. Like so many theatrical "touches," this one of the simulated dress—seen in a really meaningful perspective—offers not only rightness, but substance. It defines a classic peripety. A male, though in psychic blindness and the very act of being destroyed, redefines his instinctual sex: Toby is inherently, fatally homosexual. His "mother"—she is morally such—can do nothing but suffer him; he is her "medium," she, his.

DELIBERATELY HETEROSEXUAL

If *Husbands* is a homosexual mystery story, it is not in any sense either homosexual or mysterious by the conscious intent of John Cassavetes, who conceived it and is principally responsible for its execution. I put it this way because *Husbands* has the air of being a working collaboration among its chief actors, the three who play the husbands of the title, Cassavetes himself (Gus), Peter Falk (Archie), and Ben Gazzara (Harry). Their collaboration was confirmed by the chummy atmosphere of a television interview with the three actors conducted by Virginia Graham after the film got an excellent press and seemed a hit. What *Husbands* undeniably asserts is a very unconventional—and what some might call a very cynical—view toward plain heterosexual romance, here in the form of at least three marriages which, judging by the film's action, have hit the rocks; positively so in one case, Harry's; quite possibly so in the cases of Gus and Archie.

If one wished to be unsympathetic to what Cassavetes has done with *Husbands,* it would be easy and obvious to attach to it the current tag of male chauvinism. For *Husbands* is a "stag" movie—about audiences rather than performers and with virtually all its clothes on. An exception is when Archie takes off his clothes as a gag; socially, that is. This is an antediluvian stunt staged by drunks (Archie is very drunk), and I have not yet been informed that it means anything but exhibitionism induced by sexual frustration. However, the sex scenes themselves have very little undress. Their naked climaxes (two of which we must politely assume did take place) are invisible, and lovemaking has been confined to first stages, in which Gus practically has to assault the bar girl he has picked up in a London gambling casino and Archie has to coax a mute, shy, slender, lovely Chinese girl to so much as give him the first kiss. When she does, she gets hot very quickly and sticks her tongue in his mouth. Even as a whore's routine, it shouldn't be out of order. But Archie has a reaction which is either stupidly puritanical or compulsively homosexual: he pushes her away and declares he thinks soul-kissing—it isn't so named, but they used to call it that—indecent.

This response of Archie's is but one item of passing evidence to prove how oddly square these revolutionary husbands are, or at least seem. And why should they seem "revolutionary"? Throughout, in deliberate and multitudinous ways, it is made clear that they consider their nonsexual affection for each other much worthier, more tangibly enjoyable, than their sexual affection for their respective wives, which at least Harry (for he says so) confines to action in bed. Here one must draw as fine a line between the physical and the sexual as the aesthetic philosophers of old Athens were tempted to do when it came to love between men. With disarming candor, Harry gets drunk enough to hug Gus and Archie to him and give the latter a smacky kiss on the cheek. "Fairy Harry!" he then jovially brands himself. "Except for sex, and my wife's very good at sex," he adds, "I like you guys better." Archie and Gus appear to reciprocate. Yet just to keep the record straight, one of them puts in, rather solemnly, "Fairy Harry, you're out of line." Touché, Eros! That's one on Homeros.* Or—wait now. Is it?

As for the legitimacy of the film's representation of how off and on beat our husbands are, I can't say I any longer have any direct contact with the middle-class, white-collar, neighborhood society of suburbia where Gus, Harry, and Archie maintain themselves and families and presumably originate. While it is casually revealed that Gus is a dentist and Harry has a desk in what looks like the production department of an advertising agency, it is hard to say just what average income prevails among them. A key to their cultural status is provided by their boss-cat airs in taking over a little neighborhood bar (proletarian-cum-lush in tone) for a sort of wake in honor of the fourth member of their private stag club: the poor guy, as we learn at the flick-on, has just been wafted from this vale of tears.

The opening funeral scene establishes how statutorily thick with normalcy and conventionality these husbands and fathers are, for they reminisce of the fourth male, loved and lost, in terms of family-album snapshots: everybody and his neighbors inhabit them. On the other hand, Pete Hamill has suggested that the whole reason for the wildly out-of-line behavior of the three survivors, who follow Harry's desperate lead and fly to London with him for a Jet Set spree, is that all are in love with the fourth, now gone; he was a hardier specimen, it seems, with blond crewcut and perhaps other, less exposable, charms. The question, if not the mystery, of homosexuality is bound to occur to every judicious viewer of the film, and I dare-

---

* From the Greek: (h)omo = the same + Eros = the love god; author's contraction for homosexual Eros as opposed to heterosexual Eros. Not to be confused with (H)omeros = Homer the Greek poet.

say to some injudicious viewers. Its sex hatred, present enough to be morally uncomfortable, is standard if seen from the viewpoint of the family quarrel as a symptom of the continuing War between the Men and the Women. Usually the aesthetic forms of this war, nowadays, are comic—all the way from the sphere of romantic comedy to the sphere of the comicstrip and the dirty joke. In a propaganda article for Women's Lib,* Betty Friedan finds reason in *Husbands* to proclaim that today in America the mere term "My wife" has the status of a dirty joke.

Mrs. Friedan exaggerates, of course, but her partisan resentment is not totally without grounds. Surely the action at Harry's home, the morning after the barroom wake, is *dirty* if not in the least a *joke*. If it's a joke because it suggests a tabloid news story ("Near Knifing in Queens Domestic Spat"), it doesn't mean to be joking. It is so drearily, savagely documentary in style that heterosexual Eros might well weep tears of blood for it. Evidently suburban wife and suburban husband have a statutory quarrel that has reached the breaking point. The heterosexes are shown as common brutes with a grudge against each other as great as it is old and subterranean. Since the lady's accomplishments in bed have already been extolled (and written off) by her husband, this scene of maddened, shameless violence offers a glittering object lesson for moralists of the classic War between the Men and the Women.

The very fundaments of this war are prime causes, speaking technically, for the sexual neurosis, which may be either homosexual or heterosexual. The main point of *Husbands,* Cassavetes' own particular stress on his theme, is that these three pals, while they love *each other,* are heterosexually in great trouble. What, superficially, the strident action and conclusion amount to is that Gus, Harry, and Archie become exiles from heterosexual love; or rather, they are like losers in an unexpected state of heterosexual bankruptcy. It isn't their fault as investors, perhaps it's not even their wives' fault (Mrs. Friedan thinks it is!). It may be, to take it frivolously, just a maneuver of Eros on the sexual stock market. To be sure, it's *serious*. Because of the demands of physical nature (all three males are in

* *The New York Times,* January 31, 1971.

their youngish prime), their psychic situation, sparked by the trauma of losing their fourth pal, now endures a maximum strain at its most vulnerable point: the obvious homosexual alternative. If they weren't such bosom pals, of course, they'd be vowing a new sex life instead of drowning their all-male sorrows together.

Cassavetes could not be literate and avoid not merely naming, but also exercising, the temptation for his heroes to turn homosexual. Suppose, in fact, Pete Hamill were right, and the three men are secret and suppressed (perhaps unconscious) homosexuals who have formed an adoring private circle about the "blond god" who incontinently dies? This would make them a quasi-homosexual clique with the departed god having played, and perhaps been, "straight man." I can't see that there is a single factor or wrinkle in the film to contradict, as sheer speculation, this assumption. One could hazard that neither Archie, Gus, nor Harry understands his homosexual role except, perhaps, unconsciously. But, granting the foregoing possibilities, every bit of character revelation in *Husbands* would neatly fit such a hypothesis. And there is yet another possibility that would leave undisturbed the film's statistical surface. The *departed* husband could have been a secret homosexual—one of those unspoken but recognizable elements that frequently determine a form of group behavior. Here the hetero survivors' problem might well be: "Is there anyone to *replace* him?" And even: "Should it be *one of us?*" A great deal of ambivalent emotion might be worked up over such a strange possibility.

One sees how difficult the situation might become. The peculiar anguish of our hero-husbands would seem to exploit the difficulty, though if any of the above hypotheses be true, it is kept behind a veil. Not only does the threesome feel that, having lost the precious fourth member, the surviving solidarity is mysteriously threatened, but precipitately, as well, they feel called on to make postponed moral decisions. Harry's is the most radical decision to be made: Will he split finally from wife, family, home? He will. And apparently, at the end, he *does*. The in-crisis episode, when the three realize the depth and perhaps the intractable nature of their postmortem problem, is the men's room vomiting scene. This follows the longish, dolefully vulgar barroom wake when it is the royal whim of three boss cats to compel the bar crowd to make asses of themselves by competing in a "talent contest." This has been extremely painful for a mere witness (speaking for myself), while perhaps it was infinitely touching to connoisseurs of the folksy illiterate, those thinking it funky rather than, as I do, fatuous. To me, the vomiting scene, brutally realistic as it is, comes as a welcome purge of the preceding visions and sounds, consuming minutes and minutes as annuated barflies of both sexes, bribed by liquor, sing annuated songs and Gus, Archie, and Harry drunkenly run the proceedings.

The tune changes with the trio's urgent retreat to the men's room, where they come face to face with the nemesis of the toilet bowl, into which human gastronomic errors are disgorged the wrong way. Note exactly what happens. For here Cassavetes' script is the most original, the performances the most scrupulously realistic. I don't refer to the acrobatics of vomiting, though these are (in sound anyway) horrendous, or to homosexual contacts, absent here although often made the function of such quarters. Harry, riding high on the wave of drunkenness, could call himself a fairy because he could make the aspersion a real guy's tipsy put-on. *Now* the real guys are faced with ugly hangovers and the ugly immediacies of nauseated organisms. Nausea, remember, may be a sign of heterosexual disgust at involvement (willing or unwilling) with homosexuality. So what do we witness? Harry, stern with the other two because he's holding his liquor better, goes in and out of the dinky men's room while his pals suffer. He's ironically grim, even bitter, and furthermore, he's jealous of the incidental chumminess formed by the others' sickness: Gus and Archie vomit, revomit, and in laconic torpor sink squatting to the floor so that the camera sees their heads at toilet-bowl level.

Because they seem to wish to stay put, Harry gets annoyed, mocking them for wanting, as he says, "to be alone"— alone, that is, *as a pair*. This trifling infidelity, to Harry, jolts the unity of the trio. Meanwhile, for this privvie scene, Harry has appeared wearing a red plaid tam-o'-shanter borrowed from one of the female barflies. Is there any significance to this gratuitous hint of transvestism? It must remain ambiguous, and yet the ambiguity could hardly be unintended. I think it calls something into question. What it calls into question is lodged in a general abiding state of question by the whole film: heterosexuality itself. For so deliberately heterosexual a film, *Husbands* is flagrant with homosexual innuendo. How much committed are these characters?—how much committed their creator and mover? One *can't* go "stag" the way Cassavetes has done here without letting in homosexuality by the back door, and once in, it's sure—in this cultural milieu anyway—to make straight for the men's room. A note of no little interest is that when, later, the three engage adjoining hotel rooms in London, the first thing they do, merely to rest, is to sit together on a bathroom floor in cozy proximity with the trite toilet bowl and the novel *bidet*. One might well ask: How stealthily anal can you get and still be staunchly hetero?

What is morally put in question, overtly and beyond doubt, is the marital, family, and community fate of Harry, Gus, and Archie as well as their special friendship pact, their private little clique. The latter is what principally concerns them as the film's action gets them deeper into the throes of their spree. Precisely, we have the paradox of *an intermale love problem among men who are heterosexuals in bed.* That should ring a famous mental bell: what traditionally is the platonic homosexuality of ancient Athens. One feature of the film's mystery becomes: How could this tradition show its nose in the citadel of modern, puritanic, aggressively hetero suburbia? But Cassavetes has caught on to that "nose" in just this region with all the intent purpose of a faggot casing something prodigious in the men's room.

Certainly I don't mean to brand *Husbands* as a homo charade. Quite the contrary! Cassavetes and the other two seem conscientiously heterosexual, both privately and in terms of the roles enacted here. But that's just it. Exactly the fictional terms chosen for these roles place heterosexuality in great danger, even in sore suspicion, of being a failed institution. That is why it's hard to understand a Betty Friedan's evangelical optimism over *Husbands.* Here we behold no toiling intellectuals or artists; no closet queens leading a double life; no fixtures on an analyst's couch suspended in puzzled bisexuality. In fact, it is just because Gazzara, Falk, and Cassavetes are convincing as real guys, not gay guys, that the film got through so penetratingly to the Women's Lib leader, Mrs. Friedan, who started her above-mentioned article by granting that *Husbands* "is a movie made by men about men's love for other men." Her whole thesis is disarmingly simple: the anguishing dilemma of Gus, Harry, and Archie exists not because *they* have failed as men, but because their *wives,* as women, have not risen to their gaping opportunity. Women, Mrs. Friedan explains, have not yet bridged the intersex gap by equalizing themselves with men.

Mrs. Friedan is not one who noticeably ponders; she does noticeably propagandize. But I am much more interested in the realities of the film than in Mrs. Friedan's highflown Lib rhetoric, which is sociologically motivated and oversimplified. It gives "husbands" all the credit and makes "wives" into reactionary backsliders who have no fem-lib intuitions, therefore no proper conception of sexual behavior. Yet why assume that Harry, Archie, and Gus have a proper conception of sexual behavior? Such is far from being self-evident. Their manners when they bed the bar girls in London are, to say the least, goofy and gaffish. The denizens of the worldly establishment where they land, the gambling casino, obviously peg them as the kookier type of American lout: a set of real gentlemen-goofballs. To be sure, a vast malady of modern marital life is indicated, however ambiguously, by *Husbands.* But . . . just what is this malady? What do its actual symptoms convey? The Women's Lib viewpoint is neither a diagnosis nor a prognosis of it; it's only a pep talk about it. In utterly discounting homosexuality as a relevant factor among the Archies, Guses, and Harrys of real life, Women's Lib is writing off not only one commonsense, perhaps plausible solution to drastic intermale love problems, but flouting psychoanalysis as a tested platform of personal help leading either to stable homosexuality or stable heterosexuality.

One guesses the nature of the Friedan strategy. To align

the Lib viewpoint with an analyst's couch, or an equivalent, would be to grant the concrete possibility of unconscious homosexuality in the world's Guses, Archies, and Harrys, a concession which is not orientable to the heterosexual phase of the Women's Lib movement. Of course, this movement has a lesbian phase too, and in *Husbands,* so far as factual speculation goes, the fault in marital structures may be that the *wives* have unconscious homosexual tendencies. *Husbands* is much, and deliberately, devoted to appearances, surface phenomena. Mrs. Friedan, for one fem-lib exponent, overlooks that the three wives in the film are given very little show. Why is this? Their images do appear in snapshots, the widow of the dead man does act up at his funeral, and Harry's wife looks very commonly shrewish, honestly hateful, and goes after him with a kitchen knife. This stinginess of script doesn't seem quite fair to the girls' side in this inherent War between the Men and the Women.

In *Husbands* we have a decided pro male emotional commitment, whatever its terms. To me, the doggedness of Cassavetes and his colleagues in this regard verges on the morbidly sentimental. Perhaps, despite all the genuine warmheartedness, the genuine enough good-guyness, *Husbands* proves for Gazzara, Falk, and Cassavetes too much an occasion of condescension. Morbid sentimentality is one symptomatic superstructure of the restless unconscious, of deliberately suppressed impulses. I wouldn't say that Gus, Harry, and Archie, as conceived, are necessarily suppressing homosexual yearnings; no, but I would say that they are suppressing *something.* Could it be just plain, old, undenominated "sexuality"?—what Freud calls the polymorphous perverse as characteristic of the earliest stages of growth? The trio's behavior in London, where they climax their binge by bedding pickups from the gambling casino, displays not only symptoms of naïve American-guy boorishness but also clear-cut puritan inhibitions and a kind of ingrained infantilism. Archie, as was noted, is elected to illustrate the latter: he shrinks from tongue-kissing as if it meant sexual dishonor. Is all this an account of *male* sexual maladroitness? Scene by scene, action by action, a prevalent atmosphere of built-in frustration is created as evidence against the sexual normalcy, adequacy, and adulthood of these three husbands. Their very squareness becomes, as identifiable sexual mores, the sign and proof of their own lack of erotic style—alas! their poor-dope ineligibility. Cassavetes' earnest emotion has ultrasentimentalized itself. Neither the framework of life nor the film's inner statistics give support, shape, and conviction to the moral empathy so obviously required of the spectator.

What has really happened to our heroes? Their trauma, bringing their basic dilemma nakedly into the open, has made them regress to gawky boyishness, artless adolescent emotiveness. Altogether, I should say, the three actors, through goodwill toward the husbands they play, endow them with a little too much natural dignity for their characters as written into the script and duly performed. These grown guys hit out at each other, sometimes, like schoolboys on a drunken rampage—loving one moment, loathing the next. An *abiding* truth to it? They're still the old gang, they hope—they hope, they *hope*! This is what provides the film's tag line, which is meant, one supposes, to be the coup de grace of pathos. It comes when the sobered-up, submissive Gus and Archie decide to leave the stubborn Harry—who has completely split—in London and go back to their homes in America as repentant, gift-bearing prodigals.

"What's he going to do without us?" they repeat to each other when about to enter their adjacent homes. This going back is an "act of separation" for them, too. It's the superclimax of the film's deep-planted sentimentality. What *can* Harry do without them? An excellent question: the inevitable question. But, man! Can I think of a lot of things—and all of them, whatever their sex, good! Betty Friedan would think only of one thing: Harry could become a manly adherent of Women's Lib. Indeed, he could. But why not, I ask, a *gay* adherent? Or why not *both*? Or, to be quite thorough, neither? There are such things as manly gays, you know, as I trust I have sufficiently indicated elsewhere. In this film, the Manly Gay, or Groovy Guy, remains a mystery because only a chimera—one of the possibilities living in the purely speculative realm. That's fiction for you! Even when interesting and valid, it may leave ends dangling. But the world . . . the world . . . the world is where ends are caught up, tied, untied, used and used till time itself is up. There's a mystery about *that*. But it isn't necessarily sexual. Only, sometimes, it *is* sexual. Definitely.

A VERY QUEER NON-MYSTERY STORY

Because I call *Daughters of Darkness* a non-mystery story does not mean that it lacks its own special mystique. The mystique is instantly recognizable as mankind's old friend, the horror thriller, that deathless genre of supernatural fiction. Its female protagonists are either addicted or potential vampires and its male protagonist—outnumbered alas! three to one—is a lusty ambisexed sadist fatally attracted to the vampire life style. One of the funniest aspects of this ornamental, deadpan camp film is that those duly classic ministers of justice, the canny servant and the canny policeman, are ineffectual, morally emasculated figures who anticlimactically retire from the action. The most relevant aspect of *Daughters of Darkness* is as lucidly anti-male as the latest outloud fem-lib spokeswoman. What happens is that the reckless young sadist, having an established relation as lover-son-minion to a male patron nicknamed Mother, falls for an attractively statuesque, model-type girl, marries her instantly and thereafter gets progressively punished for his wild apostasy from the abnormal.

Something not at all mysterious, but flash-frozen from the projection booth, is that in this case *being heterosexual* is abnormal. The above-mentioned mystique has been converted according to the latest thing (unisex is the key) in mod movie madness; incidentally, all the vampires look like mannequins escaped from a Carnaby Street shop. Being gay is the norm for both male and female: being a vampire, therefore, is just carrying homophile tastes to their bloody extreme. The heterosexually attracted male is afraid to tell Mother (a middle-aged précieux who lives in England amid hothouse tropic splendor) that he's bringing home a real bride. However, he gets up the gumption to do so when he's really scared by the hypnotic success of the vampire heroine, Countess Bathory, with his new bride after they've stopped off, out of season, at a grand hotel in (of all perfectly exotic places) Ostend. The countess is about three hundred years old but looks in her youthful prime because she has been murdering female "virgins" and drinking their blood.

Scenically, most of *Daughters of Darkness* looks like a very cute idea by a travel agency to promote tourism in Belgium. We are swept from Ostend, the seaside resort, to Bruges, the quaint town threaded by canals, on official vampire business of the most heinous kind. The color photography is colorfully ingenious, especially when fadeouts go into red (get it? the color of blood) before disappearing. Publicity says that the director, Harry Kümel, would not have made the film had he been unable to induce Delphine Seyrig to play Countess Bathory. Miss Seyrig, I should say, looks nothing if not utterly and wilfully induced. It is hard to analyze her dainty suave style as the vampire countess. Purry-voiced, she has something like the bland, blond, dazzling Continental beauty of the two famous Gabors. Yet her velvet manner and fake tenderness, obviously, are meant to be countessy rather than courtesanish. Oddly, Miss Seyrig looks unprofessional from virtually every angle: she can't even slink or strike a pose without being somewhat off-center. One wonders about her earnestness.

The paradox and cachet of this very queer affair are contained in the fact that it fits a new camp genre that can only be termed bona-fide tongue-in-cheek: a style now on the up-upgrade. Personally I feel that a bold, theatrically high-keyed actress such as Tallulah Bankhead would have been much better than Miss Seyrig in the lead part. Did you ever see *Die, Die, My Darling*? Once Tallulah really believed in herself as a glamour girl, so much so when she had to turn into a glamour harpy she did so with a certain glad and earnest grace. I doubt that Miss Seyrig, even when she was the sleepwalking romantic dummy of *Last Year at Marienbad*, ever really believed in herself as a glamour girl. Here she acts the glittering, sinister high-life vampire as if her glitter were guttering—not just because vampires can't stand bright light but also because she seems to employ the devout put-on to be found in Warhol films; in any film, in fact, where character camp is a built-in reflex replacing acting ability. *That,* I suppose, is the stupendous subtlety of it. For Miss Seyrig to have really acted a glamour-girl vampire would have been heresy to the all-important camp code of the Underground. Hence, on the whole, the bloodiest and most violent scenes, including various bed actions, become what is known to commerce as a soft sell. There's a truckload of the most picturesque soft sells in *Daughters of Darkness.*

One encounters hunks of more or less sudden, scrupulously photographed violence, nude and sexy enough but with bloodletting rather than orgasm seemingly the main objective. One of the movie's grander scenes is when the poor heterosexualizing male is outfoxed by the vampire countess and his converted bride, who now, maintaining that his whippings "degrade" her, wishes to leave him. Pushed to the floor on his back in a struggle, he has the lid of a large cut-glass bowl pressed over his head by both women; the lid promptly breaks, and bouncing obediently to either side, neatly slices the wrists of both his outstretched arms, from which the blood, unsurprisingly, starts spurting. Before you can say Bathory, the two vampires have pounced and glued their lips to the respective wounds. *Le monsieur est fini.* To my mind, it's the chintziest of effects no matter how much golden camp it's lined with. But there you are: we have the *mystique,* and to spare!

So much of it that, after all, this example of a new life style in vampire films may persist in the mind as its own sort of mystery. The heroine's lesbianism hardly seems any truer than the hero's homosexuality, which he so villainously betrays. Here omnisex life style seems to take over where unisex life style leaves off. The four principals—the countess has a faithful girl assistant—tend to be so loosely ambisexed that bloodsucking might be (as perhaps it always *was*) a mere carnal metaphor for fellatio and cunnilingus, practised here in due order by everybody. So matters are insinuated, anyway. This is why *Daughters of Darkness* can be called an altogether mysterious non-mystery story, and as homosexual ritual, riddled with a baffling coyness. One might think heterosexuality, along with vampirism, were crazy whims occurring in the homosexual norms. Again: that stupendous subtlety.

All groovy guys and gals should savor *Daughters of Darkness*. Of course, its rating is R. But that's no skin off this skin flick. The under-sixteens (for whom it seems chiefly destined) will just have to vamp their mothers and fathers into taking them. Considering everything, that should be easy. What the under-sixteens like today, everybody under sixty is supposed to like. How can a "popular trend" be wrong? Right On, Daughters of Delphine!

4. THE YOUTH

OF HOMEROS

With the youth of Homeros, we are on a plane where homosexuality is contingent on romantic legend and therefore
touches the sublime. Thomas Mann's *Death in Venice* contains
the most classic of the notable and respectable homosexual
legends in twentieth-century fiction. Homosexuality becomes,
simply and significantly, the functional subject matter of a
virility myth. Though Mann's story is about sexual decadence,
the decadence is viewed not as clinical but as a resurrection-
in-death. The variation on the traditional Christian myth is
important. In *The Black Swan* Mann wrote of the same myth
as happening to a woman as mature as the hero of *Death in
Venice,* Aschenbach, but in her case the experience is heterosexual. Both the novellas illustrate Mann's Faustian theme that
flowered explicitly in his novel *Doctor Faustus.* The theme's
heroic spirit is at once angelic and demonic.

    Luchino Visconti, one of the world's leading directors,
has brought his most impressive virtues to the filmic realization
of Mann's masterpiece. He has instinctively grasped, or rather
—as I prefer saying—he has instinctively left intact, the crucial human content of Mann's remarkable fiction. What is this,
perhaps dateless, content? In later life, people of all sexes may
experience a sort of erotic second youth which may appear

gradually or suddenly; which brings, it may be, desolation as well as ecstasy and is symbolic death-in-life and life-in-death. It is conspicuous on the stage in *Pelléas and Melisande,* both as Maeterlinck's play and the opera that Debussy made from it. Melisande is a female Eros who appears to King Golaud like a wraith encountered in the forest, but who is real enough to be married to him. It is she, however, not her old husband, who sickens and dies when she is deprived of the consummation of her passion for the youthful Pelléas. Just so does Aschenbach (whom Visconti turns into a composer) sicken and die over the beautiful but unattainable boy, Tadzio.

Melisande represents Golaud's reclaimed heterosexual virility as Tadzio represents Aschenbach's brief illusion of reclaimed virility through homosexual attraction. In the case of homosexuality-come-late, which may happen to male or female heteros, the role of Homeros (or homosexual Eros) automatically takes on a mythical dimension, as of something beyond reach, impractical, like the Faustian impulse to regain one's youth through love of some young person, male or female. Owing to Christianity, the wanton eroticism of the *Satyricon* became impossible for centuries except as driven underground. Gradually, the blind rigidity of bourgeois society has built up moral repressants that cannot be removed unless some late change of life opens the eyes of an individual to a new sexual experience, which may well be the invert's experience. Just as male heterosexuals, failing in virility, imagine that only some fresh young girl can renew their interest in sex, so men who have overlooked, or automatically repressed, past homosexual impulses become suddenly aware that some extraordinary young male has made them alive again to sex. Frantically, an inner voice asks them, "Is it too late?" In *Death in Venice,* it *is* too late; too late, that is, for carnal love.

Visconti has let Aschenbach's moving story unfold visually with restraint laid upon his natural impulse toward lush extravagance—toward the "theatrical." Curiously enough, it is with this highly picturesque period story that the director manages to revive some of the austerity of basic humanity that he showed us in *La Terra Trema* (1948) and *Rocco and His*

Brothers (1960).* Simple reverence for Mann's genius seems to have guided him. Yet one might quarrel over his conversion of Mann's writer hero into a composer based on the example of Gustave Mahler, conveniently using Mahler's dark, passionate, melodious music to strengthen his own conception. In the form of flashbacks, moreover, Visconti has culled supposed experiences from Aschenbach's former life: his carefree happiness as a young father and husband, his early ordeal as a rejected composer, the enigmatic fiasco of a later visit to his favorite whore. The last is altogether Visconti's contribution. However questionably relevant, these additions succeed in diversifying the story's kinetic values and are at least plausible; particularly as Aschenbach's dialogues with a young disciple enable Visconti to bring some of Aschenbach's philosophic reveries (though not always happily) into dramatic focus.

Mann's original story, of course, remains purer, more poetically tense in continuous texture, tragically more "final." Visconti has wisely retained Mann's leisurely pace at the risk of dropping the tension and breaking the story rhythm. There are moments when one feels the film's feet are dragging; then, once more, the adagio movement is reinforced by an accent and one is aware that the extremely lean action of the original, its lack of meaningful dialogue, is being obeyed to a rhythm like one of Mahler's voluptuously spun-out melodies. Much intelligent attention has been given the creation of period atmosphere: the costumes, down to the bathing suits, are a triumph. In a way typical of Visconti, his camera promenades stylishly across friezelike groups of hotel guests, waiting in the lobby for dinner to be announced, listening to an evening concert outdoors, walking along the beach under big white parasols. He was never in better control of his rich sense of background, and of course Venice itself, with its ready-made panoramas, offered perfect opportunities to accent the decorative. Nor is this painterly film director unfamiliar with painting: we get glimpses of Dali's rowboats on a sun-drenched beach broken otherwise only by isolated human figures; the water-

* Though made in 1948, *La Terra Trema* did not have *intact* public exposure in the U.S.A. till 1965.

scapes, in turn, are Whistlerian; the final shot of the flat, palely lit sea and beach, with Tadzio's distant figure in the center and a hooded, untended camera far to the right, obliquely evokes Atget's archaic photographic art.

For his Homeros, Tadzio, Visconti has uncovered in Björn Andresen a tall, statuesque fifteen-year-old whose serene beauty casts a Garbo-like spell. One imagines that Mann visualized a rather smaller boy, one more "conventional" despite the classic beauty attributed to him. Visconti's Tadzio appears like a miraculously revived movie legend: an image surely male enough but also curiously hermaphroditic—or, as I would prefer saying, poetically transsexual. Young Andresen is not only fabulously photogenic and perfectly restrained in walk, gesture, and facial expression, he can also project the magic appeal that is said to enthrall his aging admirer, making him dye his hair and paint his face, and inducing him to stay in Venice till—at the very moment he decides to yield to Tadzio's allure—he collapses and dies of a plague. He has neither touched nor spoken to Tadzio; they have only persistently, solemnly flirted.

Mann's virtuoso symbolism may have a bit too much "outside" in Visconti's film; certainly, the film falls short of the original's intense innerness. To some extent, this is the fault of Dirk Bogarde's performance of Aschenbach's role, a performance in many ways admirably right. Professionally Bogarde is a quiet, sure, intelligent performer, and his quality of ease and rightness never showed to better advantage: he is *likable* as Aschenbach. Yet I should say that his total interpretation of the role (for which Visconti must share the responsibility) lacks ultimate depth and is a trifle unnuanced in its transformation of a serious artistic genius into an old, bepainted, trembling lover of a boy. For one thing, I believe, the role would have been better without the occasional auntie-ish mannerisms that Bogarde introduces as, apparently, his personal contribution.

Harsh critics of the film medium maintain that an absence of innerness is integral to film, whose genius is essentially to show us the outsides of the world: the maze and glory of its sensuous surfaces. As literally optical, a film's genius is surely to perform this function. If ever a particular film illustrated this, it is Visconti's *Death in Venice!* But I disagree with the above-stated canon of the harsh critics. Many films have proven that the genius of acting and directing can achieve true innerness and project it optically as well as through words. I should say that, here, young Homeros achieves exactly this feat: it perpetually glows in his face and clothes his figure. One is as aware of it as if he were a figure from Botticelli's gallery of gods, angels, and princes. It is the essence of Visconti's filmic beauty, and it shows eloquently, dramatically, through all the costume lushness, the richly modulated backgrounds.

To touch the sublime! This is, to real souls that are conscious of it, to become involved—yes, whatever one's beliefs or philosophy—with the sacred. Is Tadzio, whose arm finally points toward the infinite while Aschenbach tries to rise and instead falls dead, an Angel of the Resurrection? In a sense he *must be* if one has accepted Mann's invitation that Visconti has nobly imitated: the invitation to immerse oneself in spiritual as well as carnal things, in innerness as well as outerness, in life as a *sublime* project. Life's disease and dirt?—its threat? These proliferate in fact as well as symbol. It is the tragic human condition.

Doubtless, in the opening shots, when Aschenbach is just a serious-looking gentleman on the deck of a steamer bound for Venice, and we know nothing else about him, there is a naïve automatism which we must attribute to filmic tradition: "Here's a man (or a woman)," this tradition always says, "let's see who he is, what will happen to him." Events themselves must tell the story. What Mann established at the beginning of his novella—Aschenbach's past, his identity, his mood—Visconti begins only insinuating and furnishes later, rather sparsely, with flashbacks. If Visconti's film is less innerly rich, more ornamentally outer, than Mann's story, it is still a very memorable mirage for a movie to offer us. It is worth keeping as a film and as homeroic lore.

The inspiration of another gifted if younger Italian filmmaker, Pier Paolo Pasolini, brought to us in 1968 another mythical yet very real figure of Homeros in a film called *Teorema*. Well cast in the person of a charming young actor, Terence Stamp, this ambisexual Eros exercises a universal spell over four members of a well-to-do upper-class family—husband, wife, teenage son, and daughter—as well as over their maidservant; in short, he seduces each in turn as if by magnetic attraction, and then, like a god in a cloud, vanishes abruptly from their lives. The straightforward fable, told realistically but with much nuance, makes one of the profounder works of film history. One might think of it only as an allegory, and complex enough for its meaning, at the end, to seem ambiguous.

What great power does this Eros represent in the modern world which he visits like an ordinary house guest, which technically, in fact, he is? Is he a classically felt incarnation of the libido? If so, he is presented as a sort of messiah, and yet a messiah whose message frees only momentarily. When he has left, the wife turns into a sort of nymphomaniac who can't resist brazenly picking up young men in the street; the introverted daughter soon goes into total paralysis and seems destined to spend her remaining life in a sanatorium; the son, a painter, "degenerates" into the wildest of modern art manners where urinating on his canvases is one modulation; the husband, who has had a strange impulse to present the factory he owns to his workers, takes off all his clothes in a railway station and wanders nude and howling into a wasteland of volcanic rock; the maidservant has a strenuous religious conversion that prompts her to leave her job and become a "saint" who achieves levitation. The film's closing sequence is her self-supervised burial-alive, perhaps signifying modern religion's last gasp in the ancient art of sublimation.

Is this ambisexed Eros, then, only the hero of a hollow charade, a fraudulent boast of the libido, since his successes, wreaking havoc as an aftermath, bring only momentary, illusive freedom to the beneficiaries? The film has a symbol or two which reminds us that Pasolini's mythically inflected medium here covers his own personality as one fusing Communism with Catholicism. Even his early realistic film about a petty criminal, *Accatone* (1961), ends as a moral fable through a dream device, while another of his films, *The Passion of St. Matthew* (1964), views Christ as definitively a poor man's messiah; logically, thus, the modern form of Jesus' teaching, the universal bourgeois religion, would be a falsification, a tragic failure, and explains why, in *Teorema,* this religion seems to give up its ghost through the maidservant's deliberate self-immolation.

In relation to our theme, Pasolini's *Teorema* offers peculiarly arresting evidence through the figure of Homeros as ambisexual. Pure style is something which the many popular preoccupations of the film, especially its information function, have found the hardest to achieve. Thus, even the rare talent of a Pasolini cannot control the working of the allegoric device he has employed for his Eros figure. Homeros, as hero of two homosexual seductions here, quite satisfies the present focus of interest. Yet, as also a heterosexual seducer, the youth (in the person of Mr. Stamp) exerts a power over us, the audience, such as he exerts over the people in the film. Is it possible that, despite his honorable aims as a dispassionate allegorist, Pasolini has been a little too personally susceptible to his Eros? It is not only that, in an epoch-making move, the camera focuses exclusively and at length on the crotch of Mr. Stamp's seated and sprawling, though trousered, figure. Invariably he is also shown as charmingly, disarmingly boyish. When he seduces the wife, it is she who makes the aggressive gesture by appearing naked, unannounced, in his room; he himself has just been having a romp in the woods with his dog.

Besides, portrayed so realistically, through such concrete visuals, the physical effect which Homeros has on his admirers causes his power to be self-sufficient—and that it is a *sexual* power Pasolini puts beyond question. For example, the seduction of the husband is told concretely enough, while no direct erotic contacts are filmed. Consequently, when the husband undresses in the railway station, the motive of his despair is now clear enough to require no further sexual emphasis. But Pasolini elects to reestablish the erotic motif with highly specific innuendo. At the station, the man's eyes are drawn to the figure of a robust, attractive youth lolling outside the men's room in a most suggestive, apparently "professional" pose: he is (as the vernacular has it) showing his basket. It is when the boy gets up and enters the men's room—the timing and context make it a "high sign"—that the factory owner, resisting the bait with an obvious shudder, takes off his clothes and is next seen running madly over the volcanic rock.

It is significant—possibly it is decisive—that the Eros figure here is by all visible signs not only sweetly erotic and gentle but conspicuously "innocent," as if he hardly knew his own identity, what his own power means. This personality could not have been injected accidentally or contingently; in any case, it can only be integral to the work's total effect. Yet can a mere wave of the allegorist's wand—assuming this *was* meant by Pasolini—dispose of the film's most powerful emotional factor: its ambisexual eroticism? Is this Eros supposed to be Amor, the medieval ideal inherited through Platonism, and is it only "modern" fleshly corruption that makes Amor do his stuff in bed? At all events, if so, I rather think that Pasolini has out-foxed himself. I believe we have in *Teorema* an intact figure of Homeros, closely related to other appearances in films. If Eros, the god, is under the bedtime orders of modern laymen, male and female, then he is no longer a true god of love, free to be as carnal as he is spiritual. He is no longer Eros—or Homeros. Yet I think that film fables about him, such as we are considering, reveal his will to survive as an identity.

Billy Budd, likewise played by Terence Stamp in a surprisingly good film version of Herman Melville's novella, is another image of Homeros come down to us by way of symbolist-realist literature. The allegorical substance of Melville's work, clearly pointed up by the text, has been analyzed by capable critics. Here I want only to indicate the homeroic pattern represented by Billy as mesmerically attractive to two older men, the benign Captain Vere and the malign Claggart, whose accidental death by a blow of Billy's fist precipitates the story's tragic end. Claggart's ambivalent hatred of Billy, though poorly delineated by the film, only confirms this character's homosexual substructure. Billy's innocence, combined with his youth and beauty, and especially his death as a symbol of resurrection, qualify him as an incarnation of Homeros. Further, his purity is ratified rather suggestively through a symptom noted by witnesses: his corpse does not show the phallic erection commonly produced following the death of hanged men. The very presence of this unessential, perhaps overzealous, detail seems to prove that Melville had more on his mind than an allegory of supernatural innocence and its charm.

I do not mean that anybody in the movie mentions the said detail. Yet those who know the original must remember the luscious descriptions of Billy's physical youth and beauty. He fulfills a type named by Melville the Handsome Sailor (a theme reappearing in his novels), and Billy's smooth adolescent face is said to be "all but feminine in purity of natural complexion." Such beauty, states Melville, becomes Claggart's "envy and despair," causing in him "pale ire." Envy, one can reckon with as, perhaps, fairly normal—but *despair,* too? The latter suggests complete involvement of body and soul. Willy-nilly, the Handsome Sailor works his way surely into the hearts of all, with the result that he is finally nicknamed "Baby Budd." If this be Melville's way of invoking the Christ Child, it is remarkable to find a full-grown youth chosen as the vehicle. We should notice that this world of sailors is all-male and there is not the slightest sign in Melville's novel, or in the film (any more than in *The Great Escape*), that the principals are not perfectly reconciled to the absence of women. And yet why should either Jesus or Amor function specifically in an all-male environment? It is a biased way to handle either. But there it is.

To turn to films with more contemporary figures than Billy, still another modern Homeros is visible as a variation on the Eros of *Teorema;* he comes from a work by the author of *Death in Venice* and so can be rated as a distant cousin of Tadzio. The film is *The Confessions of Felix Krull,* an abbreviated version of Mann's unfinished novel, whose original title had added a term to define Felix: *Confidence Man.* Consciously or unconsciously, Pasolini could have taken a cue from Mann's conception of Krull. For part of the conception is that, though Felix is a confidence man of versatility, a gigolo and adventurer, he is not only young and handsome but also honestly enjoys his work, especially in bed with the ladies. Supposedly, family

circumstances compel him to "seek his fortunes in the world."
Yet this typical fairy-tale convention can deceive no one, least
of all the author, Mann. There is every sign that Krull has precisely the honest, innocent kind of eroticism belonging to Pasolini's hero. This is not at all a "passion to seduce" in the sense
that Don Juan's was; no, the Don's was seduction as a demonic
possession. In passing, we should note that the historical Spanish origins of the Don Juan figure avail evidence that, in one
of his verifiable root instances, he was a secret homosexual.

As a passion (and permanently rather than passingly) a
strongly cultivated ambisexuality tends toward a transcendent
plane, a supernaturalism by which—again the pastime of the
gods!—it becomes omnisexuality, which reaches back; and,
down a little, to our own time's unisex. The actor who plays
Felix Krull is Horst Buchholz (transiently renamed Henry
Bookholt), just as young as, and even handsomer than, Terence
Stamp. At the hotel where Felix works as a bellhop, an elderly,
dignified Scotch millionaire is taken with him, invites him to
his room, and, champagne glass in hand, makes him a very fine,
very serious offer. One feels that it might have been accepted
had Felix not been on the eve of an affair with an amorous
female guest, who, while not really young, provides among other
things a sex that is more to the young man's taste. We have, in
short, a glimpse of Homeros, the all-powerful, in his aspect as
potential hustler of homosexuals, as professionally "compromised" as our latterday Midnight Cowboy. The modern character type, as we have seen, is notably ambiguous, a sort of Proteus
of sex empowered to take homosexual form at will, even if it
be only through heartless professionalism.

Jon Voight's role in *Midnight Cowboy*, as well as other
film hustlers, should be cross-referenced with Felix Krull as
casual representatives of the con-man aspect of homosexual
practices. As true in *Midnight Cowboy*, the hustler of women
may come to be hustler of homosexuals, and as the latter, his
confidence game may be criminal; that depends largely on his
overall temperament as well as his sexual temperament. Some
hustlers (take the hero of *My Hustler*) look upon homosexuality
as straightforward prostitution and confine themselves to play-

ing trade to their customers, reasoning that thus they remain virginally free of homosexual taint; to be literal, they exclude their mouths or anuses from use. Others are pathological (we shall see a good deal more of these) and murder and/or mutilate their victims. Still others are hardened professionals who don't come across sexually at all but rob, sometimes also beat up, their customers.

I bring up the Voight role once more as the very antithesis, morally and aesthetically, of Terence Stamp's role in *Teorema*. Between them, the fluid gamut I call ambisexuality achieves its antipodes. Categorically, Thomas Mann confirmed the type of the really youthful Homeros in Tadzio, the exquisite mirage of renewed virility offered Von Aschenbach. Tadzio in apotheosis appears on a beach, his limbs displayed, and he disappears almost literally into a cloud. At this point, Von Aschenbach wants to follow him, gets up from the beach chair where he has been reclining, falters, and drops dead; he has contracted the plague that is ravaging Venice. For some time, he has known about the danger: he has stayed only because Tadzio and his family have not left.

Cupid Redivivus, the young god of magically redeeming virility in the crisis of mature males, is a specific extension of Eros, or Cupid, or simply young love triumphant. Yet his complement, Eros Homeros, is simply the homosexual version (male or female) of the same enshrined image of youth. Later, we shall see how a popular rock star of our day takes the fabulous form of a Homeros grown decadent, transvestite, and neuterized. Pasolini's Homeros, whatever his author's inspiration, remains as is: *potent*. Homeros in triumph is more apt to be pinpointed and pure in the works of Underground film-makers. Outstanding in recent times are the maneuvers of the inspired Gregory Markopoulos, who has paid more sincere tribute to this aspect of Eros than any other film-maker in the world. This could be more fortunate than it is because his intellectual resources are limited, and his technique, while inventive, lacks variety of motif and often looks barrenly abstract, leaving his subject matter stranded. Surely, his interest in Homeros has a good deal of support and precedent. A pioneering work in this direction was *Lot in Sodom*, a courageous film made in 1933 under the aegis of the experimental-poetic school in the United States. During the mid-twenties, independent film-makers over here were inspired by European purists who were exploring the film's technical possibilities. Taking impetus in part from Cocteau's example in *The Blood of a Poet,* this memorable film is the work of J. S. Watson and Melville Webber.

Where Markopoulos has been pagan and classical, *Lot in Sodom,* as its title indicates, bases itself on the Bible's moral cue, depicting sexual perversity and excess as mortal sins. The deference, rather transparently, is formal. While obeying the biblical account concerning Lot and his family and the function of the two angels who investigate Sodom at the Lord's behest, the Watson-Webber work uses all its creative accents to depict the sensual responses of the male homosexuals of Sodom to the physical beauty of the foremost angel. Naturally the angel repulses their advances and proceeds (not finding fifty chaste persons present) to condemn Sodom to the flames, but not before we have witnessed, at some length, the orgiastic pleasures of the all-male population. Rather sketchy in style, the production at times is amateurishly stiff. Yet, clearly, poetic feeling is uppermost. The accent of the largely choreographed homosexual orgy is on eroticism, and while never "obscene," is quite literal.

Usually avant-garde films treat homosexuality as another *raison-d'être* for the hero type. In *The Flower Thief,* for instance, he is young, comic, offbeat, contemporary. But one homeroic film by Markopoulos is unique in being totally the portrait of an individual homosexual: *Himself as Herself.* Portraiture is one of the modes this film-maker has extensively explored. There are pretty pictures in *Himself as Herself,* pictures having nothing to do, in fact, with homosexuality. But elements of an aesthetic variety of drag, numerous decorative posturings, the relentless presentation of a young man fixated on his own image and free to indulge his occupation luxuriously, endlessly—nothing of all this can be missed: it loads the overlong film from end to end.

Had we only this single film from Markopoulos, it would

define the direction of his interests both as to form and substance. However, we have from him equally informative works and, luckily, much better ones. The best homeroic footage from his cameras is contained in an elaborate work titled *The Illiac Passion* (1966). It is not exclusively homosexualist but deals with heterosexual as well as homosexual myths drawn from classical models—Orpheus and Eurydice, Narcissus and Echo, Apollo and Hyacinth, Venus and Adonis. Markopoulos has a refined sense of the nude and a positive, though sadly fallible, gift for casting. For instance, in *The Illiac Passion,* there are some fine intimate shots of lovemaking between males that easily avoid vulgarity and have a true poetic resonance. Two "mod" types, a pretty, monumentally fat, yet shapely young woman and a tautly slender, good-looking youth (the dancer Kenneth King) impersonate Venus and Adonis. Their flirtation is a bit overdone, but it is interestingly decorative and rather amusing. On the contrary, other incarnations of divine figures taken by Markopoulos from myth are, in the modern-dress interpretation given them, puzzlingly inept and deflating. The film is a very mixed bag, and does not come off, as a whole, despite Markopoulos' arduously applied techniques.

The quintessential effort of this film-maker to erect a figure of Homeros is a work called, with proud calculation, *Eros O Basileus (Eros the King).* It is organically fluid and tight as a film owing to its intense concentration on the image of a nude young man rather like a male nymphet growing up. Again, Markopoulos' filmic imagination is unequal to the task he has set himself: the film is languorous and clings for dear life to the film-maker's bug-eyed fixation on his subject. No amount of filmic effects or visual nuances can overcome the fundamental barrenness of a work built on a largely meaningless pantomime for an attractive "male model," persistently nude and unmissably homosexual in timbre.

There is no plot to *Eros O Basileus* and no other character complicates the action, which is altogether a series of plastic arrangements, some of which are interesting, some a bit silly. Doubtless Markopoulos' basic achievement here is that, with no information about the film-maker's identity, we would realize unhesitantly that such prolonged and minute attention to a youthful male nude could only be the occupation of another male—a male whose exclusiveness of eye denotes supremely personal engagement. Not conceivably could *Eros O Basileus* be the work of a female film-maker unless she were a rare, most aggressive type of voyeur. So this film, as a triumph of Homeros, is a sort of success by the significant omission of female ambience. Poetic though it be in tone, it is as internally all-male as the steam room at a Turkish bath.

We must not neglect to credit even Hollywood films with helping to build up, though in a poor indirect way, the mythic image of Homeros. But before noticing this achievement, we must turn to another lyrical contribution by a poetic-experimental film-maker. This is the choreographic figure of Dionysius as created by Charles Boultenhouse in a dance film; it takes the name of that god (but not in vain) and is based on Euripides' *The Bacchae*. Boultenhouse is a much less prolific film-maker than Markopoulos, but one more astute. His Dionysius (the handsome, lithe young dancer Louis Falco) has his inevitably charged confrontation with King Pentheus (the dancer Nicholas Magallanes) without any artificial feminizing of either. What is valuable about the method used is that an essential homosexual emotion comes through by a kind of confrontation which only film could handle; that is, Boultenhouse never shows Dionysius and Pentheus in the same film frame. They "face" each other only in terms of relation in filmic space. The god exerts his hypnotic spell, first entrancing Pentheus and then magically tearing him apart, merely by sequential juxtaposition, not by spatial contiguity.* Their spatial roles, according to this filmic convention, is wholly implicit, exactly like ordinary close shots or close-ups in which two characters have a dialogue, the camera first being trained frontally on one, then the other.

This simple montage in *Dionysius* actually serves to accentuate the intimacy and dramatic impact of the narcissean

---

* The internal technical devices were slow-motion panning from side to side for the hypnosis scene, circular motion for the intoxication, very rapid stop-camera frames for the tearing apart.

element. The illusive mirror-identification between Dionysius as Male Master and Pentheus as Male Slave is thus greatly simplified and proportionately reinforced. I need not push the homosexual aspect of the spell cast by the orgiastic god: he literally forces this king, who denies and mocks his power, to assume the dress and the female hair of one of the Bacchae. That homosexuality is inherent, in the eyes of modernity, became clear in recent years from the stage production given the work by Richard Schechner. Schechner too (Boultenhouse made his film, in 1963, before the Performance Group did the play) eliminates the transvestite business between Pentheus and Dionysius that the original play specifies. Instead, in a phrase doing honor to the vocabulary of Allen Ginsberg, the god in Schechner's production curtly orders Pentheus to accord him the service of fellatio—and the agonized Pentheus, though not in sight of the audience, tacitly obeys him after slowly crawling toward him along the ground.

On the popular screen, there is not a numerous gallery to illustrate the youth of Homeros. Primarily, this is because truly dedicated work in poetic film-making, at least in terms of classical motifs, is still, unhappily, scarce. Yet a film such as Pasolini's *Teorema* alone is impressive enough to put the homeroic image in an important frame. Looking to the near past, we find it illuminated by Cocteau's famous avant-garde film *The Blood of a Poet* (1930). Since there it appears in a rather difficult, esoteric form, we have to be knowing so as not to miss it, particularly because Cocteau shows it as metamorphose. First, Homeros is the tyrannic schoolboy, Dargelos, haughty and a true Male Master, secretly adored by smaller boys and more especially by the poet who is Cocteau's protagonist. This episode is introduced to show the poet-protagonist as already homosexual when he was a schoolboy.

When the schoolboy-poet is "fatally" hit by Dargelos' snowball, his death (like his suicide as an adult) is symbolic. Cocteau means that Homeros, becoming malign and destructive rather than acting as Eros the Savior, has killed his own image in the boy-poet's mind. This becomes plain through the action. At this moment an Angel of Death (a young Negro dancer) appears to preside over and virtually restore to life the prostrate boy "killed" by the snowball: the arrow of love. The black angel is a Homeros of the Night—specifically the Night of Love —and of course means not death, but resurrection. That the adult protagonist and the schoolboy are the same would again appear by the action of the film proper. Being Cocteau's personal myth, it is related of course to several of his films and literary works.

The same scene now sprouts theater boxes where people watch the action as at a play. Below them is a card table where the grown poet is playing a game of destiny with his Muse—the living statue-goddess we have seen early in the film—so that the stricken schoolboy, found now by the seated poet's feet, has to be gently removed by the Angel of Death. The angelic black figure is the malign force of Homeros (Dargelos) turned by poetic metamorphosis into a benign force. It was Cocteau's creed that the life blood of poetry could accomplish such magic.

In his much later work *Orpheus* (1950), it is merely another form of Homeros that appears as Cégeste, the youthful alter ego of the mature Orpheus. The origin of this youth was a greatly gifted young author, Raymond Radiguet, whom Cocteau knew and idolized when he himself was young, but who died very prematurely. For Cocteau, Radiguet's death became a legend, a tragedy surrounded by the aura of ritual sacrifice: genius immolated by a mysterious act of destiny in which he himself was somehow complicit. It is easy to trace blond Cégeste (Edouard Dermit), who is young and handsome like Radiguet, back through the protagonist of *The Blood of a Poet* to the real author's demise as a tragedy holding the grace of immortality at its heart.

The third metamorphosis of Homeros in *The Blood of a Poet* is of course the grown poet himself, who loses to his Muse in the game of life-and-death and must resign himself to "life" in the form of immortality as an artist. The theme haunted Cocteau partly as his own autobiography, partly as a tribute to a man he once loved, and who of course was reincarnated in later lovers. In *Orpheus* we see the young poet, Cégeste, kidnapped and held captive by a beautiful, mysterious woman who is really Death (comparable to the statue-muse of the earlier film): Cégeste has become Orpheus-Cocteau's youthful self as well as the dead youth, Radiguet. Death's sumptuous limousine (the film has a contemporary setting) is like a life-infested funeral hearse. Lent to Orpheus, he listens over its radio to messages from Cégeste "in the other world," messages "coded" like modern poetry. The plot is complicated by Eurydice, Orpheus' wife, whom Death also kidnaps and holds captive till a version of the classic strategy brings her back to life and her husband's arms. There can be no question of Cocteau's open, if tactfully professed, homosexuality. Therefore the presence of Eurydice is only a concession to the larger art form at which Cocteau had begun to aim.

Usually, Cocteau found some means to inject the homosexual theme into his films. His last film, *The Testament of Orpheus,* a sequel, is rather bad, self-plagiarizing and self-indulgent, virtually a piece of aesthetic masturbation. In *Beauty and the Beast,* there was a scene between Jean Marais, acting Beauty's suitor, and a young male crony, when they imitate the voices of women and camp around in broad female style so as to play a trick on their two ladies, who are hidden in a closet. I remember the late Iris Barry, then curator of the film collection at the Museum of Modern Art, New York, telling me: "Cocteau and Marais really felt they went too far in that scene." The scene is missing, I believe, from all commercial editions of *Beauty and the Beast,* though the Museum has (or did have) a print of the film including it.

In the coming discussion of beaver films, we shall see what a natural source exists for exploiting, with small artistic pretense, the youth of Homeros for rank-and-file moviegoers. Markopoulos' *Eros O Basileus* is a strictly élite version of the aim to isolate for the mind's eye the image of an attractive, homosexually available young male. The pornography issue is becoming less and less real except as a moral platform of the ultraconservative forces, whose chief weapon is police persecution. The fluid moral temper of official opinion, according to time and place, always decides the use of that tactic. But pornography as such can have no relevant bearing in this book.

Beaver films, all-male or all-female, are viewed here as "bad," in any department, entirely on grounds of taste. Their interest as freedom of sexual expression simply offers us a distinct dimension that makes them discussable.

The poetic dimension of Homeros is not just "discussable," it must be discussed because the homosexual young god, as a real figure of humanity's cultural heritage, keeps cropping up. Lately Donald Richie, among the serious avant-garde films he made in Japan, provided a lyric and impressionistic treatment of the Death of Homeros theme in his brief work, *Dead Youth,* based on a poem we hear recited in English at the beginning, in Japanese at the close. It opens with a naked Japanese youth spread out face-up, apparently dead from drowning, at the edge of a vast body of water. His reappearances during the ensuing live action seem to represent his past life in the minds of various lovers who mourn him. The scenes are rather casually arranged, the editing rather loose. The work's true distinction is in its complete dedication to its idea: a pure tenderness for the homosexual passion. It is a world in which we see only young males engaged in their routine love games—the only note of tension is when one of the dead youth's lovers seeks out his grave (before which a photograph of him is displayed) and in a transport of longing, masturbates.

Like all "suppressed" gods, the invisibility of Homeros is only illusive; he's apt to appear anywhere, anytime. Part of his magic is that he should seem (if not actually be) beautifully, instantly, utterly accessible through mortal reincarnation. Thus it was a truly rare achievement for Pasolini to isolate Homeros Available, as he did in *Teorema,* so realistically and so mythically. The film encourages such manifestations through a native medial immediacy that exerts its own kind of poetry. In this respect, film has an automatic *wiliness.* In Albert Lewin's courageous but inadequate "art film" made from Wilde's *The Picture of Dorian Gray,* Dorian's handsome immaculate image conveys a special homeroic power that inheres neither in Wilde's original novel nor in the movie script.

It happens that Hurd Hatfield, who plays Dorian, does not seem made of the fine beaten gold of the aristocratic English type of beauty visualized by Wilde. Besides, Hatfield is dark, not fair. Of course, the tenor of Dorian's relationship with Lord Henry is a polite charade necessary to the concealed meaning of both movie and novel; this is represented in the movie with all the elegance that Hollywood could possibly summon to its aid around 1945. But, beyond such considerations, Dorian's image (a point I've made in *Magic and Myth of the Movies*) comes across not only, at first anyway, as immaculate and handsome, but likewise graciously soft, temptingly dewy, basically all-young-male in the homosexual sense. The context is perfect to allow an apparition such as Hatfield (with the deft assistance of makeup) to incarnate another image of Homeros. I'm sure he has suggested one to many spectators, even to female spectators confirmed in voyeurism. We see Dorian, meticulously dressed and serene, strolling through his mansion as if it were the house of a lover's dream, and he, Homeros, some miraculous, superb, warm marionette with superflexible joints. Unluckily, the well-meaning Lewin managed to flaw his film with assorted depressing, if canny, vulgarities, but Dorian's distinguished look survives all that. Lewin may be supposed to have converted the Shakespearean actress with whom the novel's Dorian falls in love into a music-hall singer because her human type and social status corresponded to the sordid male types which Wilde himself started frequenting. But, if so, this was esoteric film-making at a time (1944–47) when I was the sole critic eager to make depth readings from the movies.

In 1970, Dorian Gray had a fanfareless follow-up—a strict modernization that, as a film about Beautiful People Who Can Also Be Ugly, could, and should, have been much better. As is (or was!), it's remarkably lifeless and third-rate and has a botched stylishness. Made in England, it derived its name from its hero. As seen here, Dorian is a sort of Black Homeros who physically is close to the White Homeros of Terence Stamp. He is—of all people—Helmut Berger, the depraved von Essenback of *The Damned,* and doubtless got this chance from his slickly satanic performance in Visconti's film. The present long blond hair suits him better than the close dark trim he had in *The Damned.* Yet, so badly directed is he that, to be the image of eternal youth and beauty required, he must lean on a long series of body exposures, which happily he sustains well. For one without muscles, he's stunningly symmetrical.

Almost never out of camera range, Berger makes a curiously absentminded Narcissus. While he seems made for love, very willing, and has numerous bed encounters with females, he projects little sex appeal or verve, and seems not nearly so wicked as in *The Damned*. His Dorian is a manikin Homeros, not sleepwalking, like Hatfield's, but alienated *à la mode noire*. The story, despite a luxury atmosphere meaning to look decadent, limps and looks makeshift and tacky. This Dorian is like a remote island: the lone inhabitant of Baudelaire's Cythera! The rest of the cast, male and female, not so much sleep with him and admire him as, restlessly, lap his shores. The dialogue mentions a "young boy" he has corrupted; also, he cruises a black male in a men's room and we see them standing at the urinal—but that's all. The obvious ambisexuality remains disconcertingly stingy; in fact, the script is as bad as the direction. In that old familiar way of the movies, the sabotage of art achieves an indirect rightness by thus isolating its Narcissus from first shot to last. Hence Wilde's intention is realized with only one hand, the left, which is tied behind the director's back.

Does anyone imagine that, in our day of blackest comedy as a family staple, the movies would have failed to make Homeros into a really dastardly villain: quite as lovable as young? After all, the Don Juan tradition has its homosexual modulation ready to hand. And Dorian Gray. Yet neither is actually needed to tell us that no such thing as an untainted, purely angelic Eros of the homosexuals is possible. As the ordinary hero reaches toward the mythic hero, so the mythic hero reaches toward the ultimate excess that is wanton ambisexuality. This ultimate appears clearly enough, and not too ambiguously, in the odd-mod situation of *Performance,* a film I can hardly wait to get to. But I *must* wait.

Some of Dargelos' cruelty and its "open" sexual ambiguity (in *The Blood of a Poet)* appears in later French films and tends to take sophisticated cult forms derived from schoolboy sadism. We shall encounter it, for example, in *Les Cousins,* where a heterosexual Eros is the victim of an ambisexed, fascist Don Juan. But to consider the rare use of a female Homeros, young and beautiful and victimized because she is a woman in a man-dominated society, we are lucky to have Honoré de Balzac for her progenitor. An early-nineteenth-century writer but immensely well informed, Balzac would still tend normally to treat homosexuality as a semimythological subject. This he accomplished in *Seraphita,* whose hero/heroine belongs among the sacred transvestites still to come. Yet in two other stories, *Sarrasine* (male homosexuality) and *The Girl with the Golden Eyes* (female homosexuality), Balzac went further than any other author of his time—barring the then nonliterary precedent of Sade—toward recognizing the social reality of the offbeat sexes.

Good society of Balzac's period could tolerate the statutory "vice" of homosexuality only as a masked eccentricity, to be pardoned or not (if accidentally unmasked) strictly in accord with the masquerader's social status. Balzac's genius for fact-finding realism could understand and convey that his great villain Vautrin's infatuation with Lucien de Rubempré was based on invert sexuality. Vautrin (or Jacques Collin), a socially displaced intellectual of nature, is precursor and paradigm of Jean Genet's archetypal "butch" homosexual. His author focuses on Vautrin's virile homosexuality with 20-20 vision. Yet not once did he have to mention that Vautrin made a pass at Lucien, the youth whom he worshiped and raised up in the world.

Balzac's primary life experience with homosexuality, being himself heterosexual, logically became the male's trauma on discovering homosexuality as a female vagary. This was in *The Girl with the Golden Eyes.* Another instance was in *Sarrasine,* which concerned the tragic shock of a man who discovers that an actress with whom he falls deeply in love on sight is really a man in drag. It is hinted that Sarrasine might be a castratus, but this technicality is not in accord with the story's emotionalism and morbid erotic atmosphere. For the disappointed lover (Myra and Christine, take note!), the pseudo-woman remains a man. In 1962, the French director Jean-Gabriel Albicocco had an inspiration somewhat like Roger Vadim's when the latter filmed a modernized version of *Les Liaisons Dangereuses (Dangereous Acquaintances)*. Both these movies earned the contempt of square critics as sordid, slicked-up forays into mod sensationalism. Albicocco's film utterly eluded them in every department but its brilliant photography, which any sharp-eyed bat might have caught while on the wing.

I should note, while on the wing, that the film critics on family newspapers, viewing themselves as champions of public morality, might have been playing possum about this film. That was as far away, remember, as 1962. But I believe in their sincerity. Up till very lately, when homosexuality is a high minority fashion, critics have resorted to every possible "fair" tactic to suppress homosexual angles whenever movies dared be explicit and realistic about them. The lesbian as persecutor and persecuted is the complex theme of Albicocco's film, but this fact was scarcely granted a peep-in by the reviews of it in major New York papers. Archer Winsten announced that he was so repelled by the whole movie that he could not bear to discuss its actual contents. Film critics have contributed their share to the tacit conspiracy I mention elsewhere: the slander of homosexuality as a bizarre mythopoeia limited to the unhappy few. Maybe, as Stendhal thought, only an élite few can hope to be happy. But, in his famous *envoi* to *The Charterhouse of Parma*, his indication of quantity had nothing to do with sex.

Albicocco had a viable reason to update Balzac's period eroticism by putting it in contemporary moral and aesthetic dress and aligning it wittily with dominant-male psychology. His strategy serves the historic continuity of lesbianism in terms of the male trauma resulting from head-on impact with it. He stacks the cards—alas, male chauvinism in 1962!—by presenting the struggle of male-versus-lesbian in the context of a gay-young-blade cult of heteros as imagined by Balzac in his *L'Histoire des Treize (Story of the Thirteen)*. The young men, who are très chic and wear cat masks to their club meetings, go in for seducing women as a sadism of male dominance—yes, the old game of male one-upmanship. A member of the Thirteen discovers that beautiful Marie Laforêt, the girl with the golden eyes, is the love slave of a woman rather than a man. This insolent secret is viewed as a direct challenge. At once the club starts wickedly plotting to break up the affair by getting Marie well seduced.

Albicocco's film, to be sure, is self-consciously chic, full of camera virtuosities and rapid mental takes. It makes great use of fashion notes on exoticized Parisian male gallantry. And why shouldn't it? It manages stunningly to be unsquare in serving as a kind of high-fashion blague: the masculine genre in Paris that takes lesbianism to heart and does very well dressing it up while systematically trying to squeeze it of its inner pride and outer poise. You might call such a strategy the depraved and wishful thinking of high-mod males. All right, it's a little vulgar! So? As we learn here, sapphism too has its master and slave types, its girl Homeroses placed on pedestals, then ritually taken down and, like Cupid, stripped and whipped.

Soon we shall be able to class "the girl with the golden eyes" as aristocratic ancestor of that drearily vulgar pawn of a girl over whom Sister George, TV lesbian master, fights (winner take all) with a rival lesbian master. The lesbian master in Albicocco's film is a celebrated fashion designer and so corresponds to the television executive who routs poor Sister George—that spongy old, tacky old Greenwich Village tomboy. More of *her* when we find Homeros, male and female, growing old. Does the glittering male alleycat triumph in Albicocco's dashing film? Suffice it to say that he brings the ladies to utter ruin. But that's the movies—even those that are very French and very superior; I mean aesthetically superior, not superior in terms of dominant-male psychology. Remember, by the way, that part of being a lesbian is to compete in terms of dominant-male psychology. And if the lesbian here kills her unfaithful young golden-eyed mistress, she's only being a twentieth-century lesbian with delusions of nineteenth-century male grandeur.

Youthful Homeros, male or female, seems a movie natural as Innocent Victim. And, of course, Continental films are more apt to take a straightforward view of young homeroic victims than those of England or the United States. A little-known work from Italy, *Il Mare* (1962), by Giuseppe Patrone Griffi, deserves praise for its blandly truthful use of homosexuality.

The story, set on a resort island out of season, virtually strangles itself with artistic photography and self-consciously elaborate manners. Yet its portrait of a male adolescent's undisguised crush on a young man, and his frustration because a young woman intervenes, is sensitively worked out, beautifully honest, and unaffected. An ironic tilt to the plot is that the young man, seeking refuge from a tragic love affair, ultimately can no more take on the young woman (though apparently he is heterosexual) than he can the boy. At the end, everyone is unhappy and the enigmatic pathos of the restless sea triumphs. The film was seen at the First New York Film Festival and it is a pity that no commercial distributor here would risk its exploitation. Highly seeable despite its self-consciousness, it has a hauntingly poetic eroticism.

Homeros, malign and male, has several recent manifestations in film. Surely one of the most pointed—so pointed that it might seem a black parody of the Eros of *Teorema*—is the darkly, starkly magnetic figure of the blond young adventurer, Karl, in *Something for Everyone*. Many found this movie extremely entertaining, and not too shocking, in its first month of showings in New York City. It is not a distinguished film on any level, but it qualifies itself very well for any study of homosexual heroes. For one thing, it must look far more familiar and plausible to modern audiences, who take pride in their worldliness, than does the delicately, difficultly structured *Teorema*, with its fabulously benign Homeros. However, one notices at once the resemblance between the two films. Michael York, as the suave, good-looking, but demonic Eros of *Something,* creates quite as much havoc as the angelic, equally attractive Eros of *Teorema.* Moreover, the two are equally and elastically ambisexual, though Karl's great versatility hardly comes directly from the heart. Their dissimilarity is just as inescapable. The benign Eros (Terence Stamp) wishes everybody he sleeps with nothing but good. It is only the paradox of destiny, only his "inevitable" withdrawal from their lives, that causes their immediate despair and rapid ruin.

On the contrary, as youthfully winning and naturally sexy as he is, Mr. York as Malign Homeros is willing, pronto, to sacrifice anyone who stands in the way of his erotized climb to the top of the world. He's even ready to kill the thing he pretends really to love, as he kills the young woman (along with her parents) who threatens to spoil his game when he's halfway up his incline. As a child in a poor family—we learn at the beginning—Karl always wanted to live in a fairy-tale castle. Now that he is a young man, turning about twenty, he sights a real such castle. It belongs to a bored, worldly German countess (Angela Lansbury), who has recently lost her adored husband. If actually she must live in a nearby mansion, it is only because she can't afford the upkeep of her majestic castle, perched high on a mountainside. Karl determines to enter her service, and enter it he does, by a neatly managed murder and a neatly managed betrayal. When he notices that the countess's young son, handsome, with an elegant hippie hairdo, seems attracted to him, he sets out to seduce him, does so with ease, and thoroughly enmeshes him. When it becomes suitable, he advances himself in his developing scheme by sleeping with the countess herself, acted by Miss Lansbury in reminiscent (guess who?) camp style.

The action is generally geared to farce laughs and a polite burlesque of outdated German aristocracy and moneyed bourgeoisie. It is amusing enough unless (like some critics) you constitutionally loathe camp. A young playwright I know startled me by remarking, "Why, *Something for Everyone* isn't 'black' at all! It's a bore." Well, I've always thought most "black comedies" a bore. No, this movie is not really black if it be taken as the trivial charade which, at a perfectly serious level, it is. But the way people take things—the phony aesthetic brio built into taste formulas "for everyone"—should be taken seriously if only because it is something that traduces the serious. How "black" a comedy is *Waiting for Godot?*—and how "good," really? And so on, and so on into existentialism's black, or at least dirt-colored, heart. I thought that Bert Lahr, who performed the main role in *Waiting for Godot* on the New York stage, gave the work more comic genius than he took from it. I would say that *Something for Everyone*, when it isn't being Miss Melodrama of mid-1970, is by any gauge a rousing camp.

As for its blackness, let's say it's Technicolor Black, hiding a rosy-red as well as blue spectrum, as Technicolor Black, like nature, chemically does.

I was about to call *Something for Everyone* a kind of black Germany fairy tale in modern (post-World War II) dress. Karl gets the young count married to the rich girl whom he (Karl) has seduced, thinking that he can handle any number of irons in his red-hot fire. But things go awry when the young woman (as sickened by her marriage night as her bridegroom is) discovers the two young men in a passionate kiss. The young count, of course, is a natural homosexual and Karl has had to force him into marriage for *his* convenience. Now Karl realizes that the rebellious wife, his own mistress, must die. Since fortunately he still has the job of family chauffeur, Karl manages to catapult the outraged bride and her parents off the road into a ravine while he nimbly slips out of the car before it crashes.

The late bride's wealth descends to her husband, the count, and thus the family castle can now be opened. Finally Karl is to marry the countess (which is all right by the young count, because it's a way of keeping Karl in the family), when unexpectedly Karl gets his comeuppance. However, it's not *too* bad. Instead of marrying the countess, he must marry the countess's fat, bespectacled teen-age daughter, who has had a crush on him all this time, and cleverly having put two and two together, has decided that, while she'll have a criminal on her hands, she's willing to risk marrying him. Isn't he, after all, Eros the Ambisexual, and irresistible?

An incisive bit comes when the fat girl puts the clamps on Karl and states her terms. Guessing his ambisexuality to the full (she too has seen him with her brother), she chirps brazenly, "You could do it with anybody, couldn't you?" Behind the clear, open look of Karl's eyes, she has also guessed his clockwork calculation: "I could see you were always thinking, thinking. . . ." In a way, he has met his match: they deserve each other. So, you see, Karl must be declared the winner. The last technical obstacle to his permanent elevation has been removed: he's going to live in the castle and be its lord. He still has the young count where he wants him, and Mamma too, *if* he wants *her*. If *Teorema*'s Homeros is white, as surely he is, the Homeros of *Something for Everyone* is just as surely black. Except for that, they're twins.

We must resign ourselves to the fact that Homeros, white or (to use a metaphor) black, is built into the world's sexual conduct. And he is far too important, even when young, to be looked on as the sore-thumb phenomenon of misfiring heterosexuality. Karl's evil, cold-blooded ways remind one of how hot the blood is in the veins of Encolpius and Ascyltos, the heroes of *Fellini Satyricon;* and that, while technically a couple of imaginative hustlers, the pair actually represent the canonic fools of fortune in a morality tale. They "do evil" because it is forced upon them by the nature of the world they live in: hazardous, licentious, and bloody. Ambisexuality, for Karl, is an economic weapon, a mere instrument of power. Encolpius and Ascyltos are young temperamental homos, genuinely passionate, who start out by obeying the cultural mores of their time and place. In Petronius' Rome, being bisexual—that is, having all kinds of sexual experiences—was a way of learning life. Such experiences were an ideal that meant human completeness, realizing all one's potentialities. The only "tragedy," the only "evil," in the *Satyricon* (and Fellini has followed this) is the sheer melodrama of the picaresque life style. Modern times seem anarchic, not to say "immoral," to declare that something of the same sort is "for everyone."

How different things are in *Rebel Without a Cause* (1955)! Post-blackboard-jungle, it is a modish antique of juvenile delinquency, deriving most of its chic from the way the film brings out the homosexual aspect. That aspect is not (as we shall see in *The Sergeant*) a blemishing bray of a sore thumb wrapped in closet-queeniness, and belonging to someone old enough to know better. Not at all! Here it is a mounted cannon in the boys' locker room with a set of opened switchblades, eloquently phallic, surounding its base. We all know that the late James Dean's rather hard, but very pretty, physical shell was a homosexual parody of Marlon Brando, in that it quickly, even in several poems, became a fetish of boy-man homosexualism: thrilling as a knifeblade with its point lying lightly on a Leather Boy's stomach . . . a Leather Boy's naked stomach.

The chief male performers in *Rebel Without a Cause,*

Dean and Sal Mineo, infuse a bracing content into roles that might have been less but are, as braced, more. Mr. Mineo was then a black-eyed, curly-haired, fresh, and full-lipped broth of a boy looking like an overgrown *putto*. His scenes with James Dean seem as tender as two schoolboys can get about each other. By all means the homosexualizing causes the film to be more interesting than it might have been, and penetrates (to more immediate effect than the novel) into the mechanism of what makes the youth violence of our day, in terms of erotic kicks, tick away like unisex.

Come now! Only nannygoats and other retrograde old maids will deny that my meaning is crystal-clear. It's a message! True, messengers are blasted, sometimes, for the messages they bring. Mr. Mineo is thus blasted in this movie trap. And so was James Dean in life's trap. Dean was killed in an actual hot-rod accident—shortly before *Rebel Without a Cause* was released— echoing the do-or-die chicken-run sequence of the movie when a certain competitor can't stop his car before it takes him over the cliff to his death. Dean was in his car with a male friend when the fatal, bizarre accident occurred. In *Rebel Without a Cause*, he (the senior) is Mineo's good angel, although Mineo can't be saved. No, Mineo is a rebel with a *secret* cause: Home-ros'. And if there's one thing Hollywood blindly delights to do, it's to make Homeros the "black" little fall guy of gunshot violence. The official moral sop is furnished by the sado-masochistic automat of our age of pop and poppers—neither of which, it may be wise to add, means dad. Drop in your quarter (or rather your two-fifty or three) and you get a gay corpse—provided Old Man Morality has had things in hand.

Dear reader: do you perchance resent my emphasis on the homosexual aspect of the Eroses I have been conjuring up? If so, I shan't ask you to reconsider the evidence I have adduced. It seems more tactful and tactical to draw your attention here to the tradition of homeroic imagery in painting. No female painters of any stature appeared in the Renaissance. They were all men; that is understood. As for Michelangelo, his homo-sexuality is well published, accepted by all but the deluded, diehard enemies of sexual deviation. But I do not have in mind the superhuman male anatomies of Michelangelo. The masculinity of those figures is too stylized as ideally athletic: they lack, in short, human accessibility. Besides, they are "effeminate" only as an Amazon is effeminate. As much as one may admire them as male objects, they tend to slip away from the erotic imagination unless it be exclusively fixated on oversized limbs.

In the case of Caravaggio, whose homosexuality is not so well documented but still very plausible, the erotic charge of his male images is, I think, to be grasped at once. Caravaggio painted many youths, often teen-agers barely out of pubescence, and Cupid himself was one of his "boy" subjects. At the Kaiser Friedrich Museum, Berlin, there is an *Amor Victorious*, which is a thinly disguised portrait of an individual, a boy who may have been twelve or thirteen, with straddling legs, exposed genitals, and visible but superfluous wings. And a smile. . . . The painting is a masterpiece of warm human anatomy, in perfect taste because of Caravaggio's technical skill and purity of feeling. It is a charmer—and possibly the only painting in history to have justified the label of "charmers" (proposed but discarded) to describe the male beaver films when they made their public debut. Another unmistakable portrait by the same painter is a very young *Bacchus* at the Uffizi Gallery, Florence. It marvelously fits our category.

Exactly because such a figure was a convention of Renaissance art, one is struck by this particular figure's direct human and, I think, erotic appeal. The painting quality is at once immaculate and sensual. A crown of huge autumnal oak leaves stars the head of this Bacchus; his nude boyish torso is modified only by a white cloak draped on his shoulder. It is the god with the banquet board between us and him, graciously, seriously, almost "coolly" offering us the ritual glass of wine. He seems small but physically generous, delicately effeminate yet indisputably all-young-male. He could be a round-faced hippie in Freshman High today. Caravaggio makes him live, voluptuously at rest, in the deep dimension of Homeros.

Now turn back to consider Pasolini's Eros, Visconti's Homeros, Cocteau's Cégeste, Dorian Gray, Horst Buchholz as Felix Krull, Homeros as Karl the black/white hustler. And you could seek out, if you like, Markopoulos' Eros as "king" and the luminous-limbed Dionysius of Boultenhouse. Decidedly, you don't have to consult a button to know that HOMEROS LIVES. Just go to the movies and take a *good* look. Take a good look, for instance, at the fabulously cast Giton of *Fellini Satyricon*, who is not at all the dazzling young hustler of Petronius. Fellini's Giton is something wonderfully antique, all Roman, a long slender boy with oval face and the provocative, smiling amiability of the ideal whore: the slave able to take any sexual role or position at the simple pleasure of his master. He is the perfect icon of Homeros as *potent* Hermaphrodite. Fellini's film also has a living demigod Hermaphrodite who is worshiped like the miracle-worker, Our Lady of Lourdes: albino, two-sexed and sexless, beautiful and unbeautiful, a piece of sacred pulp, something to haunt Myra Breckinridge. Giton is just the opposite. So was Sal Mineo, at least potentially, in *Rebel Without a Cause*.

5. ... AND HIS/

HER OLD AGE

Perhaps when a writer takes this subject by its horns, there are still readers (I don't say without their own interesting views) who inwardly exclaim or protest to their friends, "What's all this, *really?* A storm in a teacup! It's blatant propaganda by sectarian emotion." Or: "Morbid imagination on the rampage, and rather garbagy." Or: "It's sick stuff—sexually vicious— more than a little pretentious, too. Nobody can convince *me* that it's profound or meaningful!" Do I go out of my way? Do I visualize windmills? I shan't take the chance. I'm going to play it close.

I would answer this way: literature to one side, humanity will be humanity as boys will be boys—indiscriminately, perversely, blindly, and hypocritically too: how they like, cultivated or uncultivated, just so they aren't disturbed by "more trouble." Funnily enough, more trouble comes and comes and comes, doesn't it? The facts are as I say and as reasonably "certain" as the arrival of old age—even to Homeros and his lesbian counterpart, whatever be their culture or social status. I shall presume, then, to supply more remarks on the fulsome and varied evidence on film screens, evidence about my subject that merely repeats, with variations, the happenings of life and the underpinnings supplied by history.

149

As we all know to our sorrow, there is a sexual decadence, homo or hetero, which is purely the result of annuation. Is there something especially pathetic about the *homosexual* male or female growing old and sexually ineligible?—more so than in the heterosexual cases? If so, it is only because the heteros provide those prototypic symptoms which the others, as it were, have to imitate. Yet, to be quite exact, grimness and grotesquerie in such matters, like pathos, depend a good deal on personal factors and specific situations. The style in which age is carried by everybody is as private as the size and shape of one's nose, the size and shape of one's penis, the size and shape of one's breasts and hips; the latter may be as important to male and female homosexuals as to ordinary women. But things like puritanism, perverse vanity, primitive superstition, prevent people from examining the root facts of sexual disaster as of sexual victory. Sexual disaster, naturally, may be a symptom of old age in any sex at all.

In the old as in the young, sexual disasters can take the form of criminal acts, send the perpetrators to law courts and on to lasting confinement in psychiatric hospitals. It happens that the history of motion pictures avails the case of a great male star who was a romantic hero, an idol of the ladies (I daresay of a few gentlemen, too), handsome, muscular, and privately homosexual. He turned out not to be a criminal, but the victim of criminals. Surely, what took place is not without its peculiar, very own moral. His story can be told freely, without indiscretion, because it happens to be a matter of legal record. He was Ramón Novarro, who, in his later life, when retired, was horribly tortured, mutilated, and murdered by two young male hustlers he had taken home one night. Owing to the young men's confessions, and the common knowledge of the Hollywood community, there can be no doubt about the clarity and decisiveness of the acknowledged facts. Ramón Novarro, at the hour of his death, was not too feeble to have worn his sexual annuation gallantly—as gallantly as he had worn his heterosexuality in films—and to look again to youth—sublime youth! —to resuscitate him in the true bed of love.

For a while, during the twenties, Novarro was Rudolph

Valentino's most conspicuous rival. He was—athletic muscles nakedly aglow—Ben Hur in Cecil B. De Mille's movie of that name; he played opposite Greta Garbo in *Mata Hari*. He was given other roles that allowed him transiently, lingeringly to expose his shapely masculine limbs. Was his face a bit too "pretty" for a man's, just a *wee* bit? That seemed only to augment and entrance his host of female fans, and naturally his male fans. The truth was that he carried off his film chores in a brilliant matinée-idol style. Wasn't he constantly in the arms of beautiful women? Wasn't he constantly kissing the opposite sex? Dear readers, that was what is known as a myth; a bona-fide myth, as all public myths necessarily are, a myth despite the fact that Novarro may have been bisexual. May the myth, late or soon, be fatally punctured? May it be shown up as actually "pretentious, morbid, sick stuff . . . even garbage"? Alas, public myths have a way of giving birth to such scandals, as if by built-in reflex. Go through the microfilms of any given newspaper from its inception; you could spend the same time better by just going to the movies.

If, at the present moment, one were to look around in the movies for an example of homosexual annuation to both compare and contrast with Novarro's real life, one could not possibly do better than alight on a recent work which was daringly homosexual and realistic, but which, I fancy, will come to be, in filmic annals, more notorious and curious than famous and canonic: I mean *Staircase*. It started as a play about two middle-aged back-number "poofs" (British slang for faggots) who attempt to conclude their distant romantic marriage with all possible dignity; mostly, they fail in dignity (after all, they *are* poofs, and rather shabby ones), but they succeed in terms of the seemingly deathless and indiscriminate Sentimental Romance—I mean as sanctified by the movies. Moral: "You too, faggots, can end like Elizabeth Taylor and Richard Burton, future tense, if you have the gumption. You don't need the burdens of million-dollar publicity, scandals, the wanton invasion of privacy endured by movie stars; all you need (so Charles Dyer's play implies) is humble obscurity, and poofdom." And, of course, old age or "agingness." *That's* the ultimate test.

But you'll come out pure gold—as did, rather wistfully, Rex Harrison and Richard Burton in the film version of *Staircase*. For those two valiant professionals were persuaded to masquerade as the poofs in question . . . and are they *heroines*!

If anything, conceivably, were needed to "prove" that these two actors are privately heterosexual—as superfluous as that might be—that thing was their reincarnation as Dyer's pair of homosexuals. I did not see the stage version (one of the protagonists was Eli Wallach), but the general impression, as I recall, was that the actors in it left something, as the gracious phrase still has it, to be desired. Granted: the respective skills of Harrison and Burton, judged by average professional standards, are formidable when doing almost anything. That assumption does not conceal from a canny spectator that behind the moral, psychological, and emotional "drag" worn by the two men in this film are a pair of hopelessly, absurdly compromised professionals doing a straightfaced charade composed of genteel hokum. They just don't have the genius to act poofs convincingly. I don't mean by "straightfaced" that there are no intended and actual laughs in their highly paid performances. Laughs, in fact, are built into the plot and dialogue of *Staircase*, and laughs come off in the film, if not quite hilariously, as if they had been computerized.

Moreover, both actors are fully equal to the special demands of pathos which their roles involve. They meet these quietly, patiently, capably, like English gentlemen in the army preparing to conduct themselves creditably while under fire. No histrionics! No excitability beyond that normally to be expected of the given tough situation: *this* movie's situation. The fact is that, seeming rather self-conscious of the abysmal shift from heterosexuality in art to homosexuality in art, Burton and Harrison, ostensibly by mutual consent, underplay even the most dramatic, funniest, and most hysterical moments of the action. Charlie, the "masculine" member of the pair (Harrison), calls out to Harry (Burton), "You silly old queen!", as if he were a splenetic Albert chiding Queen Victoria, *sotto voce*, for locking the bathroom door against him.

Oh, the beautiful, the rare irony of it! Because Charlie

gallivants, bringing home a hustler (who incidentally looks like a lesbian in drag), Harry tries to commit suicide and is rescued by the skin of his poor old teeth. Charlie has been arrested for female impersonation in a raid on a bar (luckily for all, we are spared sight of this event), and when he has to appear in court, he—the prickman of the marriage—gets so panicky and weak-kneed that it seems he won't make it to the place of judgment. But Wifey (that is, Burton) rushes after him to be the family staff. And the picture ends—you might have guessed it, since it's British—with the Lovers Reunited in what had better damn well be Marriage because it's Permanent. Get the message, moviegoers? I'd be surprised if even the stoned hippie seated next to me missed it—provided, of course, he was conscious.

I take a certain horrid pleasure in adding that *Staircase* the movie made hardly a ripple at the box office or, so far as I could make out, in the larynxes of the spectators within hearing distance when I attended. The film is as securely buried, as of now, as it's possible for so recent a film to be buried. I would wager that it never, never comes back, not even on television. If it does, it will be as a sign that the great heterosexual public can't get quite enough of that rare, exotic, and somewhat ludicrous bloom: the predilection for sleeping with one's own sex. I can't believe that the great homosexual public finds *Staircase* anything but grotesquely out of whack. The thing that clings persuasively to this Harrison-Burton escapade in sex deviation is that, after all, the film is documentary evidence of a statutory dilemma for homosexuals: the age of the *tante*. The French word corresponds to the English colloquialism "auntie," and is more accurate, applied to those of middle age or past, than the "poof" lately bandied about in British films. In *Performance*, by the way, a poof is what the gangster's vengeful pals try to force him to admit he is when they wreck his apartment, bloody him up, and almost finish him off. It would seem that, to nether British manhood, the term connotes the depth of male humiliation. (Thank goodness there is a well-received upper-class alternative: "the love that dare not speak its name.")

To impersonate an individual of "the people" is a special pride and glory an eminent actor may expect to garner during a rich career. In the eyes of actors, this angle contributes as much as sex deviation to the magnetism of the two roles in *Staircase*. There is, too, a "poetry of the old" that attracts actors and actresses fond of testing their versatility; especially male actors, who take a bit of female impersonation in stride (I think of Burt Lancaster as an old harridan in *The List of Adrian Messenger*) as if it were a Charley's Aunt stunt "to help out a friend in a moment of need." However, modern experience has sharpened any number of eyes and wits. If we reflect that Anthony Perkins' killer in *Psycho* is rigged out, when he impersonates his dead mother, just like Charley's Aunt in the old-fashioned versions—gray hair, shawl, and long skirts—we see something of the sinister as well as the pathological in what used to be only one of the theater's camp routines. Now we see, as it were, the meat behind the masquerade.

This fresh percipience is due largely to the current age of enlightenment about both criminal motives and ordinary bedroom behavior. *Staircase* was designed to be a depth study in *tante* psychology, a tragi-sentimental vignette with laughs; even at that rate, its relation to aesthetic taste is bad because one of the most boring stereotypes of the theater is reincarnated here by the novelty of a homosexual rather than a heterosexual couple. It is the mutual danger of "change of life" in any successful marriage enduring through the decades. *Staircase*, seen from this basic angle, is a variety of soap opera. More elaborately documented, it would fit top television requirements for serials. Burton and Harrison are supposed to leave us with wet eyes and a dry mouth—you know, that bitter existentialist flavor. At the end, *my* eyes were as dry as my mouth. And if I tasted something bitter, as I did, my association was instantaneous: *Clorox!*

The Charley and Harold of *Staircase* aren't really "old," but just past their prime. One might think of them as oldish Homeroses wistfully (like Mann's Von Aschenbach) viewing the image and the capers of the young. While picnicking in a park, they accidentally eavesdrop on a heterosexual encounter between naked youngsters. The hustler brought home by Harold is technically young, and yet, as I said, he looks like a lesbian, and to be even more literal, his face bears a bloodcurdling resemblance to the late Dame Edith Sitwell as a young woman. When, in 1926, Pavel Tchelitchew first met Dame Edith, he thought she resembled a Russian priest he had known, and she was then still youthful. *Staircase*, however, leaves little room for the poetry of vision typified by Homeros grown old. There is a glimpse of elderly Homeros in *The Confessions of Felix Krull* in the person of the Scotch millionaire, and yet the type, to judge by its rarity, seems not very viable for stage or film. In films, among the homosexual elderly, we are apt to get the commonplace businessman type that is victimized by the hustler in *Midnight Cowboy*.

It seems relevant to view Homeros grown old as Homeros grown suddenly and disastrously outdated, prematurely decadent in all ways. Oscar Wilde's life tragedy is rather like the cataclysmic aging of Oedipus when he unburies the buried truth. There have been two film versions of Wilde's life, both British, fortunately; one starring Robert Morley, the other, Peter Finch: *Oscar Wilde* and *The Trial of Oscar Wilde*. Unfortunately, however, neither film really brings home the aftermath of Wilde's personal misfortunes: the new, sad dimension he lived in after his release from prison when he went to Paris to live in exile. An authentic photograph of this period, showing him on a visit to Italy with Alfred Douglas, is a startling and poignant document. We see in each man the ghost of the homosexual dandy, something at once forlorn, *raté* and rakish.

An odd sidelight on the homosexual as superannuated or outdated was cast by the decision of Shirley Clarke, the Underground film-maker, to do a straight film portrait of a black homosexual, Jason Holliday, a man with a great deal of likable humanity: his sole qualification as a "distinguished person." The film proved a startling success with the audience at the New York Film Festival, 1967, and is in fact eloquent cinéma vérité, straightforward, and with precious few dull moments. It was made entirely in Miss Clarke's living room at the Chelsea Hotel, New York, and is literally a one-man show, assisted only by two offstage voices: Miss Clarke's and that of a white male friend of the subject's. The work might be called an exterior monologue, a nightclub "this is my life" routine by a subject past his prime, a subject with no professional success (and not enough success in love), yet a subject who successfully sits for his portrait. Jason's whole character is presented in a few closely joined sittings, during which all he does, face to the camera, is to relate—with blunt candor and racy good humor— his life story. *Portrait of Jason* is one of those "happy accidents" where, thanks to Miss Clarke, the right medium was found at the right moment for the right subject. It is not a great film, no—but it is grandly authentic where a *Staircase* is pathetically inauthentic. But to return to Oscar Wilde.

Of the two screen impersonations of Wilde, Morley's was the more sophisticated and relevant, yet it lacked true depth and poetry—above all, true pathos—as much as did Finch's. Morley had more style-atmosphere, even looked physically much like Wilde; Finch conveyed more actual sexiness. Yet sexiness is too low-grade a term to apply to Wilde's conscious poetic eroticism. Also, Wilde was handsomer, more of a great presence than Morley could hope to imitate. Morley succeeds best in the drawing room's public moments and his private, weepily sentimental moments with Alfred Douglas. But it is futile to go into much detail. As professionally capable as Morley and Finch respectively were, neither could supply the brilliance, the sheer voltage, of a personality like Wilde's, whether or not Wilde be thought of as having a "homosexual" style. To some extent, of course, rather feeble scenarios were to blame for the two films' inadequacies. Still, one thing is most relevant to the biographic facts of these film fictions. It is that if ever there was a real-life figure symbolizing the Youth of Homeros, that figure (from Wilde's viewpoint) was assuredly Lord Alfred Douglas when first he came into Wilde's life.

The young Alfred Douglas was the typical English golden boy, flaxen-haired, good-looking enough to seem, at times, angelic. In fact, both Alfreds on the screen are rather sketchily portrayed; neither is a great beauty, although one is in the true English mold of handsomeness. Almost instantly, Douglas completely won Wilde's heart, which idolized him and honored him in poetry. What is most significant is that intuitively Wilde anticipated with his hero, Dorian Gray, the whole shock, burden, and scandal of the homosexual as one degraded and prematurely aged by fatally indiscreet overindulgence. All the poetic irony of Wilde's life lies in the fact that he believed *The Picture of Dorian Gray* was a sort of self-indulgent fantasy ornamented with precious aesthetic emotions, whereas substantially it was a prophecy of his own social downfall as a homosexual.

In the Italian photograph which I have mentioned, one sees *two* Dorian Grays, already on their macabre way to senescence. Douglas salvaged himself by turning to religion and becoming a willfully reformed prig; Wilde sank voluptuously, by his own weight, to the bottom of homosexual disaster. By coincidence, Morley's true face (hawkish rather than Roman) resembles more the Wilde of the Italian photograph than it does the vibrant, dominating, aquiline Wilde of his youthful heyday; resembles it, that is, *more physically,* as if Morley's were the face of a less attractive brother of Oscar's. By the time of Wilde's self-exile following his imprisonment, Douglas himself was already too old to be the type of Von Aschenbach's Tadzio —the chaste marble boy seen on a beach's golden horizon.

Yet age, as we learn dramatically from Proust's great recollections, is a strangely mercurial, illusive, yet also manipulable thing. The homosexual Wilde's career happened to hold a special, very real, and fatal disaster. So did, in its more phantasmal but equally decisive way, Von Aschenbach's. Mann's theme of late erotic impulses as carrying physical disease assumes in Von Aschenbach's story its purest poetic form. The invalid Proust's case also confirms Mann's general thesis. We know that, as for homosexuality, while it may, like heterosexuality, hold its sexual dolors as the individual grows older, it is still far from being necessarily dead or played out at middle age or past. The existence of the erotic mirage of Tadzio may imply a swansong, but the character and actual duration of that swansong are variable; in brief, a swansong may signify tangible renewal rather than tangible disaster.

There are, we must conclude, swansongs and swansongs, which exist in the movies as elsewhere. One that is highly instructive, but presided over by an ickily medusan muse, designed for the pantheon of camp poetry, is the movie called, with a thump, *Boom*. It was made with highly redundant care and "artistic" deliberation by Joseph Losey from Tennessee Williams' disastrous play *The Milk Train Doesn't Stop Here Anymore*. Mr. Williams is accustomed to having to rewrite his dramaturgic efforts to please directors and other critics. He has listened to agents, secretaries, and assorted nonhelpers. Maybe, at times, the result became more audience-worthy; if so, I should say it usually became, by ratio, less worthy of the art to which it aspired. From youth to his present annuation, Tennessee always started with certain gifts; from then on, during at least a quarter-century, everything steadily became more fertile and less gifted. This sometimes happens to the naturally gifted, whose only compensation is that their success, duly recognized in the slick magazines and drama columns, gets their author called (to turn to a culture patois) one of the Beautiful People.

This term, not exactly, I admit, mint-fresh, is a collective one; so far as I know, it doesn't exist in the singular. It signifies a tight-woven, high-level establishment minority that has come "to be" without banners, a cause, or slogans. The B.P. is a gimmick phrase of those who invent the advertising slogans and other *mots nouveaux* that appear as prose in the high-fashion organs and their echoes; more than likely, this one is borrowed, not thought up. Everyone prominent in *Boom*, even the camera, belongs to the Beautiful People. Don't imagine, dear reader, that the cachet means one is "beautiful" in the vulgar, literal, physical sense; one *can* be beautiful in that sense, it's okay, but what it really means is the "success" that has got one adopted into the local and preferably international élite and that, therefore, homogenizes being lovely-to-look-at with being even-lovelier-to-gawk-at. A certain kind of success confers, you see, a holier-than-thou-serenity that registers even before one heaves in sight and the cameras start clicking. It's something one sort of "grows up in," the way Elsa Maxwell grew and grew as a professional hostess. The older you are as a member of the B.P., the more you realize that it's better than growing old as a member of the D.A.R.

I have to admit that Homeros in various forms has not been excluded from the Beautiful People. Indeed, this point emphasizes another important factor. Sex among the B.P. is strategically suppressed, as if the established cult were an open church rather than a closed cliché. The milieu I mean is altogether as real and as mythical as are homosexuals. It's also rather utopian. The prevailing moral assumption, in this respect, is the world's most, most, *most* liberal. It might well be named unisex, which is, in my opinion, the reigning zoömorph of the new fashion world. The B.P., incidentally, need only one sort of credit card; it's never shown at a door or worn as a button. Like certain aspects of camp, it's not even communicated in words. Among the élite—if you're really there— you never hear the word "élite." *That* is always the air one breathes, even if, like Cissy Goforth, the heroine of *Boom*, one chokes on it. Technically, Mrs. Goforth (a name it would take a dramatist's genius to think up) is a middle-aged warhorse with cancer of the stomach. She could just as easily have cancer of the B.P. tract. Because she's *very* vulgar, even shrewishly vulgar.

All this makes it curiously possible for everyone visible in *Boom,* no matter how silly or hideous or inept or sexy or unsexy, to make it up the hill of agingness toward another million dollars or another invitation. Noël Coward, playing Bill, who is a statutory camp of the B.P. nicknamed at first the Witch of Capri, entered the cast of *Boom* as a replacement for what originally was a female part. One grasps the happy inspiration: far-out sex, in whatever direction it goes, is tacitly accepted by the B.P., and since homosexuals do roam international society, why not "up" the camBP aspects of *Boom* by making the "Witch" into the part of a male bitch? In my terms, he would be Homeros grown old among the Beautiful People—and where else, in the world of 1971, could one grow *so* gracefully old? Sir Noël Coward's experience as actor and worldling, his literary and theatrical achievements, his title, and his invulnerable orthodox manner all went "boom" for his casting in the revised part.

There are no bones made about the BPitch of Bill's sex boom. If certain telltale mannerisms assumed for the part by Sir Noël did not identify his sexuality, certain lines and action in the movie would. Only an upper-upper poof could glance at a monument of cuisine ceremoniously offered by a butler, and say sniffily something like: "Why, I wouldn't touch *that* monster!" He has been discussing marine medusas with his hostess, Mrs. Goforth, and because on this occasion he is an intruder, he and his dying hostess have been solemnly bitching each other. Bill has come to her privately owned island in the Mediterranean to gloat over her rumored death agony as well as to cruise the internationally known, high-tramp poet, Christopher Flanders, played by Richard Burton and nicknamed (before the camera manages to arrive on the scene) the Angel of Death. (It may be wicked to say so, but doesn't one just naturally sniff the possibility that all this is a deep, Cocteau-inspired allegory?) Bill, you see, is a warlock (male witch), and Chris always arrives, duffel bag over shoulder—he's a *wanderer*—just before one of his many patron-hostesses steps into the next world.

Perhaps a certain ironic canniness lies in the way the numerically well-on Burton plays a role that was expressly written for a gorgeous young blond who would look like the last gasp in glorified hustlers (the original stage production made this *quite* clear). Scene in, scene out, as played with his hostess, Chris seems to be head usher at a court function, who has just received an amorous message from his sovereign and is sublimely determined, both not to lose an iota of countenance, and to gratify the old girl only on receipt of a fee worthy of *his* royal condescension. Finally Chris, the Angel of Death, strips his dead, or almost dead, hostess of all the jewels she's wearing. And this he does (O *black* angel!) without having come across with his part of the bargain, to perform which he has been invited into the unfortunate Cissy's bedroom at literally the last minute! I can't resist quoting *The New York Times*'s capsule notice of a TV screening of *Boom*: "Phooey, double phooey, and shame on you, Tennessee Williams."

I need only to qualify Sir Noël's impersonation of a vainglorious old Homeros of the B.P. In alien circles, he would be said to have a sympathetically interesting mug. To do him all justice, Sir Noël is a person as well as a People. Throughout, the true camp of *Boom* may be defined as the richly ironic acts of various persons' condescension. One may feel that Sir Noël's stagily delivered funny lines are simply British underacting. Maybe so. Yet I doubt that Sir Noël summoned to this perform- ance the tension (as formerly, anyway, he certainly could have) that he gave roles for which he had more professional respect. His bruised-black Homeros—or, in the vernacular, his battered old faggot—seems to me flat, stale, and unprofitable. An actor who could have felt more interest in playing Bill would cer- tainly have given him more camp *esprit*.

In *Boom* everybody looks oddly sick and *raté*, uninten- tionally so. I only want to add that Bill does try to put the make on Chris, urging him (with a passing genteel outcry obliquely evoking Sir John Gielgud's vocal manners), "Come to Capri, Chris. . . . Come to Capri!" Mrs. Goforth—who usually looks like a half-stripped Christmas tree with its hair down—is so alarmed by Bill's interference that she shrieks out the scandal to her household minions and orders that Bill be escorted, pronto, off the island. When Cissy (Elizabeth Taylor putting her own make down rather than up) looks like a *fully dressed* Christmas tree, her get-up suggests a discarded idea furnished by some mad-queen designer to dress Mother Goddam in that classic camp film *The Shanghai Gesture*.

Evidence of the swansong for Homeros, as an optimistic and more legitimate event, comes, not unexpectedly, from films in the avant-garde, or Underground, tradition. A film-maker who recently illustrated this is the poet-painter Charles Henri Ford, with his first major film, *Johnny Minotaur*. A docu- mentary made of his own poem-posters is his only previous filmic venture. *Johnny Minotaur* is spotty in its merits and not a technical success; it lacks basic drive, overall form, and that style-resourcefulness whose absence spoils so many earnest poetic efforts of independent film-makers. It has eloquent shots, and shots that are undistinguished, insubstantial, overcasual. This does not prevent the authentic presence of the Homeros theme in *Johnny Minotaur*. Homeros grown old or "too old," and seeking himself again in a youth to love. After all, no less is true of the Warlock of Capri who loves the Angel of Death in *Boom*.

Johnny Minotaur is a personal adaptation of the Theseus story in the form of a modern poet's diary, an autobiographic memoir composed in Crete, home of the ancient Minotaur, in which Ford has a house where he stays most of each year. At first the poet, well on in years but "fit," is attracted to a handsome young male painter who is heterosexual and happens to be devising a Minotaur's helmet-mask of the type some believe was worn by King Minos, or a viceroy, to impersonate the mythic Minotaur. This sets the poet's mind working, and the result is a fantasy bred from immediate reality and distant myth. Basically it is Cocteau's formula, and just as Cocteau's *Testament of Orpheus* is the autobiographic memoir of a poet past his prime, so Ford's Minotaur film is a recapture of an even more symbolic past. Cocteau made *Orpheus* about a decade before the *Testament* (1960); Ford started *his* testament from scratch. Nevertheless, Ford's age makes him the proper sponsor, guardian, and lover of Homeros. Once, Ford himself *was* Homeros.

The god's youthful delegate appears as a teen-age Greek boy of today, black-browed, slim, phallic; enigmatic, a sort of toy, yet remote, a "baby minotaur." Johnny seen in his bull headdress, naked, and carrying about in his arms a naked young boy, is a touching passage of fantasy. For his part, in the real duration of time, Johnny has fallen in love with the poet-memoirist's niece, a young Pasiphaë of striking looks but a certain diffidence, and starts wooing her. Ford has not been careful to build up personal identities in his film, to define their fluid shifts or make a clear plot from reality to fantasy and back. As an integral structure, the film is a sad failure, nor is its invention either significant or agile. But one sequence, external to the main threads of plot, and dispensable in that sense, concretely visualizes the image of Homeros deprived, Homeros decadent and eager to revitalize himself.

Here a surrogate for the film-making poet, the one who is making a Minotaur film within the film, witnesses and records some casual lovemaking between two bathing, completely naked youths whom we have not seen before. The scene is a lovely, sunny beach; one cannot help thinking of *Death in Venice*. The lingering taboo on actual kissing and embracing between males (usually ignored only in male beaver films) is broken through here in some charmingly spontaneous foot-age. Hippie-haired, good-looking, the two youths make love, ranging from frolicsome to serious, as if the crouching, avid, camera-eyed voyeur poet were not close enough to reach out and touch them. Wittily, Ford accents Homeros (not really old but ineligibly annuated) by making the surrogate poet wear a rather absurd, tourist sort of get-up in this scene. We shall come to this type, laymanized and commonplace, when we reach the voyeurs who frequent male beaver films.

As for Homeroses of sapphic gender, there are compara-tively few on the screen, though it can boast of some. Usually they appear as schoolgirls and/or schoolmistresses. There are some choice, actually eloquent female figures, mature and adolescent, in a French film, *The Pit of Loneliness*, all about a fashionable, sapphically saturated girls' school. But this belongs in a future chapter. The irresistible nymphet, the idolized girl, is more apt to be a heterosexual such as we find in the film version of *Lolita*. It is odd to think of the story that one pub-lisher to whom Nabokov submitted the manuscript of his novel said that he thought there would be a good enough market for his book if he turned his heroine into a *boy*. Though, of course, Nabokov indignantly refused, the idea is valuable in illustrat-ing the fluid emotional structure of the passion aroused by Lolita. The shift from hetero to homo, far from being the un-imaginable leap many conceive it, is so obvious as to occur to someone who senses what the vast tides of public taste are up to. That publisher's suggestion has more point today than it did a decade ago.

The aura of television hovering over the existentially flavored comedy *Staircase* becomes really existential in *The Killing of Sister George*, the film made from the play of the same name. The title part is a famous television personality who in private life is a domineering lesbian, fast getting on in life, speaking chronologically, fast slipping back in it, speaking professionally; in brief, she is on the skids with her star part in a popular TV serial. The chief unpleasant thing about lesbian characters, especially as they mature, is their hardness— "acting butch" is the basic colloquial—while on the contrary, softness in the male homosexual, even to heterosexual audiences, is likely (unless grossly caricatured) to be winning rather than distasteful. Is this the psychology of what is called male chauvinism? No matter! Let us take up Sister George's classic lesbian personality.

Sister George maintains her erotic hegemony by persecuting the listlessly passive, infantile young woman with whom she lives. As domestic tyrant, she is the metaphoric priapus as an abusive weapon (yes, *that* again). When her girl slave has been naughty, she makes her drink dirty bath water: a ritual humiliation whose metaphor, of course, is the female's ejaculation. I hope I'm not betraying any male chauvinism in saying that lesbian antics tend to sound notes sour and gritty rather than gay and fluent, even when they take the form of legitimate jokes. So it is understandable that female Tadzios should not appear in films in very idyllic forms. Consider this sapphic situation: an imaginary *The Girls in the Group* would be far less fetching to the general public than Crowley's actual *The Boys in the Band*. Once there was a film in chic lesbian style, *Club de Femmes*, all-girl with Danielle Darrieux, an oldie screened only in the art-film houses of the puritan-speaking nations. Rather, I imagine a girl-group flick, American style, as set in a women's prison (dimly, I recall some such thing), suitably grim for the subway trade, with the raunchiness in drag and the jokes (if any) typical of barroom horsiness in old Westerns. For example, an author so updated in sophistication as Mary McCarthy, when she wished to portray females as a group, unhesitantly chose the angle of suburban heterosexuality; this indicated her practical acumen as well as her subjective inclination. When a female homosexual, on the other hand, essays to display her kind as a collective, she seems magnetically to have gone to schoolgirl experience: witness *Maedchen in Uniform,* the above-mentioned *The Pit of Loneliness,* and *La Batarde,* the novel by Violette Leduc from which the film *Thérèse and Isabelle* was made.

Profitably, we might turn aside for a moment to a pop-nouveau film produced by Robert Wiener and directed by Ron Dorfman and Peter Nevard: *Groupies*. In the head-over-heels vérité manner, plump in the midst of life, it's excellent. It's likewise all-girl in the sense that virtually everybody in it, including the male rock stars, have long hair and look girlish. Technically it's not homosexual till, all of a sudden, we find among the camp followers called groupies (attached or semi-attached girls who religiously follow the rock stars wherever they go and sleep, or try to sleep, with them) a little male transvestite, plangent but seemingly ineffectual. Since the dominant erotic style is unisexual, he's just a faux-pas.

Seeing the girls club up in twosomes and fiercely discuss their new or old crushes and their number of successes, one notes how easy it would be for them to enact, indeed *be*, lesbians. They're just like the archetypal schoolgirl with a crush on the school's football hero, except that, as groupies, these girls seldom take no for an answer: extracting a yes happens to be their profession. When we view how a certain rock singer, resembling Mick Jagger, keeps having phone conversations with his admirers and putting them off, it may occur to us that these flowing maned youngsters, with their big cushiony lips and bedroom-goggled eyes, might find it less wearing (they travel and live in all-male groups) to tear off a piece with one of their mates, or a passing fairy, than to give themselves to some ravenous groupie. The groupie would almost certainly want to go home and tell her roommate, "Last night, Mister Rock did it to me five times—and on pot, too! It was the *craziest!*"

Groupies is cute; it even has a little flair, a little pathos. And its fun, when not simply gray, is black. In the comic dimension, all the same, charm seems conspicuously to elude the exploitation of outright lesbianism. *Thérèse and Isabelle* and *The Pit of Loneliness* are in the deliberate romantic style despite the naturalistic notation of the former. What might be called "romantic touches" on lesbian relations have occurred in an unusual number of films prior to the exhibition of actual carnal relations between women (as in the Russ Meyer porno flicks, which show bed-sex outright). There was the naïvely exotic melodrama *Blood and Roses*, that bore a frank, obliquely gothic touch. It has lush, postury, rather absurd scenes between animate lesbian dolls, and trick photography that by all means, being derived from surrealist painting, was both bloody and roseate. The "charm" of *Blood and Roses* is like the worst of Dali's pseudo-romantic erotic decadence: *maquillage* and mayhem.

As for charm, Harrison and Burton earnestly tried to milk as much of it as inhumanly possible from those middle-aged poofs-of-the-people. Sordid, yes, even vulgar they were— but oh, their pathos! that is, their *intended* pathos. It is hard to imagine an equivalent of *Staircase* in lesbian terms unless one were to do a version of the Stein-Toklas love affair. But those real-life ladies came from the artistic intelligentsia and finished off domestic matters (Miss Stein suddenly died at past middle-age) in perfect good style. Even a comic treatment of their story would naturally tend to be most genteel, with no touch of pop spiciness. Supposing one were to film stories about the well-known bachelor lesbians of the Beautiful People—some passed away, some as old as Sister George—I doubt the affair would get as far as production; there would be too much chance of *their* being called male chauvinists, and *you* no gentleman.

One way of not being genteel is to set a lesbian comedy, as with *The Killing of Sister George*, square (or should one say slanting?) on the pivot of an inside-television intrigue. A cheeky-chic television executive sets her cap for Sister George's girl slave, desiring to liberate her, and that's the "killing" of Sister George, including her job. In a casual repetition of effect (actually preceding the commercial film), Andy Warhol's *The Chelsea Girls* has a young-old lesbian, a dope-pusher and addict, domineer over a young lesbian in much the way Sister George domineers in her tyrannic moments at home. Sadistic cultiness, in fact, easily thrives in lesbian relationships owing to the efforts of an aggressive sappho to establish a dual moral and sexual authority like a naughty Momism between girls; the idea is to approximate the "masculinity" which a passive sappho, presumably, always yearns for. "Slaves" and "Masters" are now an open parlance in both heterosexual and homosexual relations. The paraphernalia of chains, whips, and other (more or less actual) weapons of torture are regularly mentioned in the sex rags of recent flowering, and have made their marks in male and female beavers as well as in Underground films.

There is a leather-and-metal sort of sex cult, alike homo and hetero, whose film imagery is already familiar enough to have been travestied in a short film by Paul Bartel, *Naughty Nurse*, which sets out, very bluntly, to exploit kookiness in sex and society. A male surgeon and his male and female associates (one each) spend their lunch hour by going to a shabby hotel, getting in scanty-panty leather/metal drag and playing a charade in which the surgeon and the female assistant are interrupted in their mild sadistic ritual by the male associate (a Negro) who impersonates a uniformed cop. At first you think he's a real cop; then, at the scheduled invitation, he promptly divests and dives in with the pair to continue their ambisexual play as a threesome; he also wears the leather/metal scanty-panties. The surgeon, who is playing slave, is due to be "disciplined" by the cop in more ways, we can assume, than one. The curtain line is a cry of joy from the female: the surgeon has told her that tomorrow she can "be the cop." *Be*? How frivolous existentialism can get!

When back-number lesbians anticipate "the end," it is basic, if not *de rigueur*, to apply a certain unladylike technique of survival that approaches sadism. Beryl Reid, enacting Sister George, does creditably enough in a part which any actress might regard as professional self-iconoclasm. For that reason she seems to have injected her part with big-little boy boisterousness. Its chief attraction as a part would be as tour de force, but this tour de force has to be, if convincing, both bitchy and butchy. This isn't a very easy or palatable combination. Miss Reid gives what might be termed a very knowing performance but not an open-and-shut authentic one: she is *too* rife with good-fellow jollity, *too* bristly chinned with bad temper. In parenthesis, it could be said that some women, though technically lesbians can't help being ladies, just as some gentlemen, though technically pansies, can't help being men.

Let that parenthesis prevent my being branded as a male chauvinist. But really, it is not so much a parenthesis as another—I hope not too ambiguous—element of my theme. It is legitimate tactics for all older lovers to act as protectors of the younger, especially if the young are neophytes, perhaps out of luck or simply "growing up." Hence the schoolmistress/female-pupil arrangement, the schoolmaster/male-pupil arrangement, of education into homosexual love.* This aspect of Homeros "in uniform" I treat right here since the school environment provides the ideal arena for mature homosexuality to assert itself as the image of superior wisdom—real or faked, tender or brutal, passive or aggressive.

Both male and female homosexuals, sometimes disguised or self-disguised, logically assume protectorship as a routine part of courtship. It is always *age* which makes this strategy look right: the suitors are being maternal or paternal. In *The Girl with the Golden Eyes* as well as the recent, if less distinguished, *Fraulein Doktor* (renamed *The Betrayal*), a masterful lesbian type is to the fore. Typically she is a cock-o'-the-walk professional with the arrogant, debonair manners of a Don Juan. Such is the character played by Capucine in *The Betrayal* as a virtual prototype of today's high-fashion lesbian: mature, handsome, angular, shirted and cravated, doing the dominant-male act in which she overwhelms her prey, an "innocent" girl, by literally undressing her. This sort of character, sincere or not, assumes the role of paternal protector. Which is neither more nor less than natural. And just as natural is that a protector should use sexuality as a *salutary* form of punishment.

There was a glimpse of this sort of thing, rather brutal and cursive but nevertheless typical, in Vilgot Sjöman's wrily naturalistuc study of reform-school mores, *491*, taken from the novel of that name. There the boys living under a modern-type "free" experiment, supervised by male social workers, are rather evidently committed to girls. Not so in the instances of all the social workers who attend them. One phase of the plot is how a few boys contrive to gain a crucial advantage over their supervisors by trapping one of them into performing fellatio on an inmate while a tape recorder is under the bed. Then the con-

* At least one first-rate, very sensitive novel has been written on the master/pupil homeroic relation, *Lord Dismiss Us,* but to date it has not been filmed.

niving group sends an emissary to the chief of social workers
with the object of a blackmailing coup. Sjöman displays the
whole incident impersonally and unsensationally, but with
a certain realistic brio. The dignified elderly gentleman is
quick to perceive all that is afoot but he too has an ace in his
hand. The complete exposure of the boys' game, no matter
who else suffered, would make it really hard for them. So the
social-work chief takes an aggressive stance. No longer is he
a benevolent mover in this noble experiment with juvenile
delinquents. His hand placed suggestively on the boy's knee is
merely a deceptive irony. Actually he is a voracious wolf lust-
ing after young male behinds. Suavely he pulls down the
venetian blinds in his office, then a little less suavely, directs
the boy to stand by a desk, lean forward, and lower his pants.
This man, we see, is no fellow of fellatio, but a sovereign of
sodomy. The grimly deadpan joke is now on the boys.

Male or female, the powerful mature "patron," masked
with genuine enough dignity and conventionality, is bound to
be a figure in the homosexual pantheon. Many such oblique
affairs between older and younger men have appeared on the
screen with cheerful solemnity in the form of a poker-faced plot.
One very interesting case, *Double Indemnity*, I analyzed in
Magic and Myth of the Movies. I have already mentioned here
the rather esoteric angle presented by the master crook's gunsel
in *The Maltese Falcon*. That this same gunsel may have more
than one master in the movie (or that Sidney Greenstreet, the
master crook, may have more than one obliging minion) is
revealed by something that might well slip by someone who has
seen the film but not read Dashiell Hammett's novel. In the
latter, Spade's female secretary, casing the member of the gang
played by Peter Lorre, bluntly tells Spade that the Lorre number is a queer. Such candor, for the forties, was too definite for
the movies. So once more homosexuality is indicated by a
standard, yokelish innuendo. The point is "made" when Spade
makes something of reacting to a whiff from Lorre's evidently
perfumed pocket handkerchief.

Those mysterious wings, spread by crime and other underworld doings so liberally in the movies, offer haven, inci-

dentally, to the hidden homosexual who acts as type-patron of the young and the luckless. A true pioneer in campy adventure films was the well-remembered *Gilda,* heavily gilded and affording (with Glenn Ford and Rita Hayworth) some slyly insinuating erotics. At the outset, Ford, then much younger than now, has his skin saved by a gray-haired gentleman in evening clothes (George Macready), who routs some thugs with a rapier plucked from his elegant cane. The rescuer has altogether a devastating, super-Clifton Webb style, but there is something cold and mechanical about it. He "owns" rather than "loves" his reigning mistress (Miss Hayworth), and then he starts owning rather than "loving" his new henchman, Ford.

It wasn't hard for the worldly-wise to guess, even in the forties, that Ford's rescuer was a stand-in for the malign-benign homosexual patron. After he has given the young man a good job in his plush gambling casino, the fun and the sex intrigue begin. Loyalty to his benefactor and love for Miss Hayworth— one of the more luscious, less ambiguously sexed queens of camp—start tearing young Ford apart, seemingly at his most vulnerable point: the midriff. Yet the midriff has several departments. Miss Hayworth finds reason to complain that she isn't being sufficiently recognized in what would seem, by nature's plan, to be *her* department. Once she is so irritated by Ford's seeming mental block that she suggests, point blank and out loud, that he see a psychiatrist. *Gilda* was all circusy, obscene fun, as if it were a drag act turned into a super-spectacle. If you wondered just *who* was in drag, that made the suspense all the more provocative. And if you found the end something of a letdown, you could decide that, after all, *plots* too get in drag.

Not always is it possible for the mature homosexual patron to maintain style, dignity, and a successful masquerade. How much, for instance, Sergeant Callan, protagonist of *The Sergeant,* would have loved to act the paternal guide for his worshiped young private, whose obstinacy turned the sergeant, instead, into a blustering, blundering she-bull whose only *possible* solution is suicide. I'm saving up Sergeant Callan for a future appearance. But one fleeting case—on the distaff as opposed to the staff side of homosexual patronage—appeared in 1961 as part of the television film series called *The Asphalt Jungle*. It was, of course, fully decked out in thriller charade. But it was quite readable to those who look even casually beneath the surfaces of urban folk art. Six young women have been wounded by an elusive sniper. The shooting invariably takes place when the girls are in the company of male escorts. When finally the sniper is run down, everyone is surprised that "he" is identified as the female owner of a coffee house who has been characterized, meanwhile, as possessively interested in girls. The woman confesses that her reason for shooting the girls is their loose conduct with boys. The relation between an aging Sister George and a motherly lesbian sniper is more than obvious to the oneirocritic of Hollywood fantasies. And I fancy that all of us, by this time, are oneirocritics.

The coming discussion of *The Pit of Loneliness* will serve to show how gracefully, wittily, and romantically mature female Homeroses may preside over sapphic love rituals, where girl pupils sit at one's feet as the youths of Athens sat at the feet of Socrates. Now, *there* was a sumptuous edition of male Homeros authenticating his old age as grand, loving, and wise! So far, the films have not dared to incarnate Socrates in a major role; and thus not as the lover of his "Tadzio," Phaedrus. If ever there could be a peak homosexual role for a mature actor, that would be it. How well one can imagine the late Charles Laughton (whose face would have been ideal) almost, but not quite, succeeding at doing Socrates. I fear it would be impossible to erase from one's mind the effeminate Nero which Laughton acted in that old Cecil B. DeMille paganophile movie, *The Sign of the Cross*. Next to Nero's throne, one couldn't help noticing, constantly present, the demure male figure of the emperor's young favorite. Opposite Homeros as Tadzio, as Cupid, as Phaedrus must always be the figure of the mature homophilic male, whether emperor, philosopher, painter, or millionaire. Even Bill, the Warlock of Capri. . . .

6. HIS/HER NAKEDNESS: BEAVERS AND METABEAVERS

The all-male beavers (all-female beavers, incidentally, seem primarily destined for *male* watchers) are usually painfully amateurish in acting, photography, and direction, and often stultifying in their lack of interesting or attractive physical material. Still photographs of good material have been much quicker to proliferate. And yet, even as I write, more and more pretentious sex films (currently in the name of science, and mainly hetero) are being developed out of the pristine beaver, originally a living anatomy chart produced for leers and drooling. When pretending to be "stories," beavers are more or less inane anecdotes or, if shaped anything like a novel, a series of integrated actions, they suffer from the regular afflictions of pulp cults. Pulp cults, of course, have been gussied up as pop culture.

All of which is no more than natural to the world that men have made out of our planet. Beavers and metabeavers (beavers with pale delusion of grandeur) are produced not to make films but to exploit a technical vice. The technical vice (on the male side) is voyeurism of male nudity, including the till recently taboo genitals, and in advanced sex culture via

film, more or less realistic simulation of sex acts seldom taken
to the intercourse stage. However, considering everything, one
might expect some ornamental virtues even where there are
no reassuring signs of zest taken in acts of sexual contact.
Ornamental? Well, there are different standards of the decorative, especially in the male beavers where mere scale is decisive
in grading the beauty of the sex organ. General muscularity
helps, so does an attractive face, but these things are peripheral
in the hardcore beaver cult. I daresay the young performers, not
at all cut out to be actors, are cramped by the official taboo on
the erect genital. The technical strategy is to sneak in a semierect genital caught, as it were, in the act of playing possum.

I'm afraid many gentlemen in the audience (though
there are seldom "many" at the most crowded times) detect this
tactical cheat and stoically deplore it, for it signifies that the
organ in its normal state may be nothing to write home about:
the beaver cultist is impressionable as well as mercilessly analyt-
ical. Sometimes a person of magnificent genital endowment,
and fair good looks otherwise, is persuaded to lend his valuable
property to the relatively unrewarding uses of the beavers. We
might as well pause to examine the origin of the term "beaver."
Where did it come from?

The word strikes the uninformed mental ear oddly;
partly, this may be because the male formula is a mechanical
takeover from the original female formula, which was plain
"beaver." When, sometime in 1969, enterprising people in the
film world (I think the first was Gerard Malanga) decided to
exploit all-male beavers, a different cognomen was proposed:
charmer. But "charmer" was altogether too sissy a word, so it
was decided to rely on rock-bottom tradition: boys as well as
girls have the pubic hair that inspired the epithet in the first
place. The reason the label is puritanically inexact is that the
whole point is to see, if possible, what the pubic hair does not
conceal—not even on women.

Yet pubic hair, and brassieres, panties, and jockstraps,
remain symbols with a potent charm of their own. The original
metaphor of "beaver" was simply that the female's bush of
silky hair evoked the rich quality of a beaver's hide and had

the force of the last clue in a treasure hunt. As for action itself, the rules of the beaver (so as to stay within the law) were to allow as much display and sex play as possible without getting to genuine, or simulated, intercourse. Nowadays, intercourse in films done on a commercial scale is so well simulated that one may well wonder if it's not really taking place. One of the silliest things that followed the rules, when film producers of sexploitationals were still shy of the law, was that intercourse was supposed to take place with the female in full undress and the male still in his unloosened trousers. Today *that* situation has a neanderthal haze about it.

Actually, "beaver" is less special than the miscellaneous pornographic article "blue movie," which denotes the classic stag film. The history of the word "blue," as something besides the color itself, makes a bizarre etymology. Even in Shakespeare's time, it denoted "low spirits," thus giving much depth to our modern song genre, the blues. Yet the word took on connotations of superiority and high office, as in "blue book," "blue blood," "blue ribbon." Its first appearance in print to denote obscenity is given by the Oxford Universal Dictionary as 1840; it even meant the "plague," says the same source, and "things hurtful," such as the Devil. But what precise association could have made the heavenly color an emblem of filth and the dregs? There is a hint in the fact that, in the middle of the eighteenth century, "blue-stocking" became the cognomen of a reformist element in society wishing to substitute "literary conversation" for "card-playing" as an upper-class habit; or, to translate, serious morals for profligacy. Along this line of anti-licentiousness, of course, Puritanism grew up, and out of Puritanism came our own modern "blue laws"—repressive laws, laws that made one "blue," that repressed drinking and other forms of social exuberance—among which sex might safely be listed.

A point of poetic irony, today, is that in no movie house does one find a less lively, a "bluer" audience than that attending beavers and blue movies. This is more particularly true of the all-male precincts, where incidentally the proportion of female attendance is about one female to twenty or twenty-five males; the male attendance is about one (at an average showing) to every five or six seats. The gentlemen, unless they are in couples, sedulously separate themselves at least a seat apart: God forbid that the police or anyone else should think they've come to use anything but their eyes! Of course, the patrons of the blue movies, however oriented sexually the item be, are preponderantly loners, and tend to enter and leave the theater like well-behaved zombies or somebody gagged and trussed. There is a tight, hottish-dry aridity in the air that you can almost hear breathing, as if it were a sort of deep-down chronic asthma of desire. We are simply inside the cloistered contemplation and sex-on-ice climate of the devout voyeur.

Audience reaction at all-male beavers, even in view of spectral attendance, is surprisingly light; if the scene is "heavy," it's only through deadweight. There may be a gentle wave of titters, topped by a ha-ha, responding to some mildly funny camp action, or a superior chuckle or tsk-tsk from a sophisticate who registers the more blatant ineptitudes, but as for honest guffaws or loud dirty snickers, these rarely intrude upon the churchlike silence. Gasps of admiration may be heard, but notably these are close to the murmur of private prayer; when one is distinctly heard, it's like a dropped prayerbook. Partly, I grant, this inexpressiveness must be due to the disappointing, the transparently sham qualities of the spectacles being unfolded. Yet basically, however low-grade, the beaver habit is unmistakably a ritual.

I think that antipornographic moralists misunderstand, as a rule, the nature of what I shall call quasi-aesthetic voyeurism. It is a stern occasion when the burden of moral choice rests heavily on the ticket buyer's shoulders. First of all, the very meaning of peephole ritualism is that physical functions of which the subject is variously capable are now reserved exclusively for the eyes. Voyeurism nowadays is the purified, isolated kinaesthetics of sex. The eyes as sole technical receptor must therefore be a very active *per*ceptor, and the more willfully active when the kinaesthetic possibilities are the poorest. Thus, in the sheer optical sense, looking at beavers is a kind of athletic discipline, comparable to a solo workout at the gym. You don't find *athletes* laughing while deep at work. Watch any baseball or tennis match: the mood is "gravity" in the abstract or moral sense of that word. The whole muscular as well as mental system of an athlete is, or should be, intent on the goal of physical functions designed to produce exact results. The dreadful hiatus apparent in the kinaesthetic flow at an all-male beaver film occurs because almost never does the screen spectacle produce an illusion of true sexual function, not to speak of a true climax to that function. How rarely, in the male beavers, a racket seems to touch a ball or a runner to get even to second base!

In psychological reflex, athletes spasmodically laugh, grimace, and lose their tempers; much oftener, they are setting their jaws and trying to concentrate. To the kinaesthetic athlete who is the beaver-watcher, it is futile to concentrate mentally on a mawkish charade of sexuality, to set one's jaws over the absence, not the presence, of an orgasm! Moreover, kinaesthetic voyeurs feel much less free to express themselves than do athletes and audiences, say, at a baseball or football game, where spectator vociferation is a sacred convention. This is because the voyeurist ritual means psychological privacy. I can remember, however, an occasion of genuine peepshow sex when this tacit code of closed privacy and silent reception was violated.

The violator was a female opera singer who was witnessing (the locale was Paris) fellatio being performed by a woman. After watching the professional at her task for several minutes, the singer showed signs of unrest to the little group that had joined her for this amusement. At last she could no longer contain herself and broke out in something more than a stage whisper, "My God! How badly she's doing it—she has no idea how it should be done . . . She's *terrible*. . . . Just look at that. . . . I could do it much, *much* better—I could teach her something." Her departure from the voyeur's code was indeed "operatic." She was performing, however strangled, a *récitatif*.

Would that the male-beaver-watcher had the opportunity to produce a similar spectator response, however to be repressed. The only occasion that I know of, to date, was a semiprivate screening of a lovemaking film by the Undergrounder Stan Brak-

HOMOPHILE ROYALTY

Hetero queens of a homocult   *Myra Breckinridge*

Hetero kings of a homocult   *Staircase*

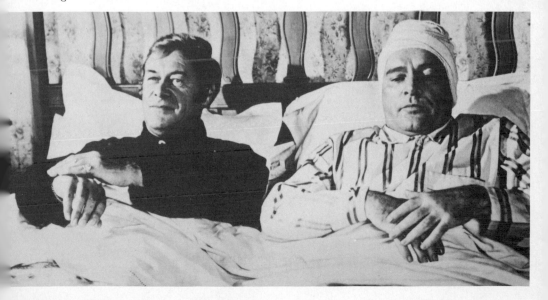

LESBIAN GALLANTRY

Courtier kneels to lady in the school play   *Maedchen in Uniform*

"Diesel dyke" kneels to "femme" in the dance hall   *The Conformist*

LESBIAN VIOLENCE

The penis as knife: set to slay with it   *Les Abysses*

The penis as knife: slaying with it   *The Girl with the Golden Eyes*

HOMOCULT PLOYS

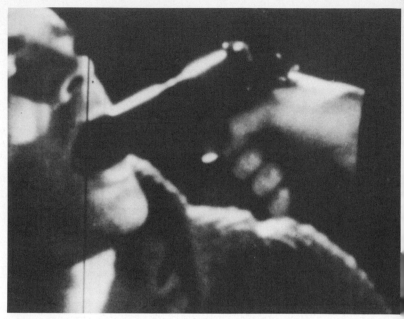

Flirting: the man's gun in his mouth   *Un Chant d'Amour*

Flirting: the man's gun at his mouth   *The Detective*

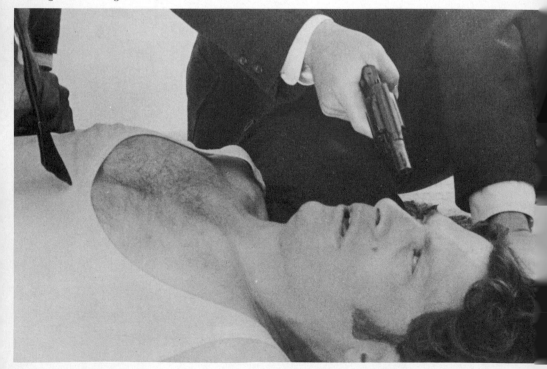

irly-girly chorus   *The Boys in the Band*

Satanic camp   *The Boys in the Band*

ofessional kiss   *The Boys in the Band*

A peek from the closet   *The Boys in the Band*

nsy camp   *The Boys in the Band*

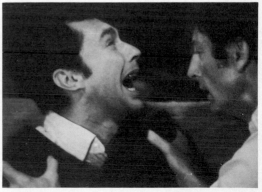

Hysteria (no camp)   *The Boys in the Band*

GAY UNDERWEAR

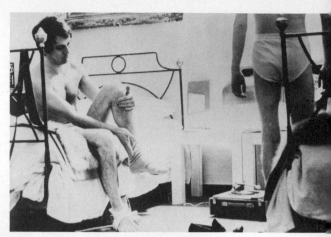

Even Homeros wears it
on earth   *Teorema*

ABOVE LEFT: Unmasked as a Nervous Nellie
On the Double
ABOVE RIGHT: Loser at all-male poker
Horse
RIGHT: Lesbians lacy and enlaced
Flesh

HOMOPHILIA IN THE HAY

Innocent (?) chums
Shoe Shine

Chums decidedly un-innocent
This Special Friendship

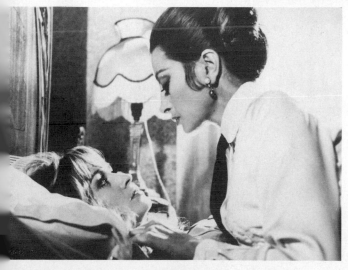

Literally lesbian, figuratively hay
The Betrayal

THE ALL-MALE ORGY

Dwarf acrobats with transvestite boy: interrupted early on   *The Silence*

Nazi SAs with transvestite partners: interrupted later on   *The Damned*

ABOVE: Fallen: White Cegeste *Orpheus*
LEFT: Fallen: Black Homeros
The Blood of a Poet

Unfallen:
Solicited in Sodom
Lot in Sodom

LITTLE HOMEROS CASTS HIS SPELL

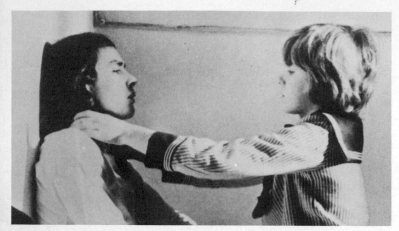

Love look: between boy and chauffeur   *The Conformist*

Love look: from big boy to little boy   *This Special Friendship*

Love look: from youth to boy   *Rebel Without a Cause*

THE INTERMALE KISS

Nominally hetero   *The Brotherhood*

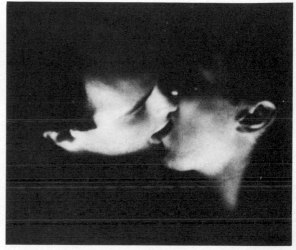

Avidly homo   *The Iliac Passion*

ominally homo   *The Boys in the Band*

Superavidly homo   *Johnny Minotaur*

THE INTERMALE EMBRACE

Sometimes it begins at this age   *Death in Venice*

Then one wants to shoot the other.   Then both want to shoot each other.
And does.   *The Brotherhood*   And don't.   *Flesh and the Devil*

HIS/HER OLD AGE

RIGHT: The bride is also male
Fellini Satyricon
BELOW: The husband is also female
The Killing of Sister George

...e mistress is also master   *Fellini Satyricon*

HOMEROS AMONG
THE BEAUTIFUL PEOPLE

Mother, son, son's admirer   *Death in Venice*

Dorian's painter, Dorian Gray, Dorian's admirer
The Picture of Dorian Gray

FROM HOMOPHILE CHARADE
TO HOMOPHILE REALITY

Algy and Ernest pretending not to be   *The Importance of Being Earnest*

Oscar Wilde and Alfred Douglas not pretending not to be
The Life of Oscar Wilde

KINKY TRIANGLES IN HOMOPHILIA

Gunsel, master/mistress, very private eye   *The Maltese Falcon*

Prison roomie, sex paw, prison roomie   *The Great Escape*

KINKIER TRIANGLES IN HOMOPHILIA

Kissed, would-be-kissed, kisser
A View from the Bridge

Real guy, real guy, real guy
(missing another r.g.) *Husbands*

Quasi-homo,
neo-Nietzschean,
quasi-homo
Rope

KINKIEST TRIANGLES IN HOMOPHILIA

1 + 1 + 1 = unisex
Performance

Fickle dummy,
betrayed ventriloquist
lucky ventriloquist
= tragedy
Dead of Night

Cockette,
male friend,
Jackie =
Women's Lib
Blonde on a Bum Tri

THE HOMOSEXUAL AS A DOUBLE

Mirror image: the hustler hustled   *My Hustler*

Two-sex-powered Dionysius   *Dionysius*

BELOW: Mirror image: male and female
Some Like It Hot

Mirror image: master and man   *The Servant*

PROFESSIONAL SISSIES AND PROFESSIONAL TOMBOYS

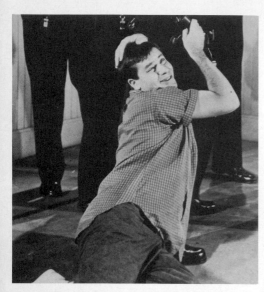

Not a delinquent but oh, so delicate
The Delicate Delinquent

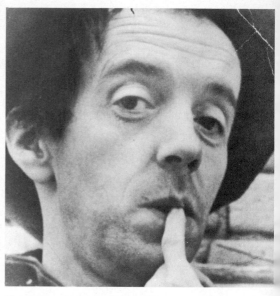

Not a thumb- but a pinkie-sucker
The Flower Thief

Not exactly but Franklin Pangborn
Where Did You Get That Girl

MORE PROFESSIONAL SISSIES AND PROFESSIONAL TOMBOYS

Not a dame but Tiny Tim

Not your mother but
George Sanders in drag

Not a WAC but a male war bride
I Was a Male War Bride

Not a drag queen but Bea Lillie

Not a dyke but Hepburn with
haircut   *Sylvia Scarlett*

THE HOMOSEXUAL IN SHOCK

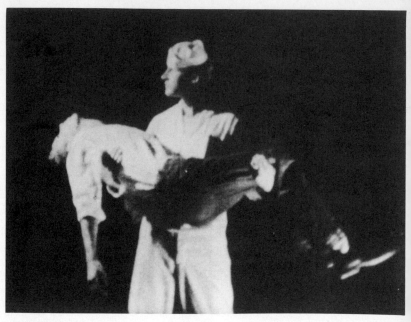

Not a Pietà but a beaten-up homophile   *Fireworks*

Not a Conversion of St. Paul but a stunned army major
on the road to homophilia   *Reflections in a Golden Eye*

EMBLEMS OF THE ALL-MALE DREAM

Exhibit A: On the edge   *Blonde on a Bum Trip*

Exhibit B: On the edge   *The Iliac Passion*

LONG LIVE THE KING/QUEEN !

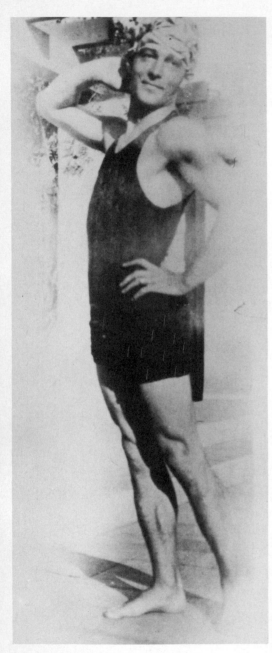

Rudolph Valentino

Ramon Novarro

hage, when, in close-ups of unambiguous literalness, one hippie-type male is shown sucking off another. Actually, while it does look real, the film is neither very interesting formally nor very exciting in action. There is no attempt at rhythmic progression, no mounting excitement, and, unless my memory disserves me, no pronounced sign of orgasm. Nothing, but nothing, looks really real in the male beavers; that sort of reality, except in the rarest cases, is never put to the kinaesthetic test. I remember an agonizingly prolonged session on screen between two fairly presentable young males, their genitals showing throughout as limp as empty jockstraps. Supposedly taken with each other and ready for bed action, they begin pawing each other all over a couch, though not all over each other's bodies. They were, so to speak, necking; that is, massaging all parts of the anatomy but the right ones. I can't even remember what, if anything, happened; surely, nothing of consequence. It was a sort of chummy, let-me-show-you-the-right-hold session, to the accompaniment of muffled vocal endearments such as, "Oh, do I go for you! . . . Do you send me! . . . Are you my groove!" Alas, you weren't. At least, not up to the point when I decided I'd had enough.

As to simulated orgasm, the male beavers—unless I am sadly behind in this moviegoing region—are stupidly backward. Already commercial movies of the new vintage have utilized it, especially in the female throat. The male beaver failure is due mostly, perhaps, to the dearth of acting talent in the performers. Whether man or woman, homo or hetero, getting oneself worked up for an act of simulated sex may well involve, no less than sheer skill in acting, fairly real stimulation, both psychic and physical; especially so when one considers that sexual encounters, like other points of the plot, must be as carefully rehearsed as other parts—and if they're not, they should be. At times, a lapse of professionalism in this respect is as gaping as an open fly, and one more reason for absenting oneself, in despair, from the theater.

Just as a sense of professional duty has kept me in the theater through many a commercial paralyzer, it has prevented my neglect of the beavers, male, female, and undiscriminating.

After all, how otherwise can one learn about the media? It is a pleasure to return to a subject I mentioned above but dropped culpably, I confess, in the interests of thorough documentation. I refer to the young man with the magnificent genital proportions. With highly charged camp irony (which induced extraordinary but not massive laughter), his phallic eligibility was just what, as if it were a Greek fate, proved his undoing, so that he becomes—surprise!—an unwanted monster of the bedroom. First he's shown cruising on the street, where he picks up a girl. Inside, they promptly undress. . . . The style of performing in male beaver films, by the way, reminds me of the flat, remarkably generic vices of the supposedly real housewives who obligingly bark for detergents on television, and seem to have a physical fixation on washing machines and their contents: they're like displaced voyeurs. Similarly, the performers in male beavers are like displaced persons who ought to be in rut, but instead are barking in pantomime for something that isn't there. Male beavers often have the air of being inept, discouraging trailers for next week's feature.

To get back to our superequipped male and his understandable tragedy; they undress: she more quickly, he with tactical restraint. She gets a gander at his organ—instant panic, hasty dressing, gasped excuses; she exits. Now, one fairly sees the insides of the poor fellow's mind working. Of course, there's an *alternative*. He too dresses and sallies forth on his former quest, only this time he picks up a member of the hardier species. For some mysterious reason, the small talk of cruising tactics between males is given a long, long rope which threatens to hang this well-hung film for good. It's what passes traditionally, I suppose, for upping the suspense: will this male react like the preceding female? Well, again with Greekish fatality, he does react like her, following the suspense ritual of both men undressing; the super-equipped number has managed it this time as if it were a naughty deed which he has to confess. In all sobriety, this beaver duly illustrates an aspect of the sexual canon to be called the Penis as Deadly Weapon.

In a way, to be sure, the form of the thing is a joke. Yet such a tragic reversal of pornographic pleasure has to it an excruciatingly real, insidious irony. Suppose *you* were faced with a dilemma like the pickups in this film? I am presuming, but try to put yourself in their place. One usually does that automatically if addicted to theatrical spectacles. Refusal to thus identify creates a special tension. For example, I discern a precious sort of pantomimic propriety, an inevitable grace, in the way that male and female are spontaneously repulsed by the sight of this prodigiously unavailable genital, as if it were made of stone or wood—a sublimated dildo—intended only as an object of devilish religious worship. Part of the irony too is that while shown clearly and for a considerable time in closeup—it reaches almost to the knees—it remains semierect and never, at its biggest, gets to be more than semihard.

After the retirement from the field of his second prospective partner, the desolate fellow, doom in his not very pretty face, casts himself on his cot and starts—the power of surprise again!—to try to penetrate himself with himself. The sight, I can assure strangers to this sort of thing, is at once infinitely dreary and infinitely pathetic. It's not metabeaver, it's metacamp. One is stunned; one's responses are frozen. Still, if the intelligence surely tells us that we are beholding a foolish charade, the sight does possess an inner lining of reality which is just sanity itself. The fear and rejection of the young man's prospective partners are overwhelmingly natural because so deadsure natural. The situation is the result of common sense, and common sense is of no help whatever to the strategies of emotional drama.

For several minutes, I think, one sees the fellow writhing about trying to make ends meet. They don't. We sense they never will. Success wouldn't be consistent with the tragic style written on the sufferer's face. The most that a sympathetic witness can furnish, therefore, is the thought that at least the fellow *deserves* to succeed. Fate, we know, orders these things otherwise. Remember, always, the hidden sacred guilt. It may not be too terribly proud to visit the humble beaver in all its porno shabbiness. Watching our hero trying to guide his semierect organ into the desired orifice—so it seemed to me, I confess, toward the end—had the effect of watching self-blinded Oedipus groping about the stage.

There are far too few such aesthetically stimulating

moments in the depressive religious atmosphere of the beaver houses. I speak, I admit, not as a devout voyeur who sees every new show. Of gay sex material, however, one expects some gaiety. Like token enthusiasm, gaiety erupts in these films as if it were undericed champagne opened in a call house: it's presumed to whet the appetite for the meal to come. Yet every beaverite knows that the true meal must be found elsewhere; that *that* is never part of the voyeur's bargain. The liveliest sex numbers on beaver screens are apt to be the mad queens, the semiprofessional transvestites, who have directed and produced as beavers their own nightclub and party routines. And yet for the real connoisseur these provide some of the most anti-climactic and unrewarding experiences in the beaver house. Preferable, by a wide margin, is some straight-sided gangling boy, with just the orthodox faint tinge of girlishness to make him seem sportive and accommodating. He is the neo-hustler, magnetic just because he doesn't yet seem initiated into the real professional game. The saturative convention of beavers— sometimes even in their transvestite form—is eventual undress and the stark ritual exposure of the genitals, however fleetingly. A lot of the gaiety items are set in the key of picnic-going or kittenish male play in shower rooms of the sort that suddenly gets ready instead of rough, and cannot remotely be suspected of innocence. I saw one shriekingly tame beaver staged in a swimming pool, when the now-you-see-it nakedness of teen-age males looked like premeditated if polite mayhem inflicted on a standard TV commercial.

Such are the fringe benefits of the screen's homosexual license, which, according to its current proliferation, already has the stature of a major craze. Now and again, an effort in the direction of a cult film appears that has the yearning heart of a passionate amateur rather than the gaping purse of an obsessed money-maker—the heart and will of someone devoted to prick-worship and the hermetic myth of an all-male fantasy world. *Pink Narcissus* is rather like *Flaming Creatures* but with the female's presence taboo'd and exiled. *Where* it was created, or by *whom,* remains a secret: it was conceived, written, directed and produced by Anonymous (say the credits) who may be, according to rumor, a VIP. Showing *en passant* technical facets of amazing canniness (it was "blown up" from 8 MM), the film creates off-color colors and a general fantasy style that seem to be the muse of lyric verse gotten up in drag; except that, with all the palpable campiness, the dignity of the teen-age male beauty who is the theme-hero, the tenderness with which his entranced postures are photographed, come through at moments as untarnished poetry. Yet, despite touches of taste, the film as a whole is almost self-consciously ridiculous, outdoing any other homo parlor charade for opulence of effect within narrow spaces and gaudy allure for the optical palate.

There are almost as many spangles, feathers, lights and bizarre, gilded costumes (ambiguously male/female) in *Pink Narcissus* as in an old-fashioned Ziegfeld Follies or Folies Bergère number. Frontal nudity is glimpsable enough to make the film a true beaver, but more than that, the nudity is sometimes both insinuative and imaginative. One dazzling instance is when the very comely young hero, whose fantasies are supposed to be mirrored by the film, approaches an ordinary public urinal, only to find himself next to someone who violently stimulates his imagination. In a magic twinkle (of which only a movie is capable) he is suddenly seen in full bullfighter's regalia with the skintight pants a bit more than skintight; he then starts making some cape passes with a "charging bull" in the person of a Leather Boy riding a motorcycle, the background, meanwhile, remaining the set of urinals. Finally the "combatants"—more realistically dressed, or rather, undressed —get down to some convincing men's room business with each other. I don't wish to flatter what is mainly only ultrarich faggot fudge, ludicrously embarrassing, but the truth is that the erotic effects and the camera work occasionally, aided by music, become the vehicles of genuine plastic imagination and true poetic mood. Lapses of taste and taste, alike, make *Pink Narcissus* a major cult film, and thus a film detached from the mere beaver category.

Aided by superstarmania from the Underground and pressure from the booming porno market, the larger gesture in beavers was inevitable. Hence not every male beaver looks like a home movie cruising brazenly across the screen or someone acting out another penis charade. Two standard efforts have established measures for the art-house beaver in different directions, one toward Warhol-school scale and ambitions, the other toward the commercial Western as imitated and parodied by homo pulp fiction. There are hundreds of all-male novels on the market, most not of the slightest importance as literature and of very little talent as pornography. However, a remarkably eloquent and well-crafted myth of homosexual pornography has appeared in recent years. It is a series of related novels by Richard Amory, led off by one titled *Song of the Loon*. This is hardcore pornography not because it's so dirty (it isn't dirty at all, just literal, canny, and sexy) but because it is a radically carnal formulation of classic male homosexuality.

A best-seller, *Song of the Loon* inevitably had sequels as well as a parody (*Fruit of the Loon*: a play on the trademark of men's and women's underwear). By classic male homosexuality, I mean the combined cosmetics, aesthetics, and ethics of homosexuality that stems from the pagan past of Greece at the height of the gymnasium cult. This aristocratic cult looked upon effeminacy and prostitution as vices. Neither of those vices is in *Song of the Loon,* which bears to the mod hustler novels the relation that *Little Women* bears to *Moll Flanders.* A great athlete of the gymnasium typically had male lovers. But not only would both naturally have total aristocratic style; there prevailed, moreover, in the particular area of physique, a proud standard of beauty from head to toe. The ancient gymnasium was a true temple of culture. Poetry contests were part of the Parthian games and, in the time of Socrates and Plato, philosophy imbued the male cult at Athens with the loftiness of what our time knows as the Classical Tradition.

In the Rome of Petronius as filmed by Fellini, we see the gymnasium in the vestiges of its cosmetic flower, its high aesthetic and moral decadence, as when the mature warrior, Lichas, goes drag-queen as bride of the handsome young colt, Encolpius. Again I stop to wonder if Fellini as a young man—say, one of the *vitelloni*—did not have a fetish for drag queens, and if, in the *Satyricon,* he may not be reconstructing the mythical background of such fetishism as, in other movies, he has reconstructed other of his sexual fantasies on a similar scale. *Song of the Loon* is also the fantasizing of fetishism.

What is startling about *Song of the Loon* as homo pulp fiction is the austere intelligence—but really!—situated back of its stark erotic action. In surprisingly tasteful utilitarian prose, the author manages to invent scene after scene of all-out homosexual encounters between rustic white males, or such a male and an American Indian male. All the characters are described as if taken bodily from the squarest, most he-man Western epics now gracing our film archives. Everybody is a real guy—most are also "good"—but, besides, everybody of any consequence is a clannishly committed homosexual whose prime occupation, rather than herding cattle, trapping animals, or mining gold, is cruising men, prospecting cock, and digging ass. If some neophyte has the idea that anything else is worthwhile, thorough and effective measures are taken to disabuse him of such tommyrot. All this is the more extraordinary in that the basic charade (we cannot suppose the existence of any such saturative cult in the Old West) assumes, through narrative and psychological tour de force, the stature of a myth.

You probably think I exaggerate. Well, go find a copy of the book and its sequels—don't bother with the parody, which is redundant and spoils the straight high camp of the originals. In terming *Song of the Loon* high camp, I don't mean to swerve from the point that it not only represents a surviving sensibility cult (its modern social form is sublimative YMCA homosexuality) but also harks back to Athenian aristocracy as well as to those primitive all-male rituals that involved homosexual relations as part of initiation into manhood. Outside ritual forms, American Indians seem generally to have regarded homosexuality as only an imitation of the heterosexual man-and-wife pattern, with the passive partner dressing as a woman, the active one retaining a normal male aspect. The homosexual Indian modishly, if gratuitously, introduced into *Little Big Man* certainly reflects a historical custom, but since, under his costume, he's much too recognizable as a genial, relaxed habitué of contemporary gay bars—at least, that's the way he plays it—

he represents just another bit of that curious movie's historical camping. The basic offbeat sexual structure is archetypal of the human race. Such relations can exist today actually as well as in culturally abstract terms.

We can discern signs of the latter in the transvestite stunts put on in commercial movie plots by presumably heterosexual males. Available from the archives is the classic female impersonator such as Julian Eltinge, duly garnered from the stage by Hollywood in the teens of the century, and the perennial male star—Cary Grant, Anthony Perkins, Jack Lemmon—who gets into drag as part of heterosexual camp plots. *Charley's Aunt* itself is a heterosexual camp affair, and its continued revival on stage and screen makes it the full-dress canon of the submerged homosexual joke invented (theoretically) for and by heterosexuals. Don't forget that a woman is always the express sex object of the transvestite male in these plots; that, in fact, she is the root mechanism that induces female impersonation in her lover. An arch example is *Some Like It Hot*.

Today, of course, a much wider, more realistic cultural outlook has possessed the realm of deviate sexuality in films. Hence we brush against the nuance sexes such as the confirmed heterosexual-male transvestite. But in *Song of the Loon* there are no nuance sexes, no drag at all. Its erotic myth corresponds to a type situation in modern urbanized homosexuality among the maritally inclined: two technically he-man bachelors live a reasonably permanent married life (that is, reproduce the man-and-wife pattern of domesticity) without either one looking or acting or dressing like a woman—unless, as nowadays, in the unisex mode that heteros too have adopted.

The quasi-beaverish quality that befell *Song of the Loon* when brought to the screen was part mere timidity (though that is the least understandable factor), part amateurish ineptitude, and part the simple failure to appreciate the book's *masculine* homosexuality as the indispensable thing. In this respect the novel is pure, unambiguous, the film is tainted, ambiguous. One reflects that the particular megalomania which is native to all phases of film production provides a fatal trap for anyone lacking the true artistic instinct, and this comes to about ninety-five percent of filmmakers in all economic classes, all cultural grooves. In an interview with the magazine *Gay*, Richard Amory has characterized the producers of porno flicks in a way that might explain a great deal: "They really believe sex is funny, especially gay sex. They've discovered it brings them in potfuls of money, so they traffic in it, but they really believe that two guys making it is hilarious."

That would account for the stupidity of the filmic transference. But, more empirically speaking, it may be that those responsible for casting *Song of the Loon* as a metabeaver suffered from attacks of sexual megalomania no less than hilarity and could not see that the men enacting the two leads, Cyrus and Ephraim, were far, far from being apt incarnations of the characters in the novel. Granted: one could hardly expect amateur or professional actors, required to look like Gregory Peck or Clint Eastwood, to consent to impersonate unrestrained scions of the Masculine Homosexual Cult. Doing so would ruin what is officially, sentimentally known as one's "public image." But even if the producers of *Song of the Loon* had to resort to what they could get in the way of male physique and acting talent, they seem to have been perversely blind to the traits of the men they finally cast. Maybe, as in the *M*A*S*H* syndrome, thinking of homosexuality as a "fairy joke" will not only stultify, but blind.

Nowadays, with the upsurge of independent film-making, a mere cozy conspiracy among some friends may precipitate a catastrophe which none of the interested parties will notice if the money starts coming in. Regarding *Song of the Loon*, the casting disaster may be due to the special megalomania of beaver psychology. This is that *anybody's* physical, especially genital, exposure is the first and last guarantee of success. What this assumption does not take into account is that, for the basic male beaver, genital exposure is, ideally, big-genital exposure, and that the paucity of this ideal commodity will lead to comparable paucity at the box office. At all events, as a critic, I must report what I regard as the facts about *Song of the Loon* as a movie.

Surely, it had a largish budget. In the middle of its

action occur some spectacular special-effects that are ornamentally aesthetic just where the novel is aesthetically realistic.
This is the big sex scene when the young male neophyte is first
seduced by the somewhat older cultist and the "great affair" of
the story is started. For the descriptive realism of the acts and
the organs involved, done in prose of high and appreciative
wattage, the film has substituted an artful use of negative color
photography (the whole is in color) and some carefully choreographed mattress acrobatics. Imagine finding "art photography"
in a beaver—I suppose it's the result of luxury psychology:
trying to float the metabeaver!

Speaking of choreography, Cyrus in the film can't even
look natural while running (a fact only emphasized by slow
motion in the hallucination sequence), and when walking, he
looks at times about to burst into tears because the pebbles
hurt his feet. Both men, standing still, are (or might have been)
eligible, to a degree, for beaver contemplation, but the harsh
truth of the camera eye has been merciless. The older Ephraim's
manly physique looks flabby, dissipated, and off athletic form,
while Cyrus, though tall, nordic, and statuesque, seems frozen
by stagefright and an overwhelming inexperience in getting on
and off a horse. One has the feeling that both, regardless of age,
are would-be professionals and effete city types. It is as if the
realities of the physique-model studios stood transparently behind the *Loon* fantasy of orthodox, leatherized Western heroes
mythically behaving as confirmed members of a homosexual
he-cult. The Indians, which in the original are part elegant
porno, part Chateaubriand-Arcadian, look ludicrously like bor-
rowings from early commercial Western films converted into
instant faggot-charade; they behave, in person, as if they had
been invented by the Longfellow of *Hiawatha,* then reinvented
by some dreamy schoolboy turning gay. The ritual sex orgy concluding the original trilogy is cleverly transposed *Golden Bough*
stuff: this is omitted from the film in favor of a scenic initiation rite administered to the romantically susceptible and
drugged Cyrus.

Now a word from our sponsor, the Muse of Penisology,
who, alas! having been cheated by this hifalutin prick· flick,

angrily withdraws his/her patronage. The exposed midbody endowments of the leads, far from being candidly cameraed, are casually seen from an objectionable distance, where even so, they look dispiritingly modest. Why this anomalous discretion? "Aesthetic"? It's just possible, in the complication of art megalomanias, that this discretion was "practical." To have cheated photographically (quite possible, of course, by framing-off and foreshortened close views) would have meant a direct appeal of "scale" thought unbecoming to romance. Thus my report on *Song of the Loon*—a metabeaver less lusty than luxury—must be far and away negative. As in the commercial brotherhood, all golden opportunities are muffed by a fatal rationale: makeshift convenience guiding unconscious stupidity; e.g., the blind leading the blind.

I'd hate to seem merciless. A critic's mercies must be limited and had better be reserved for the more virtuous exhibits. Homosexuality, still a militant minority in the public purview, does not invite—of all things!—mercy. The truth is that the trend in hand has utilized a commercial gambit to engage a spectator interest that couldn't be attracted with perfect honesty. We must also make room in the discussion for those symbolic veins which many big film directors insert into their works for fun's sake, and out of compensation, I would say, for having sold their souls for money. This is what I mean by what I oppose to the virtuous: the vicious; that which militates against *honest* truth. At the same time, dishonest truth may create some necessary strategies which are their own sources of amusement and interest. Any kind of real truth is a force unto itself and possesses its special strategies, for which film director and script writer may be only a pawn in the game.

A distinct case in point, leaning on ambiguities that may infuse the atmosphere of big movie-making, is that of *Strangers on a Train*, one of Alfred Hitchcock's formidable thrillers. The relationship between two young men encountering each other on a train, both nurturing murder plans, is highly suggestive simply because the desire of one (the true criminal) to victimize the other is, in another dimension, the displacement of a homosexual fixation. One has a wife he wants to be rid of so as to marry his mistress, the other an objectionable father. Why not, says the father-hater, commit each other's crimes? Then each, of course, would be free to provide himself with a perfect alibi. Both young men are good-looking; one is Robert Walker (senior), the other Farley Granger, an American Apollo serving the regular function of romantic movie lead.

It occurs to me that a legend gathers in the minds of homosexual spectators about certain actors. They are thought, truly or falsely, to incarnate (according to the legend "documented" in Norman Mailer's novel *The Deer Park*) those undercover homosexuals in Hollywood who have private legends of heterosexuality publicly manufactured for them to offset rumors about their true sexuality. It is not merely that Hitchcock could not remain ignorant of such an aspect of Hollywood fact and fancies. Did he, perchance, deliberately exploit the sexual aspect by casting the personable Granger in this particular role? And did he take private aesthetic pleasure in viewing his film as a sort of double charade? The original charade would be the one inhering in the story itself, in which, purely on a psychological basis, the charade can be read as the plot of one character's pathology. Since it looks like sex fixation disguised as crime compulsion, the homosexual fantasizer is not a member of the audience, he is *in the film*. Granger has the wife he wishes to be rid of, and so it falls to Walker to kill her, something he accomplishes with a sort of burning grimness. However, Granger cannot stomach his end of the chore, so that finally he himself becomes his would-be partner's second quarry. Meanwhile, he seems to become more and more aware of Walker's evil personality and perhaps his sex fixation too. One can imagine everyone professionally concerned savoring the beautiful camp of the charade's other face, informally taking the delight of dilettantes in another naughty sex lark, which most of the customers will take to be just another crime melodrama. At all events, we should recognize the persistence of the homosexual charade in big-time movies.

In origin, charades are a light, presumably impersonal sort of truth game. Many parlor games, such as the primordial Post Office, were a childish pretense to get the sexes together.

Yet, as for homosexuality, boys were not supposed to kiss *boys*. Since recently this puritan bourgeois convention has been annihilated in the theater, the camping generically true of parlor games has taken on an actively protean quality extending to homosexualism in the arts. Remember the mouth-to-mouth kiss given man by man in Arthur Miller's *A View from the Bridge* both as play and film? There it was meant as an accusation, and yet the plain assumption was that the accuser, not the accused, harbored the homosexual nature; so the kiss was a seriously meant camp charade. Camping, from straight to burlesque, is apt to be a homosexual maneuver, something that art would naturally reflect.

It is quite logical that homosexual oralism in the movies be counterpart to the beaver films' homosexual genitalism. That the entertainment industry is itself keenly aware of this point was clear as recently as 1970, when a Rowan and Martin *Laugh In,* in an October broadcast with Zero Mostel as guest star, did a skit where Mostel and others burlesqued that Mafia film melodrama *The Brotherhood.* Some New Yorkers may particularly recall the "kiss of death" in that film because, for a while, to advertise its approach, a huge billboard on Times Square displayed the heads of one man kissing another so closely that their physiogomies could not be identified. The men turned out to be Kirk Douglas as an elder brother of the Mafia and Alex Cord as a younger. The decision of the governing committee ordains that Cord dispatch his big brother; the Douglas character, well aware of the order, gives his little brother, just before he's plugged, a deep farewell kiss in the more intimate manner of Italian males.

In the *Laugh In* burlesque, Zero Mostel is seen as the father of the two brothers, while the younger is shown as a pistol-toting gangster and the elder as the family homosexual, gotten up "hilariously" as a ballerina, tutu and all. Because of the skit's climax, there's no mistaking the precise reference to *The Brotherhood.* The ballerina, while camp-faggot in manner, is very male in physique and stature. When the gun-toter leaves the room to perform his stint, Mostel and his wife lament as they wait for the gunshot by which one son will destroy the other. Mostel tries to soothe the poor mother. "It won't be like losing a son," he says. "It'll be like losing a daughter." The shot still fails to come. The mother can't bear the suspense, so Mostel walks to the door, opens it, and looks into the next room where the deed is to take place. An instant of charged suspense. His head turns and he says to his wife: "They're still *kissing!*" Quite an imposing superstructure for what did *not* start as Post Office.

To the non-Latin races, it is easier, more natural and "innocent" for *women* to kiss each other. Physical affection is supposed to come more normally to the softer sex, with the result that a mere surface appearance of lesbianism, trifling or ambiguous, is more apt to get by in the movies than corresponding gestures between men. Yet license in offbeat sexual expression has been so much more deliberate in late years that accentuated oralism between women is a pretty sure index to lesbianism. In *The Balcony* (a badly done version of Genet's play), one good kiss is enough to reveal the lesbian relation between the madam of the whorehouse and her female assistant (Shelley Winters and Lee Grant). Still, in Hollywood, innuendo is much preferred for the big-scale flick intended for family consumption. And even innuendo cannot go *too* far.

It might seem to both readers of the novel and viewers of the film *The Haunting,* with Julie Harris and Claire Bloom playing the female leads, that lesbianism had a role in drawing these unusual ladies closer in the frightening, macabre situation to which they commit themselves and where they must "cling" to each other. Their physical contact was evidently regarded as a problem. At one point Miss Bloom is supposed to paint Miss Harris' toenails. That seemed altogether too insinuating in our highly sex-conscious times. So Miss Harris had to paint her own toenails. Paradoxically, Hollywood psychology has it that intermasculine affection (the buddy-buddy thing) is more acceptably "innocent" than corresponding intimacy between women. This must be because "out there" women are considered to be more naturally "carnal." The issue got down to a case in *Secret Ceremony,* where a girl's daughterly fixation on an older woman displays a sort of Electra complex turned inside out. Already, in the space between *The Haunting* and *Secret Ceremony,* there seems to have been an advance in permissiveness.

Much of all this may be due to a special male chauvinism: more indulgence must be allowed the female, who, as the frailer vessel, is both more easily and more innocently drawn into "temptation." So goes the social legend. Nakedly speaking, males are just as vulnerable as females. Yet transvestism offers itself as just another device for concealing this vulnerability better, more deliberately, than women do. Part of the social legend of female impersonation is that it is only an "affectation," an arbitrary imitation of "feminine softness." But suppose the process is not an affectation but a confession? Suppose it is a matter of turning the "in" side "out"?

All masquerades have this paradoxical quality of making dress up look like a display of nudity. The hidden homosexualism of the standard cowboy film has long been mined to reach an audience that goes in for the moral metabeaver: the naked look for homos masquerading as heteros. Aesthetically it involves all male homosexuals who attend movies and titillates the imagination of a certain type of female voyeur. That the subtle substructure of homosexual charades in Westerns is not the hallucination of homosexuals who arbitrarily twist the facts of the plot, but rather something inherent in the plot's basic material, is proved not only by *Song of the Loon* but by a film more sophisticated than that, perhaps too consciously sophisticated, but at any rate deliberately and methodically campy: *Lonesome Cowboys* (1969). To be sure, that was an Underground affair with an Underground budget. A big grab for the big trade came as recently as early 1971 in *Zachariah,* a straight-camp charade using Wild West locales and borrowing clichés from versions of the West seen on the ballet and musical-comedy stages. Yet the two male leads (very pretty and very young) pretend with fabulous schoolboy seriousness that they were born, even as John Wayne and Robert Mitchum, to play traditional Western heroes. Publicity termed the film the "First Electric Western" because of the rock groups visibly providing its music. It should have been heralded as the First

Hallucinogenic Western. It has the new marijuana style: "reality" is simply the brand of hallucination you prefer.

A historic precedent, Howard Hughes's *The Outlaw* (1946), indicated that a conscious conspiracy was afoot in the industry to camp up the sex angle with subrosa attraction between cowboy heroes. Jane Russell of the famed mammary equipment played the female sex bait; a stallion symbolized the male sex bait. When the junior and senior outlaws find themselves with conflicting proprietorship over lady as well as stallion, a flip of the coin allows Junior to choose the stallion so that reluctantly he must assent to the inevitable gun duel with Senior. It's all Oedipal, Wild West, and closet queen at once. Junior wins and parades off with stallion under him and girl behind him. *Zachariah* brings that up to date. The female sex bait is a sadly sick parody of Mae West, and the two cowboys, after a suitable embroilment, forget her, embrace, and ride off happily together.

The other film, the Warhol/Morrissey *Lonesome Cowboys,* while ostensibly, as a confiding piece of Underground naïveté, to be considered a now-now-now exhibit, derives logically from the emergence of the gay-cowboy charade as codified by my analysis of *The Outlaw.* The youths in *Lonesome Cowboys,* mostly good-looking, unisexed, hippie-haired, and drawn from the Underground social set headquartered in Greenwich Village, simply get into midnight-cowboy outfits, and on an old Western movie set (now serving as a museum piece) act out a sort of homo psychodrama with a plot impertinently borrowed (as Paul Morrissey openly admitted) from *Romeo and Juliet.*

All pretense at plot, scarce enough, is intentionally absurd and irrelevant; to wreck all form is part of the Underground's official camp strategy. The purpose of *Lonesome Cowboys* is as much to show off nice-looking hustler types, aesthetic style, as to create an antihero, antiform film in the sacred, if unspoken, name of camp. The actor Taylor Mead, a sacred fetish after a decade of gay roles in Underground films, is given the Shakespearean role of the Nurse, which he unaffectedly and ad-libbingly treats as pure faggot-charade. The pre-Raphaelite cowboys with whom he camps around here, rather lazily and pointlessly, are much more interesting than Mead. They can be identified as new-style psychodramatists doing their thing for the benefit of the Warhol anticulture machine.

They swagger, they loll, they quarrel and maul each other like schoolboys in dorm. They even go through the preliminary motions of raping Juliet, played by Viva in a formal riding habit; in brief, the boys play at some butch camping. The whole charade has a homosexual perfume as familiar as Chanel No. 5, and about as artificial too, for none of the cowboys commits himself to more than tentative homosexuality. The transparency of charade, the isolated sublime note of camp, is the essence of Warhol's showmanship. The cachet is for amateurism to arrogate superiority over professionalism by giving away the show of the homosexual charade as seen in commercial Westerns.

Oddly, when it comes to sexploitational nudity, it is a go between one of the manlier cowboys and Viva, who informally enact the sex part of the love-death tragedy right under one's nose, and then, instead of carrying out the death part, allude to it as if it were the myth of the Pill or the exotic custom of taking a douche. The whole action has been a sequence of more or less ad-libbed charade passages vaguely related to the Shakespearean plot; homosexuality has gotten only as far as pummeling, the inexplicable appearance of the sheriff in drag, and some strangely touching verbal flirtation between cowboys. *Who* said anybody here was a faggot? It's only Juliet who accuses them in the film itself. Viva in this part corresponds to any woman who might mistake a man's long hair, good looks, and narcissism for homosexuality; she could also mistake it for heterosexuality.

As a male beaver, the film *Sticks and Stones* does not belong to the coded charade group of sexational films, which bridge to the commercial stuff because they consciously *parody* it. So when I say that *Sticks and Stones,* an upper-class beaver of feature length, is more virtuous and virtuoso than *Song of the Loon* (on all counts but fancy photography), I mean that it has cannier, honester ways of modulating its beaver status toward metabeaver. While there is a little routine exposure,

Sticks and Stones isn't technically a prick flick. It's what might be called the gay scene in terms of homosexual society at the Fire Island level of gracious promiscuity. In *Loon,* the bald promiscuity of sex is qualified by orthodox romantic love and mythic ritual: likewise with the bald promiscuity of sex in *Sticks,* except that an infusion of antique ritual is missing. In *Sticks* the ritual form, being indigenous to Fire Island, is naturalistic.

For the reader's benefit, it should be remarked that Cherry Grove, the homosexual center of Fire Island, is a community almost unique in its liberated aspects. It has good policing, good safety standards (what is a couple of murders in decades?), and little persecution from hoodlums or the law. When hoodlumism has made brief incursions, it has been nipped in the bud by the police. From way back, there are resident heterosexual property owners who have welded, in the purely civic sense, with the liberal bourgeois homosexual ideals now for long ascendant there. As to indecorous orgies, there are few not confined to quarters, thus few creating even minor scandals. Once or twice a year there are therapeutic police raids on that stretch of the beach known as the Meat Rack, when, as it were, sheer human excess, going on there nightly during "the season," must be reminded of a certain classic dictum, perhaps as true now as it ever was, *Nothing too much.*

The fragile action of *Sticks and Stones* (the title seems to be a neat pun on the male genitals) is padded out with atmospheric humanity, natural scenery, and overlong takes breeding monotony. The surrounding human elements are characteristic (a gay hippie yogi, for example, young and beardless) but lack the class of the two leads, who, while undistinguished as actors, are comely and fairly convincing; one is tallish, slender, with a stylish pigtail, the other very attractively built and pretty of face: a sort of Madison Avenue groove kid on summer vacation. Theirs is an established affair (a cottage is the love bower), but the tall one grows bored and party-prone while the other gets jealous and mopy. Obvious dénouement: a quarrel and lovemaking desperately forced on the philanderer by the faithful one when at last the gay merrymakers (and their quaint heterosexual companions) have gone home. END HERE. . . after some very perspiry calisthenics on the living-room floor. The sectarian irony of *Sticks and Stones* is that a few bones of vestigial romanticism can be broken at the heart of the gay world, as elsewhere. Rather small beans from the large artistic view. Yet *Sticks'* sincerity and authenticity, though quite without genius, are merits that linger in the mind. The neurotic infighting of rank-and-file homosexuals is well caught, and the total feeling of dialogue and action is untrashy. On the beaver scale, *Sticks and Stones* has somewhat the quality of a modest Hollywood sleeper, unimportant but worth seeing once, and perhaps twice.

When dealing with the beauty aspect of beaver films, one is tempted to slip in the word "cosmetics" for "aesthetics," that is, if one wants to keep the category strict by assuming their only real objective is exposure of the sex organ, male or female (or anyway the latter's furry sheath). Are the cosmetics to be questioned? Well, there's something called "grooming." Besides, there are beauty contests for organs as for muscles. Prejudice to one side, it makes perfect sense. Of course, it is odd that shop windows displaying the covers of sex magazines and nude photographs reveal black or white patches affixed to exactly the same private parts whose clearly photographed images may be purchased inside. Of course this is legally required hoodwinking. The theory must be that the underaged, especially small children, would be corrupted by sudden confrontation with said organic facsimiles. It's odder still when one considers that sexual organs in the flesh, live, and on adults, must confront thousands of small children every day without causing harm to their morals or psychic shock—*everyone* gets used to the sight sooner or later. Again, maybe the subtle power of the *image* makes sight more traumatic than the subtle power of the *flesh*. All of this, naturally, would not be an issue were our society not paranoid on the subject of sexual license and promiscuity.

Speaking for male homosexuals, one gathers from the beavers that the male nymphet (or faunet might be better), with promising muscularity of all kinds, ranks highest in favor. Now, this may be wrongly to assume the special working of cosmetic preference in the regular beaver patron. It is a rather moot matter. If this patron be of the wolf type, then the gazelle or traditionally *mignon,* slight but muscleless, specimen may suit his fancy best. Let us call this type the Gangling Boy. One shouldn't lose sight of the fact that things like *Song of the Loon* and *Sticks and Stones* are not so much metabeavers as attempts (succeed or fail) to liberate beaver psychology into the aesthetics of legitimate art. Likewise with *Pink Narcissus.*

Elementarily defined, the beaver house is a parlor not for displaying an Apollo-concept for males but for creating an existential atmosphere of homelike reality, whose focus of on-screen interest is the image of a miraculously available, sexually consenting male. This focus is alike true of the female category of beaver. Maybe I have been a bit remiss in ferreting out all-female beavers with an outright lesbian stamp. On the other hand, beaver films where naked women kiss and make preliminary sex play with each other is a typical extension of interest for heterosexual male audiences.

The hardcore pornography of the stag film—classic antecedent of blue movies, nudies, and sexploitationals—is essential to note because it constitutes the sheer animal authority for including all "degrading" sexual acts, some of which are irrumation and sodomy between males as well as males and females. True, the general uses of stag films (obvious from the epithet itself) make homosexuality in either genital sex a rarer spectacle. Stag films denote a category prior to all-male or all-female beavers, and prior to the titillations of the nudies and sexploitationals, which used to be more promise than performance; today, there are some lusty performances even if the goods are ersatz— take Russ Meyer's commercial films.

"Stag film" is now an antiquarian term, if only as indicated by the growth of new terms to label all sorts of contemporary films; inevitably, homosexual stag films became an item of the once-underground porno repertory. Wherever a stag film, however, showed a group orgy of males and females (depending on relative recency of date), it would have been not only logical but also literal for homosexuality to develop through sheer animal on-the-spot impetus; not an animal impetus, mind you, necessarily coming from the guts, but taking incidence from the psychic atmosphere of prostitution, from "professional enthusiasm." In effect, the line between amateur and professional enthusiasm in sex matters can easily be ambiguous. If the purse overflows, so can the heart, or vice versa; anyway, the guts register the propulsion without regard for its source. Isn't just this, in fact, naturally supposed to happen in the love piles being strenuously staged by contemporary theater? I can add that I knew a young man (an aspiring author who is now a respected figure) who was, at that distant time, in the habit of being kept by his women; there was pretty clear evidence that he could get a hard-on at the mere mention of money. Only guys, you see, are unable to fake the genital origin of the heart's esteem; gals, professional or not, can fake it if they want to.

For long, our age has been one of specialization (some claim overspecialization); now that it has become an age of aggressive minorities, all varieties of sexual taste have heroically created their specialized media for given audiences. Of course, women too might be expected to patronize all kinds of beaver films. But, as of this moment, their presence before such screens is inconspicuous. Maybe the current Women's Lib furore will change all that. At least, a statement of policy may be expected from Women's Lib leaders on the "beaver" aspect of the sexual question. One can imagine the Libs, like suffragettes, being altogether anti and setting out to completely erase the female's degrading exposure to the male from all film screens. Women's Lib, unfortunately, is confusingly related to Gay Lib. While the latter is ultrapermissive and naturally includes a lesbian contingent, Women's Lib has an antisexual, that is, antimale, bias which would logically tend to limit "permissiveness" to the lesbian area. One wonders to what degree pure aggressiveness can be nurtured among radical-minded women without making their orthodox sexual front *homo* rather than *hetero*.

Cosmetics, of course, is one of the chief instruments for helping to distinguish females from males—as a young woman in a cosmetic commercial pointedly announces: "I *like* being a woman." Hence devices for emphasizing sexual differentiation (theoretically promoting heterosexual interests) would not be in the Women's Lib line. Altogether, in the fem-lib sense, sex is a crucial subject of interest only as it represents the neutral construct of an equity that has erased the pivotal nature of heterosexuality as *sex;* that is, it tends to make sex abstract. Somehow Women's Lib has a lesbian rationale without any carnal application, much as if they were nuns. When female feminists cry out against the moral image of woman allegedly held by men (e.g., that she is only a servant and a "sex object"), they seem to forget that regardless of all economic considerations (in or outside the domestic establishment), a man can be as much of a "sex object" to a woman as a woman can be to a man! And if he isn't, *why* isn't he? I think it's for women to answer why.

I know, of course, that a certain kind of woman develops a phallic fetishism equivalent (it might seem) to the same thing in male homosexuals, while plausibly such women might be less willing, even nowadays, to have it known or seem to exploit it (for instance, by buying tickets to all-male beavers). I remember how offended an otherwise enlightened woman was when, during conversation, I remarked with a smile (maybe I shouldn't have smiled), "Well, you know, there are female as well as male fairies." Still, from a great deal of evidence, one suspects that most heterosexual women, in terms of hardcore psychology, are more envious of the penis than attracted to it. Recently I was startled to hear, in the film *Five Easy Pieces,* a grown-up male address his grown-up sister "Penis Envy" as if he were giving her, good-naturedly, her old nickname. In effect, the epithet may have had a complexion more political than Freudian; that is, it may have been a symptom of sadistic male snobbery, all the more sinister in being playful.

Studying both the beauty and morals of beavers, one notices how easy it is to call them old-fashioned, both heterosexually and homosexually, because their focus of interest, no matter at what angle or level, remains on the sex organs as objects lovable precisely for *what they are*—and they are, as has been frequently noted, different from each other. Today's unisex tendency, making men and women dress and wear their hair alike, corresponds to integration in the racial domain. At one time, social integration of race, and assimilation through mixed marriages, was the radical thing, the up vogue. Now the radical thing, the up vogue, is segregation and even *black* apartheid. The problem clearly, in the unisex dimension, embraces the political sphere. The title of a recent book by a woman, *Sexual Politics,* unambiguously trumpets itself. What can the term possibly signify except the rivalry between the opposite genital sexes crystallized on the economic and political levels? Yet unisex stands as an icon of peace between the basic sexes, Women's Lib as an icon of war between them. For recent examples from the movies, take *Goldfinger, The Tenth Victim,* and an elaborate story from the TV series called *The Prisoner;* all, from the female side, represent antimale war cults.

Apart from the fates ordained for unisex cosmetics and unisex copulation, the moral ideal of Women's Lib would seem to be Woman as a Penisless Man. This may seem to be knocking offstride the proper pursuit of my present subject. For if there is one image absolutely foreign to male beavers, it's a penisless man, whether created by nature as a female or by surgery as a transsexual. Obviously it is impossible to avoid the transsexual here because it is one of the psychological motivations of male homosexuals and it *does* change their naked image. Fatally enough, that bivalved carnal pivot of sexuality—referred to by Freud as *la chose génitale*—will not yield up stage center in this chapter. Transsexualism, after all, may be the main psychological problem of homosexuals. In relation to the sex organ, the heart and even the libido are abstract superstructures to be defined by emotional patterns and moral acts, regardless of what sex organs are involved, which are addressed to which, and why or how. . . . In transsexual mythology, the penis is a ghost image. And ghosts *haunt.*

Morally, *Myra Breckinridge* and *The Christine Jorgensen Story* are respectively unsquare and square versions of this problematic aspect. How much authority—tacitly, how much right—does an individual have to decide which sex organ he or she shall wear? I say "wear" to allow for the strange case of the dildo, by which a female (and even, as we learn from Myra's case, a transsexual) may assume the limited function of a male and present a phallic image. It is to be noted that Myra's first phase (as analytically imagined by her author) is psychologically fem-lib. Far from joying in magically available heterosexual conquests, the brand-new Myra is out to triumph over the male as an opponent: hers is a delusion of female grandeur; exactly this, so far as the Women's Lib goes, establishes the satiric dimension. In Hollywood's dearly beloved way of simplifying, the movie *Myra* more clearly emphasizes the basic theme of Vidal's oddball version of the War between the Men and the Women than does the rather complicated farce version of the original novel. The accident which magically turns Myra back into some sort of male is made by the movie not to seem (as Vidal had it) some grotesque "natural" retribution, but the phantom Myron's concupiscent plot to get rid of his overt Myra-personality so he can marry Mary Ann (which he does in the novel and logically will do in the film). This might seem, correspondingly, a technical victory for the female, in that the mutual outcome of movie and novel reestablishes the heterosexual balance. But, first, it does so in doubtful form (what kind of an actual male can the restored Myron be?), and second, the dominant moral option belongs exclusively, throughout, to the *male*.

Vidal (here being at the antipodes from the George Jorgensen who became Christine Jorgensen) manipulated the course of transsexualism—"the operation"— to make a man's will to become a woman into a collapsible charade. Via the dildo concept, the penis, instead of being "sacred flesh," becomes a mechanical toy, an attachable-detachable armament. This was Vidal's basic comic idea and as such it is legitimate. In the most sophisticated sense, the form of expressing sexual desire is not fundamentally determined by differing and technically corresponding organs attached by nature (or by God, if you prefer) to the fronts of human beings. The form of sexual expression—the implementation of carnal desire—is a total election of the human individual; now, if a novelist, as in Vidal's case, chooses to make that incontrovertible election look convertible, as well as ridiculous, it is his gifted privilege. It affects the cultural status of the individual's choice; it does not change the factual existence of that choice.

Vidal's book is a sexo-social satire that has its crudities. Yet it has its fine points, too, if one cares to look closely at today's erotic delusions-of-grandeur as they exist in the social mass; a look, say, at the cosmetics industry, including clothes, whose avowed creation is now more than ever the Feminine Woman. *Myra Breckinridge* is a peculiarly violent reading of the human tautology of sexual cosmetics at its mass-myth level; it ought to be noted, I think, that prodigious muscles on a male are as much a cosmetic myth as nonmuscles and plus-eyelashes on a female, whose plusness must be fleshy but not muscular. Since the mass-myth level is one to which, prior to Vidal, I have given a great deal of attention, it is not surprising that Vidal should have been inspired to make me Myra's muse in his book. I know very well that this device (indicating a critic and his book by their true names) was a move in the modern game of one-upmanship. I may be pardoned, then, for observing that Vidal deliberately gives a false idea of my book's tone and intentions by quoting from it only such sentences as seem solemn and academic, a little absurdly so out of context, and that what he is really being so self-conscious about is the tacit debt to my example.

The movie *Myra* is the story of a double, like a divided hermaphrodite, an organically split sex personality—shades of Aristophanes' fable of the sex origins! In this light, Myron and Myra become the original, technically fundamentalist Adam and Eve, the pair of which the female is a rib taken from Adam and transmuted. A dildo, incidentally, is rather believable as a megalomaniac form of a rib. Anyway, Vidal's fem-lib joke of Myra as conquistador in the War Between the Men and the Women is a fake. The male psyche is what gains victory *in both novel and movie* even if under divided emotional drives, divided physical modes. The visual medium has the faculty of incarnating the old, male, original Myron; to put him in clear and complete organic dimensions in the way movies have always shown ghosts or spirits as living people. Technically, Myron is a "solid" hallucination, and after the operation (in the movie) converses, intrigues, and argues with Myra, finally turning on her and killing her. The novel had nothing of this last.

The movie was entirely the invention of script writers who remained loyal to sacred Hollywood conventions while obeying (in grisly enough scenes) Vidal's premise that a male could choose, through a surgical operation, to womanize himself and that the resultant organism (to all appearances an attractive, strong-willed female) should become a sort of demon avenging women on their oppressors (men) by scuttling a handsome young male (Rusty) at his most morally vulnerable point. That the anus *is* Rusty's most morally vulnerable point is not asserted in the movie, but in the novel, where (as I've mentioned in a previous chapter) he is reported by Myra to have become "a complete homosexual." Nobody but the excessively naïve could suppose this to signify homosexuality as a "defeat" or "disaster"; it is but another item of Myra's total megalomania.

It is a tribute to Roger Herren, who plays Rusty, and perhaps to the director, Michael Sarne, that Rusty's crushed demeanor after the rape (portrayed by the movie in the charade form of bronco-busting) actually conveys a tearfully *triste* gratitude. I can expand on my previous reference. Many males, anally raped by main force (Myra has strapped Rusty down), might well sob and vomit immediately afterward; they might develop an anal complex, or they might not. The rape and its consequences might be utterly suppressed in the interior being and remain only a vague, secret shame. But the great proportion of males would never look merely doe-eyed, sad, and submissive as does Rusty after this experience. He's like a whipped schoolboy, thoroughly quelled. The fact that the rape is a form of blackmail should make him more angry, not less so. Here the movie scores a point over the novel: Rusty's homosexuality is subtly predicted then and there. The novel's Rusty shows *only* the whipped schoolboy: "Then, tonelessly, he murmured, 'Thank you, ma'am,' and went." This is poker-faced camp. The movie's afterimage of Rusty is not only funny but touching. It actually resembles the dewy-eyed, secretly grateful humiliation of ravished maidens (I mean females) whose spontaneous grief and pain have produced a second, anticlimactic reflex: "Well, it's over at last [SOB] but now I know [GULP, HOORAY] what the possibilities are!"

In *The Christine Jorgensen Story,* the sexual "possibilities" turn out to be quite as improbable as the comicstrip "possibilities" (SIGH). The George Jorgensen of reality, a willowy male, is impersonated for the movie by a sturdy young man of masculinely pretty features and an administered dose of acting like a homosexual photographer: all graces and ideas about how a girl should act if she wants to look glamorous and sexy. From the film's curious behavior, one is to assume, however, that all this is a formula for George's straitjacketed puritanism (partly a family complex) so that he never allows sex itself the slightest expression. Clearly, his genitals seem to him only an inscrutable practical joke. When—seemingly a "first time"—George has a definite and strenuous pass made at him by a most eligible young homosexual, he repulses him like an female virgin jealous of her status in a pre-1950 Hollywood romance. After knocking out the fond attacker with an accidental kick in the groin, George rushes distraught into the night and almost throws himself into the bay at Southampton, a town, it would seem, more full of wassail and wickedness than one had supposed.

No, no, one could not have expected *The C. J. S.* to be a beaver, male or female. Yet optimistically one might have expected it to be a Grade A metabeaver with appropriately scientific undertones. Nothing of the kind. It is a Grade C Hollywood specimen so painfully unsensational as to emerge as the most uneventful science-fiction film of that, this, or any year. More positively it is the fashion fable of what a respectable transwoman would wear during the 1953–54 season. All this is oddly egregious because, far from experiencing joy at being released from her male prison, Christine is plunged into gloom at the irreverent attitude of the press, and uncheered by the serious attentions of an American newspaperman sent over to Denmark to "get her story."

Only a brief view of the new Mr. (now Miss) Jorgensen's expanding breasts makes the film even faintly reminiscent of the pornographic sixties and seventies. All the elements of the old 42nd Street nudie are here—all except the nudieness. Excuse me: one exception! While in the Army, George, taunted by his fellow GIs, makes a feeble try at doing the expected with a pretty whore—whose admirable breasts, incidentally, seem worth much more than her set price of ten dollars. While the very presentably male torso of John Hansen (who had the misfortune to be cast as both George and Christine) is denuded in this scene, and kissed down to the navel, the action remains technological and at its previous rigidly moral stalemate.

Part of my reason for bringing in *The Christine Jorgensen Story* is as an object lesson virtually the opposite of *Myra Breckinridge*. "Virtually"? Well, homosexuality does get a parody show in *Myra* through the artificial rape of Rusty, and Rusty's conversion—tacit in the movie, explicit in the book—to passive anal sex. Otherwise, Myra the person is as technologically and intellectually abstract as Christine the person, who as George has no taste for sex at all, and as herself not the prospect of any taste for it till she gets past the trauma of having a different genital structure. A doctor declares that George's female hormone imbalance (three times what a male should have) justifies calling him a woman trapped in a man's body. Goodness me, if *I* were a woman trapped in a man's body, I'd be the proverbial caged lion till I got out of there, and then— But Christine is as patient throughout as Job, and, after and before, as pure as Deanna Durbin surrounded by those hundred men.

In fact, whatever happened to George's stockpile of female hormones and the added doses of them given Christine following the operation? They all seem to have gone into shock, because Christine shows not the slightest interest in men till the final clinch. And *that* is about as stimulating as the spectacle of two zombies thrilling to the first stage of reinstated sex-reflexes. But a word for the miscast John Hansen. He makes a very attractive boyish specimen of the eligible young-queen type: pretty, square-jawed face, rugged physique. In dresses, however, he behaves like a remarkably amazonian maiden who has been rejected as a beauty contestant because she is forty pounds overweight, has husky shoulders, a very masculine neck, and a bosom that seems to be two oversized wens on either side of a dimple.

Miss Jorgensen herself, whom I had the pleasure of meeting personally, is much more convincing as a woman. So much more that her declaration of regret at the fact that she was to be played in the movie by a man, rather than producing an involuntary joke, seems to point out the film's saddest and soberest truth. I hope that Mr. Hansen's future as a juvenile lead is not spoiled for being untrademarked as it is here. He would have made a nice Rusty Godowsky; indeed, he resembles Roger Herren. In or out of drag, Hansen is surely more of a gentleman than Myra Breckinridge, who becomes a blatant hussy as soon as she's transformed. In that respect Hollywood tried to leave her "as was." Vidal's satire on the female Hollywood star should not go without notice.

As Myra, the beautiful Raquel Welch has been made up starkly (this is more obvious in some scenes than in others) to suggest the kind of feeling that Myra develops for Mary Ann: lesbian. If Rusty is a kindly satire on the male homosexual star, Myra is an unkindly satire on the female homosexual star. That's male chauvinism in Mr. Vidal, no doubt, but also unmistakable perspicuity. Many people have found these angles, and everything else, in *Myra Breckinridge* repulsive, unusually repulsive. I am sure that no one could top Christine Jorgensen in feeling repulsion for it. Through the Myron/Myra syndrome of ultraradical transvestism, we can gauge just how strategic it is for some hefty male star (take Wallace Beery or Burt Lancaster as female impersonator) to get into drag and either act or cavort. His identity is thereby masculinized so that, as it were, his heterosexual credit becomes boundless by the implicit fact that the outside, in such cases, perversely contradicts the inside. It's certain to look comic; it's certain to be a camp.

And that, precisely, is what is abhorrent to a George Jorgensen, and cosmetically so despicable that he will undergo surgery to avoid all outward appearances that can be interpreted aesthetically as comic or campy. What he wishes to come true is not heterosexuality, but the fairy tale of female impersonation. The transsexual operation is at once the supreme faith and the supreme cynicism of being a homosexual. There comes to mind Wilde's definition of a cynic as one who "knows the price of everything and the value of nothing." The transsexualized cynic is one who knows the price of every penis but the value of none, including his own.

Miss Jorgensen might be shocked by the violence of this idea—that is, by its style—but logically she ought to agree with it. From what one hears of the special physical results of the transsexual operation, it is doubtful if a true male, arrived at sexual encounter with a transsexualized male, could have anything but a purely psychic illusion that he is dealing with a real female. I don't refer, of course, to those males who *desire* the purely psychic illusion and for this reason are hung-up on transvestites; no, I mean those males who want and expect a natural female. If one imagines a transsexualist triumphant in the bedroom, one has to imagine the sort of triumph that must have prevailed in many a Victorian marriage, where the sexual organs were felt but not seen, and even when felt, were not investigated by hand or eye. Hence the realities of female impersonation in surgicalized men go inward from the facade of outer clothes, past the (of course) ravishing next-to-body underwear, to an embarrassed state of affairs which, to put it bluntly, gives the show away.

Chronic transvestites, who are as fully compulsive as transsexuals, disdain femininity through technical frontalization and remain organic males under their dresses, even though, in bed, they submit themselves to men in the usual passive way. Yet this passivity is not inevitably the case; some male transvestites take the aggressive role. There is even a legend that nontransvestite male homosexuals will submit themselves passively *only* to male transvestites. It is a pity that so far, I believe, the beaver films have been too unimaginative to tackle these offbeat themes. On the other hand, Underground films amply attest to the aesthetic, supercosmetic status of the transvestite for whom the masquerade is *total* sexual reality regardless of what technical role is played in bed. Altogether, the male beaver, with its naïve phallic fixation, has neglected certain magics of sexual transformation: for example, female appearance into male reality, or the Penis as Miracle.

Mario Montez, a transvestite pioneering in Underground film, gives an especially eloquent version of the total sexual reality to which I just alluded. Facially he looks somewhat like a Mick Jagger whose decision to feminize himself arose from drastic necessity rather than cosmetic whim; not that Jagger too does not wear his life style on the outside, but its cosmetized femininity is borrowed, not born, camp. It's not at all that the transvestite's garbs are not detected even when worn socially, on the street; canny eyesight can penetrate them. But this vulnerability to "exposure" does not deter certain transvestites who have appeared in Underground films from wearing their outfits beyond camera range, as if they were pelts, not clothes.

This is true of at least three whom I have seen in a state of mufti: Jackie Curtis, Candy Darling, and Holly Woodlawn. I shan't say anything of the performances of these actress-transvestites except that at times they display a rather touching, faintly bewitching grace that is a very narrow art of its own; yes, by all means a cosmetic art, yet so thoroughly styled (after all, it is in repertory on screen and off) that it attains the enigmatic veracity of Garbo saying—this was in *Camille* in a scene with Armand—"What are you doing, anyway, with a woman like me?" I recall seeing Jackie Curtis at a party wearing a backless evening grown and showing a drooped majestic curve of back muscles which, with the broad shoulders and long shapely arms, made me whisper to my companion, "My God! That's the way Garbo looked in *Susan Lenox: Her Fall and Rise* at that dinner party!"

As I say—an incident from the already mentioned documentary, *The Queen*, proves it—the confirmed transvestite very seldom chooses the hard road which the transsexual is unafraid to travel. That he, too, believes in the Penis as Miracle (on himself) is close to the mood of the male beaver in its obvious bond with narcissism. As for the *aggressive* sex partners of transvestites, it may be easier psychologically to ignore a natural "mistake" (the normal penis on his passive partner) than to ignore the vestige left on transsexuals by the correction of that mistake. Remember the scene in *Myra Breckinridge* when Myra stands up on the table, lifts her dress, and lets down her panties to show Buck Loner and his colleagues her operation? Properly informed, one understands why these men are stunned and why one of them—susceptible soul that he must be—faints onto the floor.

Myra Breckinridge, so gratuitous and suspect an addition to the politics of Women's Lib, brings up a question I think very important. Transsexualism quite to one side, it would seem that all strenuous efforts by womanhood to find equity with men produce, in the context of our highly competitive society, an explicit moral masculinization of the female. This has nothing *necessarily* to do with the cosmetic tactics of women to look "femininely attractive." At the same time, all this being so, why are Women's Lib members so much opposed to official beauty contests, claiming that women should discourage themselves from being passive ornamental "sex objects," whose sole alternative to the beauty business is domestic slavery and a husband? Usually the winners of the Miss America contest are bent on professionalizing their superattractiveness as females: in brief, they want to go into business "as women." This public spectacle should suit very well the audience requirements of lesbians. Is the whole fem-lib stance a way of lesbianizing females without their sleeping with one another?

If, on the other hand, the modus vivendi of women be to discourage femininity as a specific occupation, professional or not, then they are automatically masculinizing themselves, reaching toward a sober-sense unisex. I wonder about this. How far the problem is from just going to beavers of all sex complexions! But then, beaver films, as an industry, have so little imagination. I am inclined to suspect that a victorious Women's Lib movement would make women less sexually palatable to men unless men agree proportionately to change. Yet heterosexual males, who in the great mass are counter-unisex, do not wish "proportionately to change," they wish to find femininity in their partners, womanliness in every sense. Go to Vox Pop with a microphone and you'll see what the census is. If such a quality in women symbolizes bondage, as fem-lib advocates contend, it still governs the laws of sexual desirability in the eyes of the male heterosexual majority.

What occurs to me is that the widespread success of defeminization among women might entail a curious turnabout. Heterosexual males might begin being more attracted to *effeminate* male homosexuals than to *masculinized* female heterosexuals. This would be a sad day for "the family." But who really respects the family so much in our cynical, minority-mad milieu? I have always felt, personally, that the primary sexual characteristics (the organs of reproduction) were last, not first, in the hierarchy of sex magnetism—except, of course, for the hang-up of size queens (e.g., homosexuals for whom the size of the penis decides sexual desirability). In fact, culturally, the sex organs are just Stone Age cosmetics. But what have I said? Something "clever." In honor of the sex organs, which by beaver standards *are* the ultimate beauty, I must take it back.

7. TRANSVESTITES:

SACRED, PROFANE,

AND NEUTERIZED

Conceiving homosexuality to be a social phenomenon and a social problem, the hardest thing about it is to persuade the man in the street to realize how varied is the range of homosexuals (male and female) from masculine to feminine types, and in turn, the range being so great, to grasp that sex, far from being simply one of nature's things, is a phenomenon of human metaphysics. In other words, a homosex has the identical problems, the same exultations, every other sex has. There's no reason to think the mere word "metaphysics" a snag to the common sense of understanding this point. The tendency of our age is more and more to recognize the validity of the stark-naked fact as superior to the "invalidity" of suppositions, fancies, and speculations. The current emphasis, I grant, is legalistic, scientific, ethical. Well and good. It is no speculation or fancy that millions of men sleep with other men, millions of women with other women, nor is it the result of some absurd, unhealthy, or impractical illusion that makes them so sleep. Absurd? Anything in the world can be *made to seem* absurd! Reliable statistics can disprove that, in the mass, the homosexes are either unhealthy or impractical.

Homosexuality is the valid result of an inner drive, just

as heterosexuality is. It may wane and wax here and there in time and space. The moon does likewise. It may be throttled, it may be converted back. Doubtless a certain minority of homosexuals are reformed, especially if reform takes place at an early enough age. Again, a few homosexual experiences in youth do not necessarily crystallize morally in the adult individual. Still, the future of anyone who is reformed is open to speculation, to the checking of facts as they eventuate. Fully as many heterosexual drives are reformed for social and economic reasons as are homosexual drives for the same reasons. How happy or successful such reformations are, how ultimately *realistic*, depends on the constitution and fortunes of each individual case, on how consciously sincere the reformation may have been. It does not depend on whether the individual subject turns out hetero or homo. He may not even be reformed from homo to hetero, or vice versa! He or she may simply become "different."

With its trick faculties and gracile arts of transformation, the film's technical nature makes it the ideal medium for penetrating a mask, physical or social, and thus for illustrating once more that, to rely on a serviceable truism, things are not always what they seem. If a man be an undercover agent for a foreign country, he does not want to seem one; just so, if a man be a homosexual—according to a convention that is still alive—he does not want to seem one, anywhere, at least, except in his intimate circle. With proper humility, controversialists of sex must realize that society is a vast complex of deceptive appearances known as "conventions." For a very simple instance, it is conventional that, if one be an adulterer (something itself due to the convention of marriage), one does not want to seem an adulterer. Whether an adulterous couple be said to live together in more or less "open sin" or to be having a more or less "secret affair," their labeled status has nothing to do with nature's laws; it is owed entirely to social morality and its strategies. If a man sleeps regularly with two women, there is apt to be an automatic conflict of practical interests: jealousy, economic rivalry, compromised social appearances, homes perhaps threatened. Many novels, therefore many films, are based squarely on such facts in the shape of romantic adventures and moral dramas.

Nothing could be more pertinent to the mechanics as

well as the aesthetics and cosmetics of homosexuality in the movies than a classic little charade that has been pretty much submerged in the annals of the film. It is a movie I once selected to illustrate "supernaturalism" in sex: *Turnabout* (1937).* Its fictive mechanism is simple—too simple. The glib assumption of a rub-of-the-lamp oriental magic that a young husband and wife can instantly exchange all sexual characteristics but their organic physical forms and behave like each other, rather than themselves, creates a fairy-tale supernaturalism for a marital comedy of unusual structure. The situation is that the couple, quarreling over the responsibilities supposed proper to their sexes, vent passionate wishes that they could be in each other's shoes—then, at any rate, they think, each would appreciate the other's intolerable burdens. The statue of some anonymous Eastern personage (maybe Hindu and seemingly a geni) "overhears" their utterances and promptly decides to grant them their rash wish. The fanciful charade feeling is underlined by dressing up a real man's bust as a statue and having it speak to the astounded couple.

After wearing each other's nightclothes, speaking in each other's voices, and learning that such drastic shifts of identity create more problems still, primarily social, the two agree that they have been taught a crucial lesson and submit with grace to the benevolence of the geni, who restores matters to what they should be in every honest bourgeois marriage. In retrospect, an attractive gaiety, as of the innocent youth of our century, seems to apparel *Turnabout.* It is not only that the joke is lucid and seems as much on the side of nature as of society, but that the homosexual aura given the couple in their transvestite interval suggests, rather than depravity, the old fun game of sex masquerade—all the way from the college musical show to the vestiges of Halloween.

There are, in our film legacy, too many instances of moral frivolity about homosexuality, too many cases where it is literally used as a Halloween masquerade to play slyly on the subject of the homosexual as if he were not real but a sort of charade person. Thus the sophisticated Hollywood director

* See *Magic and Myth of the Movies* (Tyler).

George Cukor, who had discovered Katharine Hepburn and developed her into a star, used her for the kind of thing that Mart Crowley terms, where a certain sort of director is involved, "getting his jollies." For such directors, homosexuality becomes a professional in-joke that will entertain the public while leaving it in its natural, semiblind state of prejudice about the facts of homosexuality. True enough, that day is about over. Now it is "in" to exploit the homosexual's non-Halloween personality. According to Cukor's own statement (made at the Museum of Modern Art on the occasion of introducing a retrospective of his films), he regretted the movie *Sylvia Scarlett,* in which Hepburn masquerades as a boy. The reason was undisclosed, but Cukor indicated that all concerned thought the movie a loss, a sort of tactical misstep.

Perhaps the only reason was that *Sylvia Scarlett* did so poorly at the box office. Maybe the public did not especially care to see a lyrical ingénue it had taken to its heart throw her enthusiasm into a rather disturbing sex charade. Miss Hepburn had the good fortune to have features carved like pre-World War I modernist sculpture. As her first film tests proved, she was eminently photogenic, with a jutting manner both vocal and calisthenic. She was a sort of indigenous prep-school Garbo with an American forward lunge instead of a Swedish backward discretion. Kate went straight—on, on, on . . . on to Sylvia Scarlett. Her original breathless yet breath-controlled Bryn Mawr accent, which she placed in the roof of her mouth to get elevation and cut off on her lips as if with nail scissors, had a wealth of "difference" to it. A singing nasality made it sound, when required, like a love lyric recited by a schoolgirl suddenly visited in the classroom by Aphrodite. Young, fashionably angular, always like a lanky schoolgirl in the flush of saying "I am a woman" for the first time, she fit into the role of Sylvia Scarlett as into a young man's glove, all slim questing fingers, tingling confidence, and hard knuckles. Her bosom was nowhere. But she didn't need it.

I am disposed to rate Hepburn as a professional tomboy —a type I shall discuss later—because in her roles she was, after all, so much disposed toward men. She used to yearn after them in a voice calculatingly pitched somewhere between the coo of a dove and the yelp of a coyote. In *Sylvia Scarlett* she gives up her false male identity because she falls hard for a man (Brian Aherne). But before that happens, she involuntarily snares the heart of a young lady, who thinks that this handsome, dashing boy can improve his manly looks. Whereupon she draws a moustache on the submissive Hepburn, and charmed with the result, plants a lusty kiss on the lips beneath it. By family standards this was good clean fun, but I am sure it was also a "jolly" relished by everyone in the studio according to his respective sexual lights. At last Sylvia, appearing before the man she loves in a dress, has to endure his ridicule—he still thinks her a boy who is now playing a joke on him! All this looks like a belittled and belittling parody of the plot of Gautier's wonderful romance *Mademoiselle de Maupin.* I wonder if any one about the studio was aware of this. In any case, it was a long time before this actress emerged from the bringing-up-baby syndrome.

The same childish aura of playfulness for playfulness' sake authorizes professional drag acts and supposedly the mythical shenanigans of *Charley's Aunt,* that gay old gray chestnut. Modern psychology, of course, automatically lent another dimension to the charade demonstration of *Turnabout.* Just a flick of the plot and they'd have had a married couple at the old act of quarreling and, tit for tat, calling each other a dyke and a fairy. That can happen when it's true and when it's not true. Jolly or no jolly, the inevitable thing about *Turnabout* is that it's a two-way act in which form can change place with substance. It takes no wrenching to assume that the whole affair—and to hell with that geni!—holds both partners' unconscious homosexual wish, so that the grotesque comedy becomes the wish fulfillment of a dream. On the other hand, one could insist that it's a morality tale inexorably pointing back to the heterosexual order of nature.

I don't want to seem to take too pure an interest in truth for truth's sake. My original analysis of *Turnabout,* I admit, was a strategy to make homosexuality as authentic and interesting as heterosexuality. What I would now argue is that *Turnabout* is too graphic an exposure of the homosexual mechanism to seem *only* a romantic joke or funny moral tale. Viewed as sheer mechanism, sex masquerade must seem ambiguous. By a certain formula, real enough in practice, male or female transvestism is a simple extension of the art of disguise, as when a prisoner escapes or a gangster wishes to elude the police. For centuries, it has been a standard plot complication as well as a theater convention: males acting the roles of women. Shakespeare took delight in making his female characters assume masculine gear in the course of a tricky plot; later, we shall see how such a thing works out in *Mademoiselle de Maupin*. But take a curious case from film history.

Marlene Dietrich, as a café performer in her first American film, *Morocco* (1930), did her classic drag act of singing in top hat and tails. No intent to deceive, because she doesn't tuck in her hair or change her voice! Yet, for the sake of an exotic touch, she troubles—moving her act into the audience—to pause, ogle a female spectator, and give her a kiss. A gaggy gag. But why should an actress of Miss Dietrich's resources have pushed things that far?—because she's supposed to be smitten, on the spot, by Gary Cooper? Reality, however problematical, gets built into appearances. Late historical developments in the film underline the ambiguity of the heterosexual fun taken in Halloween masquerade. How harmlessly innocent and "straight" might seem the sort ladled out in Billy Wilder's comparatively recent *Some Like It Hot,* where drag "deception" is as open as a college musical's! Here, Jack Lemmon and Tony Curtis are found in the act of escaping a gang's persecution by impersonating two young ladies and joining a traveling all-girl orchestra. Though Messrs. Curtis and Lemmon looked heroic in drag and seemed to throw their hearts into the impersonation (after all, Marilyn Monroe turned out to be a member of the girls' band), one could have detected the masquerade ten yards away: the leg muscles alone were enough. I think that the United States may be the only place where such a fun game, supposed to be infinitely rib-tickling and preferably hilarious, survives in such a pure and primitive state. It's just possible that we of the United States harbor the headquarters of heterosexual female impersonation—and that *this* fact occasions the "jolly"! For, after all, it's the old act of female impersonation so as to get near a woman. Escaping from gangsters, indeed!

Despite its satirical nuance and its intricacies, even *Myra Breckinridge,* in this light, may be viewed as a profound strategy designed to prove that a real man can step out of those undies, and moreover, as nature meant to happen, move straight into the arms of a lady, not a gentleman. Well, I too am taking the heterosexual stance now, but not at all in that dimension of drag. No matter which sexes are involved, I want to emphasize that the sex act is an act of basic and extreme physical inter- mingling. A fascinating problem for poets, novelists, and play- wrights (and, one might presume to hope, for modern sexolo- gists), has been precisely the *limits* of sexual intermingling, no less than its *modes.* The old mythic image of perfect union be- tween a man and a woman, which in tragic paradox created the love-death legends, is neither a mental fantasy of unhealthy in- dividuals nor a myth invented only to stimulate the emotions (even the ritualized emotions) of sex. Perfect union is merely the *logical extreme* of the mutual drive that brings two people together in bed for sexual reasons. The love-death, then, is a highly sophisticated term for a special historic situation of the idea of "perfect union." Largely with reference to the succes- sion of kings, death was once an adjunct to sexual union be- cause of an established custom: eventually a queen, by way of mortal combat between the incumbent king and a challenger, would acquire a new consort.*

The much later custom of chivalry made men seek death precisely in order to die *for love.* This was connected with Mary- worship in the Middle Ages. The famous Tournament of Love was obviously a metaphysicalization of actual combat for posses- sion of a woman, a symbolic act of sex in which the beloved was glorified (i.e., spiritually pleasured) by the lover's victory at arms. The moral mechanism behind this courtly custom— thriving in the twelfth and thirteenth centuries and often only a sport—was simple: it was the idealization of the beloved as the Virgin Mary. In the most exact sense, it was also metaphysical adultery, since convention said that a knight should choose an-

* See Mary Renault's novel *The King Must Die.*

other man's wife as his idealized lady. Needless to add—if only because nature seems to have an undying impulse to "bring back to earth" all romantic sublimation—private carnal indulgence went along with public metaphysical display. Yet the poets of chivalric love, the trouvères and the troubadours, continued celebrating the purely metaphysical aspect of this erotic pattern.

The Freudian system would term chivalric love a transparent device of sublimation. But the Freudian system is a little better at analyzing phenomena than designating, at something of a conscious risk, their root causes. Sublimation in its higher forms relates to religion, which itself—in the family complex of relations analyzed by Freud—was a ritual relation to the mother as *maternal principle*. This was as true of paganism as of pre-Renaissance Christianity. But sexually considered, the more informal or lower phase of sublimation is merely the postponed or frustrated realization of desire. Psychologically, there is an automatic element of sublimation in the daily experience even of firmly joined lovers; we have examples in the popular songs of yearning on the lips of separated lovers daydreaming of each other.

I speak of the mass level of love and its *daily* experience. Perhaps the true root of sublimation, running a gamut from transient frustration to poetic and religious metaphysics, is absolute in an obscure sense. "Consummation" may be technically subject to too many hazards to call it satisfactory in a necessary or enduring sense. The discovery of the orgasm as a physical principle (to which ejaculation is related, but not just another name for the same thing) was an important stage in the true understanding of sexual experience, and thus of love's common moral goal. Ejaculation is a sign that the orgasm *may* have been achieved; the individual, in any specific instance, must decide whether or not it has. The orgasm, like love itself, is of an infinite variety.

Any enlightened philosophy of love must conscientiously reckon with what the sexologists call orgastic potency. Now, on what depends the realization of this important step in the advance toward total sexual satisfaction? Surely, it depends much on the "object," the specific partner, but it depends just as much on the physical reciprocity of that object, which has to match other-taking with self-giving. The sex object must be highly eligible, but its responsiveness must live up to its eligibility. True mutual orgasm logically depends, then, on maximum physical collaboration between the partners. I hardly think we can get closer to a mere definition. It so happens, however, as Freud discovered, that one of the chief deterrents to such realization of the sexual ideal is the incest motive; this is so because in the mind of a son the true orgasm is anticipated, sometimes, as a thing to be attained with his mother; in the mind of a daughter, with her father. This prior sublimation of incest conditions all subsequent realistic efforts toward achieving sexual happiness, or "total" satisfaction.

The medial forms, including painting and literature, express more than literal image and literal fact. Asking the movies to halt at the rudimentary concept of reportage, therefore, is to ask literature to surrender all romantic metaphysics, all poetic symbolism, all figurative as opposed to literal statement. We need not ask this—especially since the film has a lot of activity which allies it to the high reaches of expression in the other arts and so to the mechanism of sublimation in the symbolic structures of all media. In *Magic and Myth of the Movies* I wrote of a transvestism that expressed, not gay homosexuality as I have usually spoken of it here, but a supernaturalism of sex comprehending homosexual motifs. My strategy was not just to bring in homosexuality where it was not meant to be (ostensibly), rather it was to expose the fluid ambiguity of sex as a pervasively real circumstance. This tactic situated homosexuality in the great sexual stream, and by the same token situated heterosexuality as constantly subject to complicity with homosexuality.

In other words, there is a world of true forms in social behavior which directly reflects the world of those true, invisible forms in nature which *go beyond physical sensation;* thus forms to be grasped visually, objectivized, only in the vestments of symbol and the rituals therefrom—or, as one might say, in the transvestments of symbol, and thus through transvestism. When, with the surrogate of his penis, a man penetrates a woman, *he wears her body*. The penis dons the vagina via the vulva and wears the womb as a headdress. The rearing priapus broadens like a mushroom or a cobra's head toward the womb above. Literally, the physical conjugation releases a seed, the male sperm that spurts up and lodges there, and having fused in the womb, contrives to produce the child.

In dynamic terms a curious kind of transsexuality has taken place. The penetrating male, driving forward, wishes, as it were, to plant himself in the female, to thrust in to the root of his penis, to get in as far as he can possibly go. But in terms of phallic sensation, what happens in the act of "going all the way in" is that the local root orientation is *reversed*. In "planting the tree" of his body, the male *transplants* it, for the tree-top sheds its seed and in effect (especially if the resultant child be a male) duplicates his own penis in the opposite direction. The seed becomes a root whose male trunk, in turn, may go on to fecundate a womb. Besides, whether the seed develops into male or female, the woman, as the penetrated one, herself senses this exchange of penis orientation as a transference, or "transvestism." Hence at the crux of the act of potency, *she* becomes the penised one; and as such, one who wears, has donned, her own vagina. Thus do man and woman exchange roles on the level of physical conjugation. Perhaps it is not irrelevant that in the technique of transsexual surgery, the subject is contrived to wear his scrotal sack outside-in, turning what was male into a surrogate for the female.

The foregoing is a way of detailing the elements of mythological fantasy as they seem to determine what takes place in that great film *The Dybbuk*, made faithfully from S. Ansky's play with a troupe of Warsaw Art Theater players in 1938. I give the whole sexual substructure to accent the deep pervasiveness of the phenomena of transvestism. In being heterosexual as well as homosexual, transvestism cements the basic sexes into a stream of full, constant, and fluid variations that develop new forms quite aside from surgical transexualism. The erotic situation of *The Dybbuk* is that a girl's disappointed lover, a Hassidic student of forbidden magic, decides to have her despite her forced marriage to another (she loves him, the student) by committing suicide and turning into a dybbuk, a spirit that can enter another's body in the phenomenon known widely as demonic possession.

The young student's dybbuk accomplishes its purpose, but to the necessary great distress of the young woman, seized as she is being led to the marriage altar, deprived of her rational personality, piteously weakened and terrified, and compelled (worst of all) to speak in her lover's own voice. Inevitably, in this pious Jewish community, the drama proceeds according to a religious pattern. A great Hassid, a very old man, is enlisted to exorcise the dybbuk in order to restore the young woman to her organic personality. Magic, religion's opponent, has succeeded in its erotic quest, but only transiently; it must be defeated to reassert the normal ethical rights of the individual. The ritual of exorcism is held in a synagogue, where finally the dybbuk is persuaded, half out of obedience to religious authority, half (it would seem) out of combined pity and exhaustion, to leave the young woman's body, though with a pathetic reluctance. Having gone into catalepsy, the girl now revives—the ordeal and the movie are over.

But exactly what has happened in terms of sexual conjugation: its fierce aims and its changing fortunes? I cannot see that *The Dybbuk*'s story is anything but a religious parable of the "crime" of illicit sexual passion. Quite contrary to the unsettling ambiguity of *Turnabout*, this story tends to resist any effort to interpret sex as homosexuality in any phenomenal or realistic sense; unless (as in fact I propose here) we conclude from the structure of the basic physical act of sex that there is an "extremity" of merging between heterosexual individuals which transcendently induces them to exchange their sexual forms. Passion would be the force effecting such a metaphysical exchange. There is even a literary tradition to testify to the passionate nature of heterosexual transvestism. It was put magically—that is to say, unorthodoxly—by André Breton when he said, "I would like to change my sex as I change my shirt."

Of the element of great passion in *The Dybbuk*, there

can be no doubt. Here was a very special version of the love-death, from which the female partner is rescued by the strength of a given ethical custom: the power lodged in the old rabbi who performs the exorcism. Always, traditionally, there is something "illicit" about the love-death ritual. The male demonstrably takes the female in *The Dybbuk*, despite the taboo laid on her as the betrothed of another man; he utterly penetrates her (orgastic potency) to the point where his penis (of which in this fable *he* is the surrogate rather than vice versa) is "lost" in her but takes brief command of her, like the successful stormer of a fortress. He submerges not only his penis, but his whole body. Anticlimactically, he at last is expelled, but not without having achieved complete immersion in his beloved, an absolute transvestism, so that he may be said indeed to have worn her body for a while, like a gown, a ritual garment. The successful exorcism is a moral commentary: illicit sexual passion is a sin and must be vanquished. Yet the exorcism as such does not dispose of or even disturb the metaphysical condition which I have described. Passion (we might hopefully infer) continues to motivate the race and variously implements sexual behavior.

Some schools of thought contend, and perhaps rightly, that the incest impulse as well as the fantasy of a penised mother are often integral steps in the male's sexual development. In male homosexuals, this step, however consciously imagined or unconsciously displaced or sublimated, is the norm; soon its power, according to the individual's constitution, may shift fixation from mother to father—that is, to the *true* penis-bearing animal. At the same time, the womb as a dwelling place, a refuge, remains in the mind of a male homosexual as symbol of the family conceived as an enclosed domain of sexual satisfaction. For the male to create a new family—that is altogether a different matter! To accomplish this, he must slough the whole incestuous atmosphere of sex and regard himself as husband and father, not son and lover (whether of mother or father). The danger is plain: in order successfully to become a husband and father, he must (whether he knows it or not) acquire the faculty of orgastic potency.

Of course, there are common standards of independent

"family success" which, if properly investigated, would have to be written off. Here the pivotal thing about sex is that works of art, by offering us (as the best do) the imagination *in its naked form*, present a symbolic order linking essential physical acts to essential ideas. One of the shames of filmic theory is to have developed a school that pretends this symbolically coalesced order of reality is beside the point of motion pictures, even intrudes on them. This is like maintaining that the mind is an intrusion on nature, something arbitrary, as if, for instance, civilization could be called the "human" disease of the lower animals. At the best, such a theory of film is a false totalization of a partial truth.

Fortunately the movies provide us with an acting personality whose sexual nuances suggest the metaphysical ambiguity which we might well term, I think, the spiritual inversion of sexual form. *The Dybbuk* expresses the spiritual inversion of sexual form as an *act* and a *story*. But a personality can just as well express it. The personality I mean comes from the movies: Greta Garbo. As my monograph on her* said, this designation does not refer to the common gamut of persons who, being carnally homosexual, sleep with those of the same organic sex. It would be foolish to conclude from my ideas about Garbo that she is, or that I think her, a lesbian. It is simply that when I have seen her walking across the screen, I have always been overwhelmed by the feeling that within her woman's shape, behind all her beauty and feminine postures, a man hid himself and walked around with her.

My monograph was playful, somewhat sly, about the realistic sex angle. But it ended by evoking the beautiful and fascinating image of Théophile Gautier's creation, Mademoiselle de Maupin, a transvestite, and the likewise transvestite heroine of Balzac's story *Seraphita*. It is striking that Balzac chose the feminine gender of a Latin proper name to title his story. His protagonist happens to be a double transvestite, a supernatural sort of being, a Swedenborgian angel who dresses like, and implicitly has, the organic form of a man when in rela-

---

* *The Films of Greta Garbo* (Conway, McGregor, Ricci). "The Garbo Image," introduction by Parker Tyler.

tion to a woman, and correspondingly a woman's aspect when in relation to a man. I have always thought it a real misfortune that Garbo never enacted a role doing justice to the high, or metaphysical, level of transvestism. It is no novelty for an actress to play a man's role or to masquerade as a man while playing a woman's part. We can recall both Sarah Bernhardt and Asta Nielsen as Hamlet, the latter actress playing it in a German film version.

It was rumored and seemingly confirmed that Garbo planned to act St. Francis of Assisi and other male parts, though it seemed obvious, at least to me, that her personality cried out for a role going beyond the charade (however serious) of a woman masquerading as a man or simply pretending to be a man for some stage or film role. Garbo did, of course, masquerade as a man for her role as Queen Christina of Sweden. The movie, *Queen Christina*, had some photographically stunning shots of Garbo but would have been quite insipidly romantic without the vitality of her unique presence. I do not regard Garbo as a great actress but as a great personality. Though she was a sincere craftsman, she could show involuntary ineptitude in solving some of her problems of style, and by no means did she always give the perfect accent when required to be intensely emotional. Under the guidance of a sensitive director (Cukor, for example) her greatest acting triumph might have been playing Mademoiselle de Maupin. That she ought to play it was long an uncommunicated obsession of mine.

As a romantic fantasy, Gautier's story stands sexually in a class by itself. From a historically misplaced fem-lib impulse, Mlle. de Maupin decides to go about disguised as a sword-wielding conventional youth (the period is supposedly the seventeenth century), specifically in order to protect a tender young girl who is the sister of a suitor of hers who has died; the charming girl follows Maupin as her page, of course in boy's clothes. There are several passages between them so tender as to evoke an erotic atmosphere. Only a genius of eroticism such as Gautier could have made a truly poetic thing out of the extravagant story which follows. His heroine's motives are tacitly referred to an elusive, deep-lying, and unaffectedly vagrant eccentricity. Her behavior and personality make her a rare image of gallantry; her period masquerade suggests a female knight of the Crusades or some goddess on a mission of mercy to which she sacrifices the natural enjoyments of sex. But given these higher imaginative premises, Mlle. de Maupin's story is worked out with remarkable realism.

Involvement with an ambisexual triangle soon befalls the disguised heroine when she meets a man who is already in love with another woman, but who immediately, despite Maupin's seeming maleness, feels irresistibly attracted to her sexually. Gautier is high style. Thus his story is high comedy as well as romantic drama, and for his time the blend was thoroughly unique. The other female member of the triangle, Rosette, is duly attracted to the disguised Mlle. de Maupin and boldly woos "him" but is repeatedly rebuffed. Meanwhile the affair between Rosette and Theodore, the male protagonist, goes through a series of passionate vicissitudes with Maupin a shadow in the background.

At last, when Mlle. de Maupin acts the role of Rosalind in a privately held performance of *As You like It,* and Theodore sees her in her true female appearance, it bursts on him that this is really an organic woman, so he determines to find out if he is right. Gautier rounds out the story with superb finesse, and honorably discharges his natural debt to French eroticism by paying *hommage* simultaneously to Eros and Homeros. Theodore spends one night of love with Maupin . . . but Rosette does too. There are few details that indicate the quality of the respective sexual encounters. Still, that we may not be in doubt at the climax that sexuality has not remained in its charade state, Gautier daringly has Theodore discover on the sheets of the bed where Maupin has slept with Rosette the exact sort of evidence that was introduced into Oscar Wilde's trial by a chambermaid: only a spot, but damned and damning. Indeed, when Gautier's novel first appeared (1835), it was damned as filthy and evil by almost the whole French press; the author elected to write, for later editions, a vigorous and entertaining satirical preface on his book's reception.

Mademoiselle de Maupin suddenly disappears from the lives of her two lovers, and from her story, as goddesses used to disappear into thin air. It is not so much that she has been a romantic novelist's dream as that she has something of that supernatural faculty of sex that Balzac defined in *Seraphita* in the ambivalent figure of Seraphita-Seraphitus. Gautier's genius had brought the sacred transvestite, like a goddess descending to mortal sex, down to earth. Why should not Aphrodite, like Zeus himself, have a protean sexuality; or, in equivalent terms, practice bisexuality? Gautier's genius also informed him of a point important to this discussion: that the most fanciful dream of sex, the most metaphysical idea about it, somehow can be traced *in the physics of human sexual behavior*. Hence there must be a limitless suite of magical sexual changes that refer not only to the spirit of things but also to their substance.

We should not forget that Balzac's memoranda on this subject (as I indicated previously) came fairly close to Gautier's in *Mademoiselle de Maupin*. He invented a person who was La Sarrasina on the operatic stage and Sarrasine, a gifted violinist, in ordinary society. However a practical joke is played on the gentleman who has seen only La Sarrasina and become smitten. Invited to a private dinner where Sarrasine has been persuaded to appear as La Sarrasina, the hero is completely duped, up to the moment when the emotionally unstable Sarrasine, wooed frantically by his admirer, betrays the imposture. Tacitly Sarrasine is a castratus. But the drama is worked out in terms of the hero's "mad" reluctance to give up his delusion, seemingly being fascinated by the double personality that is Sarrasine-Sarrasina: the joke ends in the victim's tragic regrets. The story is a bold psychological study in homosexuality of a kind that I have mentioned here: the pseudo-heterosexual type fixated upon transvestites. The truth is that if homosexuality can be outwitted in the clinic, as reports tell us, heterosexuality can be outwitted in life by some oblique, in-lying homosexuality. At the center of all sex, perhaps, is a primordial bi-structure. So in Balzac's story, as elsewhere, we see the Goliath of heterosexuality brought down by a homeroic David with the surface charms of a woman. It may take a while for the movies to get around to such things. But don't think they're not already on the move.

What, then, are the "sacred transvestites" who illustrate this abidingly obscure spiritual inversion of sexual form? They are unusual types of "angel": the higher metamorphoses of both-sexed Eros. We must not doubt that these angels can achieve some sort of carnal status *in themselves* and without the aid of transvestment. Have we not seen as much in the screen's Billy Budd and the Eros of *Teorema*? Both are so young, feminine, beautiful, and gentle that they require no outward sign of carnal womanliness to function as bisexual images. In strict mythological tradition, on the other hand, the sacred transvestite incarnated itself in Hermaphroditus, the two-sexed child of Hermes and Aphrodite—called by the masculine gender of his name, doubtless, because he was born under patriarchal dominance. A decadent version of Hermaphroditus appears in *Fellini Satyricon* as an actual cult figure, alive but not very well. The "demigod," as he is called, instances both Fellini's genius for casting and his power of real visualization. Albino, naked, and modestly offering a male genital, he has been made up to look infantile and seemingly is a mental defective who must be handled like a baby, or else is supposedly drugged. He looks like a chubby fourteen-year-old faggot who has been dressed for a drag party and then collapsed because he has been sent on a trip.

This sacred hermaphrodite is rather awesome in the vestigial religious role Fellini has given him. His figure fairly oozes both physical and spiritual unhealthiness. Kidnapped by Encolpius and Ascyltos, who murder his attendants, he is trundled through the desert, where the pathetic, unreal thing finally dies from thirst and exposure to the sun. This sequence is marvelously atmospheric and impressively successful in that its macabre physical realism does not dispel the hermaphrodite's inherent aura of supernaturalism. It is possible to scorn the worship of "monsters" as a phase of religion that has been swept away by time. But can we honestly do this when confronted with the assortment of monsters the movies have so copiously and superstitiously enshrined and which haunt television screens?

Besides, Curzio Malaparte's anecdotes about Naples in his novel *The Skin* indicate the actual survival of monster worship. I would suggest, therefore, that such an anecdote as that just described from Fellini's movie proves not only that a sort of aesthetic-magic belief in "monstrous" figures clings to the human psyche but that sexual roles play a large part in them. For example, the homosexual marriage that takes place in *Fellini Satyricon* between the young Encolpius and the mature Lichas (a demure bride) is not to be taken as sheer myth or anachronism, or one of today's camp fancies, or jollies. Why not? One material reason is that officially sealed homosexual marriages, male and female, are taking place all the time.

That absurd marriage in the *Satyricon*, coming to nothing, is still a matter of surviving sex ritual. In this key, I can supply testimony from the premises of a recent experience of moviegoers. It is no other than that ingenious and controversial tribute to hippie psychedelics, the movie boldly titled *Performance*, which is far more about sex rites than about bed sex. Its homosexual reference is ample enough, while the only true bedroom homosex appears in a few caresses exchanged between the principal girls; however, the film is full of ritual transvestism. The New York film critics tended either abjectly to laud its extravagances or insolently to excommunicate them, the lean being much to the latter view. As happens frequently in journalism, the truth is somewhere between those two supercharged aesthetic responses; or rather, the truth by its own weight simply knocks the bottom out of them.

Performance, as a whole, does not deserve so much partisan aesthetics from any conceivable angle. Artistically and intellectually, it is a poor thing; otherwise, it tends to be rich—*nouveaux*, that is to say, *riches*. Its spectacular qualities consist of superslick photography (with some cutting borrowed from advanced Underground experiments) and a fusion of the psychological-nightmare sort of crime story with the high costume paraphernalia of rock, the latter including a mod version of the last century's oriental-bower decor. *Performance*'s contribution is the inevitable technology of reproduction: electric keyboards, microphones, hallucination as a science-fiction, as well as a

dietary, technique. Of course, all this is duly ritualistic, a mum-
bo-jumbo ritualism invented by whiteys.

Mick Jagger was chosen as this superpad's proprietor: a
tired-out and supposedly retired rock star: in brief, himself on
a fictitious plane. The stint has so often been assigned to celebrities of all sorts, why not to Jagger, too? Though not at all
an actor, he is perfectly suited by nature and art to the sort
of hippie kink-spreading that the rock milieu has inspired in
this film. His popularity is right, moreover, for the movie's
million-dollar scale. What seems odd is why, even so, he had
to seem as limp as the proverbial rag and lackluster as an exhausted whore with the glooms. Once Jagger presented a more
youthful and attractive image. It has taken him but a few years
to grow cadaverous—shrunken in all places, it would seem, except his remarkably billowy lips, which manage to suggest the
lip-shaped sofa that Salvador Dali painted into his trompe-
l'oeil portrait of Mae West (when her whole head puns with
the furnishings of a room; it is the best Dada portrait I know,
exactly like her, with the nostrils representing a fireplace).
Everything on Jagger's body, even his bones, seem to have
dwindled away around his mouth, so that in contrast his heavily
painted lips look as if they were brought forward by a 3-D
lens.

Except for a lively song, which he delivers in a hitherto
unknown guise that masculinizes his face and body, he is
spectacularly lifeless. This new "transvestite" act is hippie-into-
Deep-South-gangster with sideburns and slicked hair brushed
straight back. At that, he delivers the song (though it seems
meant as a parody of Bob Dylan) in the round, throaty-deep
tones of an old-fashioned big black mamma. Yes, histrionic
problems may be extremely delicate. To project lifelessness in
the sense of the walls that surround drug addicts, slicing them
from the external environment, is no easy-on assignment. But
patently Jagger does not take it as a histrionic assignment at all.
It was much easier just to go around looking, and talking, half-
stoned.

When he speaks dialogue—and sparse it is—it is always a
few decimals short of normal volume and has the flatness of

amateurs who have not the faintest idea of what stage speech should be. Don't get me wrong, please! I know the value of an actor's deliberate understatement of physical and vocal style, the dramatic effect of a sudden flatness of voice or a whisper, the possible artistry of placing a quiet tone to express mood or character; perhaps, an interior monologue . . . Jagger's screen conduct has nothing to do with all that. No, it is *very* special. While he comes alive in that one song, he has no signs of personality but inert ones: the long hair covering the far sides of his cheeks, the ghostly-pale fleshtone, the rubbery red lips (curiously unsensual for so rococo a cupid's bow), the exotic uniforms, beads, bracelets, gewgaws. Sometimes he even looks like a sick-sick parody of an old movie vamp. Paradoxically he seems to *will* wearing his paraphernalia the way Garbo wore a bathing suit in *Two Faced Woman*, as if, after all, it had nothing to do with her.

By no means do I think that Jagger's selection for the part lacks relevance. The problem is to locate that (perhaps self-directed) relevance at its deepest and most far-reaching. To begin with, the hippie-rock-drug idea means, sex-wise, alienation from passionate bed-action as the naked drive toward sexual climax. For chic hippies, the sex experience and the aesthetic experience are automatically one: there is no dialect of interaction between moments, levels, moods. Naturally, drugs make this organically possible. Above all, the hippie-rock-drug idea allows no moral testing, no intellectualizing, not even any poetizing above the pop level, no exposure whatever to disturbance or challenge. It is a closed, a static, proposition, and the chief closure is a ritual blur tending to homogenize the senses and their discrimination—their connoisseurship, as it were—so that even the basic sexual choice of hetero or homo object is smudged, becoming the value we have started calling unisex.

Unisex appears on the rock stage as a universal convention both as to costume and manners. The male rock star, even when muscular and frenzied, is a kind of cadavre-exquis (the surrealist image-person built vertically of sections determined by chance), except that with the rock star, chance is replaced by the established canon of unisex. Unisex means simply the elision of masculine and feminine traits, hairdo, makeup, and ornaments, as well as the pants long worn by both sexes. It does not mean, necessarily, bisexuality or homosexuality, yet it makes homosexuality easily accessible without fuss or moral aftermath. The faces, even the bodies, of many male rock hippies are ambiguously sexed. Jagger is only a conspicuous archetype.

When, in *Performance*, the close-clipped, vibrant young mod gangster (James Fox) meets long-haired, worn-out rock star, we have (not without intuitive design) two kinds of alienation opposed, as if they were customs of tribes which never before had come into contact, hostile or friendly. Each archetype, at first, feels instinctive aversion for the other. Then both begin to realize a peculiar affinity: a magnetism that abruptly stops short of the erotic. The gangster, a fugitive from his own gang's vengeance, feels the unknown sensation of a totally different quality of life. The mutual keynote, nevertheless, is violence. Yet the superpad of the retired rock star is keyed not in the violence of the gang world's wild physical action, destruction, torture, blood, and murder. All these things carry the high risk and supreme nervous tension that the rock world seeks to exile.

What soon strikes the gangster in *Performance* and "gets to" him is that all physical dialectics of *his* caliber have been emptied from the rock singer's enclosed life, while substituted for them is a strange, subdued ritual of the senses: singing, music, drugs, and childlike, playful "nonviolent" sex. In one dimension, the gangster represents the chaotic violence of war, risky, never held in bounds; the rock star, the chaotic violence of peace, unrisky, always held in bounds. When they collide, as they do here, an explosive melodrama seems the logical result. And so it comes about. Finally the gangster shoots the rock star through the top of his head and is led off to gang justice—for a seemingly loyal confederate has betrayed his whereabouts to the gang boss and precipitated the climax. Yet this does not happen before Chas, the gangster, has submitted to a psychedelic initiation rite, which he half-relishes, half-rejects; he is bewigged to look like Jagger, lipsticked, given hallucinogenic mushroom, dressed up, and eventually gets into bed with the boyish type of the resident team of two odd girls companioning the rock star in his retirement.

The boyish, extremely young female here (scarcely out of pubescence) is well worth noticing. She is but another figment of the radical neutering that seems to be the canonic heart of the hippie sex style. One assumes that, in the hippie world, "penis meets vagina" in the same old romantic sense of "boy meets girl." Yet a difference sets the two formulas apart. This is the sexual permutation that veers the orthodox sexes toward their homosexual coefficients, without necessarily or typically arriving at homosexuality. The little girl that Chas goes to bed with has a chunky if rather attractive child's face that might belong to a thirteen-year-old boy (her hair is sparse, short, and, when wet, clings to her head). Chas good-naturedly accepts her sexually but tells her that she's really "like a boy." Indeed! But also like a butch nymphet. One might say she *is* a butch nymphet.

Unisex fashions are not altogether now-now. They used to crawl out of the gothic woodwork before disrobing for bed and love. Mademoiselle de Maupin herself is an elegant example. Now these same fashions are no mere romantic convention associated with literature, the stage, and outdated films. They proliferate in shops and stamp the posters as well as the persons found in hippie living quarters. They indicate the neuter phase of sexual transvestism and signify everything from a pathological dislocation to an accepted social convention or a poetic symbol. I feel obliged not to leave this point without weighting it with available statistics: they are under our noses, and provided the higher olfactory nerve is working, they can't be overlooked.

The latest phenomenon in the way of complex transvestism on film comes, not surprisingly, from the busy premises of Andy Warhol's film factory, long since surfaced as a place where marketable movies are being made. The Warhol/ Morrissey film team (having given us *My Hustler, Lonesome Cowboys, Flesh*, and *Trash*, all with relevance to offbeat sex) have now achieved, with a notion by Warhol, another *dernier cri* with a film called *Women in Revolt*—or, as eventually it may be titled, *Blonde on a Bum Trip*. Whichever, it may well be the dernierest of all the Warhol/Morrissey cris.

Its complexity materialized not owing to filmic ideas (all Warhol/Morrissey works are deliberately backward and reactionary as films) but owing to a direct insight into the nature of sex and satire. *Women in Revolt* features three full-time transvestites (the type that never gets out of drag) acting the parts of females of low-intelligence level who become attracted to the lib idea, go through some patently unconvincing moral calisthenics by "organizing," incoherently backslide, fall apart as a group, and end up diversely in certain well-known attitudes taken (today no less than yesterday) by fallen Eve of the legendary Garden. Does it sound like a put-on? Don't understate the point. It's a superduper of a put-on.

The above scant version of what happens in *Women in Revolt* is purely for momentary convenience. The pithy paradox of the occasion is far more devious. *Women in Revolt* must be seen and heard, at least once, to be appreciated. There is an aspect of the goings-on that makes things look, every few seconds, like a skit from *Laugh In* when that TV fixture is being flippant about such grave problems as politics, drugs, and student unrest. However, you can never be sure which side Rowan and Martin, godfathers of *Laugh In,* are on. You know that *Women in Revolt* is *not* on the side of the Women's Liberation Movement, unless, intentionally, for publicity reasons. Nothing is taken seriously in this film except the relentless desire of confirmed female impersonators to act out what Wallace Stevens once termed the Supreme Fiction. If you can detach yourself from the *Laugh In* response, the film's shenanigans acquire a rather awesome majesty.

In three different styles, Jackie Curtis (probably the most gifted actress of the three), Candy Darling, and Holly Woodlawn enact Eve as a loose-woman-of-the-people inhabiting two social zones. Jackie and Holly are poor-bohemian, Candy is the renegade darling of a rich middle-class New Jersey family. Candy puts on the "lady act," Jackie is a carnal shrew, and Holly a dotty nymphomaniac. Jackie proceeds to have a baby by a famous muscle man, whom she pays for the privilege, Holly disgraces the fem-lib gatherings by dyking openly with both males and females, usually undressed, while Candy, mesmerized by Hollywood's lure, is on her way to being a sex goddess for hire when the film—as if it were, after all, a real bathroom act —gets flushed down the drain.

But, again, mere description is beggared when it comes to rendering in words what *Women in Revolt* "is." Candy— with very photogenic, very feminine features—is the only one of the three to give any substantial illusion of being a woman except at the most casual of moments. Voice, height, muscle, and size of limb and face, and that ineffable something known as personality, give the show away more frequently than they maintain its supposed illusion. The point comes up: Is any illusion, in the proper sense of that word, intended? I think none is. And here lies the subtlety of this supreme, consciously ridiculous, fiction.

Life is a camp—and this means *your* life, too, lib ladies! One characteristic of the Warhol/Morrissey entertainments is that put-on is not simply the only real thing in life, but that it cannot be quite real unless it obeys the most dated, vulgar, and received modern stereotypes, even while making these look generally obscene. By no means are these stereotypes the most important things in life because they are the strongest, most serious, and significant things, but because they are the silliest, most vulnerable things. It's a gay way of twisting Pirandello's old tale—mixing the real with the unreal so thoroughly that both become irretrievably absurd.

And yet—this is the deepest, most elusive nuance of it —not *altogether* absurd. One of the timeless morals of exploiting unreality in theatrical media is that when the chips (or, here, the chippies) are down, it is exactly when the stuff of life becomes most preposterously unreal that life begins to take on the hues of some tragic inevitability: some bottom-layer truthfulness. The manners of *Women in Revolt* are, in the innocent sense, the vulgarest; in the artistic sense, the most amateurish. Moreover, this situation is not something plotted by a person or persons with an idea; rather, it's a kind of mental collaboration by spontaneous combustion: a sum total arrived at by craftsmen who chime in by wishing to "make something" of the inner self. The resulting play-acted satire is only —like the classic Hollywood star vehicle—an excuse for three transvestites to work up their everyday stuff before a camera. Though in utterly shabby clothes, this film has as profoundly and humanly authentic an inspiration as Balzac's *Sarrasine* or Gautier's *Mademoiselle de Maupin*. Of course, nothing could be further from Garbo's high moral transvestism than the bizarre gyrations of the Misses-Messrs. Curtis, Darling, and Woodlawn.

But, you see, that's just it! Here the gimmick and the grandeur are all together. We never forget, nor are we meant to forget, that these "actresses" are males. And they are most male when most absurdly pretending to be female. At the end, Candy has a scene where she is a pretty convincing sex-goddess parody, now being interviewed on her dazzling prospects, as if, a few years ago, she had been crowned Miss America. This scene, with an apparently lesbian interviewer in man's clothes, ends (as do most previous scenes) with slapstick violence on the *Laugh In* model. But it's the *Laugh In* with a difference. Somehow it provides a transcendent insight, piercing, and not without blood, into what the Marilyn Monroes and Jean Harlows of film history always used to be about. And this insight is actually the inspiration of a group of males. *Women in Revolt*, much more than *Women in Love*, is all-male, indelibly all-male no matter how many dresses are in it, or how many organically real women collaborate on it. Real women are present here, but only to show that *they* are not the point. Women's Lib, Right On! Ours is a man's world; maybe it is a world ruled by male chauvinism. But Andy Warhol, in the century's eighth decade, knows this more pointedly than did D. H. Lawrence in the century's third decade. I may remind the reader that male chauvinism precisely predicates what the fem-lib contingents resent these days: woman as either a glamourized sex object or a childbearing domestic slave. We see these extreme types on television, but are they really so prevalent in life?—that is, so offensively prevalent?

Don't think that by "a man's world" or "male chauvinism" I signify only homosexual constituents. The movies offer variously benign and malign versions of the heterosexual male who is attracted to wearing female disguise, and not even for sexual purposes; at least, ostensibly not. We might mark the difference between the sinister Halloweenism of Tony Perkins' transvestite killer in *Psycho* and the naïve Halloweenism of the youth in *I Vitelloni* who goes to a masquerade ball in drag though he belongs to a heterosexual fellowship. At last, falling-down drunk and hysterical, the poor guy collapses at the very moment he glimpses his sister leaving the ball with her lover to whom she is engaged. The indication is plain that the male masquerader has strayed from the "brotherhood" and yearns after, not his sister, but the man she is to marry.

I Vitelloni, however, was the film where Fellini wanted the implication of homosexuality definite, not suspended. Art has the habit of adjusting many of the dislocations that crop up in life despite the desire of film editors—at least, a decade ago—to throw them out with the rest of the cuttings. As to the homosexual implications in *Performance*, to quash *them* would have been to suppress the film. A sort of silent void begins to surround the mutual hideout of that rock star and his gangster guest. To make this void into a flexible metaphor: Every human individual lives in a world surrounded by a vacuum communicating only partially, obliquely with the things known as society and group and even family. Minority groups may systematically create new solidarities, new "life styles," but in so doing they also establish new vacuums. Paradoxically, they are separatist. So it is, we reflect, with planets and universes. They segregate or integrate themselves according to inherent dynamic factors or the viewpoint adopted of them, the context in which they may appear.

For years, an individual may live surrounded by a virtu-ally loveless space. Then suddenly the "void" is occupied. The common act of cohabitation acquires a new dynamic meaning because now one shares it deeply, abidingly with another in-dividual. A fresh magnetic bridge—of which the penis is a symbol—has been built. *Performance* shows us this situation in anticlimactic parody. Two antithetic life styles, the rock star's and the gangster's, have accidentally tangled, and yet they cannot properly connect. In a way, each tries to do so but fails. The situation develops combustibility; the "silence" previously separating them, being a sort of peace, turns into war. The final shot is of Chas, the gangster, still in wig and masquerade, at the tail end of his "trip," but he has just been collared by his old gang and apparently is going to be erased. Momentarily he is a transvestite of both sex and silence.

A similarly disoriented, disturbing silence happens to have been artfully pictured and seriously explored by Ingmar Bergman in his masterful film *The Silence*. In a contingency as forced and abrupt as that in *Performance,* the unrests I have mentioned have fought their way to the surface, attained various articulations. Whenever not properly freed into action, these tend to be smothered, to assume weird or spasmodic forms, and sometimes, as literally happens in *The Silence*, throttle themselves. If offbeat sexuality and its transvestite symbols reach allegorical levels, as they do in Bergman's film, it is time to reflect on the theoretic basis of transvestism in the movies as either sacred or profane.

As we know, a number of films involve homosexuality as primarily a psycho-physical adventure while the more contemporary milieu testifies to the role of drugs as a function in such adventures. But the drug experience, and the whole psychedelic cult, presupposes a radical disorientation from common consciousness as well as from rationalized moral conventions; in short, it requires an excluding silence, hermetic walls, to guard what is within. There is no release of the drug world into the speculative world of metaphysics and the imagination. The drug ritual itself is stifled, needs "transfusion" as well as "transvestism." Internally, the sexual neutering I have described only coincides with *non*sexual neuterizings of our milieu as monitored by drug addiction. One might term the whole hippie idea a strategy of isolation from enemies through disguise: a paranoid transvestism where the armored disguise is an essential part of the ritual, is integral and indispensable.

We can observe of the ever restless and articulately inarticulate underground film movement that male transvestism

—seemingly a propaganda as well as an art weapon in the keeping of homosexuals—is by no means only a gambit to attract males and keep out the opposite sex. If we take seriously Jack Smith's notorious film *Flaming Creatures* (1962), the drag act of presumably homosexual males is a strangely static and narcissistic routine as well as a sort of atavistic *hommage* to the female. Instead of the homosexual orgy we find in *The Damned* and *Scorpio Rising*—both of these oriented to male militarism, both finally excluding women altogether—Smith's peculiar transvestite cosmetics concerns flirtation between males in drag that turns into flirtation with a real woman and finally her rape by cunnilingus, with the transvestites acting as Handmaids of Mari,* betraying, as it were, their own Queen, the female deity, into the power of a profane, half-naked male cunnilinguist.

While this "ritual" rape is proceeding—is it, by the way, the male trying to transvestize himself, as in *The Dybbuk*, by total entrance into a woman's body?—some of the transvestites also get naked, only to expose organs seemingly incapable of erection. There are enigmatic nuances here, perhaps personal with their creator, Jack Smith (who himself appears in drag, then somehow gets lost), but rather, I believe, based on an instinctive sort of monosexuality. Consider the way in which the black Venus of *Fellini Satyricon*, by virtue of sex magic, rescues the homosexual Encolpius from the impotence that overtakes him. Fellini, in fact, saw and admired Smith's film before he made the *Satyricon*.

Unisex—to essentialize the present point—is but the formal superstructure, the contemporary symptom of phenomenal monosexuality. Monosexuality comes to be the strictly passive state of the inherent bi-structure. It, too, is a primordial condition that may be historical—no mere figment of metaphysical discourse as it is in Plato's *Symposium*. The ads for unisex fashions could not precisely reflect—indeed probably have nothing to do with--metaphysical preoccupations. There may have arrived in our times, both in the race and the individual, a common spontaneous will to revert *existentially* to primordial monosexuality. In this dimension, unisexuality would not accurately

* See reference on p. 30.

correspond to bisexuality (experience of one sex with both sexes), since bisexuality denotes a conscious, everyday moral practice; rather the term, as I define it, would mean ambi-sexuality; e.g., the faculty of *un*conditioned reflex in any one sex toward any other—any time, any place, any manner. The public love-ins would then be a social demonstration of sud-denly unfettered monosexuality; collective lovemaking—such as we find in certain Underground films and off-Broadway plays —would be simply the articulations of unisex.

As for fairly happy, at least workable, marriages between females with masculine traits and males with feminine traits, statistics afford testimony for the existence of such unions. As we also know, the ingredients of sexual chemistry, in normally organic males as in normally organic females, are mixed: part male elements in each, part female elements. The only practical difficulty is that, while it is the simplest thing in the world to distinguish, in the undress, an organic female from an organic male, and to grasp why they are corresponding opposites, the hardest thing in the world—undress or no!—is to distinguish a special sex from a special sex *as equally corresponding opposites*. Nevertheless, this has become the self-appointed task of the current dating services that advertise in the sex mags, along with "personals" that name much more specific requirements and qualifications. Here the problem involves something to *rate* categorically, not to *date* categorically.

Speech and silence are ambivalent moral and aesthetic situations. Silence is holy where speech is unholy: a profanation. But speech too is sacred, or holy, where silence is a profanation. Sacred things, including sex rituals, are characterstically sur-rounded (and thus "protected") by silence. Yet they too require speech: articulation, expression—they require breath, air, al-though, as proper to the greatness, it be a sheltered air. Silence-as-profanation is the theme chosen by Bergman for the film I have mentioned. Not without cause, in *The Silence*, do homo-sexuality and transvestism become pivots by which to measure unholy silence. One can see the peculiar general relevance of improper, that is, immoral silence: that very element of taboo which Freud had to demolish in order to let in the air of truth on things sexual. There is an exclusively moral "transvestism" about all truths in our world—the name of the "dress" is hypocrisy.

Habitually, our society pretends that peace is not an appearance but a substance; that, under a maneuver of moral consciousness that is universal, peace does not become (as it *does*) a mere dress for the persistence of all kinds of wars, economic and social as well as military. The word "peace" becomes a mere technical convenience, a semantic hypocrisy. We are all in the midst of a cool peace, as it were, sheltering wars that are still warm. For his setting in *The Silence*, Bergman ingeniously chooses a city that obviously is a strategic center for troop movements in some undefined military situation, maybe war with a foreign country, though it could be a civil war. All general identities in the film are apochryphal or unmentioned. A family of refugees—wealthy, upper class, because they land in the city's best, probably oldest hotel—have temporarily, because of some official hitch, been prevented from getting clear of the main scene of crisis. Its members are two adults, sisters, one of whom is married; the third is her little son.

Only faint hints are given of what the family circumstances are, "who" they are, or what their plans are besides escaping to some "other country." At the end, Bergman makes language itself the unmistakable symbol of proper human communication, in that the language of the country where they are quarantined is a strange one, not even identifiable to the audience. Only on a train (which finally the two surviving members of the family manage to take) does it become clear that now the two, the mother and her little boy, will have to learn a new means of communication, the rudiments of a foreign tongue that implies a new, super, communication. Or, perhaps, it is only that human communication, having been totally destroyed by fatal "silences," must be learned all over again. The elder sister, suffering from progressive suffocation, has elected to stay and die in the hotel.

The relevant thing, implying a profane transvestism, is that sex is the crux of the family situation, which, acutely, with sure touch, Bergman reveals to us. Among other things that this high bourgeois family has failed to do, obviously, is to perfect sexual communication; that is, they have not adjusted their insistent inner drives to those surface appearances deemed so proper and necessary. The elder sister is by nature a lesbian, but either has altogether suppressed her true sex, or has become, at this stage of her life, fixated on her own sister, so that the family heat is now definitely on the libido. That no male members of the family are present except the little boy may have something to do with the passing moment of precipitation to which we are introduced. In any case, the safety of the three, perhaps their health if not their very lives, is in jeopardy; this too intensifies the internal family crisis. Momentarily they are halted in a vacuum—magically, they are "free" in this artificial impasse—and things happen.

With recognizable point the lesbian sister (Ingrid Thulin) is a writer, in fact a translator. Yet she has been unable to translate into adequate action, seemingly, the true impulses of her libido. Obviously, too, speech frustration is the gauge of the prevailing silence. There are stretches of action with little or no dialogue. Words are egregiously sparse because the frank, spontaneous speech that would be welcome liberation under the circumstances is not forthcoming owing to the incestuous lesbian situation. The elder sister begins to have choking fits; she dare not declare her feelings to her sister, so she finds it hard to work and takes to her bed. But the younger sister is now driven to express her sexuality in this frightening general vacuum and picks up a virile, good-looking waiter in a café, and rents a room in the hotel for their rendezvous.

The watchful, anxious, suffering lesbian seeks out her missing sister and opens a door behind which she hears her voice. The couple are in bed together, and there is a scene of harsh, blind, futile recrimination between the two women as the naked man, staring speechlessly, lurks in the rumpled bedclothes. One sister, the young mother, is for all-out self-realization; the other is for temporizing, respecting the decencies, and so on. Having grimly evacuated her intruding elder, the younger, now quite forgetful of her little son, returns to her pleasure and allows her pickup (as if it were a sought humiliation, a self-punishment) to sodomize her. Is it only precaution against impregnation? I doubt it. The scene is magnificently real, magnificently conveyed in its impact, as if the irregular ecstasy, a precious sacrilege, were an explosion muffled by walls. She screams as he enters her. It is the triumphant sexual speech breaking through the silence at any price.

Meanwhile Bergman has used the restlessness of the bored little boy, wandering the august hotel corridors in search of a magical adventure, to supply a brilliant symbolic touch to the realistic allegory. The boy fleetingly tries to engage the attention of a male worker, is briefly entertained by a benevolent old butler, then runs into the film's most remarkable invention: a troupe of dwarfs who are performing at a local theater. They are all men, but when we first see them at the hotel, they are parading in a body down the corridor to their rooms in the awkward, but gravely retarded, manner of those with short, partly deformed legs. Somehow, as Bergman films it, it is like a religious procession, grand, rhythmic, almost pontifical. And one of the first things we notice is that one of the foremost dwarfs (all still in their theatrical costumes) is in drag as a bride.

Whether or not any of them are homosexual hardly matters—at least, not to the dwarfs. To us, to Bergman, to the little boy, his mother and his aunt, the point has relevance which might make it mercilessly true, and in the artistic view, not a little sublime. What the dwarfs proceed to do with the little boy, in the harmless sport which they begin, is to dress him in one of their female costumes. Again the silence has been broken through, and with devastating thrust. This casual transvestite incident so common to childhood, and perhaps quite meaningless, may conceivably be a supreme moment of revelation for the frail, wistful little boy: the golden, glamorous sign of his homosexual future. The essential thing is that, as such, it would be in the film's evident pattern of sexual deviation—in fact, if it were *not* within it, why should Bergman have chosen to introduce this bizarre little incident of transvestism? The boy's mother, having missed him, has started looking for him and comes upon the investment scene at the height of its fun. The dwarfs are laughing and innocently horsing around; the delighted boy is as if bewitched. Like a righteous mother (this bit could be on television) she reproaches the dwarfs, gets the boy undivested, and taking him by the hand, stalks out—out into the restored silence. And she leaves a silence behind her. For the hilarity of the dwarfs has been quelled.

8. HOMEROS

IN UNIFORM

We have already had a taste of Homeros in uniform in the discussion of *The Damned* in the first chapter. In that episode Visconti's film avails a sort of epic view of homosexualism as a metabeaver cult. We see a group of beautifully photographed muscular young men whose status as either Nazis or homos is questionable owing to the use of so many appealing specimens as hardy German militarists and wanton gays rolled into one. Just where is the true masquerade? Possibly it is on more than one level. Somehow one can't quite put the young men in focus except as actors in an oddly compromising situation. The universal legend is that the military uniform is most becoming to males and it shows up in romance as an immeasurable asset. How quickly that uniform is doffed among the SA men in *The Damned* as soon as the peasant girls have vacated the premises!

In recent decades of the sexual enlightenment, the uniform in reality has come to be both a gloss for homosexuals who go in for the straight bag and (with sailors especially) a veritable symbol of what justly began to be called cruising. Whores as free-lancers, no matter of which sex, are and always have been cruisers. Sailors, fresh in port, are just as legitimate pickings for homosexuals as for whores; only in the homeroic realm, it is the sailor, not the homosexual, who "sells" himself. Moreover, the military uniform has come to be recognized as a sort of sexual

243

uniform in the large, looser moral sense. In short, the army and navy are training schools for homosexual relations as naturally engendered by the time-honored conditions of isolation from women and the coarse physical intimacies of dormitory life.

Homeros in uniform therefore has a vast background extending deep into the social past. In pagan times (as we find from a moving episode in Flaubert's novel *Salammbo*) it was a military cult; male lovers died together on the battlefield as gallantly and loyally as they made love on their pallets. The mercenary army that is trapped in *Salammbo* has pairs of lovers who fall on each other's swords rather than die by the hand of the enemy. Thus the homosexual love-death has its own legend to set beside that provided in the heterosexual domain. Nor is the sexual implication of the uniform, indiscriminately homo-hetero, confined to the Regular Army. The school uniform is just as eligible as the military as a sign for sexual inversion as promoted by sex segregation. One of the very first candid displays of lesbianism on the screen came in the classic German film *Maedchen in Uniform,* where of course it was treated as a scandal, but not, decidedly, as an unpardonable offense. Right in the film is a handsome young schoolmistress who tries to protect the "guilty" girl from the punishment of expulsion the relentless headmistress wishes to impose on her.

Not surprisingly, the mechanism which betrays a brimming-over adolescent in the flush of her first lesbian passion is that old standby, the school play, in which the roles of both sexes are taken by one sex. The charmingly nubile Manuela (already the object of a crush in one of her schoolmates) has just the touch of boyish brio to make the young actress, Hertha Thiele, excellent in the part. As a cavalier declaring himself to his beloved in a costume play, Manuela, trim and handsome in her male tights, looks so much like a boy and speaks out so fervently that the whole school finds itself on the edge of its seats. Harmless little "love" passages and jealous tiffs among the girls have built up the necessary atmosphere for the climactic revelation. This comes when, at the celebration after the play, Manuela gets tipsy and openly avows her passion for a certain attractive Fräulein among her teachers (Dorothea Wieck). Manuela being rebuked and temporarily isolated for this "scandal," it becomes clear that the feelings she has expressed for the Fräulein are not unreciprocated, if only in terms of chaste affection.

The film's original ending had Manuela, grief-stricken and terrified, commit suicide by throwing herself down the building's stairwell. For the United States, at least, this was changed to have her plucked away from her perch in the nick of time by her schoolmates. Manuela is conceived, naturally, as a neurotic schoolgirl whose emotionalism makes her vulnerable to the well-known temptation of schoolgirls as of schoolboys. The theme was not news to the world in 1932, and yet it was plain that society, even then, was taking such aberrations more as normal phenomena, less as something calling instantly for military punishment, social ostracism and/or clinical treatment. But bourgeois morality has always been flaccid about such problems of youth, and tends to be so to this day. This is true because nobody but medical experts and other puritans presume to be certain about how "dangerous" an aberration homosexual practices are in the unformed individual.

In this film, the time is still the era of imperialism and the creed is drilled into these pupils that they must grow up to be the proud mothers of German soldiers. The issue is dramatized in advance by the oppressive presence of German militarism and German racism. The autocratic old headmistress, a Prussian idealist, wears on her bosom (as do the other schoolteachers) a military cross hanging on a broad ribbon. The school is thus a female barracks, and the headmistress thinks of its members explicitly as the female counterparts of soldiers. It might have come as a complete surprise to Frau Principal to be told that so much masculinizing of mere girls might suggest, to a few of them anyway, that the male ideal be carried into the sphere of sex as a helpful, if discreet, dormitory exercise. What in boys' schools, especially military ones, is "effeminate" and "despicable" would be "masculine" and "admirable" in this Potsdam school for girls. But to reason like that is to honor fact and logic, neither of which, of course, has anything to do with ethical codes, which traditionally tend to be arbitrary and remote.

In strange contrast with this school drama, where race

pride and military caste promote homosexuality, is the comedy-drama of another famous film, *Zéro de Conduite (Zero for Conduct)*, from neighboring France and by a director, Jean Vigo, who did not live long enough to leave us anything else so fine. Done in 1933, the work is at heart a farce, but so full of unpretentious and inventive wit in characterizing an ordinary boys' school that its human texture comes across as extraordinarily true and funny, really close to the bone; perhaps too close, for not only is the crux of the plot a conspiracy by four schoolboys to stage a rebellion against school authority and spoil Commencement Day, but one of the little rebels is a girlish, long-haired youngster already apprehended as homosexual, and threatened therefore, like Manuela, with expulsion.

Everyone in his right mind knows about the fabled "crush" among schoolboys and schoolgirls. He knows it without consciously calling it homosexuality, or a disease, or a thing demanding swift, decisive retribution. The amusing point about *Zéro* in this regard is that the outraged school director who "reads from the book" to the trembling litle Homeros is an imposing midget, whose absurd dignity, frantic gestures, and squeaky voice make the little boy look like a *cause célèbre* for the resident gay organization. Funnily, just that is the view taken by the filmmaker, Vigo, who has Homeros and his lover join with two comrades in a plot to disrupt the school. The dormitory is wrecked that night by the student body, which then stages a delightfully wild victory march, filmed magically in slow motion. The dormitory master has been routed and is now mock-crucified upright on his own bed. Next day, the four rebels have taken to the roof and pelt the parents and dignitaries (some represented by cardboard figures) assembled for Commencement exercises. The film ends indecisively, but hilariously, on the note of anarchist revolution.

The reader will already have recognized *Zéro de Conduite* as the source of the much later English film about a similar but deadlier school revolt, *If . . .* In *If . . .* we find the quasi-homosexual atmosphere of schoolboys banding together for illegal pleasures and plotting to escape from masters who give them ritual whippings. Here too we locate the reflex action of group

revolt that, in recent years, has lifted college campuses to the
level of national headlines. Vigo's film, like other preceding
events in the media, might be said to have prophesied those
headlines, in France as elsewhere. But *Zéro* is very different in
spirit from *If . . .* The importance and the great strength of
schoolboy revolt in *Zéro* is that it is spiritual and moral, not
physical, or even actual except as an orgiastic rite; for the action
is literally all farced fantasy. The schoolboys themselves are the
only real things in Vigo's film: they and their *feelings.* The work
lives in a kind of twilight zone between reality and imagination,
and thus is rather surrealist. It uses fast and slow motion and
other tricks for comical effect. The school's physical instructor
stands on his head while also drawing pictures, and in the school
yard he imitates Charlie Chaplin. The school director, as just
mentioned, is a midget, while the cardboard effigies in the reviewing stand on Commencement Day pinpoint the absurd
unreality of it all. There is an official adult spy, known as the
Creep, who haunts the pupils and is straight out of detective
fiction. Hence Vigo's world is really the mind of a schoolboy,
true to his comrades, to love and to the idea of individual freedom. The presence of the little homosexual, quite grave and
hippie-haired, puts a finishing touch on the concept of love
(whatever kind) as essential to individual freedom.

It is said that Vigo reserved for his own pleasure, in
Zéro, a layer of sardonic emotion, that he really *meant* the black
flag of anarchism the rebels set flying on the roof. If so, he must
have been gratified, because for many years the film was
banned in France. Lindsay Anderson, the director of *If . . . ,*
was perhaps equally serious at heart, yet he declined to involve
homosexuality. In rounding out the foursome that comprise *his*
student revolt, he enlists a neighborhood waitress with whom
one of the youths has had a flirtation which ended in fantasy-
rape. In making the rebels into arsonists, and a couple of machine
guns (rather than miscellaneous objects) into the weapons of
revolt, *If . . .* attempts to reorient the fantasy rebellion of the
original *Zéro* to reality. The massacre of parents, schoolmasters,
army officers, and other students has begun as *If . . .* abruptly
ends. With its title, the film makes a feint at taking the curse

off propaganda in advance, yet insists on itself as a symbolic threat: if things do get too bad, then student demonstrations will turn into student wars—with real bullets. *If* . . . (significantly dealing with older boys) strives to be jaunty and dry, radical and lighthearted and serious, all at once; it ends up looking like Charley's Aunt if that lady were a suffragette in pants and her medium a documentary film. As for me, I'll take the Vigo version, even if I get "zero for conduct" from the SDS.

Our time's rising political activation of all minority groups, including homosexuals, has been repeatedly alluded to here. Accordingly, I cannot see that *If* . . . 's revision of *Zéro*'s homosexual element has done anything to slow down the action of gays about their group and individual rights. Surely, with the flood of homosexual material in the movies, recognized and unrecognized, it would be pretentious to do more than I'm doing: trying carefully to sort out and identify, as well as evaluate artistically, its various modes as they are self-manifested. In this chapter I shall be concentrating on the meaning of the uniform as a universal index to homosexual mores and their culture, not forgetting the poetic cult that Jean Genet visualizes in prison uniforms nor the secretive cult that produces confused poetry and outright messes despite all its fine fronts and brass buttons as militarily costumed.

The adventures of the sapphic sex may be brave enough, even fine enough, but to ignore feminine militancy for the moment, let us pass to the training of young male minds and bodies and explore further how sexuality is school-disciplined into sadism. A tight, trim illustration comes from Germany in *Young Törless* (1968). The young hero of the title part is revolted by the decision of the bigger, more brutal students of his military school to gang up on a not very girlish, but flabby, little boy and make him the victim of a torture ritual. When the morally scrupulous Törless stands up to the mob to save the crushed, almost annihilated victim, he is jeeringly accused of being "one of his lovers." Seemingly the stereotyped slur has no basis in fact: its significance is the imagination of boys whose sadism naturally takes symbolic as well as real forms. Nevertheless Törless prevails: it is the main action of a rather lean, dry film. Realistically modulated, it is a cool gray in tone with cruel edges. It seems to be the modern German conscience speaking of a repented past. Less rhetorical in manner than *If . . .* , it too might be murmuring an "if" message. *If* schoolboy sadism comes to this, can we be surprised that homosexuality flourishes *if only* as a gesture of liberation from the brutality of the all-male military cult? Take Nazism as an example, etc., etc.

Accusing a schoolboy you dislike or despise of being a "fag" may or may not mean that the charge is true. It may be only an appearance (like girlish features) or a senseless slander. The point is that sometimes not just schoolboys or schoolgirls themselves, but also authors, use the rumored slur that someone is homosexual as a pretext to focus on a subject without committing oneself to it except technically. Two American "school" films display diverse approaches to homosexuality as a mere appearance, open to serious misinterpretation. Both are facilely off the beam, dramaturgically, by making homosexual mountains out of tacit heterosexual molehills. That—we learn from these two movies—is a craft all to itself.

One, *Tea and Sympathy*, is strictly for those sentimentalists instantly persuaded by the fable that unusual sensitivity in a schoolboy, existing in a total society of young brutes, gets him falsely branded as a homosexual. Even as a dated myth, the thing is questionable. The young hero's consequent agony and the way it is soothed by tea and sympathy (administered by Deborah Kerr as the headmaster's wife) was mounted for the screen as if it were a precious objet-d'art in danger from rioting but miraculously saved. Besides being archaic, the film is a prodigiously silly fable, pulling the realities with which it deals dishonestly, systematically out of whack. For all that I and those on the set know—or, for that matter, that the author knows—the persecuted youth is really heterosexual and his victimization by his schoolmates and his headmaster is a simple outrage. Of course, it would be just as much an outrage if he *were* the "sister boy" the others call him—but the last is a point, presumably, that occurs to nobody.

As always in works so superficially contrived, it is not an individual or an idea that is libeled in *Tea and Sympathy,* but reality itself. One is saddened to think so, but it seems most unlikely that the play or the film would have attained its passing eminence had there not been a ready-made public of unthinking nonobservers to react to it. The chief stupidity involved is that the homosexuality of the occasion, far from being the archaic sister-boy myth, is the sadism of the schoolboy rabble that tears off the distraught youth's pajamas during a "bonfire ritual." A good-looking young actor named John Kerr adequately plays the part of the victim as a fleeing, toothsomely fleshed he-virgin altogether worthy of the statutory ambisexed sadism of the schoolboys. What is an old-fashioned academic institution, in other words, is made to appear in *Tea and Sympathy* as a baseless "criminal conspiracy."

But that was when campuses were still in the fifties. I doubt that *Tea and Sympathy* would dare show its face, today, anywhere but on television screens, where, after all, there are no public buildings inflammably available. Lillian Hellman's *The Children's Hour,* filmed and filtered down under the title *These Three,* offers us the prying sexual curiosity of a little girl as the villain in academic uniform. Miss Hellman's basic point is how much fatal harm can be done by the constriction of natural sexual curiosity through imposed school disciplines. But this is a closed proposition in a dual sense. When it comes to exposing what really goes on in life, just how honest will the exposure be? The Hellman play turned out to be a labored essay which could not conceal its true purpose: sensation-mongering for regular patrons of the Broadway drama. Customarily, the movies introduce some nelly male type as spice to round out the fun of a heterosexual comedy and produce bonus laughs. In her turn, Miss Hellman devised bonus "serious thoughts" and supplied some poker-faced, if overblown, stimulation of the sapphic gland. No laughs, you see . . . just tears.

The situation is classically simple. A snooping schoolgirl misinterprets what she is able to eavesdrop on between two female schoolteachers who share quarters. The schoolgirl—morbid little thing that she is—tells her story, and the two teachers are in hot water. When it comes to the agonized admission of one woman that she does have lesbian feelings for the other but has suppressed them, the film chickens out, omitting this inward basis for outward appearances. Hence the "guilty" teacher's suicide looks like the easy melodramatic tack-on—as if an honest female heterosexual couldn't live with the slander that she is homosexual. Golly! In making lesbian emotion into shadow rather than substance, this film pulled the one punch held by the original play. Well, that snooping little girl was no lady! As a matter of fact, if we want a real lesbian in the movie, she will have to be underage, possess an "unhealthy" sexual curiosity, and be a nasty little snooper, no less than something of a liar.

When prejudiced or subconscious psychology must play with the generic facts of homosexuality and end by freely inventing their particulars, we are at the lowest level of romance: the silly gossip of human relationships. Naturally, gossip can be very true in general and quite false in particular, fanciful in form but accurate in substance. This is probably its most sinister danger: this fluid ambiguity regarding form and substance. Let us suppose it true that there was a positive lesbian situation in *The Children's Hour* (naïvely bowdlerized by the movie version) and that the true imaginative value of the play is an affair between female schoolteachers on the brink of understanding themselves; in other words, that the snooping schoolgirl's imagination holds the play's and movie's true creative relevance. After all, though the "guilty" woman commits that drearily *de rigueur* suicide, it is only the little snooper's initiative that has brought her to book ("cowardly lion" that she is!). Let us also suppose that young Törless of the other film is quite capable—through nobility and sheer sensitivity if you like—of having an erotic susceptibility to the little victim of the torture ritual; let us more boldly assume that he could easily, at his age, have homosexual tendencies, regardless of how serious they may turn out to be. This is still not the prime focus of the film in which he appears, while lesbianism *is* the prime focus of Miss Hellman's play. The author tried to redeem the first movie version by, years later, adapting a second and restoring its original title, *The Children's Hour*. This time the big punch was not withheld. Yet oddly, by now, with a mediocre realization, the thing hardly made a sizzle: it was still a tabbycat frame-up posing as a well-made play.

The lurking relevance is that homosexual matters are

automatically involved in the situations of all the above-mentioned movies except *If* . . . , which rather pointedly side-stepped them. Behavior we speak of as customary, traditional; normal or abnormal, arbitrary or correct. Sexual behavior wears uniforms insofar as it be apprehended through a set of norms, through masculine or feminine styles without necessary reference to organic gender, through minute cultivations of the senses as well as certain standard acts of lovemaking. Thus we get the sexual types, the offbeat or deviate sexes, which are my subject here. In this respect the movies offer us a museum of costumes, historical and modern; they offer us sexual uniforms to which dress uniforms supply only certain general indices. Transvestism, as I have shown, is only the male or female as a surface gender, thus the male or female as only a "uniform," a typical appearance whose overt generality must be supplemented with a number of inevitable particulars.

Male sadism is not a simple thing, not a simple "uniform." Yet a military uniform is, so to speak, a positively compromising, a challenging, index to sadism as a vehicle of eroticism; that is, displaced eroticism. All sorts of sexuality may hide behind the braid, buttons, stripes, and medals of a uniform, behind its gloves and revolvers. Above I referred to the masculine glory of a military uniform, to its role in the romances of sex. High military uniforms have always denoted prestige, privilege, and prerogative. Yet exactly these moral advantages have helped authenticate and propagate some of human history's most cruel persecutions—and I don't mean sexual persecutions, or persecutions at school-age levels. All the same, a soldier's uniform denotes stern duties, even sacred oaths. A soldier is still, as of today, a sworn killer. It would be humanly implausible if his character as a killer did not in some degree, however minor, affect his sexuality, his attitude toward love and his specific erotic style. This is why sublimation is historically so important in the annals of war, where soldiering became an aspect of love, when a knight tilted for his lady, his "ideal," and men literally fought for the Virgin Mary. Even in later times, up to our century and decade, soldiers at war serve Motherland or Fatherland as a symbol of sacrificing or sublimating their sexual natures while in the fighting field.

The thing causing that sadistic little brute in *Young Törless* to cast the homosexual epithet of "lover" at the hero as a token of contempt did not necessarily mean that the speaker himself was innocent of using boys as sex objects. Homosexual relations at boys' schools may be on the animal level, may constitute a form of bullying, a way of gaining ascendancy over one's mates, becoming a "leader." Such activity is a physical purge, like excretion, and as such a notch above masturbating; it is not homosexual to the future of a boy who has a true heterosexual nature. This is why *Tea and Sympathy* is such a crudely inept charade. The other evening, I heard on television about male inmates of New York City jails being indicted for insurrection, and "sodomy" was one of the charges mentioned. What did this mean? Probably only that sexual deprivation provided a violence that brought together, in moments of chaos, victim and victimizer. "Homosexuality" as a *status* was no more involved on this occasion than was heterosexuality. It was simply the blind libido persuaded into violent ambisexuality.

The point of using the term "lover" in the *Young Törless* incident was to show scorn for any tenderness, any emotional sincerity or romantic feeling, that might go along with the technically homosexual act. Both Jean Genet and Jean Cocteau (whose schoolboy bully, Dargelos, appears in *The Blood of a Poet*) have heroically idolized and idealized the aggressive, cynical, brutal youth who becomes homosexually worshiped by younger, weaker, more erotically susceptible boys, those who may have, homosexually or heterosexually, a *tender* future in love, and thus a status, a style, of sex. Genet has brilliantly made an aesthetic cult of this type (or rather style) of homosexual love. Through experience, he learned that the natural setting for it was prison, where males are segregated and where sexuality is repressed and pressed, as it were, into a monosexual uniform.

For Genet the supreme symbol of desirable masculinity became, above all, the condemned murderer, isolated from all sexes in his cell, awaiting death only. One finds rapturous prose by him on this subject: the idealized figure of the murderer in his pages becomes almost metasexual, sublime, and "untouchable," a profane metaphysical consort of the Virgin Mary. This sublimative note is struck in the very midst of life, at the most vulgar (I use this word neutrally) level of homosexual relationships, in Genet's novel *Notre Dame des Fleurs* (*Our Lady of the Flowers*): it is a sexually promiscuous world of fairies, pimps, hustlers, petty criminals, and murderers. In this world, a perfectly ordinary if attractive youth—of fluid sexuality at first, but destined to be homo—is nicknamed "Our Lady" purely by virtue of the hysterical cult of Homeros—vulgar and poetic, realistic and fanciful, personally appropriated by Genet and exploited in his art.

It is amusing that a columnist in one of our more articulate sex mags remarked, not long ago, that the "Get you, Mary" school of homosexual manners was fast passing away. This was said, I suspect, without in the least realizing the mythological connotation of that slang term used by old-fashioned gays. Roughly it means, "Take a look at you, Mary, you're out to dazzle, aren't you? You're acting up." Mostly it's good-natured, casual, but under cover of colloquialism, it can be nasty: a sarcastic thrust. Mary, as a generic nickname for individuals of the homeroic brotherhood, certainly derived from religion, and is (or was) a common strategy for profaning the sacred so as to bring it closer, just like the casual expletive "Jesus Christ!" Even a "God damn you!" establishes more of a link between curser and cursed than does the laconic, less forceful, "Damn you!" Damning, that is, was originally God's exclusive prerogative, and so a sign of divine interest in the individual addressed.

There is a great difference between schoolboy sadomasochism and the aesthetic sado-masochism of a Genet or a Cocteau. The Marquis de Sade, in making pain through sex a moral program, essentially poeticalized it as an aggressive form of asserting complete *social* freedom. On the automatic level, the casual sodomy vented by prisoners on the rampage is as much an outburst of social defiance as an expression of sheer lust. For his part, Sade was more a puritan than an aesthete. Hence his practices are, really, not so much emotional orgies as mere outrages designed to alarm the Establishment.

In the Dargelos incident of the snowball as Cupid's arrow (from *The Blood of a Poet*), the sado-masochistic mechanism appears in a naïve poetic dimension, but one just as calculated as

Sade's "political" dimension. Cocteau chose a typically French sentimental handling of the fabulous. Pain, for the little poet struck down by the snowball, is the pain of love as experienced by Saint Theresa, also pierced by "Cupid's arrow" in the hand of a youthful angel. It is sacred because it is inflicted by one's supreme lover—such is the fantasy of the schoolboy poet—and its pain is *necessary;* as necessary, in fact, as that accompanied by the drawing of blood when the maidenhead is broken. It is the erotic ecstasy of pain. From this pattern of sexual sensation the whole sado-masochistic aesthetic was drawn. Purely aesthetically, this has nothing to do with the rights demanded by sex-liberation movements. A grand private passion is anyone's right.

Of course, the master/slave equation endures as sado-masochistic ritual. It is achieved by a giver and a receiver who play-act double pain in sex, mimicking it as a ceremony whose physical climax, the orgasm, is heightened by psychic, or visionary, components as well as tactfully measured brutalizing. By this path, Jean Genet established a working hierarchy of homosex in his underworld of prison and the private lives of criminals at large. Carnal expression is natural to any sex not dedicated, like the religious, to chastity and the idealization of love. The supreme murderer in his cell is merely a "Dargelos" beyond reach and religiously enshrined. Genet decided to make a film expressing the homosex rituals of jails, and he called it, with true inspiration, *Un Chant d'Amour.*

The very barriers imposed by prison conditions contribute to the excitement, the "art," of achieving sexual contact, and thus are shaped into rituals of yearning and vicarious pleasure. By a tour de force of sensibility, knowing just how to exploit erotically the segregation of males, Genet creates a domain of absolute homosexual purity. The cigarette smoke blown through a hole in the wall separating two lovers—issuing from one mouth, swallowed by the other—is no mere substitute for kissing or irrumation: it becomes a great essence, the veritable music of the *chant d'amour.* The camera incarnates this essence also as pure mental fantasy: the mutual daydreaming of lovers who hallucinate a past reality or a possible future; one doesn't know which, because, on the plane of erotic transport, time itself becomes fluid. The prison guard, as if mesmerized, eavesdrops through an eyehole on the masturbatory rituals in a row of cells, where each inmate is engaged in the "dance" of his own special ritual. Genet invents an insidiously contagious all-male atmosphere of sex that acts like a fever of the blood. At last the guard draws his automatic, enters a cell, and thrashes the entranced occupant with his belt, then forces the gun into his mouth.

Being remarkably tense and beautiful, *Un Chant d'Amour* contrasts with the characterless, formless "openness" so typical of the male beaver film; even when the male (or female) beaver literally shows sexual acts—at least fragments of them—they look more like illustrations from an obligingly acted-out sex manual than like love or art. In beavers, it is not that the partners, or the daisy chain, aren't honestly addicted to sexual pleasures—it's that damned camera always there! "It makes you self-conscious."

Rather skillfully, the avant-garde film-maker Kenneth Anger has plucked from the cultures about him something of the Cocteau and Genet homo aesthetics, something of the Nazi erotic resonance in *The Damned,* if only because he had actual contemporaneity, a born poetic instinct, and the courage to embody in film (even when he was still in a California high school) the sexual gauntlet which Homeros must run in modern times and the urban environment. His work has nothing to do with stag or beaver films—or, for that matter, with metabeaver films.

Anyone who knows what cruising American sailors is, knows what the adoring homosexual fond of sex-in-uniform may be in for; not just cold, overbearing, brute sexuality that must be taken in slavish manner, but also the guilt reflex in the "master" following his orgasm; e.g., the sailor's impulse to abuse the thing he has used and so automatically reinstate the manhood he thinks he has sullied. Naturally, "male masters" are always candidates to become "male slaves" and thus unambiguously homosexual. In 1947, Anger devised on the theme an inspired little fantasy, *Fireworks,* in which the white figures of sailors are like ritual masters initiating a postulant into the severities of military-barracks sex. Stylistically it is not a perfect film; it remains a very authentic one.

Anger projects himself as a sort of male novice whose shocked sensibility, under the rigors of his initiation, instinctively moralizes it; the beating up that logically comes is realistic enough. The vision of a sailor holding the beaten-up youth in his arms, Pietà fashion, is not realistic, however, but pure fantasy. So is the sailor's supposed seminal stream, spraying·the victim's mouth as if it were milk fountaining from the maternal nipple. The simulated evisceration of the victim, in turn, is a demonstration of emotion, not literal except as it stands for the penetration of the anus as a kind of rape, an appalling destruction of the male's figurative maidenhead. Moreover, to the performer of fellatio, especially if it be forced, the image of the genitals themselves is rather visceral, as if the penis were an instrument of excavation on wheels. One may think, here, of the processional rituals on ancient Delos, which included an enormous phallus drawn, like a cannon, on wheels. In *Fireworks*, the destructive nature of the homosexual act as rape is symbolized (thus the film's title) by a lighted Roman candle brought out of a sailor's fly. A decorated Christmas tree, worn by the victim as a headdress, seals the sacramental quality of the fantasy Anger has invented.

Today, when homosexuality can be more candid, is freer to express itself without great risks, *Fireworks* must seem a trifle dated in look. Uniforms may still excite masochistic passions. The ritually bedecked Leather Boy, who has so many dangling chains, metal studs, and handcufflike bracelets, is of course an ornamental or "carnival" soldier: he is in military drag. Decidedly, uniforms don't guarantee that the regular sailor or soldier pickup will be (as the old canonic myth has it) a condescending hetero "master" who will have to be paid and who *may* beat you up; he is just as apt to be (unless you have knowingly picked a brute-master) enchantingly cooperative and a straightforward homosexual. In such situations, a highly precautionary feeling-out, to begin with, is necessary to guarantee an aggressive homosexual's safety.

Kenneth Anger has given Leather Boy S/M* sex a rather pretty and perspicuous framing in a film that has become an Underground classic, *Scorpio Rising*. Anger has simply never had the material means to develop properly his poetic style; unhappily, compromise is too often the note of his realizations. Hence *Scorpio Rising* is more like an animated album of cult eroticism than a pure film poem. I guess it depends too much on its documentary references to actual Hell's Angels and assorted tribes of Bike Boys. Yet Anger's intuitive as well as statistical knowledge is evident and benefits his film as a documentary fantasy. Besides, he has had the imagination to relate the pop-cult habit of reading comic books and physique manuals (which the Leather Boy does when relaxing in his den) to the cult of Hitlerian youth as orgiastic (see *The Damned*). Anger's film, while crudely composed at points, has a sustained energy.

The male's idealization of the male, with its built-in temptation to extend itself to narcissism and homosexuality, is a mechanism clearly and economically, if glancingly, revealed in *Scorpio Rising*. A naked-to-the-waist muscular young male figure (significantly beheaded by the framing) appears as a Hercules with straddling legs and bulging, highlighted jock-strap. All the outwardness of this male cult, its mad career on the highways, its show of girl partners riding the motorcycle's second seat, is deftly elided with its occasional underside: the secret all-male orgy, one-hundred percent homosexual and candidly messy; it takes place in one of those obscure little hangouts that have "members." At the end, Anger connects all this with the death wish that rightly, I think, he considers inherent in quasi-homosexual militarism. Seen thus, Nazism is an enticement to die for an ideal at once metasexual, patriotic, and S/M. In *Scorpio Rising*, the face of a Leather Boy riding his motorcycle in full regalia turns suddenly into a death's head, while he rides on.

Intermale sex in uniform, extending from army barracks to prisons, has a subadult phase that emerges in reform schools for boys. Once more we are with the youth of Homeros: very

* Sado-masochistic; an alternate, milder, term is B/D (bondage and discipline).

dark, now, in outlook. That boys may form true friendship pacts, potentially homosexual, was given a lingering tragic glance, poignant and believable, in the well-remembered Italian neorealist film *Shoe Shine*, made by Vittorio De Sica at the end of the Second World War. Two little heroes make a proven pair till trapped in some commerce with black marketeers. The brutal conditions of the reform school where they land begin by separating them physically and end by dividing them morally. Jealous passion, especially in the younger boy, becomes as real as injured young hearts can feel it. The dénouement is fatal and abrupt: both boys escape, and one kills the other for ostensibly having betrayed him. A horse, bought with their black-market earnings, is the symbol of their former unity and their latter division. As in many an adult heterosexual drama, circumstance and emotional vulnerability have produced puzzlement, anguish, and at last a technical misunderstanding. Sex as such never enters the action. It doesn't have to. It is perfectly, palpably implicit. Despite the sordid harshness of this Damon-and-Pythias story, a pure and tender homosexuality threads it and survives when it is over.

With *The Sergeant,* in 1968, we supposedly came to the nude new world of moral vision on the screen. The Top Sergeant, as played by Rod Steiger, is a person of hard-shelled if plumpish masculinity who wears a sort of secret scar as if it were a sore thumb in a flesh-toned Band-Aid. In fact, because his facade is so carefully arranged, he is enabled to be a "secret homosexual," that race which it is a vogue these days to think is swiftly vanishing, but that I imagine is going to dawdle away a lot more of its time with us. There is no statutory reason why a closet queen may not choose to come out in the open if camouflaged by a uniform. Yet, however staunch a professional Mr. Steiger be, being a closet queen seems to go against his grain, and as much because of the closet as the queen. He has the studious air of a man who is really wondering why a whole acting performance, a character, should be so much concerned about a sore thumb. Despite the earnest craftsmanship of Robert Aldrich's film, I think Mr. Steiger's querulousness in his closet is justified.

One might think from *The Sergeant,* reviewing all the facts, that an army uniform were a magic disguise that immediately lulled all odd suspicions, all keen eyes, all knowledge of the human sexuality that takes military precincts for a special horticultural soil and a fresh realm of permissiveness. Nobody around seems anything but square despite their round buttons, nobody seems even as wised up an observer of the frailties of sex as an average truck driver (that breed notoriously magnetic to certain gays). Technically, *The Sergeant* is a clean-cut, well-tailored movie like an expensive suit that has had only one wearing, then been relegated in a plastic wrap to the closet, where it will stay indefinitely: as unproved as it is precious.

In the novel by Dennis Murphy, set during World War II in France, we had the story of a man who has managed to consider himself normal till his army experience reveals to him the full extent of his fatal susceptibility. Of course, third-rate fiction has certain rules—one might call them statutes governing private conduct—that falsify things which are verifiable enough in the highways and byways of the civilized world, but which for the sake of effect must be tragically isolated when in common prose. Sergeant Callan's maneuvers for getting his man are so deliberate and cute—by turns he is flattering and bullying, coy and cruel to his desired prey, the tall handsome blond of nordic persuasion, Private Swanson—that one could take the Sergeant as a nominal closet queen of the butch variety, sly as a fox but, in bed, a cross between a she-lion and a wolf.

The novelist made it a sort of tragic compulsion gradually dawning on Callan, then possessing him and converting him (since he delays the decisive move) into a dypsomaniac wreck who actually shoots himself. Here the plot behaves like the fabled ruined capitalist or the upper-crust criminal, who is kindly offered a revolver by his friends to avoid the strain and stress of exposure before the world. This happens mostly in books and films, and here it looks like a fib. Yet all that Callan does—ineptly, one must admit—is to clutch Swanson and place a full-throated smack on his lips when he can control himself no longer, having met nothing but positive rebuffs. The same "surprise kiss," differently motivated, projected a Freudian perspective into *A View from the Bridge,* but here the final veil is torn away. In both novel and film, Swanson is having a love affair with a classy French girl whom he expects to marry. In the novel he is somewhat mesmerized and confused by his sergeant's attentions; in short, he is "reached." In the film, he staunchly repels him like a decent male. Callan's role is a great chance for an actor to prove he can do sore-thumb roles; Steiger himself is reasonably successful, but his vehicle's view of homosexuality has rips in it a yard wide. The technique of symbolism —a beer bottle fondled like a penis, guns dangled like the contents of zippered privacies—won't do for conviction and plausibility when a work's moral skin tone, as here, is as "off" as the complexion of a heavily powdered whore with psoriasis.

The Callan we see filmated is a tough-titty *tante,* one-hundred percent American, whom one might imagine today as a hippie-hating hard-hat as well as a fawning effeminate grown wild with sex hunger. But, in the military milieu, the character seems as much sprung from the ground as if he were a visitor from another planet. You'd think the camera and the courted Swanson himself were the only wised-up witnesses of the Sergeant's sexy calisthenics. Yes, I know the army traditionally has its dumbness, but all that's for the upper authoritarians, the newspapers, and the folks back home. For decades, people have literally been brainwashed about what barracks life really is; what it is, I mean, when the corners of the privvies and the soul and the cots are searched after Lights Out. Remember: There is a light that never goes out, human consciousness, and art *should* know all about that. Nobody in *The Sergeant* was concerned with anything but the flick—you know, *the flick*—and so this movie is cut-the-comedy science fiction in military drag. I keep thinking of that cigarette commercial: *Wow . . .* It's got everything *I* need . . . I should have done this long ago, etc. Moreover, as certain picket signs say, GAY IS GOOD . . . WHY NOT TRY ONE? Or am I confusing that with *another* cigarette commercial?

Reflections in a Golden Eye, adapted from Carson McCullers' novel, itself rather kinky, is a military movie with the same stalking pattern as *The Sergeant.* An officer, here a major, is snagged by the lovely flesh of a dark, well-formed, comely faced piece of young masculinity who happens to be in the uniform of a private. A picturesque scene occurs when the major feels his first stab of passion: he glimpses the young man riding a horse bareback (and quite bare himself) far away in the woods. But the late Mrs. McCullers had other things in mind besides a right-left, left-right investigation of an aberrant officer's sexual obsession. Marlon Brando's army biggie is much cagier than Sergeant Callan; besides, he's married, with an established place in the army-post community. Mrs. McCullers visualizes a true novelistic situation; that is to say, her eye was on imaginative and erotic possibilities far beyond the private-fly obsession of Sergeant Callan to get his man.

One important difference that benefits *Reflections* is that its major is Marlon Brando, whose personal manner has more breadth than Mr. Steiger's and—still more meaningfully—whose personality has more natural neurotic coloring. Mr. Brando falls just a shade short of being perfectly convincing in his part of a mature officer, all hardy male in physique, whose lurking yen is for lusty boy-boy. The major's closet-queen front has more plausible style-atmosphere than Steiger's sergeant. For instance, when Brando is giving a history class to young officers, and is especially hysterical inside from anxiety and frustration, he vents a superb histrionic display of lingual confusion that chokes him, and then he virtually breaks forth in tears; he happens to be exalting at the moment the character of military heroes, and one feels he is overcome by self-pity. His muffled outbreak—cut off by the scenario at just the right psychological moment— marks how humiliated his brimming magnifico pride as a major is by his fatal entrapment in a homosexual passion that not only may ruin him but will probably misfire.

The truth is that this particular private—whom the major lures to his house by giving him a special task in his garden —falls in love with his wife (Elizabeth Taylor being a debonair Southern belle), then gets the kinky enough idea, since she plays hard to get, of sneaking back at night to invade her bedroom and patiently watch her for hours while she sleeps. Fortunately, and tacitly, he has the tread of a cat, and the major's suburban cottage, apparently, no screen doors that twang or stairs that creak. The restless, self-harried but deep-sleeping major is helped by an eccentric female neighbor (wakeful Julie Harris doing that monotonous offbeat routine on into middle age). It is she who spots the private trekking across the lawn to take his secret station by the blissfully asleep Mrs. Major—and very decent that station is: he just wants to *look* his fill. In all seriousness, Mrs. McCullers' idea has some fetching ingenuities (and a real understanding of neurotic natures), but everything is taken a bit far in faërie for a mere army-post intrigue, even a morbid one. The only true justification, aesthetically, as Mrs. McCullers herself surmised, was to have it end in cathartic violence, which it does. The incensed major personally uncovers the private's little nighttime vigil, logically goes wild, and shoots him dead, white-handed as the young voyeur is. No flesh-toned Band-Aids around here! Except, that is, the one secretly owned by the dreadfully disappointed major, who hasn't dared confront the soldier with his passion. He isn't conscious of it for long, however, since he forthwith puts a bullet in himself. As for flesh tones and more, the color photography is good enough to catch some of the reflections of that "golden eye" Mrs. McCullers thoughtfully put in her novel.

Still, to look the closet queen of commercial fiction square in the eyes, the tactic of enlisting homosexuality for the old sentimental moral that pathological habits—the recent stand-in for canonic sins—reap their terrible though just rewards, isn't quite mod anymore unless it's also quite mad. Not even the new waywardness of sex really vindicates clichés that are care-worn. Definitely. The two nature-nude fantasies of modern homosexuality I have just described are for the birds—let's say for the Phallus Birds of Delos. Now, you can mash up *M*A*S*H* (not forgetting a few gourmet pinches of *Scorpio Rising*) with the two preceding examples of homosex in military drag. Out of this you can strain the whole gamut of mythical army-uniformed types in films from the square-jawed white-haired general who really likes boys rather than girls to sit on his face, to the swish doughboy comedian, to whom (it would seem) the male organ, while implicitly necessary to his happiness, is objectively just a big laugh, when it isn't, of course, just a Creature Feature to an impotent dentist suffering from paranoia.

Perhaps you think that while thus kidding it up, I have gone a bit far. Don't underestimate the bottomless resources of commercial ingenuity, pleasure-bent on making one more honest, and preferably very fast, buck. I'm afraid the hallucination of an honest buck is all that made the producers of *The Gay Deceivers* rush their canned inspiration into theaters at a time when, possibly, *M*A*S*H* was only a gleam in that raunchy dentist's eye. So, gentle readers, whatever your real sex, sit back, relax, and reconcile yourselves. *The Gay Deceivers* clicks, but it is more gay, by far, than deceiving. Everybody knows the score inasmuch as the plot keeps one well informed. But the score, even so, is more than meets the innocent eye. The deeper gimmick is: Gay, gay, who has the real gay?—*libido,* that is? This flick is not only genuinely classic in genre technique (the cumulative bedroom farce), it's as up to the minute as the latest list of gay bars, printed in your favorite sex rag, that still have an orgy room back of their public room. The Get-you-Mary syndrome may indeed be socially doomed (what, for sure, isn't doomed in the near future?), but it's a tricky culture virus, I think, that will be as reluctant to give up its disguise as the last closet queen will be to give up locker-room flirtations. What, I ask, can replace locker-room flirtations?

The point for this chapter is, furthermore, who in *The Gay Deceivers,* if any, is going to wear the disguise that is an army uniform? And, of those that already wear that uniform, which . . . But I'll save the best gimmick for the last. Automatically I'm reminded of much the best scene from that groovy nerve gas of a film *Alice's Restaurant,* in which the folk-rock star Arlo Guthrie, très girlish but also très straight, must answer his draft board's call. By neither hook nor crook, he gets in with the other kooks, who are sitting there nature-naked but for their Jockey shorts. Soon they all brazenly betray their game (or is it a game?) when they start joking about being bundled into this reject room because, as one cries out, they've all done it to their mothers *and* their fathers. This hysterical boast may not be a mere play on the well-known insult but all in the day's work to the country-this-or-thats of happy-go-humpy hippies. I wonder. . . . As for *The Gay Deceivers,* it isn't at all "beautiful" in the supertolerant rock idiom. It seems to have originated in the mind of someone reared on old doughboy comedies, who also knows Broadwayized French farce and has sold someone else the idea that the new homosexuality can be exploited like any other hot subject in the film racket. "Just hire a few pansy types! No, they don't have to *be* pansies, you song-of-the-loon, they just have to look like them—the better-grade gays . . . if you understand me. This isn't going to be a *beaver,* you know!"

I think that *The Gay Deceivers* was too lightly tossed aside by moviegoers; it is really the most artistic, if not the weightiest, of the army films I have been discussing. Glittery in its way, it is an authentic work of the gay canon, high in homo echelons. I'd bet that those who went into the theater didn't walk out on it unless, perhaps, the ticket buyer were a blundering American Legionnaire, for whom kinks aren't kicks. Of course, some may have stayed like those stolid cops who gloatingly sit their way through an alleged obscene film so as to testify to "the evidence." Well, the evidence on *The Gay Deceivers* is that it keeps its miniskirts, and even its jockstraps, paradoxically clean.

One leading gay (who really "isn't" but is pretending to "be") comes to a private masquerade as a sort of Masked Marvel. Coquettishly he takes aside his billowing cape to expose, fleetingly, a decently sewn on figleaf that a nude Goliath might have worn. *That* is the movie's most vicious camp note. The faggot belle to provide most of the plot's orthodox hilarity is a well-known professional, Michael Greer, whose routines, from flounce to furore, are all gay trademark—actually a clever authentic blend of good breeding with garden-variety camp. Of course there's a complex hierarchy, severally socio-cultural, in the true gay ranks of the world. Mr. Greer shows how possible it is to be both one of the girls, with no snobby pretensions, and a gentleman one might safely introduce to one's parents. In fact, he introduces himself, with great presence of mind and manners, to his friend's parents and sister when these arrive, unannounced, to see how their boy is doing in his new diggings (with a new roommate) and surprise Mr. Greer in the act of swinging to a *habañera* while cooking an omelet. Isolated, it might be a scene from one of Ronald Firbank's precious novellas. As is, it's part of the undying French farce revived in the official drag of the Gay Activists Alliance.

The movie signals "whomever it may concern" that homosexuality can be the same sort of mechanism for bedroom farce that heterosexuality can be—and why not? Gay sex appears here light, flexible, "merely human," and as if emotionally on, not off, beat. Not that the technical strategy itself is altogether "straight." For it situates two young men—one slimmish, dark, college-senior, the other all blond, shapely muscle man—as amoral draft dodgers who use the fairy gimmick to get out of induction into the army. The draft-board act of the pair (who purposely appear together to compromise themselves by their simple-minded answers to questions) is very funny, but quite in line with the movie's whole debonair mood of being, at heart, a campy spoof.

Don't get me wrong: the pair (supposedly inspired to escape induction by loyalty to their girl friends) are socially recognizable as homosexuals; that is, they mutually suggest the "Is he or isn't he?" ambiguity. Point: they could well be. The ambiguity factor plays on the common enough assumption that "being homosexual" is usually, even basically, a professional act, a nightclub routine, implying (as I've mentioned) that homosexuality is a myth invented by heterosexuals to amuse theater audiences; we shall see into the heart of this issue when we come to the professional sissies. On the other hand, there is a mere commonsense audience response to all references to "abnormal" sexual acts. It is not that such things may not be "actual" but that it is mandatory they be moralized out of significance. "Stamp them out," the antihomosexualist says in effect. "Send them to a psychiatrist or to jail." This reaction is extreme and nowadays is increasingly rare. Yet it displays heterosexuality as a complicated antihomosexualist myth occupied with denying the natural basis for acts such as cunnilingus and fellatio; rather than view them as they are (acts as natural as going to the toilet), this myth sees them as way-out perverse notions; at least, if between the "same" sexes.

As a simple health measure for evil-thinking hetero-sexuals, I should instantly recommend *The Gay Deceivers*. I doubt if this film made any real money but in fact it is cutely angled at both the archaically retrograde and groovily wised-up public of all sexes. The gay public should take legitimate joy in it, regretting only that more beaver nudity is not present. The blond hero—supposedly a life guard—is quite a toothsome num-ber and his friend the dewy sort of grown-up schoolboy that gets wolves on their hind legs. The blackness, bile, and other bleaknesses put into comedy, in our time of sick jokes, may have really gotten through to audiences, so that no longer do they laugh without that universal reflex of grim humor that Shake-speare defined when he wrote that something was rotten in the state of Denmark.

Possibly the gay public was disappointed at the ambiguity that our pretty boys are made out as bona-fide heteros trying to put on a draft-board act; then, too, the jam public—"jam" is twenties slang for "straight"—might be annoyed by the flip blackout climax. The suspicious father of the schoolboyish num-ber, convinced by all the put-on that both his son and his pal are really queers, gives them away to the draft board. This presents the army with a moral problem, which in turn sparks an idea in a couple of draft-board officers. One of the latter has spied on the youths and discovered the put-on for himself. It occurs to him and his mate that, owing to the alleged tech-nicality, the two deceivers *can* be put down as *gay*. Why so? That's the punch line and the big gimmick. One officer, lovingly putting his arm around his mate's shoulder, says with a knowing smile: "We don't want *their* kind in *our* army, do we?"

One might regard *that* as the Pay Off. But I don't think it is, quite. The Pay Off has been another mid-bed failure of virility on the part of the supposedly girl-crazy life guard. As a male type, he bears a noticeable resemblance to the blond hero of *Midnight Cowboy,* also female-addicted and impotence-in-dicted. Movie brains behave mechanically, more so than those brains themselves realize. But this means that they behave

autosuggestibly and thus pertinently, even creatively. Did someone's brain wish to slip in here, consciously or unconsciously, the
truth that pretending-to-be-what-one-is-not may lead one to be-
come-what-one-pretends-to-be? It might be called, in this case,
the midnight-cowboy syndrome. Incidentally, perhaps the near-
est that pure-strain Hollywood has gotten to the total military
drag act was in a picture with the famous and famously magnetic
Cary Grant in the name part. Its title tells us the main point of
its story: *I Was a Male War Bride.* One might add that, in or
out of drag, Mr. Grant was no better than he should be. The
attractive masculine tones of his voice—always a great personal
asset—were always a little better than they might have been.
Let us now turn to uniformed matters more serious than the
movies, in general, would have them be.

Like the conditions of prison and the army, the conditions of school impose a uniform merely by imposing a discipline
and a segregation. As we have already seen, this sequestering of
sex develops its rituals. Monastery and prison, and at times the
army, are only the more drastic aspects of monosexed regimenta-
tion. While a cynical, noncommittal sadism may seem, from
reputation, the more typical keynote of homosexuality in school
life, homosexuality also breeds charms there. It has its tender,
lyric, and intact stretches, where the authenticity of Homeros
shows up early and romantically, perhaps definitively. A charming film from France, a really inveigling film so artful it is, was
This Special Friendship, made from the novel by Roger Peyrefitte, *Les Amitiés Particulières.* It is hardly a major work but—
like its counterpart, *The Pit of Loneliness,* about a girls' school
—it becomes rarely illustrious as a classical treatment of homosexual love: homosexual love as something at once poetic and
potentially (if not actually) carnal; confirmed in sex and yet
culturally liberal; something transcending brutality and vulgarity, alike, by the sheer sensibility for style, for natural elegance.

No nation so well as the French—moral epicures that
they are—can furnish touches so sure when it comes to period
mood and atmosphere and the human graces that show forth
in them. Apart from genius, from all art bravura, there is a

smoothness, a nicety, to French style that is as evident on film as in printed prose. The Nouvelle Vague in France, of course, has altered this ingratiating style with things more fashionably icky, angular, and *brut*. But the style I mean has not quite vanished from films or books. Such a book was *Les Amitiés Particulières*, and such a film emerged from it. The "period" is no more distant than an expensive French Catholic boys' school from the first half of this century. This school, ironically, has exactly that calm, tacit propriety that Vigo wished to demolish, not arbitrate with, in *Zéro de Conduite*.

Here, the revolt is only the private revolt of intractable, very young Homeros, and technically it fails rather miserably— but not, you understand, because it is sick; rather, because it is *healthy*. The acting is in every case superlative; not through any individual genius, any profound insight or emotion portrayed, but because of an even instinct for the right sort of thing, the thing the story itself requires at every point. Jean Delannoy was the canny director of *This Special Friendship*, and he was aesthetically uncompromising. Many gifted directors devise special editing to put across some brilliant idea; they have to do so for the idea's sake. The "idea" would be a bit ambitious, would demand a measure of bravura. From erring directors, of course, one gets bravura when they overreach themselves, and the story too; when, in brief, bravura is not wanted. None is wanted in *This Special Friendship*, and none appears; only a fluid, nourishing, never-too-much richness.

An incontinent reviewer remarked of this film that, in his opinion, the two young male romancers, a twelve-year-old and a sixteen-year-old, failed to project the homosexual attraction in histrionic terms. Alas! Reviewers perennially associate "French" eroticism with only one kind of thing, which itself they cannot describe properly. The twelve-year-old Alexandre is played by a boy with the magic name of Didier Haudepin, who has a charming oval face and great liquid dark eyes. He is a gem of a child, a Tadzio, and a perfectly self-possessed actor. Did he play his role as if he were Simone Simon in short pants? He did not. And in that he was wise where his American critic was stupid. Didier is tenderness itself, guilefulness itself, like

Cupid acting out a deliberate charade in order to triumph. Of course, the mask of innocence is there and it is partly inevitable: he is in many ways a child still, but the grown boy in him has been awakened, the supernatural spirit of Eros. He is becoming self and super-self. Contrary to the surface meaning (this is part of the depth meaning) *he,* the younger boy, does the seducing.

The best part is that Didier behaves like one caught in his own spell. There is no measuring the contagiousness of this, in any sex, to one who somehow steps within its aura. Lolita, in her film, might have evoked it but did not; she was too carnal and grown-up. In this film, Georges, the older boy, finding himself in that aura, is effectually tempted and succumbs. At first Georges, four years the senior, regards the budding affair disdainfully and rather debonairly as an amusing intrigue, but finds himself willingly enmeshed almost before he knows he is a Don Juan really smitten. It climaxes, not carnally, but by a symbolic session of cigarette-smoking hidden away in a greenhouse where the pair have started to rendezvous. A decent but officious Father has scented the intrigue and spied on it. He surprises the boys lolling in the hay, and the wonderful dream is broken. By the law of protocol, the two have to be separated. As this happens, the younger goes into heartbreak.

If Georges has been the "master" in their affair, it is only because he is more mature in every way, not because he is less in love or just tough-minded. At the same time, his naturally greater detachment at the separation adds to the dimension of pathos because the younger, in the first flush of Eros, cannot be detached about such a stark, mysterious disaster. Objectively, it is all as clear as day, a *spring day!* The mistake of nannygoat critics (the supervising priests at the school are not, even at their worst, nannygoats) is to regard the subject of *This Special Friendship* as essentially a juridico-ethical problem: Is he or isn't he (e.g., homosexual)? And: Is it or isn't it—indeed can it *possibly* be—real love, this affair between two young boys? In the abstract, those could be very legitimate questions. As seen on Delannoy's screen, they are poetic and human *données,* as plain as an exposed penis or a love lyric. *Disliking* the situation —well, *chacun à son goût! Questioning* it is out. The *données* are perfectly definite for the Fathers at this school, all enacting their parts with exceptional grace and understanding.

This intrusive love affair, for these spiritual guides, is a mere difficulty of religious protocol. Humanly speaking, it is one of the most normal of all the difficulties to challenge their authority and their administration of required chastity among schoolboys. They take this enlightened view because, as the story wisely and ably reveals, they themselves are vulnerable to the same homosexual affections through their daily contact with boys. Woven into the main affair between the two boys is the erotic fixation one vulnerable Father has for a certain boy whom he repeatedly, against the rules, invites to his room for tea and "coaching." The coaching of course turns out to be sympathy that hovers on the verge of the physical. But this affair too is nipped in the bud by official alertness, and the priest must go through a personal Gethsemane like that of little Alexandre. Nothing, in its own terms, could be more conventional or more naturally, humbly enchanting.

Not only conventional, but eminently natural, it was for a film called *The Pit of Loneliness* (1959)—based on a novel tantalizingly presented as *Olivia* by Olivia—to provide a direct foregoing parallel to *This Special Friendship.* This movie concerns schoolgirls and their schoolmistresses, the former consciously growing up and vaguely lesbian, the latter quite self-consciously grown-up and indelibly lesbian. It is the privileged licentiousness of the French to assume that, in the staff and distaff opposition, more indulgence be granted, automatically and without fuss, to the ladies. The effeminate "cult of the female" among French males—as I suppose everyone knows—is the world's greatest of its kind. I don't know whether, in 1971, it has survived Simone de Beauvoir, but that lady of strong-arm intellectualism had long before already alienated herself from the "cult of the female" celebrated by this film. That cult is one reason why it was apt, in *Zéro de Conduite*, for homosexualism among schoolboys to appear, when open and serious, as the revolutionary thing. In France, it remained for the poetic violence of a Cocteau to assert male homosexuality as an aesthetic privilege.

In England, where in recent years novels about school-boys have been more and more frankly homosexualist, the situation is the opposite; that is—with a difference suitable to the primary and secondary characteristics—it is exactly like that in the absurdly titled *The Pit of Loneliness*. One must ask, as to this title, how a lesbian (confirmed or potential) can be "lonely" when she lives in a milieu drawn boldly and directly from the legend of Sappho's college of nymphs on ancient Lesbos. Heartbreak? Frustration? Moral reaction? Well, tears too are the stuff of love. One should recall how Mars used to whip naked Cupid. There is, in fact, a sort of "Mars" among the schoolgirls here, but she is quietly exiled to preserve the polite tone of the establishment.

At this elegant academy for young ladies at Fontaine-bleau, around 1900, it is not a recognized convention, naturally, for young ladies to sleep with each other or with their teachers, the Mademoiselles. But, in a more or less Platonic fashion, it is an unrecognized convention. As Colette scripted the film, one might expect complete authenticity and some wit. One gets those, and more. Jacqueline Audry, the director, has supplied the most nicely effusive sets, camera shots, and costumes, the most nicely effusive manners (academic and histrionic) to inter-pret the story with required flair. It devolves upon the pas-sionate competition between the two partners who run the school, Mademoiselle Julie and Mademoiselle Cora, to enslave the affections of their pupils. Meanwhile of course the pupils, some of them nubile young ladies, are conducting whispered, palpitant, shadowy intrigues among themselves, including out-rageous trysts and startled face-to-face confessions.

Invert love is as much an open secret here as connections in a men's Turkish bath, and in metaphor has much the same steambath pleasurableness as in those well-known premises. The stylish Edwige Feuillère is an impeccable Mademoiselle Julie, in general the more adored of the two partners, and lush Simone Simon an exotic but emotionally attuned Mademoiselle Cora, given to *migraines* and picturesque reclinings when her rival threatens a real victory. There is a charming fluttery sort of moral *tremolo* running throughout the scenes that is very cult-of-the-female turned narcissistically inward, mostly heart, but heart clothed with warm, warm flesh. It appears, inevitably, in the raw when heartbreak threatens, when alienation from it, or disillusionment, harshly enters. Yet on the whole it is as exciting as archaic lyres consummately stroked, and even twanged. It rises to the surface, specifically sapphic, when Mademoiselle Julie ritually calms the disturbed young flesh by having it sit down in a group and listen to her read love scenes from Racine. Of course! This is erotic—but it is also calming and collecting since it focuses on love as an idea; in fact, as a tragic idea that earns at once, in the imagination, apotheosis and catharsis. Of course, it ends on a "frustrated" note. But even genuine orgies imply that same note.

The Pit of Loneliness (My God, what a horrid parasitic thing that title is*) surely furnishes candidates for an ambi-sexual female Homeros, or at least a Billy Budd in sapphic form. But, to achieve an archetype, the school's sexiest girl would have had actually to sleep with both headmistresses, one or two of her mates, and the gardener too. (Lolita, there's a future for you to exploit!) The God whom I just spontaneously invoked has not presumed to interdict a very liberal lesbianism that has made its way to film screens with a little more expeditiousness than male homosexuality; anyway, in the blunt and base erotic sense. A "special-friendship" film without emotional or stylistic charm, but accenting the carnality of lesbianism, came to us with a pit-of-loneliness tag to its overt content.

At least, that was the thoroughly realized intention of the author of La Batarde (The Bastard), Violette Leduc, who supplied the gist of the film Thérèse and Isabelle (1968). The gist we see and hear is another inveterate reflex of filmic translations. The lesbian lovers of the novel are two schoolgirls caught desperately, feverishly in a pitlike relationship mostly because of inferiority feelings, which they are determined to overcome and glorify by professing homosexuality en plein air as well as in occluded washrooms. What the movie has done is to pressure the optical and soundtrack possibilities by much close-up con-

* The Well of Loneliness, by Radclyffe Hall, was a famous early-century lesbian novel.

tact between the young women, Anna Gael and Essy Persson, without the actual nudity or explicit cohabitation that the expectant voyeur might hope to see. There are "shocking" words in the panting verbal communications, sometimes an interior monologue. But there is little communication of the acrid flavor and sallow, fevered pall, the elaborate nitty-gritty of lesbian aesthetics, that suffuses Mlle. Leduc's original prose.

Unaffectedly, the movie is a gut story boldly lifting itself to the theoretic level of poetic, and young, lesbian love having its first adventure. This special friendship is especially disenchanting when seen in the film flesh. For the schoolmates as incarnated are perhaps a thirtyish pair that hardly succeed in looking less than twentyish; at any rate, not looking the adolescents they are supposed to be. Miss Persson is already an image in the Olympia of vex-sex films: a rather shopworn if attractive professional, whose nude body-vistas are provenly photogenic. From the smut-classic style, the makers of *Thérèse and Isabelle* wished to provide some classy smut that would do for the fringe voyeur trade brimming over two ways: toward art-house and out-house erotics.* Our film, with no real ingenuity except some skillful photography, comes out looking just the way it went in: process food, at best, for art-sex hungerers. No great credit to the lesbian style. Sorry, girls! But it's true.

If schoolgirlishness as such is not already in a love theme, hetero or homo, Hollywood is quite likely to import it—youth is so irresponsible and impulsive in our radical, discontented, disorderly milieu! The industry's version of D. H. Lawrence's *The Fox* converts the two retired spinsters of the original tale into two young women (Sandy Dennis and Ann Heywood) who mysteriously have isolated themselves on a farm as if they were those finagling schoolteachers from *The Children's Hour* who had mutely agreed, more intelligently, to have things out in a safe place where nobody could snoop on them. The lesbianism begins showing its carnal features when the two have a playful melee in the snowy outdoors, and the world-shaking clutch-and-kiss takes place. If girls will be boy scouts, that sort of thing

* I owe this play on words to the *Daily News* (New York) reviewer, so I must record that she stated this film should be seen not "in art houses but out houses."

is virtually in order, and surely would be missed if the isolated pair should fail to bring it about.

That's the story on screen except for the melodramatic entrance of Keir Dullea, who of course changes things back into nature's order by seducing one of the ladies—the aggressor of the pair, in fact—and giving her such a good time in bed—discreetly daring art photography here—that she finds she likes it with a man before she's really tried it out with a woman. The imagery flashes off with one of those running-out-in-the-woods-and-wailing-the-beloved's-name soft-crash endings, leaving things as open as ripped underwear. A depressingly self-conscious piece of merchandise, I think, with the fox doing its thing in woods so artificially lit that, whether or not it's a studio set or the real outdoors, the poor animal skitters about as if semiparalyzed by all those eyes and all those spotlights.

A quite different lesbian atmosphere and motivation are evoked by a very artistic film created by Miklos Jancso, a director recently come to notice outside his native Hungary. Seen at the 1968 Cannes Festival (later at the Grove Press Festival in New York City), it is *Winter Wind*: a visually beautiful and deep revelation of the anarchist revolutionary temper. Both the male and female shapes of sexuality in uniform here are strange. The male shape tends to sublimate itself into the total idea of revolution. It is a sexual divestment whose identity—at least in the chief protagonist, Marko Lazar, the arch anarchist—is the militant revolutionary so "total" that he must literally dispense with sex. He is a man who has become so harshly and purely masculine that he is "transsexual" in this peculiar sense.

As counterpart to this personal situation—regarded suspiciously by the lesser heroes present, and leading to Lazar's murder—a group situation exists among the women sent to the forest hideout to provide sex. While not ignored by all the men, they are rather neglected. One handsome woman is obviously lesbian and takes advantage of their idleness to start up a cult of mutual affection. She even has a personal love affair going. The striking thing is that these women also function as soldiers and that the only sign of sexual affection in Lazar, the total revolutionary, is for this intelligent, loyal, militant woman of whose lesbianism he is quite aware. *Their* interrelations are platonic, a mutual dedication to the Cause, to which sex is automatically sublimated. It is a difficult erotic theme, handled by Jancso with fine impressiveness and a firm, delicate style; at once extremely candid and unsensational.

Of course, both *The Fox* and *Thérèse and Isabelle* sound separate chords of lesbian emotional violence. It is so striking to witness the great violence of the lesbianism in *Les Abysses* (see the next chapter), since such extremist violence is associated more readily—and, according to our mores, more plausibly—with male homosexuality; for instance, in *The Damned,* in prison films (where it requires, to be erotically palatable, the drastic conversion of a work such as *Un Chant d'Amour*), and in *Scorpio Rising,* whose militarized Leather Boys refer it back to Hitlerism and the drag-ish saturnalia of the SA corps. The sado-masochistic structure common to *Fireworks, Scorpio Rising, Young Törless,* and *Les Abysses* (the sole lesbian entry in this class aside from the paltry metaphor of *The Killing of Sister George*) takes over the affairs of pacific Homeros and morally defines homosexuality in terms of latent violence. Here the lurking virtue of identifying, as I have done, a god of homosexuality, Homeros, comes into profitable focus. The truth is that sado-masochistic homosexuality, like sado-masochistic heterosexuality, is a profanation, and even in its aesthetic aspects (as in *Fireworks* or *Un Chant d'Amour*) is morally ambiguous: a black content of sex which the poet must transmute in anguish leading to apotheosis; if the poet doesn't succeed, the pathologists and the puritans will.

M*A*S*H, Reflections in a Golden Eye, and *The Sergeant* are examples of movies where the military uniform is a reigning sign for violence and, more significantly, *chaos within violence.* The gunshots at the climaxes of the latter two are simply mechanical appliances for ending the insoluble chaos of the psychological violence. Neither homosexuality nor heterosexuality in such movies is by any means the moral rule suggested by Sade: a disciplined, deliberate, and self-sufficient violence; no, it is a crazy, futile, and pathologically displaced violence. *M*A*S*H* only places an idiot-grin mask over it. Essentially, it is the violence of *Bonnie and Clyde* and *In Cold*

Blood, insofar as both these movies, put in a true perspective, are concerned with perverted eroticism: the "fatal kinks" of Homeros which I shall take up in the following chapter. Yet that we cannot doubt the importance of homosexuality as associated with the militarized ethos of fascism was recently demonstrated by Bernardo Bertolucci's film *The Conformist*. Bertolucci himself adapted it skillfully from Alberto Moravia's novel.

It is a brilliantly directed and photographed film—so stylish in performance that the crypto-fascist sex syndrome it portrays seems very true yet is so subtly woven with emotional and sexual ambiguity as to block the critic who wishes to assess the precise role played by homosexuality. The hero, Marcello (Jean-Louis Trintignant), is as false a heterosexual as he is a homosexual. At least this much seems definite: the "conformist" of the title is basically an opportunist, a perfectly selfish careerist who will cooperate with any system where he finds favor and the upgrade. Marcello, we discover, is a natural coward. Is he cowardly and treacherous because of his sex neurosis? Moravia's antifascist purpose seems to have been to associate fascist sadism and amoralism with a particular sex complex in the male. This is embodied in a fucked-up hetero who—going by the plot line—is really homo. His violent sexual encounter as a thirteen-year-old boy with a long-haired young chauffeur returns to haunt and demolish him when accidentally, at the end, he reencounters his seducer.

Again, one is not quite sure if guileful young Homeros—despite, here, his homicidal reflex—is the seduced or the seducer. Anyway, he shoots, and thinks he has killed, the chauffeur. Moravia not only plays tantalizingly with plot situations; he plays thus with the sex syndromes too. Further, the director Bertolucci has contrived from all this such a smooth, flexible, fast-moving melodrama that character motivation is swept along as a bright blur with incidentally piercing insights. Marcello, as a secret agent of Mussolini's government, is ordered to shoot an antifascist exile in Paris at the moment of setting out on his honeymoon. The sexual situation is much complicated by the handsome young wife of the exile he is supposed to kill; formerly, this man was Marcello's professor at a college in Italy.

Seemingly the professor's young wife develops both a

lesbian attraction to Marcello's frivolous bride and a purely
animal attraction to Marcello. All the same, fear may be prompt-
ing her to play-act in both cases. She has guessed Marcello's true
identity and mission and obviously sues for his sympathy and
his bride's, however much she is sexually committed. The point
seems to be that hazardous political fortunes pervert and enslave sexuality, using it, if necessary, as cat's paw. Yet may it not
be, in Marcello's case anyway, the opposite? One may suppose
that a certain offbeat sexual temperament has grasped at the
techniques of political persecution in order to work off the
guilt of the impulses it is too cowardly to face. Unable to bring
himself to pull another trigger, Marcello must witness freshly
summoned murderers do in his old professor on a lonely road.
Meanwhile, he sits by in a car, clutching an unused revolver,
and likewise witnesses the murder of the professor's beautiful
young wife, whom ostensibly he is present to save.

Years later, still a party man but inutile and disgraced,
he is shocked, though not too shocked, by Mussolini's sudden
downfall; clearly, he is ready to turn his coat with the times.
But now he reencounters the chauffeur he thought he had
killed! Jolted quite out of his mind, he goes through the motions
of crazily accusing and assaulting the man, who however escapes.
The moment before, the ex-chauffeur has been propositioning a
wild-haired street boy, and Marcello has overheard. The chauffeur out of the way now, Marcello sees the chance to turn his
sexual as well as his political coat. He sits with his temptation
outside a grillwork gate, behind which the naked street boy (apparently willing) has bedded down for the night to the tune of a
phonograph record. The film ends here.

After due consideration, can we avoid formulating the
moral that offbeat sex is schematic in being a fated part of the
contagious moral vice which fascism is widely assumed to be?
That, for its part, homosexuality can also be a thing of grace, a
separate field of gravity, a poet's and philosopher's privilege and
even (as in the classic pastorals) a lover's peaceful pursuit, seems
to have been inconceivable in Mussolini's Italy. Or so *The Conformist* and similar movies would have us believe; even *Death
in Venice,* whose era is the nineteenth century and whose

Homeros is very young, beautiful, and untainted, makes turn-coat homosexuality a symbolic disease.

Modern persecutive politics has no limits, seemingly, in making homosexuality into a convenient scapegoat. An odd case in point arose unexpectedly through *This Special Friendship*. Jean Delannoy already had this film in the works when the eminent Catholic novelist François Mauriac went to the battlements to prevent its realization. Fortunately Mauriac, though he stirred up the public, lost the fight, owing largely to the lively way in which M. Peyrefitte, author of the original novel, immediately joined arms with him. And what was the reason for M. Mauriac's pious sense of outrage? Quite simple. He took the view of the good Fathers themselves, but belligerently rather than passively. His argument was to claim that the two "innocent" young actors (so Mauriac gratuitously assumed them) would inevitably be corrupted by the erotic roles they were scheduled to play, so that the movie itself would induce the lamentable romance which it is the express obligation of Catholic educators to prevent, or perhaps, at least, circumvent. In *The Conformist*, we may note, Marcello confesses to a priest, who would doubtless have championed the late Mauriac's view of sodomy as a sin in itself and a breeder of deception.

We shall see, in the present record, how possible it is for friendships formed while in school or in the army to provide a kink like a scar, almost covered up but not quite, by new flesh, a new life, by heterosexuality and marriage, or anyway the prospect of these. A curious case (*Thanos and Despina*) provides a real kink, so that I shall reserve it. The uniform, as I have said, is a symbol of conformity: its malign role in *The Conformist* is self-evident, for at times it means the conformism of the off-beat, the conspiratorial, the revolutionary. The uniform is a facade; the genitals themselves are—yes, precisely!—"uniforms." Unisex is a pansexual uniform. Behind the genitals, sometimes, is a true sexuality which, on the other hand, may be aggressively the opposite of itself in the nominal duality of the sexes that supposedly make a natural correspondence. What can we conclude but that, under the two-sex system, the uniform is a sort of transvestism?

How easily the masquerade motifs in spy and detective melodramas accommodate the tricks of seeming conformity, seeming uniformity. It is their function at once to *deceive* and be *gay,* but without gaiety. In fact, humor has nothing to do with it: neither gray nor black; it is too sardonic even to be camp, unless the camp is detached, consciously sardonic. Something of this sort I have in mind. Perhaps it is a director's jolly, a scriptwriter's *chinoiserie,* but in a film called *The Deadly Affair* (1967), Maximilian Schell and James Mason have been buddies in service to their country; nationalities are tactfully suppressed, but the country involved is England. When suddenly Schell enters Mason's life again, he is an undercover agent for a foreign country. He proceeds to gull his former friend in a complex and insinuating way, especially strange since by all the signs the two have once been very close. For one thing, he quietly seduces Mason's wife, apparently from real desire, but actually, as it turns out, as part of his espionage strategy. Mason discovers this personal betrayal but still does not realize Schell is the secret agent his bureau is trying to run down for murdering a member of the foreign office.

In one of those surprise-thriller build-ups, Schell is finally trapped in a theater with a female confederate, whose presence tells him that his own identity (a surprise to the audience, too) is now known. He then manages to escape, and is killed by Mason in a violent dénouement where the latter's hand is forced. The situation can be read like that in *Thanos and Despina*: see the "fatal-kinks" chapter. *This is why*: In the theater scene, when Schell's identity is discovered, a curiously dramatic counterpoint is provided by the play being enacted. Supposedly the play is a mere coincidence, for the point has been for the two agents to rendezvous in a theater where they have seats next to each other. But its identity could be metaphorically very significant. It is Marlowe's *Edward II,* and the climax of this king's gruesome murder is timed with the revelation of Schell's identity to Mason, who is also in the theater.

We are given not just a glimpse or two of *Edward II*. The murder is acted out, and not in dumb show but with dialogue. The realization is traditional: we see an effeminate, pathetic

Edward (whose homosexual love for his favorite, Gaveston, has been the cause of his dethronement) felled by the assassin jailers, held between boards on a table, and become sodomized by the hot poker which has been thoughtfully prepared for him. Precisely at this point, Mason has realized who his quarry is, because Schell is very late and has kept his female confederate fidgeting in her seat. Now Mason understands that this man, his old friend, has not only seduced his wife but also, being an enemy of his country, must be apprehended and exterminated. I can add that their reunion, taking place in his wife's presence, has been joyous, especially on Mason's side, and accompanied by a deep embrace. The movie gives us no idea of just what the two men's relations have been; we can only infer them from the tone of their reunion. Granted: the male buddy-buddy thing can exist and be innocent of technical homosexuality. But what happens now that Schell's full perfidy has been exposed, his doom as a spy forecast? Mason leaves his seat, but not to apprehend Schell—not just now. He makes a beeline for the men's room and copiously vomits. . . . With relief, one may recall that sovereigns on the gay side, kings who are bisexual dalliers, have gotten a more fortunate show in the movies than Edward II. In that memorable film *Carnival in Flanders* (1946), the Duke d'Alba, Spanish governor of Flanders marching on a town, has a homosexual minion who offers a case quite the opposite of the fateful Gaveston's. A stylish fop, he is all camp: Homeros in the gayest of uniforms. All the same, as a harmless luxury, he reminds us that courtly customs have never been free of criticism from beneath. And don't forget the problem of those Catholic fathers in *This Special Friendship.*

The issue remains controversial in both the social and the artistic dimensions—controversial, that is, to all but Homeros and his/her devotees. I think it would be wrong of the reader to consider that this representation of the matter constitutes a dated pose or a sectarian prejudice. I imagine nobody will deny that homosexual love is still as possible as heterosexual love; and this means exactly that, "possible," if not "probable." Whatever their cultural elevation, the male beavers and metabeavers alone attest to the pattern of this possibility. If homosexual love seems, nevertheless, to get characteristically kinky, this condition may plausibly be referred to the same deep moral confusion, however congenitally anchored, that makes *heterosexual love* the victim of similar and equally characteristic kinks. If the male transvestites of *The Damned* do put homosexuality in a blood line with heterosexual incest and child molesting, that does superbly for establishing my argument, not destroying it. Sexual pathology knows *no* favorites. And sexual pathology is the enemy of Homeros, as of Eros. Sexual pathology is the worst type of "uniform": *it kills.*

In concluding this account of Homeros in uniform by plucking evidence from the very midst of life's unceasing flow (influenced, of course, by the magic of the media), I appeal to the reader's confidence. I am not being light-minded; I am not camping. I state a simple proposition: How could the author of the present book resist what I have just read in the September 16–29, 1970, issue of *The Advocate,* a Los Angeles tabloid whose subtitle is "Newspaper of America's Homophile Community"? I refer all judgment to the reader. I think one can visualize the manner in which the editors of *The Advocate,* and its readers too, would repudiate with amused scorn such shenanigans as Rod Steiger's in his role as Sergeant Callan; one can see, too, how all true homophiles would tsk-tsk! such an outlandish case of the misbehaving military as Marlon Brando's in *Reflections in a Golden Eye. That* sort of gay guy just doesn't know where it's at. Come and groove with *The Advocate,* in other words, and *you'll know where it's at.*

On the front page of the issue in question, and in several views inside, appears a young man from Fort Worth, Texas, Larry Schramm, who, says the bold headline, has just won something. What has he won? A thing made plain by the small type: the title of "Groovy Guy of 1970." We find that it was a contest for manly gays, those with hetero outsides and, typically, athletic or muscle-man physiques. Mr. Schramm manifests in a very brief pair of swim shorts; nothing else except his head hair and a graceful, hirsute "T" on his handsome chest, a torso adornment that looks artfully coiffed (oh, sometimes nature herself supplies such cosmetic touches!). Let there be no misunderstanding about the possibility that I am pushing the facts. Mr. Schramm is an arch example of everything fashionably and conventionally groovy in the manly-gay type; he has nothing of the insinuating ambiguity of the muscled blond life guard in *The Gay Deceivers*. That's the point! The homophile watchword is "No Deception." There is no earthly reason not to think Mr. Schramm is not in perfect good faith.

Larry Schramm did not lag in saying as much for himself; that is, if the printed interview with him can be believed, and I feel that it can. From what I could tell of the other contestants, I also feel that they picked the right man in every palpable respect. Pictorially considered, Larry Schramm in face and figure could easily pass for a baseball player or even a prize-fighter; provided, of course, one doesn't catch the coquettish "Mr. America" gaze that is often a sort of high sign in male-beauty-contest winners. But this gaze, although present on Mr. Schramm, is straightforward and inoffensive. All sexes like to be admired and show it whenever asked to pose for an audience. Moreover, not all male-beauty-contest winners are homosexual; Mr. Schramm happens to assert that *he* is. So asserting, he claims to be nothing but orthodox and liberal. This is par by the lights of every homosex organization. There is some necessary vagueness about what Larry does in bed, but, seemingly without hesitation, he states that he does do things there, things literally and plentifully "gay." "I like gay life," he is quoted by the interview. "I decided a long time ago that I liked men. I don't play games. I've been and seen and done just about everything there is to do, whether it's good or bad. And I mean . . . like I know what's going on." Oh, the beautiful moral intonation, the sublime ethical assurance, of that casually inserted "good or bad"!

Larry Schramm doesn't need to be "good" or "bad" because really he's a homophile Apollo, and thus a blood relative (big-brother branch) of Homeros himself. My only reason for introducing him in this particular spot is not that he has had any movie experience. But, as the story about him reports, "He saw thirteen months' service in Vietnam and was awarded five medals, including the George Washington Honor Medal and the Vietnam Campaign." That makes it pretty positive that, as a soldier, Larry was no fake; I'm sure Larry did not win those medals by doing anything on the field of Mars that George Washington couldn't have done. To round him out, this should be added to the quotations from his interview: "I like to think of myself not as gay and not as straight. I'm both. But I'm also human. . . . I am gay, believe me. But every now and then I'll go out with some woman that has a beautiful mind." I was about to say that I think of Larry as a living monument to the ideals of homophilia. But no, he's just too beautifully real, in or out of uniform.

I can't leave him without telling what looks like the rest: "I believe," he is also quoted, "that I'm going to find somebody that's going to be my partner for the rest of my life. . . . But right now I couldn't tell you whether it's going to be a man or a woman. Both of them have an equal chance."

To quote Larry yet again with a caressive coup de grace: "You can be a man and still be gay."

President Nixon, please take note of that remark. There's Mr. Schramm's army record to provide confirmation. And Sergeant Callan's . . . and . . . there must be some others . . . others who *haven't* shot themselves.

9. THE FATAL KINKS

I would grant—I hasten to do so—that there is a no-sex's-land between hetero and homo sexuality. It is *not* unisex. Rather, unisex is the successfully oriented and crystallized form of what, if uncrystallized and radically disoriented, will indeed end in sex crime and cults of violent perversity. To promote the continued success of *Performance*'s first run in New York City, an opinion was solicited from Marshall McLuhan, who responded with impressions gleaned from his star-struck insight as if his words were film criticism in the form of space food, prepared especially for those contemplating early departure for other worlds. The film's notably chemical sex, its black and blue mores, are indicted by McLuhan as "notice of cancellation of a world," and the work's relation to food energy is called a matter of "garbage disposal." Members of the Pot and Pepsi generation will scornfully dissent from these opinions while being piqued by them into interest. Systematic scavenging would logically be typical of a morally beat, rock-beat, world. One wouldn't expect the gourmet palate for theatrical things to thrive at such a time. To me, McLuhan's applied criticism seems just only when one takes the highest aesthetic level from which to officiate. And the highest level is the hardest of all for a critic to balance himself on and give fair judgment.

McLuhan's élite vocabulary is as specifically moral/political as the much less élite vocabulary of a *Daily News* reviewer. But doing what they both do to more or less inferior films is like whacking the open palm of a little boy who has used nasty words to tell a literal truth that can only be reported in "nasty" (i.e., slang) words. The words of rock songs are colloquial and slangy—or hip—and *Performance* is a complex patois developed from a rich vernacular of our social milieu. Fantastic. Far out. All right. But how "pathological" is it? Just how scientifically can it be called the "garbage" of civilization when so many vigorous young people, who may commit no crimes worse than smoking pot, look on such things as the sacred fetishes of a life style? Well, let us look into what the fatal kinks of homosexuals are, inside and outside the movies.

There is a mortal enlightenment that should benefit all analysts who wish to take the movies as a gauge for making judgments of our society and the arts nourished by our society and considered, if not necessary, still useful. Many serious people (I mean those who take seriously the business of staying alive and well) ignore the arts by regarding them at a distance as spheres of harmless amusement; amusement harmless, that is to say, unless an artwork have the value of propaganda, moral or political, in which case it must be taken seriously because it is the work of a political enemy, the work of those, it may happen, who corrupt society with pornography. Politics, technically so vicious in its rivalries, is really (as some shrewd philosophers have noted) a more or less polite charade in which public moralities are mere counters in winning the game. In brief, politics is a sport, not a sport that produces aesthetic delight in demonstrating a skill, but a sport (like hunting) that produces aesthetic delight in making a kill. Politicians who gamble unsuccessfully for high office know this: they are "killed off" by certain crucial defeats; their ambitions become trophies in the offices of their victorious rivals. The very vocabulary of reporting victories in sports reveals a specific moral violence. When a football or basketball team, or even a tennis player, is "crushed" or "walloped" or "trounced," or just "downed" or "beaten," it is the violence of the prizefight that is morally and aesthetically evoked.

As for sexual matters, the vocabularies of both war and hunting are so familiar as not to need rehearsal. But that the vocabulary of deadly violence is increasingly ubiquitous in controversy should mean something wherever it is applied. I can cite a fairly recent instance in one of the forums that appear regularly on television, William F. Buckley's *The Firing Line,* where vital issues of the day are threshed out by Mr. Buckley with leading propagandists of the hour. As always, when his guest was Muhammad Ali, though knee to knee with each other, the host and the black fighter/philosopher, while staunchly opposed, vied with one another in civilized courtesies. However, when it was all over, Mr. Ali boasted in so many words, in the parlance of the ring, that he had "killed" Mr. Buckley. So far, screen pornography has manifested no need for the vocabulary of violence to register its points. Nevertheless, sex is a motif for physical and moral violence even when its true agency is suppressed.

What the enemies of pornography are determined to ignore (simply because being antipornographic is part of the big game) is that sex may be just as deadly a sport as politics; that is, be as morally violent in terms of victory and defeat and pride of skill. Could not Don Juan justly call himself a sharp-shooter? Sexual violence pays off in terms of fame, sometimes, and in terms of money. Glamour sex in the movies, for instance, is a pure phase of political economy. Financial arrangements are already built into marriages and liaisons and one-night stands. There's no reason, then, why the homosexes—to the extent they participate in the general mores and involve themselves in legalities—should be exempt from these same financial arrangements. Their reappearance in the movies is not confined to performance in front of a camera. As in all prostitution, no less than in less harshly defined activity, money is as important as campaign expenses to a political candidate. Sex too (if only as theatrically manipulated sex appeal) decidedly helps one stay alive and keep well.

Moreover, as psychoanalysis has proved for all time, sex implies an internal physical economy just as important to well-being as food, clothes, and shelter. It is not astonishing, in consequence, that sex can be shoplifted and used for political-economic purposes, or politics and economy shoplifted and used for sexual purposes. It all depends on the giver and the receiver and which patron spirit presides over the irregular transaction: Eros the lover, Zeus the policeman, or Apollo the aesthete. After all, those three virtuoso gods belong to the same family, and their blood relationship affects the status quo of the respective powers they wield. Since all is politics and its economy, in short, sex is, too.

Hence sadism is a political power and an aesthetic economy of the moral spirit. So is pathological sex *without* an aesthetic economy. Pathological sex is simply war with no peace terms, no aftermath in terms of further arrangements, further viability, further gambling with futures. Pathological sex is sex out to kill both itself and its partner; first its partner, then itself. Defeat simply becomes the price of victory. Rape-and-murder is, indeed, "notice of cancellation of a world": the subjective world. It is erotic because you can take another along with you almost in the act of sex. He or she goes first. You follow as soon as you've thoroughly savored your victory in the political economy of sex, your supremacy at the game in which you've been, hitherto, despised. Pathologically effectual sex, therefore, is obviously a base parody of the romantic love-death, that vestige of ancient ritual.

Rape-and-murder is victory at the highest price because it means a kind of cheating which logically is exposed and openly despised. Only you, murderer, can savor *this* consummate victory. In this way, pathological sex is virtually the opposite of glamour sex, in which *your* victory, movie star, is pacific and admirable: as much the gourmet pleasure of others as your gourmet pleasure. Male and female movie stars know this unsadistic heaven of abstract sexual delight. Here, of course, homosexes have the same status as heterosexes; the nature of the costume, the masquerade, makes no difference in the political economy of the glamour business. This is even true of sadism *as a cult,* an aesthetic quantity. When it *isn't* an aesthetic quantity (pornography too has an aesthetic voltage, however low), then the real trouble begins; sex becomes a pathology, produces crime. This is the only truly objectionable sort of pornography. Don Juan's relentless, endless string of conquests, the promiscuities of Eros or Homeros, black or like the lily, are excellent standards by which to judge these issues. The Black Homeros of *Something for Everyone* is a camp joke of the Creature Feature category. He is one of the minor scapegoats of the culture of sadism. The murders he commits are fake murders, cult murders, ritual rapes and murders. He is foiled at last by an ironic twist: he is trapped into marriage by a homely fat girl. It is like a back-handed fairy-tale ending; the hero's triumph is upended by no more than an attached "string." The dimension of everything in this movie's plot is made ambiguous by the comic satire. The same is basically true of straight detective fiction: the murder in such novels forms a "mystery," not primarily because the identity of its perpetrator is unknown and must be discovered, but because the murder remains a mystery in a ritual, quasi-religious sense. The closeness of certain fictional or "romanced" murders to records of actual murders is a way of *de*materializing the cult murder—which of old had a religious purpose and could be symbolic rather than real— into pathological murder, often pathological-sex murder. The philosophy of the Marquis de Sade—it was no accident that he achieved it precisely at the time of the French Revolution—was the last formal attempt by a religious impulse to redeem pathological-sex murder from its crude actuality by making pain (short of "pain of death") into a drastic exercise of the sensibility by connecting it with the orgasm and all corollary sensations of sexual pleasure. Not everyone in Sade's works is chopped into pieces or burned alive. Only the most naïve reader can imagine that the murders committed by Sade's sex maniacs are not essentially sacrificial acts (i.e., a form of religion) or else cult orgies in which pain portends not real but symbolic death. Sade's novels are more honestly gothic than the gothic romances themselves. If ultimately they are boring, it is because of the narrow range in which they are worked, the cast of characters to which Sade has restricted them. Had Sade been as great an artist as Proust, he would have created a single immense life work.

    The existence of *Les Abysses,* a film made in France by the Greek-Ethiopian director Nico Papatakis, is a vivid token of the philosophic attempt to restore the twin values of cult and art to a second-sight sadic grandeur. In making the economic motive dominate to portray a notorious crime on the police books, Papatakis reflected the acute political concern of our times. Two maidservants are the murderers, and their acts are technically motivated by economic desperation. The presence of incestuous love between the two servants provides a homosexual kink that is part of the sadic pattern. As homosexual kink, *Les Abysses* is still a very special case; slashingly sadistic, it manages to offer a structured sadism with exact, if difficult, nuances.

The case taken from life involved two sisters named Papin. Maidservants in a French middle-class household composed of a mature couple and their daughter, they turned on their employers in an insane fury and murdered the two women while the master of the house, frightened into helpless shock, stood by. As told in the film by Papatakis, the story is bound to suggest, with its prolonged unbridled violence, a Grand Guignol slaughter. But it is more serious and meaningful than such a theatrical display. The actual murder had already touched the imagination of Jean Genet, who saw in it a super-parable of the homosexual's transsexual sensibility, of which Genet is the century's prime personal example and first artistic exponent. Transsexualism as a *sensibility* is to be firmly distinguished from transsexualism as a *surgical operation;* the former is aesthetic, the latter (even when anesthetized) emetic.

Film reviewers were troubled by the madhouse atmosphere of Papatakis' situation: the loud never-let-up of the rising fury of the two servants. Papatakis might be said to have made a tactical error by imposing on what necessarily is a most extraordinary kink of human behavior (it cannot be called typical) the pattern of social-revolutionary symbolism; at least, this pattern is undeniable in the context of the event's time and place. It is the updated, still-universal slave revolt. This accounts for the film's documentary attention to the dramatic build-up, step by step, to the final explosion of energy that brings down, with knife and hot iron, two of the maids' employers. The energy of the feat is irrational, unrelieved, utterly animal in its propulsion. It is as if Papatakis were really thinking of the French people's frantically unleashed insurrection in 1789 that filled the streets of Paris with gore and corpses. By importing a social reflex into the film's premises of violence, Papatakis has achieved something less relevant, however, than Genet's strategy of converting the same violence into the male homosexual's fantasy. In the latter, violence is more truly sadic, less wildly, bloodily physical. It is the violence of a fastidious ethical conscience.

Originally, Genet wished his play, *Les Bonnes* (*The Maids*), to have its two principals, the tragic sisters, acted by young men. This makes his whole strategy, homosexual and artistic, wonderfully transparent. It was a superior way of familiarizing and domesticating a deed of wanton, implacable violence. Papatakis stuck much closer to the facts than did Genet, who dropped all statistics to re-create the fantasy life of two emotionally starved, paranoid, socially base women whose sole motivation, as the Papin sisters, seems to have been to keep the home they were about to lose because of their employers' decision to move to a smaller house. In Genet's altered plot, the maids die in a poetic ritual of self-annihilation; their employer has been only a frivolous woman of the world whose gowns and lovers they envy, so that they parody her goings-on when she is away, taking turns in playing her and her lover. In *Les Abysses,* the story keeps in line with the facts by showing the morally oppressed women finally stampeded into their revolt by their employers' desire to sell the house and discharge them.

The household in *Les Abysses* is depicted as a nest of hornets, everybody more or less ready to sting everybody else, with the employers decidedly on the defensive; thus, selling the house may have been the last resort of the oddly entrapped family to rid themselves of their servants' corrosive, incessant abuse. The maids' omnipresent filth, physical and verbal, might logically overawe audiences and appall the squeamish. To Papatakis, however, this is the mutual filth of common master-and-servant life if, regardless of time, place, and circumstance, it could be seen in its naked economic form. To Genet, the original facts had meant only a springboard for a poetically exquisite drama of two sordid maidservants magically changed by the transvestite lens of homosexuality.

It is *male* homosexuals whose primitive fantasy, typically, leads two individuals to do what Genet's servants do: dress up in fine clothes, quarrel like bitches, and act out charades in which they desperately caress each other in sex-starved reaction. Papatakis elects to make his situation more sexually difficult by the lesbian attraction of the neurotic daughter of the family to the younger maidservant. Genet is more psychologically and artistically radical. He is a very particular sort of spiritual transvestite, metaphysically almost lesbian, as if he were not a fairy in mental drag, so to speak, but a lesbian in real drag. This is the true cachet of *Les Bonnes*. Hence the debacle maneuvered by the older sister in Genet's play—her strangling of the younger, and her own suicide—is a supreme gesture of tragic authenticity: it is absolutely willed and self-defining. But it is morally thus final and real *only because* the trap is basically male-homosexual in concept, not female-homosexual. Lesbian incest became Genet's device for the fatal trap recognized and acted on by the older sister, who is specifically Genet's surrogate, the one who guides and controls the plot.

Finally Papatakis' strong film ("strong" in all senses) seems intellectually crude, with the rather too good-looking maids, played by real-life sisters, Francine and Colette Berge, acting out some characteristically Continental erotics that sit rather ornamentally on supposedly unchic maidservants. The modern contagion of revolt feelings among radical artists induced Genet himself, paradoxically, to be among the French VIPs who were persuaded to publicly endorse *Les Abysses* and get André Malraux to permit its screening at the Cannes Film Festival. The film happens to be so significantly homosexual, not for its own lesbianism, but for its cross reference with Genet's subtle "male" lesbianism, which is a propagandistic variation on his own moral program for a masculine, genuinely phallic Homeros. Genet's case in *Les Bonnes* was signally made explicit and eloquent by the American choreographer Eliot Feld's ballet inspired by it. The work was expressly designed to be, and was actually, danced by males. It was a direct insight into Genet's subtlety and was impressively danced (when I saw it) by two talented youths who might be called incarnations of the souls of lesbians: two Handmaids of Mari illuminated by a Platonic vision—not shot in the ass, with bloody results, by the tricolor cockade which Papatakis had in hand.

Yet, however we criticize *Les Abysses,* however rate it artistically, it is not vulgar. It has genuine stature, and sadism is what gives it its stature. Kinks: those fatal things? Yes! Kinks come plentiful in films homosexual and heterosexual. They come in Creature Features, with their limitless devices for involving rape and murder, they come in Antonioni's psychological parables of sexual maladjustment. Brute sadism is a commodity of commercial film which critical observers (not always film critics) habitually protest against, even calling it "pornographic." But protesting, of course, they do so in vain. Owing to the grip of the absurd melodrama, the nightmare of the Creature Feature that fascinates all ages and most moral temperaments, sadism in film, and the homosexual kinks of it, lack the dignity that the true culture of sadism presupposes. In intellectual essence, sadism is not a senseless outburst of violence, not the acts of a lunatic, or even the violent oppression of people by organized political force. All those manifestations exist; I can't deny the fact. But they are *vulgar channelizations* of the primary ethos of pain, not its supreme expressions. Statutory sadism, as invented by the Marquis de Sade, is supreme as a particular strategy. It is a strategy to convert pain in the sexual act into an art of therapeutics. No, please, not a *science* of therapeutics! The moment something gets into the mental clinic, it gets hopelessly lost. In brief, sadism is the aestheticizing of pain viewed as a fatal constituent of sexual activity; that is, an essential, ineradicable constituent of sex. If the object of pain is not to kill oneself and/or another, it must be instrumentalized toward survival.

With dolor, I feel, we must turn to a movie such as *In Cold Blood,* which celebrates the total irrelevance of sadism as a functional ethos, an aesthetic strategy. The crime which Truman Capote so delicately handpicked from life—so as to practice on it an elaborate but futile craftsmanship—was perfectly chosen. *In Cold Blood* is a featureless sort of creature, all cool reality pared to the bone, as it were, of all the old fustian fantasy and shown in the candid photographic nude; something to morally masturbate by and thus ideal for the mass élite that reads *The New Yorker,* where it was first published. God forbid that I might be thought to accuse Mr. Capote of bad faith or the coarse desire to cash in on morbid public fixation.

Mr. Capote is, of sorts, a literary man. His work has veered from precious romancing to unprecious pseudo-fictionizing. *In Cold Blood* represents the latter activity. The book is one of those blindfolded inspirations of dubious modern literature. In telling himself he was pursuing a humane truth by investigating the murders by his pair of criminals (I shall leave them anonymous), Capote was really pursuing a set of inhumane facts which he had decided to interpret in a spirit of sublime Christian charity: "They know not what they do, etc." To forgive almost anything is possible, I suppose, according to the moral nature. Maybe Mr. Capote might contend that he had nothing such as forgiveness in mind. Yet personally I can think of no other reason for the way he has redundantly, sentimentally lionized two such murderers.

For the moment I may be arguing beside the point. Because a moral theory of either justice or forgiveness is not what determines the quality and exact aims of either Capote or the makers of the film *In Cold Blood.* What they both have done is to direct their address, commonly if diversely, to one and the same public sensibility. This is the sensibility that craves the one true meat of the murder plot, whether it be the crucial instants of pain, the kill itself, or the network of technical paraphernalia surrounding it. This public sensibility wants the plot of human suffering and death as the prolonged, not necessarily successful, process of solving mysteries of identification. The process involves a double mystery: that of identifying and apprehending the personal agent and that of identifying his motive and method. There is a peculiar thrill to the skein of multiple statistics provided by Capote's investigation of an overtly gratuitous crime, a crime committed for crime's sake. I doubt that Mr. Capote could ever have hoped to discover anything of Dostoyevskian intellectuality in this murder; everything (since the gist of the facts was well known) pointed to the opposite. Faced, thus, with the blind alley of a nonsolution of motive, the fictional method was free to expatiate on the stark facts of its execution and aftermath and the tracking down of the criminals: to make simply a more vividly documented crime story. Capote's intensive inquiry into the lives of the family that became the murder victims was as gratuitous an invasion of privacy as the invasion of their home by the wandering miscreants who entered and deliberately, unnecessarily killed them. There was theft, but the loot in dollars was ridiculously negligible, and there was no offer of resistance.

The strategy hidden in this image of people gratuitously exterminated was something which the director, however, thought dispensable, apparently on grounds that it was too ghastly to reproduce photographically. We see nothing whatever of the murders in the film made from the fact-fiction work. We see only the postmortem period from the viewpoint of the criminals and the machine of apprehending them set into motion and followed to its climax. Many lovers of mystery stories, confronted with visible murder and visible blood, would shrink back, I agree, just as murderers shrink if confronted with the actual corpses they have created. Why should this parallel be so? Because the lover of mystery stories, more or less subconsciously, makes a double identification: with the victim and with the murderer. It is only an attunement with the paranoid existentialism of our times that causes murder-mystery lovers to greet both criminal and victim *as himself:* he is the "innocent" victim, the "innocent" murderer. The comfortable, isolated, commonplace victims of *In Cold Blood* did not in any reasonable sense invite the fatal attention of the two young male murderers. Just so, the man in the street seems to himself as utterly innocent of any offense that would invite retribution from the law or vengeance from a person or persons hypothetically offended. Yet *he* too is shot down, he, "the innocent bystander." He is shot down when there is no original crime, thus no tangible vendetta. So "vengeance" is just something having spontaneous birth in someone's morbid mind, someone's crazy, distorted imagination. Unless . . . Unless *what?*

Aren't we very close to the psychology and moral premises

of *Les Abysses*—from the viewpoint, that is, of the victims?
Well, Mr. Capote's book would say otherwise. His book is un-
pardonably a narcissistic charade in which he details exhaus-
tively, at infinite leisure, all the painfully plain statistics as if
they were notes made by some misplaced author of Greek
tragedies—useless to a Sophocles of yesterday but quintessential
to a Truman Capote of today. Mr. Capote was fatally misled by
his own quasi-journalistic acumen. Talent, his book has; genius,
or even high talent, it has not. It is an exquisitely calculated
bull's-eye that misses sadly in the aesthetic dimension. Of course
no one (except obscurely) thought of taking the film, before or
after it was made, in the true aesthetic dimension. If someone
had, its greatest value, by far, would have been to make it not
what it is, a documentary tear-jerker, but a male *Les Abysses*.

If the original Papin sisters, the manslaughtering maidservants, could be given meaningful intellectual and aesthetic
form, why not the equally "mad" murderers from *In Cold
Blood*? One reason was that they themselves, the two young men,
were born in cold American blood. This is blood with too little
heat even to rationalize its own desperation, its sense of social
injustice. To be sure, at this very moment, it is getting warmer,
but even a few years ago, it was cold and notably barren. The
two murderers, therefore, were perpetuated in even colder literary blood, and in a refrigerated Hollywood blood that quite
eliminated the actual slaughter. At bottom, Mr. Capote's moral
culture is disguised sissy-boy sentimentalizing that is "flexible"
not in moral essence, but only in prose gymnastics. The only
possible way to have shown the murderers of *In Cold Blood* in
the artistic dimension was to conceive them as pseudo-incestuous,
criminally perverted, proto-homosexuals. As is, they appear in a
mentally dim, photographically glaring, morally redundant
melodrama posing as a morality tale which, looked at objectively, seems a back-numbered piece of medievalism.

Typically in the movies, especially Hollywood movies,
homosexual kinks are a life-style game for two. Archetypally,
one, the "David," is good, the other, the "Jonathan," is evil; for,
invariably, some kind of evil is the basic ingredient of the overt,
or near-overt, homosexual recipe—the rules of the game for

undercover duos, male or female. We saw it starkly melodrama-
tized in Hitchcock's *Strangers on a Train,* alluded to before as
the veiled nakedness of attempted moral rape of male by male.
Farley Granger is the legendary all-male juvenile, a tennis star
saddled with a wife who stubbornly refuses him a divorce so
he can marry again. The sly "jolly" is in confronting this innocent (to whom another male, technically, is a naked animal inhabiting dressing rooms) with a villain who adopts the familiar
and gets prodigiously buddy-buddy. Yet Granger listens to
Walker's idea that they murder each other's unwanted relatives.
The Walker boy, who hates his father, is a tempter like the
Devil, like Black Homeros himself, quite willing to use the
ambisexual gambit. It's positively S/M to see the tasty Granger
flailing alike on the tennis court and in the arms of fear and
terror. To have agreed to the impudent plan would have been
like saying yes to a locker-room flirt. His wife already murdered,
he's like a girl at a rendezvous protesting her virtue. . . .

I don't maintain that hating one's wife is necessarily a
sign of being a suppressed homosexual. But there's a foothold
there. Besides, the whole plot make-up is so fake-up that one
has to cast about for some clue to make Granger look less like
a perfect dummy. Why does he tolerate Walker's kook-looks
even for a minute, and why does their showdown scene look,
not like a murder partnership welched on, but one guy's agony
and the other's fury that that odd locker-room flirtation was a
fizzle? If you doubt the intricacies of such Hollywood jollies,
catch the act on TV sometime. About that banal War Between
the Men and the Women, duly involved here, remember this:
it is not a *homosexual* legend. It is not homosexuals that the
Women's Liberation Movement of today has in mind, but the
men they all sleep with, or the men they don't sleep with because these men are sleeping with other women, or because they
themselves (if lesbians) are sleeping with other women. Some
lesbians have good reason to fear and resent heterosexual males
as sex rivals; for the same reason, of course, some homosexuals
have reason to fear and resent women.

There is a certain amount of such psychology among all
the sexes, but this psychology works all through the continuous

world chain of sex rivalry and intrigue. What most people are tardy in remembering, if they realize it at all, is that we do live in a male-oriented society; less so in the West, but a male-oriented, male-dominated world enclave of psychology and behavior, nevertheless, is still with us. The compromising factor of the fem-lib rationale is that, without desiring to change the metaphysic of dominant-equals-masculine, the fem-lib leaders want a greater share in it for women as the class of organic females. Perfect testimony to this truth comes in the form of a remark by the late psychologist of sex relations Eric Berne: "Men like to be more masculine than the person they are with. So do some women."* What may sound just cute at first sight has a profound truth. To verify it, go to Shaw's *Man and Superman* or to your neighborhood movie house. And watch. . . .

Concerning the War Between One Homo and Another, Hollywood is satisfied to be only jolly macabre where life has a way of being grimly in earnest. Thus we reaped the actual case of Leopold and Loeb, the Chicago youths who planned and executed the murder of a small schoolboy whom they kidnapped, killed, and defiled somewhere in the woods. Much later, there was one of those bursting canned-candid novels about the crime, titled, with the deepest of discretion, *Compulsion;* certainly, it could not have been titled *Compunction.* The original trial, blazoned on the front pages of the world's newspapers, clearly established that Leopold was the game's mastermind, Loeb the game's vulnerable hysteric, homosexually prone and in it for bed kicks—or rather, kinks. Years later, while in prison with his erstwhile partner, Loeb was butchered in the privy by a fellow convict whom, ostensibly, he had sexually importuned.

It was also well established by the trial that the confessed murderers had had sexual relations with each other. However, left only to the film, as made from the best-selling novel by Meyer Levin, one would have to guess at the homosexual core of the crime and thus conclude that it was another of those blind-alley things—unless one had intelligently latched on to the suppressed facts through a couple of fleeting innuendos in

* *Sex in Human Loving* (Berne).

the dialogue. I call once again on the universal lamebrain who judges such puzzles from behind his statutory heterosexual barricade: "Those guys just had *twisted minds,*" this person is found declaring. "When your mind gets twisted like that, anything can happen!" Oh, yes. And so on! Unlike Loeb, Leopold made a model prisoner, led a scholarly useful life behind bars, and when released, began the life of a quiet, job-holding, well behaved citizen, a status terminated by his death.

The true moral of crimes like that of Leopold and Loeb is apt to be missed since it is conscientiously, systemically bypassed by most people. It is not that homosexuality can be a criminal, sometimes fatal kink. It is that sometimes crimes are committed by heterosexually masked fuck-ups who operate as repressed homosexuals. Open, free homosexuality is the cure, not the cause, of potential or accomplished crimes. This point appears rather clearly in the movies themselves as a veritable blackboard lesson. That lesson is vividly illustrated in *The Detective* (see "Homeros as Chameleon"), where a married man, who picks up a homosexual in a gay bar, then murders and mutilates him after going to bed with him, obviously suffers from a homosexual neurosis. The chief symptom of this neurosis, prior to the murder, is that he paints himself a militant heterosexual impelled to chastise overt pansyism whenever he runs into it.

The grim case that occasioned *Compulsion* was also roundly parodied in a pyrotechnic closet thriller, *Rope*, woven by the ingenious and willing hands of Alfred Hitchcock. This time the film's time/space complex doesn't have to take in a railroad and an amusement park, as it does in *Strangers on a Train*. The two present connivers aren't strangers in a vehicle of public convenience but friends in a vehicle of private, if also neurotically restless convenience: a series of unrest rooms that pass for an apartment. All the action takes place, literally, in this series of continuous cubicles through a sequence of super-oiled camera takes which (so publicity boasted) were, as planned, uninterrupted. In charge of the action before the camera is a pair of those "twisted minds" of notorious fame. Beyond the range of the dollied camera, a number of body twists, I strongly suspect, evened things out; at least, if they didn't, they should have, if only to complete the fiction.

Parallel with *Compulsion*, two students here murder a classmate in what they imagine to be the Nietzschean spirit of murder as emotional catharsis. The schoolboy pretentiousness is treated as respectfully as if Nietzsche himself had thought of it. Actually—that is, supposedly—it has been thought up by a proxy in the person of James Stewart, who, as a Corn Belt specialist, seems much out of place as a college professor corrupting his students by preaching a Superman philosophy. As unlikely as Stewart is one of his "victims," who becomes fascinated, à la Leopold/Loeb, with the idea of putting the professor's philosophy into practice: Farley Granger. Among all physically delightful film juveniles of the recent past, Granger seemed specially fated to have thrust on him the most irrelevant criminal affectations.

The studio set built for Alfred Hitchcock to make *Rope* bears strong marks of sequestering another elaborate jolly: that intellectual pastime of which directors never seem to tire. It's as if the corpse put in the chest by the two young neo-Nietzscheans were the male genital—always at home, alive and well, to similarly displaced sexualities, but not at home, and quite dead, to papas, mamas, the police, and other non-Nietzschean nonmembers. Exception! You can always give a little party, as happens here, and serve supper on the chest with the "permanent erection" in it. For a while, anyway, you'll have the illusion that you're not in a Hitchcock movie, you're Leopold and Leob being dastardly. . . . But to return to more serious matters:

The devastating fact of humiliation felt by the maidservants of *Les Abysses*, touching their temptation privately to free themselves through lesbianism, made them turn on their own sex to wreak their vengeance: they murder their two *female* employers. But it would be surprising if the movies, in the infinite sensationalism of their wisdom, had not used homosexuality as a major motive in the standard War Between the Men and the Women. Again we must consider the discontented ladies. This element reared its pretty and pretty paradoxical head in a film by Henri-Georges Clouzot, *Les Diaboliques*. It is a brazenly tricky whodunit that turns everything, including sex, topsy-turvy at the climax. What begins as an apparently intact piece of lesbian plotting between the maltreated wife of a provincial schoolmaster and a female teacher to kill the objectionable husband ends as the diabolical scheme of the husband and his mistress (the seeming "lesbian" teacher) to get rid of the wife.

From the beginning, the two women seem conspirators, and closer to one another than quite "natural." Logically, as the plot to murder the husband is broached and finally (in appearance) carried out, the only plausible assumption is that love between the ladies is all that will hold the burden of motive for the relentlessly daring murder, even though the "victim" is not played for sympathy. Simone Signoret is sufficiently butch as the masterminding plotter to make it seem, at the climax, as if she had deliberately "acted the lesbian" to induce the other woman to walk into the extraordinary trap so painstakingly laid for her. Movies are so naturally dishonest about pulling the true sex punches that even this French film —while very possibly edited for American distribution—can be suspected of carefully leaving open the issue of lesbianism.

Maybe the wife here is just a subconscious lesbian, especially as a guilty conscience at last overtakes her and she sends her confederate-in-crime packing. This event, however, does not disturb her two opponents' devious plot, which is to frighten the poor thing to death: she has heart trouble, and is duly frightened to death by the animate specter of her "late" husband, following the most excruciating hints that he or else his ghost has returned. It is usual to classify films like *Les Diaboliques* (called *Diabolique* in the United States, as if it were a lady's name) as hard-core thrillers that stretch plausibility to the breaking point and beyond.

It isn't the lesbianism that's so implausible here, but certain plot elements that become rococo. I'd term *Les Diaboliques* a "butch thriller," as ostentatiously hard and bristling with pseudo-phallic improbabilities as some vicious and overbearing, implacable bull dyke. Yet the movie does securely unfold a certain believably lifelike pattern: the female witch cult for two; one of those dykish duets that can be spotted by a few sly mannerisms; a masculine version, of course, was *Strangers on a Train*, likewise ultimately, anticlimactically, derailed. Might one not wonder if even those two dotty old spinsters in *Arsenic and Old Lace* may not have a dash of the sapphic witch in their puckish natures? You remember: they were sweetly dedicated to poisoning all the superannuated male room-seekers who rang their doorbell. *The Killing of Sister George* is also provided with a sapphic-witch motivation: Sister George and a smart television executive have a mortal duel over passive female prey. No man is involved in their intrigue, but as lesbians, the two conceive themselves as occupied with a "masculine" war: the sex rival is to be "killed" by ruining her economically. That's *one way* for you, boys, girls, girlboys, boygirls, and fringe sexes. Just be a MAN.

But often, for an offbeat sex, it's hard to prove you're a man by having the courage of your sexuality. There is a small group of films, perfectly earnest, which use homosexual motifs in the dark, as a mystery-story pattern, and deal altogether in melodramatic surfaces: the form is as symbolic as the message. That the message thus tends to be bizarre was illustrated nowhere better than in one episode of *Dead of Night* (1946), a very ingenious film built around a supernaturalist gimmick. Michael Redgrave as a ventriloquist, whose dummy, Hugo, "falls for" a rival ventriloquist (also male) and dares to say so, as if using his own voice, discovers his homosexual dilemma in this supernaturalist form. The dilemma ends with the dummy supposedly visiting the other ventriloquist's room on his own locomotion, with the result (as if it were a bedroom farce) that Redgrave follows Hugo, finds him stretched out on his rival's bed, and shoots his rival. Later, in prison, Hugo's master emerges from catalepsy, only to destroy Hugo as soon as he sees him. He then himself starts speaking in his dummy's voice. The transference is now complete: the guilty man's homosexuality is in the open. But, of course, it's too late. He is insane. The point is as neat and cagy as it is grim.

A strange triangle with a homosexual motif appeared in

Nico Papatakis' next film, *Thanos and Despina* (1968). The attempt by one male to blackmail another into renewing a sexual affair, which took place in the past, is initiated from the side of the true homosexual, a former Greek paratrooper, who apparently had certain relations with a Greek gypsy who fought by his side. Now the gypsy, Thanos, back in the village where both live, is socially déclassé, and disinterested in his former lover, who is a rich man's son. When the latter's offer to renew their affair is firmly rejected by Thanos the gypsy, the former paratrooper, Yankos, systematically sets about ruining the other and at last gets him run out of town. However, Yankos' present fiancée, the beautiful Despina, has fallen hard for Thanos and is willing to give up everything to follow him in a life of exile and wandering. Half out of deviltry, half out of ironic humor, Thanos reluctantly accepts her companionship, only to be pursued by his lover, who has called up the police and the whole village, ostensibly to get back his fiancée. In a mountaintop confrontation between the two men, Thanos worsts Yankos in a sort of mock duel, then, seeing he is cornered by his horde of pursuers, grabs the girl's hand and leaps over a cliff in a double suicide. The moral guidelines are not nearly as clean as those in *Les Abysses*, probably because psychology and violence have been superseded here by a confused melodrama. The vital point is the homosexual motivation as a fixed lust that becomes very kinky when balked. Seemingly Papatakis made the elementary mistake (was it due to the threat of censorship?) of not defining Yankos' sexual drive as a fatal kink.

No such misfiring pattern is found in *Arturo's Island* (1962), an Italian movie based on the novel of that name by Elsa Morante. However the fatal kink here is asserted, its nature is plain to all who see the film, excepting, it would seem, that contingent of Manhattan reviewers who, till very lately, had the habit of playing possum when they were faced with an overtly homosexual situation. Even that matrix of Manhattan worldliness, *The New Yorker*, studiously avoided in its review any information about the film's theme. A growing-up boy lives on a Mediterranean island, son of a German father and an Italian mother; the latter is dead. He idolizes his father, a handsome well-set-up blond who sports with his son whenever he makes his sporadic visits to their home; business, it seems, much detains him on the mainland.

Suddenly Wilhelm, the father, brings to the island a very young bride and promptly leaves her there to his son's companionship. The hurt and bewildered boy is a little jealous; the two youngsters, she as puzzled as he, find it hard to get on with each other but manage an inevitable, backhanded sort of flirtation. A village woman also flirts with the boy and seduces him. At this moment, his father returns, but under very disturbing circumstances not immediately visible. What the spectator but nobody else knows is that the father has actually returned to help free a certain petty criminal who is to serve time in the island's prison.

The prisoner is a vigorous sexy young male who exchanges a high sign with Wilhelm as the latter witnesses his arrival off ship in manacles. Those quick to know their hustlers will guess easily that Wilhelm is the young man's homosexual patron. The rest of the story is how Arturo's father, enigmatically moody and short-tempered with his son, manages to spring the cocky young hustler and hide him away temporarily; then, how the boy, scenting a mystery to his father's conduct, discovers the hustler's presence, and the latter, ruthless and alarmed for his safety, spills the truth to the boy, makes threats, and escapes. The climax is emotionally and physically violent, with the father, made aware of everything, again taking off after his fatal passion, perhaps to chastise him—perhaps to console him.

Homosexuality in *Arturo's Island*, despite its place in a family disaster, has an authentically sweet odor. It is a passion that comes to certain males, maybe as a surprise, at certain times of life (often rather late ones), and stays there, difficult but essentially pure. This passion does not necessarily, except by mistaken appearances, vulgarize itself. Here its human object has an idyllic quality. Hustler, sheer sex brute though the young convict be, he is still a version of Homeros, inspiring purblind, infinitely sexual worship. He symbolizes the plain primeval power of Eros, whatever its sexual inflection, whatever the identity or identities of the involved sex organs. The pattern is fine because Arturo—pathetically smashed though his dream of a loyal, loving father ends—comes out the true heterosexual he seems destined to be. His "island" is the scene of a coming of sexual age: the solution of his Oedipus-complex as hitherto quarantined into his boyish, comradely, fetishistic love for his father. As a homosexual, his father forever disqualifies himself as a sex rival no less than as a lifelong comrade. It is a graduation present for Arturo at his coming-of-age, a kind of abortively realized ritual, the shock and strain of a purgative recognition. Arturo is now perfectly clean, tested, and ready for heterosexual love—unless, in the distant future, he develops a "kink" that grows and grows. But the film has a pattern strong and sufficient to itself.

Voraciously, of late, our militant minorities name the major conspiracies against them. Always it is the big conspiracy over against the little revolution. In the world of business, where men have by far the majority of big jobs and the wage level is sexually lopsided, it becomes that internal heterosexual war whose din has suddenly come into the open. No rare thing in this war, with its economic underpinnings of prostitution and assorted con games, is the use of homosexuality as a weapon in the hands of heterosexuals. In *Victim* and *Advise and Consent*, it is a kind of blackmail, and in the latter, definitely hetero blackmail. However, blackmail itself is not always of a routine kind. It may be a weapon to use against individuals by getting at them deep-down, demolishing them for private (and, hopefully, quite unpublished) gain. It may mean simply a racket of ambisexed gigolos who elect homosexuals to exploit by living with them and submitting to them. Or it may be a really kinky homosexual fetishism like that of Thanos' seemingly normal male lover in Papatakis' film. Frustrated, it will use any vicious means against a heterosexual holdout as against a homosexual holdout. Even Arturo's father may be rated a victimized homosexual who is self-blackmailed by his passion for a scheming hustler who may or may not be gratifying him.

Private homosexual blackmail, the process of what may be called organized pansy-ation, exists as a specialty and may be anything from a practical joke among buddies—a casual game of one-upmanship—to the criminal plot it develops in *The Servant*. This movie, directed by Joseph Losey, and a French film, *Les Cousins*, directed by Claude Chabrol, are signally fused by a common device, divergent in moral context yet identical in a mutual sex figure. This figure, a muscle-man specimen who appears, in both films, like something from a magician's box, is virtually naked, implicitly phallic, wholly erotic, and of course professional. Don't be surprised if you overlooked him. He is a surprise package in *Les Cousins*, where literally he steps out of a trunk as a party gift for an ostensibly heterosexual male. The situation is that one protagonist, a great ladies' man and Parisian bohemian, has just passed his law-school examination and is holding a bash to celebrate, while his country cousin, a serious fellow romantic about love, has failed the same examination because his spirit is so troubled by the licentiousness of his city cousin's milieu. He has selected his romantic companion—but she too appears "vulnerable."

The country cousin is tempted into suicide and goes walking by the Seine. Finally recovering himself, he comes back to the post-party scene, and purely by fluke is shot to death by his cousin, who is idly handling the revolver the other has just turned over to him. The calculated plot irony is rancidly bitter. The spirit of Black Eros has triumphed as if he were secretly an invert, a Homeros bent on destroying the romantic naïf, who, amid the city's utter moral promiscuity, is a holdout for old-fashioned heterosexual conservatism. At least, this is the only plausible way to interpret the bluntly cruel end as anything more than a melodramatic trip-up. The point is that the city cousin is already characterized as a playboy who, to achieve his technical orgasm, has to accompany his bed activities with the sight of pornographic movies. This makes logical the sex-out-of-a-trunk appearance of the muscle man: perhaps *he* is what the poor guy needs to get one more successful orgasm! It is homosexuality as benignly realistic blackmail, perhaps a joke, perhaps something that will work as a last-gasp solution to an impotence earned by last-ditch overindulgence.

Oh, there are endless conspiracies in the world! It is

the great paranoid illusion—all the more viable the more complex our civilization, the more acutely conscious we are of social perils. There is no good reason why homosexuality should not play its role in paranoid illusions, however substantial or insubstantial. In *Performance*, for instance, it is a floating ambiguity, seized as a mere cosmetic masquerade, yet something with villainous insistence, like a virus that breaks out of the body in mysterious symptoms. Remember that the crux of the physical battering earned by the defiantly independent gangster in that film is the supreme humiliation of having to admit verbally, under agonizing torture, that he is a poof—i.e., homosexual. At that point, there is no indication that he is, or will become, a poof. But later, when he gets taken into Jagger's *ménage*, he acquires poofdom as a kind of drag act, something theatrically illusive. How far is "theater" from "reality" these days? Hallucinogenic sex (the sort prevailing in the rock singer's studio) does not clearly adhere to any *one* taste, act, or organ. To do that might interfere with the way things have to *flow* in the drug milieu: "Easy on, man, easy on!" Tyrannous omni sexuality is what reigns in psychedelic quarters: unisex as a chameleon. The gangster (sturdily protesting, "There's nothing wrong with *me!*") gets hooked by it, however, and in effect done in by it. He goes poof! in one way if not in another.

That chance which is so fickle—bitch that he/she is—ordained, and perhaps without calculation, that James Fox, the gangster in *Performance*, should also have played the part of the fashionable young gentleman in *The Servant*. He is here victimized by a con game assiduously played against him by an unscrupulous team that gets hired as his household servants. Dirk Bogarde is the mastermind who directs the affair. He and his "sister" (Sarah Miles) are natural racketeers whose aim is to feather their nest by privately victimizing and enslaving a selected individual. In this case, as soon becomes evident, they have picked the right man. The title's mind-blowing irony is that Fox, the master, gradually turns into the servant. Beginning with his seduction by the young woman, Fox is step by step chicaned, bullied, and coddled into abject docility, alienated from his fiancée and all good society, to slip into drug addiction and the role of the orgy's fall guy: the one who gets fucked in the replete, anticlimactic sense. Actually he has been reduced to infantilism: the "it" in an absurd game of hide-and-seek he plays with Bogarde. At last, a vulgar orgy is held by the victorious racketeers, and it is now that, again as a surprise package or party favor, that ambisexual, all-satisfying muscle man appears like a god-from-the-machine. Nobody need be told he is intended as the finishing touch for the victim, who is too senseless, now, to care if the come-on has a hard-on.

Now and again the movies elect to make the free-floating homo freak, brought on for laughs, into a candidly confessed duo which is, and is meant to be, about as solemn and astounding as the slogans on both sides of a picket sign. There was that odd male couple in the promenade of faithful tandems that closed *Bob and Carol and Ted and Alice,* hippiesque in air, one of them bearded, mature, with the noble presence of a baby elephant. A female couple just as obvious, and just as strange, appears in *Five Easy Pieces* (1970), in a brief episode extraneous to the main plot. They are two youngish lesbians hitchhiking to Alaska to escape the "filth" of civilization, which the aggressive one has convinced herself and her mate is staining, stifling, and actually destroying the world.

The hero and his girl friend happen to give them a lift. As usual with such pairs, no picket-sign slogans are necessary to identify them. However authentic, however acceptable or unacceptable, they belong to the born kooks of the world, recognizable on sight, and as such are to be taken comically, of course, not seriously. One instantly agrees with this premise, though obviously their motorist hosts are more awed and puzzled than amused at them. As hitchhikers, both young women rate as miraculous *objets-trouvés* of method acting. The articulate butch type emits a clattering barrage of charges against the world's uncleanliness. The barrage is so repetitious and obsessive—so, in brief, kooky—that she herself, and this is quite funny enough, becomes Obscenity Incarnate. In an odd way, she's rather Dantesque, as if she and her friend were on their way, not to Alaska, but to Hell. However, who knows? They may be in Alaska, alive and well, at this moment.

A slightly more plausible (male) pair, duly compromised in moral look, make entrance in Ken Russell's film version of D. H. Lawrence's *Women in Love* (1970). The more aggressive of the two looks like a footloose gigolo of ambisexual tastes—or just ambisexual strategies. It does seem as if he really wants to make Gudrun (Glenda Jackson), one of the heroines; he flirts with her, and she goes to his room in the mountain chalet where they meet. To Lawrence's two heroes, Gerald and Rupert the former being Gudrun's lover, the "gigolo" (nominally he's an "artist") seems unsympathetic and without social caste, which probably he is. Yet he obviously interests Gudrun, who is having "love trouble," apparently because he *is* offbeat. When debonairly he admits to her that his male companion is his lover, with a "So what?" expression, her interest seems unabated. Yet she declines to get within reaching distance. The man, alert and cynically grinning, presides like a Black Homeros over the tangled sex drama of the heterosexual foursome, who are having a little holiday amid the alpine splendor. Gerald quarrels with Gudrun because of her flirtation with this "clown," but seems to collapse spiritually, wandering off one night to freeze to death in the snow. Another closet queen gone loco? Neither the film, nor Lawrence himself, seems to know.

While Gudrun's flirtation is rather opaquely handled, it is of particular interest because of Lawrence's overt pattern of homosexual temptation in his self-surrogate hero: Alan Bates as Rupert Birkin. This is expressed in the film almost exclusively by the famous nude wrestling scene between Rupert and Gerald, which Lawrence used as a device for bringing his two heroes into physical contact. Technically, the contact involves only a manly sport, but for Rupert (of course the novel is more explicit on this) it embodies a specific frustration. He wants a male lover as well as a female lover, though as yet he has not decided just what physical form the male connection can conveniently take. Of Gerald's physical magnetism for him, he has no doubt. Vaguely, he yearns to express his affection through some vivid and chaste demonstration: the wrestling bout offers the first good opportunity. It is as if an athlete of the ancient gymnasium should conceive wrestling as a philosophy of innocent but perfect brotherhood, and wish to install it as a kind of courtship. The best the movie can do is to support Lawrence's idea with the immediacies of kinesthetic spectacle. In substance the wrestling match—for which both men completely strip—becomes a conscious parody of lovemaking, a kind of practical experiment for the fixated Rupert. Done with more deftness and purpose than it has earned from the director, the scene could have been a supreme image of homosexual frustration, a displaced erotic choreography.

In life, Lawrence is supposed to have yielded at least once to his repressed desire for sexual relations with a man. The man is rumored to have been the model for the gardener who becomes Lady Chatterley's lover. But that was in another novel, and there Lawrence had decided to do the literary drag act, dispense with his lifelong ideal of union with a man, never realized, and play "like a woman." This, of course, is a homometaphysical syndrome that may be practiced by any author more or less consciously. Lawrence's biggest point is that it need *not* be a kink; that it is healthy, not sick. Unfortunately, it got to *be* a little sick in *Lady Chatterley's Lover*.

No doubt, Lawrence was more afraid of physical homosexuality than of the obligation to confess it in his writings, should he ultimately yield to it. Intellectually, his feelings for men seem not to have exceeded a sensuous sort of ritual worship, as illustrated in an equally famous scene in *The Plumed Serpent*, elaborately chaste and one long manual caress of erotic sublimation. One doesn't know if the idea of the hidden homosexual author and his literary double of the feminine gender ever occurred to Lawrence as a positive moral solution; his peculiar inner candor would probably have been repulsed at such a solution. Other authors of our century have not been so scrupulous—or perhaps one should say these have been more adaptable and ingenious than Lawrence, who was always "healthy" to the extent that he was "honest."

Yet art is just as devious as courtship may be. One wonders whether Gerald, in *Women in Love*, is not himself feeling (Lawrence may have felt it intuitively) Gudrun's temptation when she meets the coquettish homosexual in the mountains.

I can only continue to offer statistics from movies which manage to involve my subject. Tennessee Williams comes to mind because repeatedly he has given us heroines whose lives have been spoiled and made unhappy because husband or boyfriend has turned out to be homosexual. The theme has crucial explicitness in the lives of the heroines of *A Streetcar Named Desire, Cat on a Hot Tin Roof,* and *Suddenly, Last Summer*; each has been victimized by a "man in her life" who betrays her faith in his sex. In *Streetcar,* the despoiling shock has been in Blanche's past: she tells of it in a pathetic monologue as the true source of her troubles.

The role of Maggie in *Cat* is less pathetic, more callous and deliberately vulgar than Blanche, and Elizabeth Taylor filled Maggie to the brim and past the brim. Williams has a gift for the tenderly human, even the poetic, but he also has a gift for the hideously human, the abortively poetic, which competes with the other gift and at times overwhelms it. The movie of *Cat* made the point less clear than did the play, but (aesthetics all to one side) Maggie's husband, Brick, who suffers from impotence, has muffed his marriage owing to his still being in love with his old college roommate. This cat is let out of the bag before the hideously unhappy, unhappily complicated drama comes to its depressing climax. Both *Cat* and *Streetcar,* speaking homosexually, have the bad style of a closet queen with a good conscience, in that, self-righteously, they decline to expose a jot of the beauty and charm of being homosexual.

Perhaps Mr. Williams has been commendably moral about the subject all along and should be praised for consistently lowering the boom before what many, I suppose, believe is essentially an ugly spectacle: males at the routine business of making it with males. If so, his view of the errors of homosexual conduct ought to be a crying object lesson to the ladies. He rarely gives us a heroine who escapes having her womanhood insulted by some weak-minded fairy who has blundered things. Why do Williams' heroines never quite succeed even with his hustler and truck-driver heroes? If nothing else fatal happens, they get killed (*The Rose Tattoo*) or run away (*The Fugitive Kind*) or refuse to gratify the lady (*Boom*) because the gentleman is, inconveniently, the Angel of Death. Williams' heroes may be tremendously virile, or at least want to be, yet there's more than one jammed zipper fly in their manly ointment.

It seems a bit cruel to adjudicate Williams' climactic example of his gay-gulled heroines. Yet if I omitted this example, I would be scotching some of my most important documentation. *Suddenly, Last Summer* has the most tortured woman, and surely the stupidest, ever victimized by a homosexual in Mr. Williams' repertory of works; the dastardly deed here is the most weirdly and deliberately villainous of them all. Again Elizabeth Taylor is elected as the scapegoat, her high eligibility as a sex object, I suppose, being meant to italicize the hideous perversity of the disgusting faggot, her cousin, who for some opaque reason has whirled her off on a European (or is it Caribbean?) cruise for two. He is a great mother's boy, we learn indirectly, and mother has gotten very disturbed when her coddled treasure takes off with her niece (Miss Taylor). As played in the movie (I did not see the stage version), the clinical near-tragedy strains at every point to be incredible, from Miss Taylor's casting to the unique and ghastly end serving as nemesis for the faggot villain.

It seems, as the film opens, that Catherine, the young woman, after her cousin's sudden, at-first-mysterious death, has come home with a hallucinatory neurosis so severe that her aunt wishes her to have a lobotomy. The aunt, Mrs. Venable, is Katharine Hepburn acting probably the most ridiculously pompous, falsely keyed role in her career. She's no more Catherine's aunt than I am. She commits her niece to an institution, and soon Catherine is in a cornered spot where she may be bullied into submission. Something tells us, even before the scriptwriter does, that Catherine is far too normal, healthy, and beautiful (isn't she Liz Taylor?) to merit the sanctions of a lobotomy; hence, it's only a matter of the how and the why: how she's going to escape it and why Mrs. Venable is so bent on her having it.

Since the original work is like a soap opera written for beautiful rather than unbeautiful people, we are not surprised to have turn up a trim and true young brain surgeon (the late

Montgomery Clift) who guesses that nothing is wrong with Catherine that she can't get rid of by throwing herself as rapidly as possible into the arms of a sound medic. In this situation, the sinister phantom of her past simply must be evicted: all will then be well. Now there unfold scenes that should have come straight out of television: Catherine being persecuted by her aunt and by the brain specialist whom Mrs. Venable has bribed to advocate the lobotomy . . . Catherine reacting hysterically to the prospect of the lobotomy . . . Catherine reacting to the young surgeon's reaction to her hysteria at the prospect of the lobotomy . . . all in that intimate, impeccable TV style, real close, so that one does not miss the tremor of an eyelid or a lip, the stroke of a makeup pencil, the true shape of a mouth beneath the applied shape of a lipstick.

As the aunt, Miss Hepburn works behind the genteel mask of the old-school Southern matron, but this, of course, in the present context, proves that if anyone needs a lobotomy, its Mrs. Venable. The funny part is that the character is played as if she herself has already had a lobotomy, and if she hasn't, a lobotomy might do her some good. The true suspense, as Mr. Williams and even TV commercials seem to know, is in getting the awful truth out of Catherine before she goes into the frenzy that will make her aunt's myth look genuine. That clever surgeon sees that she gets a truth scrum, at which the grisly facts that have made her a nervous wreck pour out in the shape of that somehow familiar monologue. This time the monologue— all in tricky photography, and outrageously unbelievable —more than accounts for the sufferer's difficulty. Part of the trickiness is that in this crucial sequence one never sees the face of the faggot cousin. Only portions of his manly figure are glimpsed as he propels himself in and out of the film frames, mostly out. It's all very, very much like a bad dream: a bad dream purveyed in a cinematic "art" we've seen skillions of times though never before with such superfreak content. The result: a Creature who doesn't seem to need Features.

In fact, what he does, and what is done to him, are pure conundrums: the hallucinations of Mr. Williams' feverishly fertile brain. True, the villain is supposed to have had a

long-time trauma from witnessing turtles, stomach up, being
devoured alive by sea birds. But this symbolism is merely tan-
talizing unless, by chance, we happen to grasp its truth: the
trauma is the consequence, not the cause, of the fellow's budding homosexuality. Briefly and concussively, the story of his
villainy has taken this form: he has led his female cousin a merry
dance through tropic islands with the pretense of giving her a
good time, when actually he is using her as regular bait for
attracting native boys to his vicinity. I say "vicinity" because
they never come close enough to him to be touched. This last
fact is extremely odd. Is it owed to cinematic technique or moral
timidity? Anyway, it is utterly preposterous to those frequent
visitors to tropic islands (particularly the Caribbean) who go
there with the sole purpose of "attracting native boys to their
vicinity." Actually, far from having to have handy a juicy number showing her tits and her behind to induce boys to come
near a male visitor, all said visitor had to do is to step outdoors
alone to have boys drop from the sky and roll under his feet;
they look up at one (I am told on reliable authority), flutter
their lovely black eyelashes, and the deal is made. Thus, one
cannot take Catherine's tall story seriously, even for a moment,
unless one imagines that an unspeakable handicap, mental or
physical, makes her cousin monstrous, with the consequence that
only Her Beauty and His Money can lure the trade within
snatching distance.

Not that we see any *snatching*. Even Creature Features
give us a few good nips of actual skulduggery, but not Mr.
Williams' exacting art, which here the film-makers were induced to obey. All we get are more and more boys, crowding
around to cheer Miss Taylor's enticing protuberances and jeer
at her companion's despicable tactics. Evidently there must have
been some snatching behind scenes, for the cousin's vicious reputation has spread, and finally the only reward for his mul-
titude of flung coins are stones thrown back at him and dozens of
bare little heels, going, alas! in the opposite direction.

. . . No, not the only reward; Mr. Williams, apparently,
has wished all this to be a mere prelude to a brilliantly macabre
and highly moralistic idea. There is a terrible fate in store for

his faggot villain. And of course it is a climax to the callous use of Catherine as a sex decoy. What could be more dramatic, and symbolic too, than to have him hunted down in the very streets where he has hunted?—and by having his dying flesh devoured by the flesh that, in one way or another, *he* has *devoured*? While the visual presence of the truth has been tactfully obscured, Mr. Williams has sternly offered us antihomosexual cannibalism functioning as a complex nemesis. After casting himself, a fugitive, over a cliff, the wretched homo must play "turtle" to the flocking "sea birds." All of which is not only silly and incredible but in the worst possible taste. Because the "sea birds," as you may know or have sensed, are in this case little boys.

Presumably Catherine marries the young surgeon and attains real womanhood. But meanwhile she'd need everything going for her. With the world so full of homosexuals, *every* Williams heroine does. We have to remember that, though still inclined toward men, Blanche DuBois got herself removed to the loony bin with greater finality than did Mrs. Venable's niece. Let us turn aside for the moment to glimpse another young woman in the movies, played by Jean Seberg and (parallel with Miss Taylor as Catherine) committed to an institution where she, too, is the lucky recipient of a young man's amorous attentions. He, played by Warren Beatty, is a social worker obsessed with the idea (which Miss Seberg considerably stimulates) that he can help females maladjusted to sex by treating them to the Real Thing. One knows that Mr. Beatty has it "all together."

The film is *Lilith*, a great nonmasterpiece by Robert Rossen. I can't remember how it all ends—I'm sure it ends unimportantly—but I do recall that, while shadowing Miss Seberg about the grounds of the institution where she is being treated, her well-intentioned suitor gets an unexpected (or is it an expected?) shock. She seems to have some business in an isolated barn; and sure enough, as Mr. Beatty finds, she does. It is a rendezvous with another young woman (Anne Meacham), who is lesbianly inclined. What Mr. Beatty stumbles upon is a love scene between the women. I need not draw the horrendous moral: it is as plain as the side of an old-fashioned barn, disguised though it be by new-fangled trimmings. If only Tennessee Williams could have profited by Mr. Beatty's magnificent experience. What do I really mean? It may sound obvious, but what I mean is: sex is sex. What I don't mean is that sex is sea birds eating the entrails of live turtles. Of course, you could consider that *was* sex by construing it as a sadistic metaphor. But then, you see, the act would not be *horrid*, it would be *yummy*.

All such speculation is beyond the domain of possibility in Catherine's case. Patently, Williams wanted to give his heroine the worst scare in the homosexual history of the movies. To avoid becoming a fag-hag,* I should say, Catherine would have to call to her aid the entire heterosexual history of the movies, including *Rosemarie, The Chocolate Soldier,* and *Butterfield 8*. But surely—to turn to one of the present book's main themes—the homosexual cousin in *Suddenly, Last Summer* rates as a figure of Black Homeros. To this victim of gamin-gluttony I should like to oppose someone much more believable and sympathetic and young—and "black" only because he develops, quite suddenly, a fatal kink. Being virtually a child, he is a true mythical Homeros, tender, vulnerable, utterly sincere in his Kinky Cupid's curves. He plays with firearms that turn out to be phallic symbols. In fact, he is a natural game-player. Yet, being so young and unfamiliar with life, he doesn't quite realize that cops-and-robbers, for him, is really a sex game, and that the name of the sex is male.

I mentioned him on a previous page: he is Sal Mineo, and he is the only candidate for being the technically unknown cause in the film *Rebel Without a Cause*. That is to say, the supposedly absent "cause" in the film's youth rebellion (a rebellion chiefly represented by the teen-agers' idol, James Dean) is certainly the revolutionary role of sex. For instance, the girl Judy, who connects with Dean, is mentally all puckered up because her dad won't mouth-to-mouth kiss her. Plato (yes, that's the name), the boy played by Mineo when he was only fifteen,

---

* Slang for a woman who is temperamentally attracted to male homosexuals and identifies herself with them socially. A fag-hag is not to be confused with a professional tomboy, though the two types have points of contact (see the last chapter).

is experiencing, in no vague sense, the homosexual temptation peculiar to ultrasensitive schoolboys. Nobody wise in the ways of the world could doubt this undeclared element in his palpable fixation on Jim (James Dean), an older schoolmate. It is the classic hero worship that may or may not turn into lovemaking. Both youths are portrayed as products of alienating family experiences and fall into the class of moral dropouts that are potential delinquents. The upshot is that Plato, in the midst of playing hide-and-seek in a deserted mansion with Jim and Judy, is panicked by the arrival of the police, who have come to investigate a ruckus with some nasty "leather types." His instant reflex is to flee: obviously it is a confession of guilt, but just what guilt? He takes refuge in a closed planetarium, where he hides (with a revolver) like a hunted criminal. Only Jim, then, out of compassion of heart, is brave enough to go in to him, and as friend and ally, persuade him to give up.

By a fluke, the besieging police, misunderstanding the turn of events inside the building, plug Mineo as he emerges without his revolver (which he has turned over to Dean), and he dies on the spot. It is the banal moralistic end of old-fashioned hokum fiction reset in the milieu of teen-age revolt. But *Rebel Without a Cause* matters not in the least, on screen or off, as a serious work of fiction. By far its greatest interest is Dean and Mineo as they play out the game of displaced sex: the senior master type and the junior slave type irresistibly, if subconsciously, drawn to each other. I take it that both actors, as handled by the director, Nicholas Ray, were subjectively alert to this angle; at any rate, they brought it out with taste and feeling genuine enough to skirt the inherent corniness.

Naturally, it is possible to rule out such an interpretation as mine, however much it be shared by others. It is no mere sectarian prejudice that enables one to distinguish the human eloquence making my interpretation plausible and persuasive. The apparatus of aesthetic realization as such urges it on the attention of all. It is more arbitrary, in short, to *ignore* the interpretation I give than to *recognize* it. We must not forget, in contemplating the fatal kinks of filmic homosexuality, that there are also *fatal thinks,* and that these are what give us understanding of the kinks as not necessarily "fatal," and not even, necessarily, "kinks." Go see *Women in Love* or *Un Chant d'Amour,* and you'll observe what the aesthetic viewpoint toward kinks can accomplish. Go see *Suddenly, Last Summer,* and you'll register what it can never accomplish.

We must look to the avant-garde movement to show us both a thoroughly reasonable and validly imaginative treatment of intimate homosexuality: the homosexual as he grows up. *Narcissus* (1956), by the late Willard Mass and Ben Moore, chose a Cocteauish allegory by which to tell the story of a young male eccentric whose allergy to the female is interpreted as Narcissean in origin. While past adolescence, he is an infantile, trampish recluse who knows neither man nor woman and is horrified by his compulsive venture into a gay bar. The rejected Echo of the film, queen of a gang of neighborhood toughs, has the vulnerable, pathetic youth beaten up by her savage minions. Frightfully crushed, he commits suicide in his "pool": the edge of New York's East River. This stark narrative includes several dream hallucinations (all done with remarkable tact) updating Narcissus as an instinctive, if frustrated homosexual.

Lloyd Williams' highly personal *Line of Apogee* (1967) is a sort of autobiography taking off from an animated family album (the film-maker enacts the lead) and expanding into detailed dreams that clearly reveal the hero's homosexual progress and coming-out as an adolescent. Unhappily, the poetic style is more arduous than inspired. Yet the work is a valuable look-in on the natural maturation of an instinctive homosexual: entirely candid if rather too straightforwardly literal. Some highstepping effects remain oddly banal, and yet the dream imagery is authentic and, at times, moving. Certain things hang in the mind: the dreaming boy afloat in a transparent globe with a huge snake coiling around it, the eventual bed partners appearing and disappearing on his pillow with magic rapidity. Such films prove that a kink may be kind, not cruel; and, if "tragic," a classic tragedy, no mere sordid mess.

I don't know that all the fatal kinks I've indicated are genuine, even genuine when they are the kinks of directorial temperaments fond of making professional jokes at the permissive public's expense. But suppose what I have spoken of as jollies, or private jokes with public parts, were—as indeed I've left room to assume—a mere phase of the entertainment game, a routine professional put-on to titillate the public—the public that has such an insatiable appetite for off-color fun? The film public, to a large extent, seems never to tire of wishing to be naughty in the imagination—to believe in fairies (real fairies!) even where they're not. Because, you see, that's the hell of it! And hell, at least, isn't monotonous. Then, there's what we might call the new surrealism, which seems to have expanded and taken root in our psychedelic age. For the new surrealism, anything that contradicts reality or sober sense is amusing, end-lessly amusing. It's the New Thing that pleases, because it's bound to alarm, puzzle, or embarrass the Establishment, which by its nature is solemnly dedicated to keeping up those horrid status quos.

Well, I think none of these hypotheses about directorial playfulness would apply to the dead film artist Sergei Eisenstein, who gave every sign of meaning the homosexuality he dared to intimate. I think he would have liked to tell it like it was if he had not been a citizen of the Soviet Union and thus subject to one of the toughest bureaucratic establishments in the modern world. Eisenstein was a shy man in whom caution was a built-in reflex: he could have been ruined by exposure of his private life or any overt interest in homosexuality. He *was* ruined by ex-posure of the fact that he had put first the laws of the art he espoused, that of the film, and had invented every strategy he could possibly think of to conceal that he primarily represented the theory and practice of a new art, to which the theory and practice of a new politics was secondary. He was capable of this systematic deception (though inevitably he ran into a great deal of trouble because of it) owing to the fact that he was a genuine intellectual and that "having jollies" without a real personal basis would have seemed so frivolous a habit as to be beneath him. Finally, he could not make the formula of deception work. Bureaucratic sniffers and ego-blind tyrants always have a nose for genuine artistic and intellectual independence, which they rightly fear and naturally find abhorrent.

Telling on film a heroic folk myth such as *Alexander Nevsky,* a triumph inside and outside the Soviet Union, was possible to Eisenstein because its pattern was basic enough to be universal, and because hero worship is a natural part of the homosexual aesthetic myth. *Alexander Nevsky* dealt with powerful, physically forceful, and handsome men, even when they were (like the apparitional German knights with their fantastic helmets) the piece's "villains." Alexander Nevsky as the savior of his country, of course, flattered Stalin and seemed perfect art propaganda. Who could miss its contemporary application? Then came a greater test, *Ivan the Terrible,* through which Eisenstein had decided to express himself and by which he hoped to fool Stalin. It was as close as he ever came to having his jollies: not necessarily, that is, jokes to his own taste, but necessarily jokes at the expense of Stalin as the tyrant who had victimized, among other film artists, Eisenstein himself. Eisenstein had seen the prohibition of a whole film of his, *Bezhin Meadow,* because its pattern recognized a victorious force other than Communist Socialism in Russia. What force? Simply the survival of mystic religion among the peasants.

Eisenstein believed in this force as a timeless quality of the people and had already created a monument to it in his Mexican film project (1930). This work's heroic design was frustrated and destroyed by his American backers, Mr. and Mrs. Upton Sinclair, when they confiscated the raw footage and declined to let Eisenstein edit it because he had failed to live up to the contractual terms, and besides had demanded, and gotten, considerable money in excess of the original budget mutually agreed on. Still worse, the good bourgeois Sinclairs were thoroughly incensed when they discovered that Eisenstein had shot in Mexico a trunkful of footage which seemed pure pornography (apparently it was done for the most part in Mexican whorehouses) and thus could have nothing to do with the film they thought Eisenstein had contracted for. Consequently they did nothing to prevent the authorities' destruction of this precious footage; in fact, they believed that destruction perfectly just, since they considered the footage "unusable."

No doubt, some demon had possessed Eisenstein to **have**

induced him to take such a risk. I don't know that any of the action in the confiscated footage was homosexual. But it was certainly erotic, some of it "offbeat," I dare say, and could have been taken for stag-film stuff. It was probably superb as meta-beaver and, I am sure, conspicuously phallic. Yet Eisenstein was quite enough of a technical master to have worked it into the epic pattern he had visualized as a film about the Mexican people, with whose beauty and primitive integrity he had fallen in love. His passionate devotion to the Mexican project, the explosive force of his inspiration once he had come to Mexico, are all well documented: the whole pitiful story is told elsewhere and appears, of course, in Marie Seton's ample biography of Eisenstein.

Eisenstein had a great personal eye for human beauty, and more especially for male beauty. The remaining parts of the surviving Mexican project, edited by others into three intact films (*Time in the Sun, Thunder Over Mexico,* and *Death Day**) concentrate mostly on male protagonists. The chief hero is a rebellious Mexican peon of much physical beauty; the sequence of his "earth crucifixion," shared with two other peons, all of them naked to the waist, is famous in filmic annals. What must occupy us more particularly, here, is a series of devices which he used for *Ivan the Terrible,* generally and credibly acknowledged as his masterpiece (along with the unique *Potemkin*) and as a disguised autobiography. As Marie Seton pointed out, Eisenstein had sat on the czar's throne in the Kremlin when he made *October,* the film about the Russian Revolution, and found his legs too short to touch the floor: a photograph of this incident exists. In *Ivan the Terrible,* we see the young Ivan, as a boy, seated on this throne with his feet hanging free of the floor. An arresting fact about the whole sequence involving the beautiful child, Ivan, is that the role was a bit of male impersonation: a girl was chosen to take the part.

Insignificant? I believe not, when the fact is put in context with the film-maker and the rest of the film. Whatever the autobiographic interpretation, which is complex, the surface

* A version blending these with additional footage was issued under the title *Que Viva Mexico!*

facts are more than suggestive, conclusive as they are if connected with Eisenstein's homosexuality. At the height of his power, the self-declared Czar Ivan is portrayed at the picture's end as a triumphant strategist who has ruined or killed his most important political enemies. One could take this as an analogue (wishful thinking in part) of Eisenstein's triumph over his critics and rivals in the Soviet film bureaucracy, and over Stalin himself, to whom he constantly had to "prove" his merits. Following a period of disgrace because of *Bezhin Meadow*, he had been officially reinstated and loaded with honors. This was because the first part of *Ivan the Terrible* (issued separately) was a decided official success. Eisenstein was celebrating this success at a public reception for him at the moment of his first heart attack. While recuperating from it at the hospital, he was informed by his friends that the second part of *Ivan* (almost completed) had displeased Stalin, and its banning had been publicly announced. Eisenstein never did the final editing that later took place. He died too soon.

What message does the climax of *Ivan* have for us? I think it too complicated to analyze fully here.* But its overt features are enough to earn it a place in this book. Ivan had not reached his peak of power without forming a personal bodyguard as other tyrants had done. It was militant, devoted, and of course all-male: the Oprichnini. When Ivan gets wind of a plot to assassinate him as he leads the church procession at midnight mass, he decides on a bold and deadly form of frustrating it by substituting for himself the feeble-minded young Vladimir, his cousin, whom his Boyar aunt, Euphrosinia, has long wished to place on his throne as the rightful czar. Vladimir is impersonated by a young man so effeminate of face that he looks like the newest photogenic starlet of Hollywood in 1946. Ivan invites Vladimir to an all-male party preceding the midnight mass, ironically crowns him with his own crown in a mocking ritual, then flatters him by making him—disguised by the usual black cowl worn for the mass—lead the candlelit procession into the church; in the expected result, Vladimir is mistaken for Ivan and fatally stabbed by the assassin.

* See Marie Seton's biography and my account of *Ivan the Terrible* in *Classics of the Foreign Film* (Tyler).

There remains a single element to pinpoint Eisenstein's homosexuality quite aside from its historic authentication; that is, whatever premises for it may exist, it looks like the bona-fide invention of an auteur director. . . . Oh, yes, one may grant that sophisticated directors have never hesitated to introduce homosexuality as typical of the orgies of licentious emperors and luxurious aristocrats. Cecil B. De Mille did it, in a way, long before Fellini made the *Satyricon*; it is hinted, and more than hinted, in scenes from the wild-party and bordello sequences that were edited out of Erich von Stroheim's *The Merry Widow* and *The Wedding March*. But here, as elsewhere, I do not offer such evidence to impute private homosexuality to a director or an actor. My attitude on this point has been fully explained.

Eisenstein's private homosexuality is as fully a coincidence as the appearance of public homosexuality, or its implication, among directors and actors who are privately heterosexual. Female impersonation, as I have already made plain, is sometimes an addictive *hommage* to women offered not by homosexuals, but by heterosexuals. What happens in the lively revel held by Ivan as a rather paganish prelude to midnight mass is that, among all the male dancers, we see a single ornate female figure, wearing a mask and breastplates from which strings of beads pour. She is very much the center of attention from the male dancers as Ivan looks on with a subtle but fascinated smile. Then there is a climax to the jumping and the whirling: all stand transfixed in pose. At this the peasant girl is seen to remove her mask. The person revealed is the handsome, virile young leader of the Oprichnini. Heterosexual as he may be mechanically supposed in this movie, it is easy to think of homosexual precedents for him. Why the drag act *at all?* Automatically one thinks of *The Damned* and of assorted sadists and Homeroses that we have discussed here, and that are no worse than they should be, if no better. Fatal, kinky, just fantastic, aesthetic thrills must be taken as they come. Some come homosexual.

10. HOMEROS AS

FUNNY FELLOW

Most of an audience probably forgets—when watching a movie with eccentric comedian, character actor, or exotic kook occupying screen center—that after all a movie isn't just a studio set or a machine built for airtight laughs. That automatic assumption is the result of popular megalomania; it makes a person think that the entertainment industry spares no expense or sweat or genius in order to give him, humble individual though he be, a single little moment of intense pleasure. Therefore anything like a "stunt" in the popular arts rates aesthetically like the clowns and the acrobats at the circus. Stunts don't take place in the streets exactly, but in an arena or other theatrical space before an audience being wooed with something to make it gape, laugh, and applaud. With the recent audience-participation theater, and so much public moral education (especially by such flip equations as that between psychoanalysis and "psycho"), this particular view of the movies and other pop entertainments may seem dated, just not true now, however true recently. Time "educates," etc.

The old days, I think, just can't be whisked away quite so magically. Everything you see in a movie or on television, in a living-theater setup or beyond an old-fashioned proscenium, was always, and is still, out on the streets too. And it may well be sitting near you right now. Not that always you're aware of it! Part of the fun, the illusion, is *not* being aware of it—if theatergoing or moviegoing still happens to be your bag. As for sexuality, it has always been in the streets, and by no means as the exclusive prerogative of "streetwalkers." As we know, the most striking thing in recent social evolution has been the tendency of minority groups to "demonstrate," to walk the streets in bodies so as to proclaim themselves; not, usually, as a "rabble," but as an "organization." There are even, currently, urban Happenings to startle and intrigue passersby. But what *is* happening?—what does all this actually mean as public spectacle? It means a rudimentary theatricalization of some hypothetic set of performances—yes, that's the right word, Mr. Jagger!—which will take place (one hopes) somewhere else in more satisfying and palpable, more definitive forms. The street demonstration is a lot like the circus parade, whose only purpose is to titillate appetite and advertise the joys to come at the *real* performance. It's also like the political parade, not to mention the military parade.

The reader must suspect that, by thus prefacing my remarks on funny fellows in the movies who seem to me professional sissies, I must have something up my sleeve. It isn't really up my sleeve. It's up on the film screens and out on the streets. Everyone understands this: being a professional sissy is part of the fun business. Like that young mother wearing a track suit in the TV commercial for an antiperspirant, one is hardly ever out of training when in an exacting occupation. Do you think it's *not* such an exacting occupation and may not occupy a lifetime of professionalism? Well, let *The New York Times* (assisted by memories of Franklin Pangborn) be your guide. In its obituary for a lately demised actor, whose name must evoke instant recognition from millions of film fans, the *Times*'s correspondent wrote: "In an acting career that spanned more than 60 years, Edward Everett Horton, on the stage, screen and in television, made an institution of the Nervous Nellie character."*

According to the *Times,* Horton played virtually the

* October 1, 1970.

same prissy male in more than 150 movies. It's natural to point out that "Nellie" as a slang term for a man means that he is, or is suspected of being, homosexual: the word is from the dictionary of epithets generically meaning "homosexual." Now, to say that Nellie has no necessary sexual connotation, is really the same as saying, on the heterosexual side, that the masculine pronoun "he" has no necessary sexual connotation. Surely it doesn't, at times; then again, at other times, it does. Jack Benny is certainly not a Nervous Nellie, just the opposite in a way, though he is widely known as one of the more reliable and sentimentally dated exploiters of the professional-sissy idea. Nellie mannerisms have been one of Mr. Benny's (and, in lesser voltage, Mr. Hope's) main style items, something identifying the former as brand names and slogans do cigarettes and detergents. Mr. Benny's "walk" is a personal slogan; no spectator is allowed to forget it. When recently he had occasion to turn down David Merrick's offer to take the role of "Dolly" to prolong the life of that hello-and-no-good-bye musical, Mr. Benny explained Mr. Merrick's idea by saying, "It must be the way I walk."

Like the good-gracious-me gesture of both hands along both cheeks (another Nellie trademark and anthologized in film clips), the Benny walk is a classic of sexual ambiguity. You think I'm pushing it again? Well, in the TV show celebrating Benny's twentieth year before television cameras,* Mr. Hope, collaborating, mentioned Mr. Benny's forty-three years of marriage to Mary Livingstone, adding, however, that owing to Jack's walk, some people at the wedding couldn't tell the bride from the groom. Later, a point was made of what a startling event it was for Jack to come into Mary's bedroom. I would be the first to asseverate, not the last to deny, that all this has the status of a family joke now in public domain. I can't see, thereby, it is any the less significant. The question is not what it means to Mr. Benny, but what it means to the world, including genuine homosexuals and those in whom homophilia takes slightly more radical, more unprofessional forms.

There are things we might soberly contemplate once the chortles and broad paleolithic grins have subsided. The

* WNBC, November 16, 1970.

supersexploitation of camp in the funny-fellow industry has now
had a very long life. It is as much a household word today as the
Thanksgiving turkey, and turns up much oftener. Bob Hope is
another perennial TV entertainer engaged in refurbishing the
past for a fresh future. He is no more likely to forget sex camp
than Mr. Benny is. On a TV show directly preceding Benny's,
Hope had a sailor-on-the-girl-hunt double routine with Tom
Jones. Two towering Marines appear on the scene as possessors
of two girls the pair believe they've just snatched. In the familiar I-am-really-a-little-coward reflex, Hope spontaneously thinks
of diverting one Marine's anger by grabbing him for a dance
turn, during which he makes a point of caressing his behind.
Perhaps what Richard Amory said of beaver-film producers
(quoted here in the chapter on beavers) is also true of the general public: the idea of two guys making it is "hilarious," despite
hell, high water, and homosexuality. Period. But let me add
that Dean Martin, arriving to congratulate Benny on his television anniversary, said that all he wanted was a waltz,
whereupon, for about five delicious seconds, Mr. Benny, to appropriate music, obliged.

Putting all camp, all comical cosmetics, to one side, let's
consider that anyone at a formal dinner, anyone who looks
across a living room at another guest, anyone observing the
manners of other nightclub-goers—anyone, in brief, living in
this world—knows that neither Edward Everett Horton nor
Franklin Pangborn nor Jack Benny nor Jerry Lewis nor Noël
Coward nor Clifton Webb nor Red Skelton nor Laurel and
Hardy nor Jimmy Savo nor Harry Langdon nor Tiny Tim nor
Ferdinand the Bull nor Krazy Kat invented their personalities
and mannerisms (no matter how professional they were) out of
thin air with *no* place of origin. I am not calling these gentlemen (or these cartoon beasts) "real" sissies. That would be
simply silly; about as silly as calling a movie cowboy a real cowboy. All right: some of them are ranchers, but did they ever
shoot anybody—are they outlaws? No. The reason I propose
calling all these funny fellows professional sissies is for the sake
of the homeroic folklore I am gathering. For how could they
have learned their odd and varied effeminacies except by observ-

ing real sissies and the inevitable models of real sissies provided by authentic and organic females? I mean by the last, of course, those who walk the streets as *ladies*.

Female impersonation, I take leave to reiterate, is a traditional form of honoring the opposite sex by heterosexual males. Even if it be considered a parody or a caricature, it is a tribute: women become more womanly when we look at female impersonators, just as politicians become more political when we see caricatures of them. Female impersonation, whatever its implication for the impersonator's true sex, is likewise a profession of its own. All we have to ask ourselves, then, is whether there be a code of peculiar physical signs by which we can divide, past the dresses, bras, and wigs, the *homo* female impersonators from the *hetero* female impersonators. If there is such a code, I doubt it is written down or has a single specification that, through some stark exception, could not be proven invalid.

For instance, I remember seeing Red Skelton, in a movie whose title I've forgotten, go through a very funny routine mimicking the way a woman undresses. He used no feminine articles and didn't literally undress, but the illusion was a really artful piece of imitation with just the right degree of funny exaggeration. Now, when an act by a professional male comedian (no matter what it be) goes across big, that act is very apt to become part of his repertory, and eventually, I find, seems to get under his skin. I'd be very surprised if, even at this late day, Mr. Skelton's social mannerisms should have failed to retain something of the nancy—to use another lovely old term for denoting the genre. Actually, I caught Mr. Skelton on TV in the "I Love America" entertainment program given at the Capitol in the summer of 1970. He had rushed from a plane to the platform, and as the unusual swell of applause greeted him—more than that accorded other celebrities who had been introduced —he was palpably pleased and began giggling and cutely prancing forward as if he were about to go into an impersonator act. Of course, he wasn't; he was just there to make a few jokes.

In the fall of 1970, Mr. Skelton proceeded to celebrate *his* twentieth straight year on television and was introduced by no less a personage than Spiro T. Agnew. The climactic skit was a "magic act" in which Mr. Skelton appeared with his star guest on the show, Jerry Lewis, impersonating the magician's assistant. Mr. Lewis, more or less, acted his usual overgrown-boy goofball with its unavoidable sissy inflections. The two men clowned around with various routine business, and then the magician tries (since no one in the audience can be lured on-stage) to get his assistant into the chest used for the classic body-sawed-in-half number. The prolonged result entails nothing unusual: simply the clown routine of two males becoming (Mr. Lewis cannily playing deadweight) entangled with each other, at times on north/south diagonals. What produced the steady hail of audience laughter that accompanied all this? I say nothing. I want *to be told* for a change. For these men, it was all in the day's smirk. I sincerely applaud them; in fact, I thought the sentimental tribute paid by the younger comedian (Lewis) to the older (Skelton), before they left the stage, had a touch of real nobility. The solemnity was lachrymose but genuine, inso-far as professional courtesy can ever be genuine.

To conveniently take up Mr. Lewis himself, there seems no limit to his disposition to exploit sissy-boy business for his films. Even if he's only standing by a phone booth, he hears a high-flown chirp issuing from it that sounds like a fluttery female talking. Suddenly out walks, with a toss of the torso, a self-evident swish (yes, another word for homo), and Mr. Lewis, graphically, is agog. So are we. Unless we are better acquainted with the denizens of phone booths than Jerry presumably is. Naturally, his sissy-boy clown has no limits, either, to his own helplessness, confidingness, and fright. In a pointedly titled movie, *The Delicate Delinquent,* he is caught in the meshes of ill-fitting rowdyism, only to be redeemed by a policeman who finds his fabulous young naïveté irresistible and befriends him, with the result that they make out as did the legendary David and Jonathan.

Though I have treated the moral institution of quasi-homosexual pairs as a symptom of kinkiness, we must not forget that there were, from way back, some *good* tandems, too. We shall soon come to Laurel and Hardy. Meanwhile, do you remember that young film hero who left his girl flat to go off with the black boy? And if David isn't just naturally magnetized to his Jonathan, they can be chained to one another as Tony Curtis and Sidney Poitier were in a movie called *The Defiant Ones.* Not long ago—oh, the long, long memory of parody!— this same desperate situation was burlesqued in a skit titled "The Flaming Defiant Ones of 1958" on, of course, television. A young white man (Engelbert Humperdinck) is found manacled to a young black man as they encounter a woman impersonated by the singer Kay Ballard. The lady (who, while heavyish, is not a half-bad female) bursts out with a gloat on finding two available males at once. The two fugitives turn tail, pronto, and vocalize as one, with a unanimous "Back to the alligators!" Alligators?

Oh, well, the school of love is often, as we know, hard. If you are a professional sissy, however, you can make it seem easy, for either you're a postgraduate, like Clifton Webb, or you don't even know you're in school, like Mr. Lewis. I have often wondered about the dizzying vicissitudes of Mr. Lewis' repertory of impersonations. Often, on screen, he has been the big-little male thing, so vulnerable, in all ways, because he just "doesn't know any better." That's the cosmically dimensioned gag. For long, he seemed not to tire of acting mamma's over-grown boy with enough emotional drool to float a toy battle-ship: heavy pouting lips protruding, typically "down" in the infantile-distress pattern and "up" in the infantile-coo pattern. I remember, once, his doing this straight kiddie-party act in a scene, a very long scene, with his "mother," till a profane thought came to me: "Now I understand the impulse that swayed Leopold and Loeb."

It never mattered that Lewis was always in his twenties. He played early-teen-age just cured of thumbsucking, and so funnily that it hurt. I should say that he appealed to a homog-enized audience of rib-vulnerable sex-yearners ready to howl with amusement at anything touching their own ribs. I imagine even nostalgic grandmothers feel the relevance and react. Lewis reminds them of Sonny, fifty years ago. *You* know, the "Sonny" who was so girl-shy and yet married that nice young woman who lived on a farm and started putting him into the traces on their wedding day! Oh, lordy! Never anything like it, and a string of little ones, boys, all of them like Sonny himself. They're grown now, and one's even *dead,* bless his poor soul. And here I am, still getting *on.* . . . Is it a mercy or a burden?

While inventing this monologue for Granny, I was not forgetting that Mr. Lewis' comic image, even when most caricaturishly infantile, is physically quite virile, even sensual, and in a thoroughly male way. He has a lot of standard-quality S.A. I recall seeing him in a movie when he actually wore a custom-tailored business suit befitting his actual age: he moved his slim, tallish legs with the natural elegance of a race horse. With this to go by, it is rather easy to summon up the idea of the big-little male simpleton's strategy: some boys in their early teens are already very eligible males, sense it themselves, and knowing that women sense it, exploit the fact for all it's worth. So, thinking of Mr. Lewis as a clown, think about that, too. As for being the professional sissy along with it, it only draws a heavy, heavy line under the come-hither known as accessibility. Of no particular kind, you understand: just accessibility. Not real: a professional *act.*

Now you see, I hope, what I mean. I'll try to show how one can be a professional sissy without wanting to be, or even, at times, realizing that one is. It will help clear the board. There is a certain gentleman (not an actor) whom I know personally; we hardly ever see each other these days, but we used to be on visiting terms. His at-home social manners were casually laced with such plain sissyisms—rolling eyes, pursed mouth, head-tiltings, and mild camp vocalisms as well as, now and then, a more "Dolly" walk than Mr. Benny's—that I wondered why, considering that he was married and had an untarnished reputation as hetero, he should risk having it said behind his back that he was really homosexual. I learned, in this gentleman's case, that my notion of the risk one could run like that was quite justified.

A friend of his wife's told me—this shows how secure his reputation as a hetero was—that late one night he happened to come home and go into the kitchen for some soda. That's all he did. Also present in the kitchen happened to be some boy-friends of his teen-age daughter, who at that moment was else-where. Muttering a hello to the boys, Papa got his soda and left; soon his daughter, coming back, was met with this sentence by one of the boys: "Say, *who* was that old fairy who just walked in here?" She did a double-take and then shot back: "That old fairy, you jerk, is *my father!*" There might be a whole socio-psycho-physiological study, deeply medical, devoted to the sub-ject of why a percentage of organic males, *not* technical defectors to homosexuality, take on acting the sissy without the least pro-fessional reason to do so.

Of all prof-sis cases in the entertainment world, one might say that the most consciously, callously, blatantly vulner-able, to date, is that of Tiny Tim, the strumming songster with the preciously inelegant soprano voice who not long ago got married—quite heterosexually married, unless (as I doubt) the public has been victimized by a hoax. His beaky nose, long deranged hair, slouchy middle, unmanageable lips, falsetto voice, and nostalgic song repertory had for years dwelt in the obscurity of bohemian nightclubs. Then a record he made began selling like hot cakes, and soon he was what not his most devoted admirer (unless it was himself) might have predicted: a real star of the pop-music cult. For a while he and his unabashed high-C sentimentalism were all over the place. Patently, time has caught up with him. He even got into a movie, *You Are What You Eat,* where everyone could see he was an ordinary-sized person.

Tiny Tim was groovy, Tiny Tim was unisex or any sex you might name. Tiny Tim . . . was just Tiny Tim. Completely unique. I doubt anyone ever even called him queer. Sexually, he seemed the Unutterable in Undrag. When his marriage took place, he was the first (as he may be the last) to make wisecracks about the great event. A few months ago, I was amazed when I caught him being interviewed by David Frost. Tiny showed a sympathetic, unaffected personality, quite at ease. Conversa-tionally, to top that, he was using an ordinary masculine voice —at least, it seemed so in contrast with his singing style—and when asked to oblige with a song, it was a patriotic song, which he proceeded to sing in a patriotically masculine voice. I dare-

say his legend will persist. Among professional sissies he deserves a double nomination: as a "natural" and an "original."
Although his lips make one think that at one time he must have
imagined he was Joan Crawford or Carole Lombard, one hesi-
tates to think that, for that reason, he would have imagined he
was homosexual. *Tiny Tim*? Perish the thought!

Let us turn to a bona-fide professional who once had a
repertory of male roles. Clifton Webb was also quite unique in
the present category. He was mellowed, genteel, a "personality"
actor rather than a "character" actor, made as if carved out by
nature for the métier of drawing-room comedy. Subdued for
some roles that were straighter than others, he was nevertheless,
in manners, clothes, and voice, the exquisite dandy translated
whole from the nineteenth century; he resembles most—among
actual figures whose iconography is readily accessible—the
Comte de Montesquieu. This may be a coincidence. I fancy it
is. But that point does not invalidate the natural pattern mutually etched on their two images.

Webb's way of delivering lines in a suavely clipped, acidly
dry manner, was as funny as the lines, and by itself could account
for their risible effect on audiences. The leisured timing, the
laundry-fresh neatness, are those of a professional master of
dialogue. No matter what his role was—that of a misogynous
murderer in *Laura* or a baby-sitter and universal genius in
Sitting Pretty—he was immaculate high camp: a person about
whom nobody could be more candidly insulting than to call
him something of a priss. Nellie? Heaven forbid! He managed
even not to be Nervous.

For this actor, the film industry found a special place: an
amusing version of the eccentric bachelor, a male old maid, but
so formidable a gentleman by birth and experience that he adds
a true touch of style to what otherwise would be close to a low-
comedy character. Only the secret of a personal style could
create an eccentric bachelor such as the professional, Clifton
Webb. Thus his casual characterizations never equalled his own
ineradicable identity as a man—as, I would say, a very rare sort
of professional sissy. The man and the professional sissy are
simply inseparable in the crisply self-possessed public image he

offers audiences. Remember that mere "manliness" is one of
the professional sissy's most prized achievements.

As with the recipe of a master chef, the image of Webb
fuses the two qualities traditionally known as fastidiousness and
male elegance. The reason there is "distance" to this sissy personality is that the male type, known so beautifully as "cox-
comb" in the eighteenth century, cultivated mannerisms
(meant, of course, to charm the ladies) that were frowned on by
serious persons as "effeminate." Yet Webb's decisive mark as a
prof-sis was that he never used his elegance in the service of the
romantic; it was as if disinfected of eroticism. First of all, he was
not handsome and probably never made a good juvenile. Nor
was he "sexy." His figure looks ironed—like a fresh suit—and
he was wonderful, socially speaking, at putting on the chill. So
everything was rigged for him to be the soulless woman-hater
of *Laura.* By this route, Mr. Webb could be clued in to the
undeserved reputation of homosexuals for hating women. But
I have already mentioned the dubiousness of that clue to someone's sex.

Still, Mr. Webb's starchy, touch-me-not air in *Sitting
Pretty,* when he did the fabulous eccentric bachelor, is bound to
suggest a certain moral aversion to the sexes as such, male or
female. Confirmed bachelors are open, as it were, to suspicion
in that regard. Thus, it is precisely by ambiguity that Clifton
Webb makes an ideal medium by which to project on the mental
screen what I mean by the professional sissy as related to life
style in the society around us. He created this idealness, it
seems to me, because everything he did seems squeezed of all
erotic innuendo before he did it. That is no small triumph:
being stylishly unsexy. Mr. Webb remains the lone high aristocrat of professional sissies. Though he's not quite alone. Rather
schmaltzy versions of high-toned sissy types have been contributed by Vincent Price and the late Monty Woolley.

Sir Noël Coward, whose role in *Boom* I cited as Homeros
past the age of eligibility, is alas! a medium aristocrat. His bomb-
shelter British voice is fully as invulnerable as Webb's and yet
it has ambiguous sinuosities in its texture that are hauntingly
sexy—*which* sexiness is a question settled in *Boom* by the

character he plays. The thing about Mr. Webb is that he is so grown-up, even a little more grown-up than Sir Noël. This is significant because most professional screen sissies are usually indelibly infantile; in fact, their comic style, always broad and often etched in lingering baby fat, flows from their instinctive parodies of the infantile. This was true of both Jimmy Savo and Henry Langdon, of Laurel and even Hardy. Big and rotund, with a moustache, Hardy was patently a grown-up baby and distinctly prissy in comic style; at the same time, one feels that Hardy and such a type as Edward Everett Horton are boys who grew up to imitate the nervous reflexes of mother or aunt. Laurel's corresponding bit was the namby-pamby in its tearful, helpless, sissy-boy form. Let us remember that "sissy" is not, strictly speaking, an equivalent of "homosexual" but only one of its sometime attributes. Many homosexuals aren't at all sissy. The term has just as much to do with mere childish qualities. Take Grady Sutton: that perennial big baby inveterately addicted to girls.

All the same, being girl-shy must remain a prominent guideline for assessing professional and unprofessional sissies. Its direct correlative, supposedly part of the human fabric, is a hypersensitive response to the sex (whichever) that is so frightening. The origin of this comic-romantic formula is as old as the institution of clowns. It presupposes intense consciousness of eligibility combined with intense consciousness of ineligibility, such as a physical flaw, or just being ugly or "too young." The eligibility would be high sexual drive and worthy personal equipment. I've often fancied that some boys built physically to be very effective prickmen soon become sissies because their mother (or another female relative) has lodged in them the morbid notion that the penis and testicles are some sort of defacement, ogreish things to be hidden from decent eyesight.

Be that as it may, the Hunchback of Notre Dame is an instance, readily available from literature and the movies, of a human monster separated by an arbitrary edict of nature from the male's rightful sexual satisfaction. Thus in film comedians, from Chaplin and Harpo Marx to Bob Hope and Danny Kaye, we used to find (all these men have changed with age) an infantile jitteriness about sex inseparable from extreme natural addiction to it—at least, addiction by natural inclination. Sometimes in human culture, less than a zipper seems to divide being girl-crazy from being girl-shy, yet that frail, frail obstacle is often like a prison wall. The interesting thing is, when we study the professional sissies, that the ritual backlash point on the way to final virility is at once so sexually prone and so petrified a cultural convention.

It is as if the professional sissy declined to think of girl-shy-craziness as a passing stage of the male's development and thought of it, rather, as a life style, or more accurately, a career style. Bob Hope is now a hale and elderly MC oozing nostalgic humor, dignity, and reminiscent girl-craziness. Danny Kaye, who is about Hope's age, once impersonated a youngster who was as afraid of going into battle with boys as of going into bed with girls, even while he spent (like Hope and others) a large part of his screen footwork chasing, or being chased by, the fair sex. The obvious assumption that only retarded growth made him such a dual coward (naturally he was brave *at heart*) did nothing to alter the sissy-boy structure of his professional character.

Harpo Marx was the only infantile comedian with the invariable courage of a hero in courting the ladies, but that was because he was, self-evidently, the greatest idiot of the lot. Anyway it was clearer than day that he had no proper conception of genital sexuality; that was the whole point of his infantile satyrism: it is necessarily and eternally pseudo—just like his muteness, which nobody "believes" but everybody accepts as aesthetically proper. One might well conclude, quite seriously, that technical ignorance of sex may explain its mania in the young just as much as technical knowledge of it. Sometimes, in the young, sex looks like phobia-mania. *Limited* knowledge, then, would explain its conflicts and its perverse behavior.

It would explain what we call infantilism, or babyhood in grown-ups. At least once, Laurel and Hardy, and Langdon too, must have impersonated actual infants. Not that they needed to don long dresses or rompers, or climb into a crib, to expose their relation to infancy. There was a Langdon comedy,

Soldier Man, with an exquisite piece of humor inseparable from his delicate, subtly fastidious shyness as the puzzled, inarticulate child-man who is a forlorn sissy-boy. Langdon was short, with a largish oval face painted up and lipsticked so that he suggested, not only a clown as well as the actors who take female roles in the Kabuki theater, but also the little boy who likes putting on his mother's makeup. His mouth was the ultimate in childlike grave prissiness. Like Chaplin he played the perennial waif, adrift and typically starved for food and the food of love. And like the infantile clown, he had, as it were, sex thrust upon him, being slow to grasp his own maleness. In *Soldier Man* (1926), ignorant that World War I is over, lost and alone, Harry pursues a terrified farmer, only to find himself on his belly aiming his gun virtually cheek by udder with a moveless cow. Having the eternal innocent's spontaneity, he is intrigued by her dangling nipples, and when he is so distracted as shyly to twiddle them, one realizes what a striking similarity they have to the human penis. (*Laughter*). I doubt that, in film comedy before or since, overt homosexual camp has been so concretely illustrated; surely, never so delicately portrayed.

That being *symbolically* homosexual belongs to the general métier of the professional sissies is definitely exposed in the case of Taylor Mead, a comic of Underground films who, about a decade ago, started out as a child-man hero in a Beat Generation film by Ron Rice, *The Flower Thief.* Besides having a vérité atmosphere (West Coast hippie bohemia), the film parodied the Hollywood funny-fellow tradition through Mead's spontaneous miming. As then he was quite boyish, with dome-like head, longish features, slight body, and a querulously sad expression, he played the homo-child-man straight from life: someone apparently formed by watching old movie comedians and connecting their infantilism with his own. He showed himself a natural performer and was obviously a sissy temperament with a tendency to both defend his sissiness and exploit it by cultivating a mild child-man idiocy and straightforward naïve playfulness-with-a-sly-smile. This was effectively climaxed in *The Flower Thief* with a laughless, touching episode when he cruises a personable young bum in a deserted amusement center and obediently, smitten into solemnness, follows him for a rendezvous on a desolate beach. Today, Mead, showing seams of age in both face and manner, is a fetish of Underground film antics, and foolishly (as illustrated in *Lonesome Cowboys*: see the chapter on metabeavers) is the complete nostalgic professional faggot. He is a sort of institutional clown with the same half-stoned, half-homo routine, of which a complaining false-naïve "telephone call to God" is the principal "act."

Yet Mead *is* close to life. Somehow professional tomboys, like professional sissies, suggest lifelikeness in their very artificiality. There is only one total and indubitable professional tomboy, standing alone at her particular game of camping, and she of course is Beatrice Lillie. That she rates as another fairy godmother was proved long ago with her English music-hall number transliterated to the drawing room: "There Are Fairies at the Bottom of My Garden." Even as Mae West's, Miss Lillie's comedienne camps her way through all roles, all numbers. Not that she professionally goes for the boys to any conspicuous extent; it's just that, irrespective of sex, insidiously kook and remotely spinsterish, she's the high-low life of the party, the perfect social entertainer raised by main force to professional status. Why do I call her a tomboy? Come now! Where have we been all through the years? *I* didn't invent her. *She* did. Period gigolo haircut, necktie and all, there clings to Miss Lillie, in my view, a faint aroma of the female-voyeur-who-emulates-pansies-because-she-likes-men-so-much. But that is a private aesthetic reaction of mine and perhaps too precious to have brought up. One simply has to observe Miss Lillie and compare her to the types one knows.

Both to compare and contrast, I can draw an instance from the real society of professional tomboys. Long ago, I was pretty good friends with a militantly individualistic fairy godmother (today, if rude, one would call her a fag-hag) who adored the faggots and held in moral bondage the series of faithful hetero males she acquired. Agnes (that wasn't her name, but I'll call her that) was a rather violent woman. In figure she was rather tall, well formed, with amazonian legs and a pronounced feminine curve to her broad hips. Always there was a bitchy glint in her eyes and a mocking smile to be expected on her curving mobile mouth, made curiously aggressive by a thrusting chin. I thought her a great big sissy who by a miscalculation of nature had been dropped into a female's form. But there she was, and she could be a very good fellow.

Agnes' funny bone, and seemingly her heart, could always be tickled by the image, the very fact, of the male homosexual, especially if he was cute and pretty or, more particularly, a gentleman of graceful parts. She insisted on flirting with all good-looking homosexuals she met, half-campily, half-seriously, as if hoping for the miracle that suddenly one of them would turn into a "real" man. At the same time, I think Agnes would have been a little disappointed if one had done so. She seemed to admire in them the fact that, while they could be proved to have the normal male's sexual organs, they disdained employing them for the pleasure of women. I don't know which sex Agnes secretly considered herself; most probably a woman, but positively not a female. She was definitely not a lesbian. Lesbians she regarded as weird curiosities, while pansies seemed to her as adorable as live Easter bunnies.

At all events, Agnes was regularly bedded by her men, perhaps from sheer vanity, or that absurd conventionality that many men and women, robotlike, cling to on into old age. I must have known her for about fifteen years when she was in her prime. She never reconciled herself (this would show up in her reflexive persecution of her lovers) to the fact that the male seemed destined by nature to be on top in the sexual act. Agnes disliked nature as something that hadn't quite done her justice, but she was superstitious enough to be afraid to let her disdain of the opposite sex be known, especially if the incidental penis belonged to the lover who was in bed with her. I am sure she knew the sexual positions could be reversed (female on top), but her conventionality probably insisted that this would be unwomanly; anyway, I doubt she would have thought the thrills received worth the pushes required. I gathered that she was sarcastically submissive in bed; inveterately, she'd make satiric jokes about her lovers' behavior there, speaking of it seriously only when absentminded. I concluded, at last, that nothing would satisfy her but a male lover and a sissy rolled into one. Faced by this insoluble, unnatural paradox, Agnes would resort to bizarre forms of persecuting her men if they showed the slightest defection from the militance she thought proper to their sex and hers.

I don't mean to give the impression that Agnes was promiscuous, that she frequently changed lovers; no, she tried to hang on by enslaving them. To her, men were imperfect creatures; women were here, like generals out of uniform, to keep men in line. Agnes was always having vulgar wrangles with strangers who happened to push her in the subway or knock against her, or with store clerks who offered her some casual rudeness. She expected her husband (it was really a husband at this time) to chastise any such if physical dignity became involved; that is, if the offender happened to be a man; if it was a woman, Agnes would take care of her. Once I heard that she became incensed at some mother who was slapping her little girl around in the street. Without ado, Agnes went over, called the woman a bitch, jerked her around, and gave her a vicious kick in the behind.

I used to marvel that Agnes was never, *but never,* taken into court for anything she did to people. Once, when something so violent was in prospect—I don't remember what—that only her husband could be expected to handle it, the poor fellow really hesitated to start trouble, perhaps blood, by executing her command. As he hung back, she let go, disgustedly, with one of her withering sarcasms: "Well, do you want me to start sewing the lace on your pants now, or shall I wait till we get home?" Agnes liked the professional sissies, too, and was convinced without scruple that all, to a man, were homosexual. If she had doubted it, my guess is that she would have spent many hours awake, thinking about it. But she didn't doubt it. Oh, Mother of Homeros! If Agnes is still in this world, let her sleep in peace!

Aside from TV revivals, does one see any really new professional sissies on the screen? Are they so much on the wane in the movies that I shall be accused of chauvinism in thus digging them up and cataloging them? Perhaps so, barring, of course, the reversal of gains made by the Gay Liberation Front, etc., and an ensuing resurgence of puritan barbarism. But these pages are as much engaged with aesthetic recollections as with social updating. Even so, what are we to say to the profoundly, the scandalously, naïve ignorance of that technically adult army dentist in *M*A*S*H*? He is a rather recent addition to the guild of funny sex fellows. Surely his is a form of infantile regression of some kind. That dentist was, to be sure, no professional sissy, yet might he not be labeled an amazingly amateur prickman, with suspect potentialities? His prompt conclusion that he is a fairy because he has just failed to get an erection in bed with a girl is, after all, something more than a joke once it be related to life outside zappy screen farces. Life, I repeat once more, *does* exist off screen.

But say that we grant what is, perhaps, the sober truth: Our dentist doesn't deserve life or credibility outside the comic-book world. You'll remember *The Tenth Victim* and its super-crazy War Between the Men and the Women. Comic books are explicitly identified there as the collector's items of our literary future. As we also found in *Barbarella,* the movie, sex has been science-fictioned at a twelve-year-old level. See particularly "Frank Fleet and His Electronic Sex Machine," the comicstrip serial that *Evergreen Review* has been running for over a year. These things are legitimately comicstrip and legitimately sexy —if such is the recipe for your bag of preferred gut art. Yet we can't pretend that their pop characteristic doesn't mean infantilism trademarked for adults as, at the very best, consciously low-down camp—"elevated" only when one is on a high of some sort. Maybe Clifton Webb's baby-sitter and Noël Coward's War-lock of Capri will belong, by the end of this year, in a wax museum (TV is pretty good at that kind of resurrection), and thus we may expect fresh remakes of them among the Creature Features of 1980.

Can't you imagine the Webb baby-sitter a monster who converts human babies into animated toys for little girls on Mars?—and the police not destroying him till he has consumed at least ninety minutes doing his dreadful thing? But what am I saying? Take a look at the next installment of that perennial

TV favorite, *The Addams Family*, whose character Uncle Fester is an ugly, bald, middle-aged version of the classic sissy-boy, girl-shy and girl-crazy, mental age about nine. Transparently he has just read *What Everyone Always Wanted to Know About Sex,* precocious boy-doll that he is.

As for lesbianism, scrutinizing the evidence as a facet of professional tomboyism, one is persuaded that a number of actresses in the movies, stars and featured players, have been rooked into impersonating lesbians or lesbianlikes as a form of undercover fun: a jolly stint in their progressing careers. Examples? Well, take Lauren Bacall (with roommate femme) in *Young Man with a Horn* and the dour, raincoated femme-image of Anne Baxter in *All About Eve.* So far as young and pretty actresses are concerned, heterosexual male voyeurism has something to do with their phenomenology. An illuminating instance is the comicstrip heroine (*Evergreen Review* aptly introduced her) named Phoebe Zeit-Geist. Phoebe is obviously "zeit-geist" because she is conceived as the eternal nude girl who is the indispensable heroine of stag films. She's the girl open to all comers, the girl who may be used and used because her only function is to please the customer, whatever his desires. And the customer may be a *woman.*

In an odd but very relevant way, Phoebe is a reincarnation of the old-time serial heroines who survived the most terrible physical ordeals and miraculously came through unscathed. That film heroine (Pearl White is probably the most world-famous) was a tomboy to the extent that she was a gifted athlete, could slug things out with men, and come out as unscarred as a lucky football player from the last minute of scrimmage. Just so, in the intellectual concept of true sadism, the female is seen as both fearlessly masochistic and magically immaculate. Modern times have undressed the serial heroine (Barbarella is simply a costume version of Phoebe Zeit-Geist) and made her a stag star.

Part of Phoebe's duties is to be grossly manhandled, of course, with her life as well as her chastity constantly being attacked. Not only is she threatened by males, but also by females. And the females, naturally, tend to be butch lesbians, from rather statuesque Amazon types (as alluring as Ursula Andress) to assorted freaks and wildly caricatured bull dykes who weigh at least three-hundred pounds. The latter sort are pure comicstrip bizarrerie (not that their approximations don't exist in life) and have not been seen in the movies except through the pale mimetics of beaver films. But if, through inexperience, you think the lovely comicstrip Amazon, glaringly lesbian, has been similarly absent from major movies, you are wrong. She was taken directly from comicstrip culture to the screen and her name is Pussy Galore. She was beautifully impersonated by Honor Blackman in a James Bond movie, *Goldfinger*, a rampageous camp-espionage flick in which she was leader of a troop of Amazons engaged in secret military operations against the United States. Of course, Pussy is outwitted in her dedication to this most unladylike pursuit. But that isn't *all*. She also has it socked to her in a pile of hay by the delightfully muscular and ornately hirsute person of Sean Connery, the original James Bond. There could not be a more eloquent object lesson for those swashbuckling females who get the loony idea that they're dykes just because they've learned karate and simply "can't bear the thought of sleeping with a man." Oh, yeah? Once Pussy has a galore taste of Number 007 in the hay, she knows what it is, at last, to be a *woman*. So one might politely assume from the rules of that heterosexual folk myth to which I have alluded in various ways. One to whom that myth could point directly, of course, is Marlene Dietrich, whose famous drag routine (top hat and tails) never hindered her as a busy glamour girl with supercharged S.A.

Nudging the memory, one could also come up with Dame Judith Anderson as having lent herself, during her Hollywood period, to the professional-tomboy act. She did not get into drag for the lead in *Lady Scarface,* but who, with a voice and a profile like that, needs drag? She was boss of her crime gang—and did she look and talk like nails! Hollywood careerism is a bad habit, I think, whose subtler dangers are sometimes underestimated. For instance, who would have thought of Sherlock Holmes as anything but invulnerable to a human weakness such as sex, either homo or hetero? His own creator, Conan

Doyle, thought of him as a thinking machine whose one carnal flaw was addiction to a drug. Would anyone have imagined that *anyone else* would have imagined that he could exist outside the graveyard of Creature Features?

But he has come back in a definitely erotic capacity in a Billy Wilder fantasy called *The Private Life of Sherlock Holmes* —a role in which all the resources of superlatively cute script writing have been needed to exonerate him from something he lightly, deliberately takes on himself and Dr. Watson quite early in the film: the public onus of pederasty. Of course, Dr. Watson himself denounces it as a "damned lie" to Holmes's own face. And it would seem, indeed, it has been a *blague* of the great detective to get out of a ticklish situation with a Russian prima ballerina, who has selected him to be the father of the child she wants. Yet the style in which Holmes is acted by Robert Stephens proves that any other *blague* by the name of jolly will laugh as sweet if the rose itself have style and wit, which it has. In one unexpected stroke, a classic detective, long enshrined on film, becomes a Hollywood funny fellow *and* a professional sissy. Welcome, Mr. Holmes!

From where comes the magnetic thing promoting professional sissydom and tomboyism? Probably it is futile to do more than record the evidence. How much I looked forward to seeing Dame Judith in the role of Hamlet, in which she made a world tour! I was sure that she wouldn't do Hamlet as a Lady Scarface and I felt safe in predicting there wouldn't be an atom of Katharine Hepburn in her characterization. There wasn't. Doing Hamlet has been the professional-tomboy dream of a long line of famous actresses. That wonderful old trouper and gifted comedienne Margaret Rutherford has not played Hamlet (she never quite had the figure), and yet, playing her hilarious roles, she has so often injected into her stout female person the generalissimo manner that I think she too deserves consideration as a tomboy.

Miss Rutherford is generally regarded as superb camp, and with special tenderness (I've just learned from the Fall 1970 issue of *Queen's Quarterly*) by the world of male gays. No matter what she does or whom she impersonates, she's always a delightful old soul who manages to exude a true fairy godmother's personality. You feel she'd have Black Homeros himself to tea without batting an eyelash; in fact, she'd offer him a second cup and listen, with loud appreciative chuckles, to the next sinister bed trick he planned to play on the world. Perhaps I go too far. If so, I beg Miss Rutherford's pardon and appeal to her sense of humor, which I'm sure is as ample as her wardrobe of comic characterizations. Numberable among the latter was one in a British film comedy titled *Curtains Up* (1953), where, mannishly attired, as so often, she was a playwright with a male pseudonym.

Suddenly appearing at the theater to the director who is doing her play but hasn't met her, she identifies herself by her pseudonym. The director is Robert Morley, and he delivers the riposte with richly askance adequacy: "If you are a man, *why* are you dressed as a woman?" Nothing could be cuter, or more harmlessly genuine, than Miss Rutherford's generalissimo manner. It is (or was) seen in the midst of life on grande-dames who eccentrically cultivate the humorous, hard-edged style. On Miss Rutherford it tends tenaciously to get, however casually, into drag. As a rule her drag act stops short of actual trousers (that figure again!). Yet she has always been at home in roles where she decorated her vast bosom with military medals or other masculine gear, if only lapels and a cravat. A photograph of her in a sort of Gilbert and Sullivan military drag is in the issue of *Queen's Quarterly* I mentioned above; once I clipped from a newspaper a photo of her in which she looked the image of Toulouse-Lautrec's caricature of the mature Oscar Wilde. When she was younger, she played the medium in the film version of *Blithe Spirit* (1945) with old-pageboy bob and more than a smidgen of old-pageboy authority.

It may cross the reader's mind, at this point, to quote my own remark that camping doesn't necessarily have anything to do with sex—and, further, even the prof sissies and the prof tomboys have no inevitable sexual connotation. I think it's possible to take that view without being too pretentiously innocent. But it won't hold up in any serious investigation of the subject. The whole point about the drag act is that it is quintessentially sexual; otherwise it has no meaning. To say it has no meaning, then, is to fluff off sex itself. Temperamentally I'm opposed to that, and this book is specifically opposed to it.

I am reminded of a certain popular superstition, afloat among stand-firm conservative heterosexuals, that concerns all professional funny fellows and is due, I think, to average escapist psychology—to a kind of tactical absentmindedness. The superstition is—despite works such as *I Pagliacci* and its derivatives, including Chaplin's comedies—that anyone wearing the clown motley, unless he give material evidence *to the contrary*, has no sexuality. In the case of the identifiably *sissy* clown, the superstition surely would seem arbitrary and irrational. Yet I think that it operates even there. Otherwise why should some readers be a bit startled—and I think some are going to be—when I rate the Cowardly Lion from *The Wizard of Oz* as one of filmdom's professional sissies? Bert Lahr, who impersonated the Cowardly Lion in the famous production that starred the late Judy Garland, regarded his role purely as a problem in comic histrionics. Wouldn't that, conceivably, be exactly the viewpoint of, say, Messrs. Burton and Harrison, who played the aging poofs in *Staircase*? A professional actor, it can be argued, approaches all his roles abstractly, as if they were mathematical problems of imitation, so that it makes no difference if the role be a poof—if a male actor do a woman or a female actor a man. But it does make a difference, simply because sexual content is built into a role just like any other content, human, social, racial, individual.

In excellent makeup, Bert Lahr did the Cowardly Lion very well, and of course without any leers or nancy mannerisms. Nobody playing the Cowardly Lion is obliged to introduce pansy camp to delineate this image of the professional sissy. The cachet is far too deeply built in for such reticence or strategy or exercise of personal temperament to make much difference. It is built, in short, into the history of mankind. By "it" I mean not just this role, not just professional sissydom, but all the sexes: *sexuality itself.* Chaplin's tramp alone is sufficient testimony to warn us against the unfairness, the enormous indiscretion, of thinking about professional funny fellows as if they had no sexual instincts or modes of sexual expression. Chaplin underlined the gravity of this mistake (if needlessly) when he made being a professional clown the double dimension of the tramp in *The Circus,* and of course showed himself, there, as mad on love as before.

One of the greatest of all professional sissies, a veritable creation of genius, actually dates from the teens of this century. He was a blatant, if utterly fantastic, homosexual at a time when growing human boys (*he* was a "cat") who had the same scandalously visible propensities were treated as lepers and packed off to doctors or mental homes. I can't uncover evidence that this fabulous and endearing faggot of the comicstrip, *Krazy Kat,* was ever animated on film. But he and his adventures were pure movie-serial. That his creator, George Herriman, was influenced by the movies was evident in a curious device of the special funny-paper technique in which Krazy was presented. Its backgrounds—usually artificial mesas in the desert—changed with each frame of the drawing, which depicted in front a continuous dialogue of words and action. In 1922, an American choreographer, John Alden Carpenter, honored Krazy with a short-lived ballet.

Krazy himself has many lives, for he belongs to the history of American homosexual humor as a "first." The late Gilbert Seldes, a pioneer in appreciating the "lively arts," extolled Krazy in critical prose.* But that was in the twenties, and the very word "homosexual" was then taboo. Hence Seldes, while freely admitting that Krazy was "in love with" a male mouse named Ignatz, had to term him "androgynous." Aesthetic observers, daring enough to handle the problem, had to juggle with mythology and cite the license of fantasy: Krazy was a "Don Quixote," Ignatz (who by the way was a married man) a "Sancho Panza." But the facts speak more loudly. Krazy is portrayed as a dotty daydreamer. Clearly, he is the prototype whose embarrassing oddities are explained, mythologically, by that "knock on the head when a child."

That absurd convention has to take a back seat when it is known that this same knock on the head is what Krazy yearns

* *The Seven Lively Arts* (Seldes).

for daily, since it invariably sends him off into a funk of erotic bliss. Literally it is a brick cast by Ignatz (whose heart and body, alas! can never be won), and it climactically lands on Krazy's head. Krazy, at these orgasmic moments, stays conscious long enough to emit a single evocation of his beloved: "Lil Darlink!" Ignatz is Cupid (a wish-fulfillment Homeros), and the brick his arrow. Herriman devised wonderful variations on his theme; the theme itself was central and stood out as if in 3-D. Krazy, for instance, is terribly fond of bananas, dreaming of them as he does of Ignatz. "Byou-ti-full bin-nen-nahs" (or something like) is another of his refrains, and when he does occasionally bag Ignatz, he expresses his passion by carrying him around like a baby in the reverent arms of a nursemaid. Obviously—and I hope I can say this without being pretentiously Freudian— Ignatz himself is heterosexual surrogate for the homosexually pursued penis.

11. ALL THE SEXES:

THEIR POWER AND ITS

POSSIBILITIES

It is just possible that, someday, neither the nations nor the sexes will need labels to keep our information about them in order. Morality, in practice if not theory, is first and last the individual's possession. Like the nationality, the skin color, and the sex organ one inherits from some opaque complex of natural causes, it is as personal—and hopefully as proud—as one's mouth and nose, one's height, one's bodily shapes, male or female. In very primitive times, even a tree was an individual, and our ancestors, before cutting one down to make use of it, solemnly asked its pardon. That distant symptom of modern civilization—though you may call it hypocritical, a matter of superstitious fear rather than sincere compunction—held the germ of everything that nowadays is termed respect for the individual.

The extent and implications of this book's inquiry have prompted me to assume that, in the truly realistic sense, there are as many sexes as there are individuals; that sex, empirically, is an infinitely variable spectrum; that the seeming neat correspondence between male and female organs is not the end, but the beginning, of sexuality. In fact, the mechanisms which

349

reproduce human and animal kinds have no necessary erotic connotations whatever. Eroticism is not an instinct but a long-range refinement of the simplest nervous reflexes. We casually presume that parenthood in man and animal is an instinct. Like other terms of rhetoric by which human beings have learned to speak of themselves, calling sex or parenthood an instinct is merely to identify with nature's recurrences, with the seasons and vernal growth, with the chemical changes wrought by time in all objects, including the flesh.

Within any one human individual, sexuality evolves through stages that are literally kaleidoscopic. One of the organism's first great discoveries is the sexual faculty—but remember that this is not, till the owner is taught to "think," either male or female. The sexual faculty is a mechanism whose pleasure, in fact, is known—that is, felt—in advance of the instinct known as parenthood. A little girl who cuddles a doll is no more aspiring to parenthood than a little boy who cuddles a doll is aspiring to sodomy; both are exercising the affections and doing unto others as they would be done unto. When we are babies, we have not the least idea what manhood or woman-hood is. The famous "difference" that divides the two organic sexes is not a moral difference at all, but a physical difference: a chance variation of pattern and quantity. The orgasm, remem-ber, is a physiological process common to male and female.

That the penis and testicles are assets reserved to the male, assets which palpably the female lacks (at least to all outward appearances), is the mere result of a long-accrued psychology of value. Among the historic mists, it dates from the moment that the race decided that the penis and its function were necessary to reproduce one's kind; that the female, after all, did not spontaneously give birth through exclusive subjec-tive powers. Parthenogenesis, the idea of virgin birth, is a care-fully constructed afterthought, probably engendered by female chauvinists who resented the male's decision (unfortunately correct!) that copulation was the true condition of birth. The civilized heritage of change from the matriarchal reign to the patriarchal reign is the feature of female psychology known as penis envy.

Surely we cannot ignore penis envy as an enduring psychological factor of relations among the sexes. But it is most important that we not be facile when recognizing the point. Penis envy may characterize relations between the sexes —relations in the business world, job relations—without in the least affecting sexual relations as defined in lovemaking. Sexuality of any kind, as I have suggested here, aspires to the condition of minimal distinction between subject and object, lover and loved, penis-giver and penis-taker. For many reasons, of course, the sexual personality may develop little real aspiration. That is altogether another question. When it *does* aspire, the inevitable goal is erotic ecstasy. At the peak of erotic ecstasy, no matter what carnal technicalities are involved, the sex organs literally possess each other, and so saturatively that all awareness of *difference* between the partners is momentarily submerged. At the moment of the purest and most satisfying orgasm, sexual differentiation ceases to exist as a conscious fact. *All* the sexes aspire to the music of the homosexual condition.

Hence penis envy is totally an expression of sexual enmity and disparity, not sexual accord and parity; it is a state of mind in the War Between the Men and the Women—or indeed, in the War Between the Men and the Men; in, therefore, *all wars*. The erect penis is a power sign, a sign of mastery and aggression and a sign of sexual desirability to whose subjective absence the penisless female must resign herself. Yet penis envy also exists in males with small penises. Large penises are envied by both heterosexual and homosexual males, and for precisely the same ambivalent reasons that the female develops penis envy: the envied object is extremely attractive and extremely repulsive. It is an asset, a power, which the envier cannot wield and, so long as he or she has envy, cannot enjoy unless as a humble worshiper, a tribute-payer.

We are apt to overlook, on the other hand, one of the least acknowledged aspects of sex which I have sought to involve in these pages. It is the heterosexual male (with or without a large penis) whose anal susceptibility presents him with a cumbrous bisexual problem. Examples in the movies have recently disguised themselves in *The Conformist, Investigation of a Citizen Above Suspicion, The Damned,* and (uniquely) *Husbands.* All we need to measure the hidden type dilemma is a psychoanalytic slide rule. In its archetypal form, the psychological pattern is violent, secret, guilty submission to a male and overt, compulsive subjugation of a frontally approached female. It is natural that sado-masochistic persecution should be the particular line of behavior in this sort of male. We see how, in *The Damned,* it takes on the triple form of transvestism, childmolesting, and incest, the last being purely sadistic and all three the acts of a technically heterosexual male. One might think from this and other films that such males were nurtured and did their stuff only under fascist dictatorships (consider the Roman emperors), but then one has the striking evidence of the homophile heroes of *Husbands,* who come from the heart of democratic American suburbia. The Freudian theory of anal neuroticism in the male technically accounts for *all* such behavior. The difficulty of the confirmed anal-neurotic male is that he won't concede that his anus can be a sex organ and leave intact his "masculine dignity." Phenomena of this sort need not take the extreme forms visible in the three foreign films I have mentioned. Eros is a metamorphose god with a million honest pleasures and a million dishonest ruses.

Glancing at the world of sex in all its emotional and psychological variety, our eyes are bound to focus eventually on the renowned love game, The love game is really a war game in which the concave organ, the vagina, may be as powerful a weapon (for both the homosexually and heterosexually inclined) as the penis, the convex organ. A certain type of male homosexual passes from envying the penis to envying the vagina, which in his imagination is the one thing to subject all penis owners, so that he longs to be a woman. As a result, we have the female-impersonator complex or else its puritanic form: the tour de force of the transsexualized male. The innocent-minded must not think that all female impersonators have inconsequentially scaled penises; in some cases, a rather formidable penis is the chief element in the wish for change of organic sex. Here native psychological accidents determine the attitude of the penis owner toward his organ's grossness. Both the sex organs are power fetishes which are simply, in the strict erotic sense, tokens of promise: objects guaranteeing the future, moral commitments available to the right person with the right corresponding commitment. Bargaining between the sexes (by which I mean the owners of whatever organs) takes the form of peace pacts replacing the "normal" state of war, a competition that is part of the love game and begins in school, where feats of intelligence are sexual weapons.

Vagina owners, for their part, may be vagina enviers. How so? Because the vagina and the clitoris, as less visibly defined and measurable than the penis, make a more modest, tantalizingly present feature of attraction, displacing value emphasis to subordinate sexual characteristics which are more individually, visibly defined: the face, the bosom, the hips, the buttocks, the legs. Aesthetically, with regard to the male, the same displacement to other virile beauties normally takes place; vide the hero cults of the movies: Tarzan, Superman, Hercules. That the quantitative aspect of the penis should become a real symbol of the domination of one sex (the male) over another (the female) is the bad habit of a property-owning and materialistic society. Just the same may be said of the deification of the muscle man with his outsize pectoral muscles and his biceps like large grapefruits; other muscles, in bed, are apt, alas! to yield to a giant penis or any well-scaled penis determined to prevail.

The presence of the homosexes—whose galaxy I have presented here through the movies as their most conspicuous showcase—teaches us the basic absurdity of both penis power and the power of the puritanic penis-cum-vagina exclusivism of so-called nature. That the power of youthful Homeros is still very much functioning is proven by works as disparate as *The Conformist* and *Death in Venice*. Adolescent or pubescent, Homeros' charm is not so much the charm of a down-scaled penis as the charm of a substitute vagina: the anus and the breast surrogates of the buttocks. Actually, as a fantasy, the whole person of young Homeros subsumes his two sexual organs: the penis and the anus; he is a vision and an idea (exactly as in *Death in Venice*) no less than he is a sexual function. He is also, as in *The Picture of Dorian Gray,* an aesthetic object, a culture fetish come down to us from the homeroic Athens of Socrates. Correspondingly, a film such as *The Pit of Loneliness* behaves, in the exclusive world of vaginas, as if a turn-of-the-century girls' school were an atavistic college of nymphs presided over by rival sapphos.

The strict heterosexes, with their puritan heritage from the recent past, are among the sorriest victims of the modern political state, which regards the sex organs as essential "assists" in keeping social order by guaranteeing the family. This dominant political myth has lately gotten some damaging jolts, the most shocking of which is the world crisis being fast brought about by the population explosion. Disrespect for their parents by teen-agers is a more immanent and tangible factor. We know how acute the situation is from available data: first, the increasing victories of birth control through legalizing abortions; and second, the encouragement of birth reduction by freeing the homosexes from social prejudice and criminal prosecution. To a degree, these things stem from the youth revolt itself. The present book emphasizes the total view by bringing out purely erotic, as opposed to specious political, attitudes toward deployments of the sex organs.

Movie actors appear automatically as sex *images* rather than sex *objects*. Their true realm is the liberal imagination. The works in which they appear become fantasies of the real world more effectively than they do mirrors of the real world. And yet in fact, movie actors and actresses in the great range of sexual personality—from butch homosexual or heterosexual to professional sissy and tomboy—show the dynamic tendency of our society to readjust sexual imbalances. Freedom of choice as to one's sexual partner—just glance at Romeo and Juliet—is an ancient struggle owed to the historic concept of power politics based on the family clan.

Classic Greek tragedy itself derives from the blood feud of the clan, one of whose sources (as I pointed out on a previous page) was the impulse of an adult patriarch, Laius, to diversify, perhaps revive, his sexual passion by kidnapping (even as Zeus did Ganymede) a young boy. This statutory crime led to the incest tragedy of his son, Oedipus, and his own death. It was the object of the state, as the superclan political idea, to eliminate the nuisance of the blood feud. We see this new idea operating in the Orestes trilogy of Aeschylus, where lethal clan violence is laid to rest by Apollo's symbolic act of calming the Furies and Athena's verdict allotting them institutional rights. Yes, yet another peace pact! Global society, we find, is so structured that new peace pacts, of wider and wider import, are perpetually found necessary. In a disintegrating world society, sexual segregation becomes the concern of a minority movement. The Women's Lib impulse, for instance, is based squarely on separating the vaginas from the penises, and not even in the strict interest of lesbianism—however much lesbianism may be a moral factor —but, on the contrary, as a strategy for organizing the ranks in a power struggle between the organic sexes. This struggle cuts straight through all permissive sexuality, all "peaceful" eroticism among the sexes.

Well, there's always sado-masochism, always the master/slave relationship, "among the sexes." How about those? The point is that, if there were enough sexual freedom, what is known as "punishment" in erotic behavior would have the gentle and benign function of a social game between two or more partners. It would be a healthy sport. It would be passion as sensual pleasure rather than moral or physical pain. As I have said of the Marquis de Sade, "sadism" actually originated as a form of political emancipation of the libido. Masochism, too, especially in the male, is a form of self-humiliation that beneficially chastises penis pride and consoles the penis envier. If we look clearly and directly at the happenings of *Fellini Satyricon,* we find eroticism as a con game whose existence is benign because its rules and objectives are quite transparent: sex is a con game for the love game's sake. One homosexual lover tricks his partner of a special prize: a feminine young Homeros. All is fair, as the adage says, in love and war. True! Provided there *is* fairness; that is, provided everybody knows what the prize is, what the techniques for gaining it are, and accepts them. In sex, as in sports, there should be "good losers."

What I have called the fatal kinks in homosexuality are actually heterosexually inspired perversions. Where rape is involved (especially along with murder, as in the Leopold-Loeb crime reflected in *Rope* and *Compulsion*), the penis again is a sheer aggressive weapon, a gun or a bludgeon, and whether the victim is homosexually or heterosexually functional matters not in the least to an act that derives its "pleasure" from the infliction of pain. Of course, even rape may become part of the love game: the quarry pretending seriously to desire escape. But power politics involving sex should never exist on an independent, sexually "disinterested" plane. Then sex becomes the most abused of scapegoats.

It is power politics which may make sodomy in prisons, for example, not a valid function of Homeros but mere brute aggression predicated on a break-out or internal rebellion. Film stories about prison violence often suggest (I think of *Brute Force*) sexual involvement but never dared visibly define it till the very recent arrival on the screen of *Fortune and Men's Eyes*. It remained for the avant-gardiste, Jean Genet, to illustrate it in his film *Un Chant d'Amour,* by providing a complete homosexual aesthetics for immured criminals. Aside from such emotional and mythic exploitation, two films I have termed "homosexual mystery stories," *The Great Escape* and *Investigation of a Citizen Above Suspicion,* specifically involve the strategies of Homeros under the forced segregation of males—a segregation that may operate morally as well as physically. Moreover, it should occur to us that the whole moral of the homosexual murder in *The Detective* is the villainy bred by moralized homosexual frustration in *any* environment.

What does homosexual flirtation in the form of grilling a crime suspect accomplish in *The Detective*? It underlines a very old fable of primitive character: Good is brought about by the gentle methods of love, not the violent methods of hate; the point is refined because the detective's flirtation with the male suspect is merely an imitation of love: *a charade*. In turn, the implied but invisible, if quite plausible seduction of the German soldier in *The Great Escape* leads to a good nonviolent result from the viewpoint of the seducer, the character played by James Garner. All else that happens, aside from implied sex, is that the soldier's pocket is picked. Penises too are occasionally garnered by the exquisitely gentle practice of pocket-picking. And the same, of course, goes for garnering vaginas. Still again, the whole moral lurking behind the violence of the chauffeur's seduction of the boy hero in *The Conformist* is that no such thing could have taken place without the distortions of personality imposed by a stupidly regimented society, whose pretensions at "sex education" are criminally hypocritical. Power politics can regard sex only as a strictly cold-blooded strategy. Where sex has no true heat, you can confidently predict a kind of catastrophe. Fire away with your pistol, poor little Homeros, the blood you draw will weigh on your heart (shaped like the head of a penis) and strangle it!

Consult, too, the previous discussion of *In Cold Blood*. This film is the apotheosis of fatal and violent sexual displacement. As a Hollywood charade, it is ludicrously no less than horrendously "innocent." I am prompted to ask now: Can we dare look forward to a sexually undifferentiated and unmoralized world in which sex activity will be a pleasurable fact and a triumphant force? This can eventuate if the nature and evolved inclination of the individual be really respected; not, as it is now, cheated and enslaved by a corrupt political and social system. Free the vaginas from their "hot pants"! Free the penises from their jockstraps! These twin slogans, in this place anyway, may seem like wanton camping. But camp is a satiric instrument with inherent deftness. Its use in behalf of total sexual freedom is entirely legitimate, altogether benign.

Rex Harrison and Richard Burton are far better as the heterosexual camps they play respectively in *My Fair Lady* and *Boom* than as the homosexual camps they play opposite each other in *Staircase*. The grotesque failure of *Staircase* was due entirely to the vices of the commerical film, which is cowardly and relentlessly calculating. Take, rather, the quite unconscious dignity of the documentary feature *The Queen,* all about transvestites and their search for an honest public and private image. Or take the much more special transvestite qualities of *Performance,* where homosexuality is playroom-pseudo and the true sexual guideline is unisex. Here we have the answer to our oldest and newest sexual problems. The concept of unisex reflects a world intuition: the true freedom of natural *sexual* selection.

Structurally and emotively, the sets of sex organs known as male and female are directly concerned with each other (to the exclusion of variant sexuality) only in the interests of racial propagation. I grant that logically, in this book as elsewhere, this proposition is not only self-evident but also redundant. And yet practically—in the throes of what we sometimes call "living" —it is redundant only in the formal, the rhetorical sense. It must remain, I think, a speculative myth till the time when all the sexes are released from the straitjackets imposed on them by conventions, till the time when all the sexes are delivered from persecution by the greed and stupidity of Establishment politics.

No, your Honor!

Sex is *not* a weapon of destruction; that is, it shouldn't be—either in the heterosexual family unit where it can be found (vide the attempted knifing in *Husbands*) or in ambi-sexed bordellos or prisons where sometimes it lovingly fires blanks (vide *Un Chant d'Amour*). Sex was the very first dove. As organ and metaphor, it is due—in fact, past due—its full human rights. We need on film a new, revolutionary interpretation of the Bible, one that would make John Huston's movie of that name look like the licentious Sunday-school yatter (with pictures) it really is. True film art can never be a set of good or bad or super illustrations of Establishment sex; it must interpret the sacred sexes for what they are *and always were*: media for the totally free inventions of the libido.

INDEX